The Psychology of Management in African Organizations

The Psychology of Management in African Organizations

◆

Denis Chima E. Ugwuegbu

QUORUM BOOKS
Westport, Connecticut • London

Library of Congress Cataloging-in-Publication Data

Ugwuegbu, Denis C. E.
    The psychology of management in African organizations / Denis Chima E. Ugwuegbu.
     p. cm.
    Includes bibliographical references and index.
    ISBN 1–56720–400–7 (alk. paper)
    1. Management—Africa—Psychological aspects.   2. Organizational behavior—Africa. I.
Title.
    HD70.A34U37   2001
    658′.001′9—dc21   00–062775

British Library Cataloguing in Publication Data is available.

Library of Congress Catalog Card Number: 00–062775
ISBN: 1–56720–400–7

First published in 2001

Quorum Books, 88 Post Road West, Westport, CT 06881
An imprint of Greenwood Publishing Group, Inc.
www.quorumbooks.com

Printed in the United States of America

The paper used in this book complies with the
Permanent Paper Standard issued by the National
Information Standards Organization (Z39.48–1984).

10 9 8 7 6 5 4 3 2 1

To my wife, Toyin,

for her love

and

my children,

Ngozidilenna

Njideka

Nnema

Chima

Obinna

Obiageri

I love and cherish you all

Contents

List of Tables and Figures

TABLES

FIGURES

Preface

To build a nation, to erect a new civilization, which can lay claim to existence because it is humane, we shall try to employ not only enlightened reason but also dynamic imagination.

President Leopold Senghor of Senegal, c. 1960

That need for dynamic imagination and creative ability led me to introduce a new degree course called Managerial Psychology at the University of Ibadan, Nigeria. The program is the only one of its kind in the whole African continent, indeed, in the world.

I realized that most managers in African organizations often receive considerable training in technical aspects of their jobs and that others gain knowledge through long, on-the-job experience. Practically none receive any training on managing people. Because they have worked with people all their lives, it is usually assumed that they will instinctively know how to manage them. This is very often far from the truth. My practical involvement with consulting for organizations big and small and for government departments, as well as decades of administration, made me aware of the need for a program that would prepare African managers on how to manage people at work. I was right. The first year the program was introduced, it attracted over 1,000 applications from managers from different industrial organizations who applied for admission to the program. This was more than the number who applied to any other business- and management-related professional course at the University of Ibadan.

African workers have a right to be understood by those who manage the organizations where these employees work. Their psychological and physical needs cannot be met satisfactorily unless those who manage the organization can understand, explain, and predict workers' behaviors. The fascination that African managers have with the colonial management tradition prevents them from understanding the African system of work and retards their adoption of contemporary management models that embody labor democracy.

The objectives of *Psychology of Management in African Organizations* are to help improve effectiveness and efficiency among managers in African organizations through a better and comprehensive understanding of the African system of work and the behavior of African people at work. Second, this book is aimed at broadening African managers' concept of an organization as a physical and psychological entity to which workers react on the basis of their perception and understanding of what is going on in the organization between them as workers and the organization and between the workers in interaction with others. The consideration of an organization as only a physical entity hinders African managers from approaching management holistically. This book meets the needs of other managers and professionals elsewhere whose backgrounds may or may not be psychology. It also serves the needs of graduate students with interest in managerial psychology and other management related courses such as business administration, economics, educational management, industrial and labor relations, psychology, and sociology.

Some relevant major theories and concepts of organizational behavior and industrial psychology as applied to managerial psychology are covered in considerable detail to help managers, students, and others without much background in psychology to grasp the significance of psychology in effective organizational management and to arouse interest in meaningful discussions among scholars interested in understanding human behavior in African organizations.

I believe in the importance of theory and research. Therefore, I have tried to show the practical implications of theory and research for improved work behavior. Since this book also is to be read by professionals who may not be psychologists, I have tried to minimize psychological jargon. The few examples that you come across are unavoidable. Brief summaries at the end of each chapter provide the reader with an opportunity to recapitulate a few important facts on the issues dealt with in that chapter before proceeding to the next.

The author gratefully acknowledges the contributions of several people to the completion of this book. Mrs. Rose Umelo was the editor for this book initially. Through her tireless and painstaking efforts this book attained some consistency of viewpoint and continuity of style. I am most grateful for her excellent editorial work, which made this volume a much better book. I would like to record my great debt to my wife, Toyin Elizabeth Ugwuegbu, and Chris Akomas for their support and encouragement throughout the preparation of this book.

The Department of Psychology and the Center for Afro-American and African Studies of the University of Michigan, Ann Arbor, provided me with a hospitable haven and resources at the stage when the manuscript was being corrected, rewritten, edited, and organized during my 1999/2000 sabbatical leave. I am grateful for the support accorded me by this great institution.

Introduction

OVERVIEW

Many of my readers will object to my lumping all African countries together in my treatment of this topic. They are justified in their objection on the basis that not all African countries receive equally detailed treatment. Furthermore, there are marked geographical differences among these countries such as race, location, size, population, natural resources, culture, and political institutions. We must bear in mind that this book is not concerned with all of these aspects. The focus is organizational management practices in these countries. In this particular respect, all African countries are similar. They all practice a borrowed colonial management system. They are all experiencing varying degrees of dependence and shortage of professional, managerial, and technical expertise necessary for development. These are the essential factors that form the common denominator that warrants these African countries being considered together. Finally, African peoples, irrespective of where they reside in the continent, share in the African philosophy of human interdependence. This philosophical orientation influences African workers' behavior in informal and formal organizations and in interaction with each other.

RATIONALE

Developments in Africa at the end of the twentieth century combined to contribute to the significance of this book. These include the African peoples' victory over apartheid in South Africa, and the end of military dictatorship in several African countries. Other positive developments are the lessening of tension and armed conflicts in Ethiopia and Eritrea, Liberia, Sierra Leone, and Namibia, and the enthronement of democratic governments in Nigeria, Liberia, and South Africa. These changes have freed Africa and its peoples to intensify the debate on how to hasten the continent's industrialization, including the development of its industrial organizations. African governments are implementing the World Bank and the International Monetary Fund's (IMF) ideas of market economy, commercialization, and privatization. For modern organizations to survive in a global economic environment there must be a population available of qualified managers who are knowledgeable about modern organizational behavior management. There must be available also some African-relevant information resources that will serve as a guideline for African managers, who are the decision makers in these emerging African organizations.

Grafted colonial management approaches and the indigenous African system of managing work, in addition to contemporary, diverse foreign educational and training backgrounds of African managers, are resulting in new management approaches in Africa. Some areas of management such as industrial relations (Adewumi, 1997; Otobo, 1995; Ubeku, 1983, 1994), industrial planning (Onyemelukwe, 1966), and management in Africa (Onyemelukwe, 1973, 1983) have received the attention of some authors in Africa. The emerging new management approach, which integrates knowledge of human behavior from psychological perspectives into organizational management, has not been previously discussed for the benefit of African formal organizations.

In the United States, Japan, and some European countries, such as Britain and France, the science of psychology has revealed much knowledge and understanding about the behavior of people engaged in organizational work. Such understanding is beneficial in predicting and controlling work situations so as to increase work effectiveness, productivity, and employee satisfaction. The history of this unique area, industrial psychology and organizational behavior, is of short duration in Africa. Only in 1997/1998 was a professional master's degree course in this area started in one of Africa's universities, the University of Ibadan in Nigeria. A successful discussion of the area requires knowledge of data and research from mainstream psychology about behavior in African organizations.

Another reason that justifies the writing of this volume is the contemporary trend toward globalization of organizations. This trend requires a simultaneous globalization of those aspects of organizational behavior management principles and models that have been found to lead to efficiency in management and increased productivity. The present effort is therefore more integrative than comparative. Emphasis is laid on integrating African and Western modern managerial and organizational management behavior that has been demonstrated to facilitate increased motivation, leadership effectiveness, and employee efficiency. Such integration and emphasis are of great benefit to the momentum that is expected to take place in the industrial and organizational sector of the African economy in this century.

Market economy means ability and preparedness to survive through competitive edge, while privatization and commercialization signal the end of traditional government subsidies for African organizations. If commercialized and privatized organizations in Africa are to survive in the contemporary global economy, they are to be managed by indigenous managers with the appropriate knowledge and skills in modern human behavior management in organizations.

The effort here is to make some of this knowledge, and these skills and techniques accessible for the benefit of indigenous and international organizations in the African continent. Globalization, privatization, and commercialization imply that foreign investors will sooner or later be attracted to increase their rate of investment in African organizations. Organizations managed by a pool of qualified personnel will most likely benefit from such an increased rate of international investments.

GUIDING ASSUMPTIONS

Several general and specific assumptions guide the orientation of this book. One of those is that, given the relatively short history of large public and private formal organizations in African countries, each of these new states, without exception, suffers from a severe shortage of organizational managers. The few who exist lack the requisite and appropriate knowledge, skills, and long-term experience. Furthermore, since the application of serious Western psychology was absent in the African continent until the third quarter of the last century, there were no organizational theories and practical tradition from which African managers could draw. At the moment, in most African countries modern management techniques and models are absent in most indigenously owned organizations. According to Onyemelukwe (1966), as these indigenous owner-manager organizations grow and expand, they should be requiring managers with the expertise to help them manage these organizations. Unfortunately, this caliber of personnel is not easily accessible. There are others, too, who do not realize the need for bringing in the people with the management know-how to take over the running of their companies for them. Volumes such as this expose these owner-managers to modern management techniques and educate them in the realization of the importance of having people with the necessary expertise to manage their business.

Leaders in government and private organizations in Africa now know that reliance on so-called foreign experts to manage their expanding industrial organizations has the tendency to retard quick organizational development due to increased costs. Most African countries have completed, or are engaged in, processes that will maximize indigenous assumption of management responsibility at all levels of their organizations. This requires the development of indigenous management personnel with the necessary leadership, technical, and human skills. Developing such a reservoir of manpower is feasible only where there exists a body of modern organizational management knowledge from which managers could draw. An important responsibility for African managers is to provide flexible leadership that enables their subordinates to participate effectively in dealing with the problems that rapid expansion and growth of African organizations are likely to produce. The colonial management model was hierarchical, autocratic, and exclusive. This volume is an acknowledgment that the inherited model was a failure. The need for rapid industrialization and growth requires a radical transformation of the colonial culture and processes of management of African organizations.

In African universities and polytechnics, the teaching of management relies heavily on borrowed, outdated colonial principles and theories that do not take into account African environmental factors and human behavior in management. This is partly due to the inability of some African educationalists to integrate borrowed Western theories and principles with the theoretical and practical environmental factors that determine the behavior of the African workers. Available research data and management knowledge in Africa are reviewed in this book. This information is integrated with African relevant Western research and knowledge that are likely to promote effective organizational and human behavior management in African organizations.

TOPICS

The outlined premise dictated the topics that are dealt with in this book. These are some of the important areas with which organizational behavior as a discipline generally is concerned. They illustrate aspects of industrial and organizational psychological theories and principles that are applicable to the understanding of human behavior management in workplaces. The chapters represent a wide variety of human behavior management problems relevant to African organizations, as perceived from a psychological perspective. In spite of this specialized perspective, each chapter can be understood by psychologists and nonpsychologists. The format adopted allows the author to report research findings in Africa and the industrialized world. It also allows the author to deal with methodological approaches and theoretical formulations in psychology at a more general level than one would find in a more specialized psychology volume.

The chapters are all directed toward a common objective, namely, to expose, inform, and equip African managers of today and tomorrow with the necessary organizational behavior management, practical skills, and knowledge that will increase effective leadership skills, human management skills, problem solving-ability, and creativity and innovation. For researchers and other intellectuals, the chapters lay good foundation for future research and a better understanding of the dynamics of African workers' behavior.

The first chapter maintains that the early twentieth century colonial, European management models shaped contemporary organizational management approaches in Africa. Those models are said to be bureaucratic and characterized by overcentralization of power. The colonial management model is vividly exemplified in both the public and private present-day sector organizations in Africa. In these organizations officials are responsible only for rigid discharge of their prescribed duties. The organizations are divided into departments, which are segmented into offices whose sphere of competence and hierarchy of responsibility, power, and authority are clearly defined. Management communication is directional, that is, top-down, and is strictly confidential and not open to public scrutiny. Accountability at the top of the management hierarchy of the organization is not adhered to. Administrative activities at every stage are recorded in writing in minute details and authenticated by the signature of the manager or the officer in charge.

Some of the fundamental weaknesses of the colonial management model are that it failed to develop any systematic methods for selecting, placing, and training management employees. It made every employee permanent after a probationary period of one or two years. It was based on the erroneous belief that management can be learned only through experience. Instead of formal education and training, employees are expected to acquire management knowledge and skills only by experience. Workers are generally poorly paid, and their intellectual and technical skills are not fully utilized.

In spite of over a century of colonial, European administration in African countries and over three decades of stateshood, there still exists today an acute shortage of trained manpower in the professional, managerial, and technical areas to meet the developmental needs of each of the African countries. The Western science of psychology, which has proven successful in Europe, Japan, and the United States for the understanding and dealing with the problems associated with leadership, assessment, selection, and placement of individuals, problems of motivation, productivity, commitment, absenteeism and turnover, and job satisfaction, was not practiced in Africa until after independence. The survival of African organizations in the present global market economy requires that managers of African organizations adopt comprehensive management approaches that include emphasis on the understanding of human behavior in workplaces.

Chapter 2 focuses attention on the major psychological and human behavior problems in the management of African organizations. An outstanding feature of African organizations that distinguishes them from organizations in the developed countries is the type of ownership. In Africa the organizations either belong to expatriate former colonial people or colonial government or are one-person, indigenous, small or medium-sized business enterprises.At independence African governments inherited the colonial government organizations. Traditionally, these government organizations were not operated as profit-oriented businesses. They depended largely on annual government subsidies for survival. With the recent economic decline in Africa and reduced or nonexistent government subsidies, these organizations are experiencing severe adaptation and survival difficulties.

Several authorities have described African cultures as a major impediment to the development of African organizations. Many of these experts and researchers blame African cultures for two things. First, these authorities claim that African cultures are responsible for African workers' poor attitude to work, including low productivity, lack of initiative, and excessive religiosity. African cultures are also blamed for the assumed inability of African managers and workers to assimilate at a rapid rate grafted Western management styles and work ethic. Research evidence in this chapter discounts these popular, stereotypic, traditional explanations, which were handed down from the early colonial days. In place of the traditional cultural explanations, new, data-derived explanations based on ineffective reward allocation, reward scheduling, and lack of managerial human skills are offered as the real causes of the African attitude to work.

Other organizational management difficulties in African organizations that are mentioned in this chapter include problems associated with recruitment, selection, training, placement, leadership, decision making, communication, and performance evaluation.

Chapter 3 concerns the phenomenon of motivation in the workplace. Motivation is a psychological construct that is associated with goal directed behavior. It is a construct that has yielded one of the most versatile stereotypic views of African managers and industrial workers. In order to achieve a fairly simple and coherent organization of motivation theories, Katzell and Thompson's (1990) outline of motivation theories was adopted. This system allows for a smooth and a simple systematic review of the theories of achievement motivation and the relevant literature from the West as well as those from the African subregion.

The conclusion that was reached from the review was that culture-based achievement motivation interpretation and the implied motivational inferiority in non-Western cultures should be rejected and abandoned. Achievement motivation is universal and evenly distributed in a given population and across cultures. There are, however, cultural differences in the type of behavioral endeavors that societies regard as an expression of achievement motive. What one culture regards as an expression of achievement may not be so regarded in other cultures. An understanding of this will enable managers in African organizations to establish the appropriate cues or contexts for eliciting need achievement work behaviors in their employees.

Finally, social motives that are relevant to African organizations are discussed. Emphasis is placed on management strategies that are likely to enhance high levels of motivation for managers and other employees in African organizations.

In the inherited colonial organizational management model, there is no difference between power and leadership. In that model leadership and power are characterized by dictatorial disposition and master servant social distance relationship. Both demand a high degree of conformity from subordinates, which stifles communication, creativity, and other decision-making attempts. Chapter 4 of this volume provides an engaging review of organizational leadership theories, mostly from the developed and industrialized world. African countries and organizations have their own ways of measuring successful leadership, but at this time those techniques and measures are yet to be systematically organized and articulated. Modern organizations require the leaders to be accountable. People should also know when leaders are effective and when they are ineffective. This requires reliable means of consistently measuring leadership effectiveness. The chapter presents indices of leadership effectiveness that are relevant to managers of African organizations.

Psychology assumes that managers' effectiveness or ineffectiveness in a given situation is a function of three factors namely, the environment, the task, and the manager's personality. This theoretical orientation is particularly interesting and instructive to African political and organizational leaders. Making efforts to recruit talented workers, motivating workers, serving as a resource for the work group or team, and constant evaluation of group performance are discussed as very important tasks that distinguish effective managers from ineffective ones in African organizations.

Ineffective managers (usually called "deadwood," in some African countries, because they yield no useful outcome or fruits) are usually a problem for African organizations. Often they are in a management position because they represent a special interest group, or they may be in the manager's seat due to political patronage. The more any of this is the case, the more difficult it is to remove the ineffective manager. It is also difficult to reach such managers through organizational feedback.

Since independence, African organizations have passed through periods of buoyancy to depression, during which period most organizations were operating at about 30 percent of their capacity. This resulted in the layoff of workers and mass unemployment. The chapter concludes by making some specific suggestions on what the goals and responsibilities of African managers should be to make them more effective, given the type of political environment in which they operate, so as to avoid a similar crisis in African organizations of the future.

Chapter 5 examines individual and organizational decision making in the African environment and concludes that decision making at the individual level is mostly intuitive and often based on precedence. In African organizations it is chaotic and intuitive due to two factors. One is that most of the organizations do not have well-articulated missions, goals, and objectives, which should guide decision making. Second is the absence of reliable data or information either in the environment where the organization is operating or within the organization itself. This discussion is followed by a consideration of decision-making theories that are inherited by organizational behavior from Western social psychology.

The phenomenon of groupthink is closely linked to behaviors that have contributed to some of the organizational and ethnic conflicts in African countries as well as in their organizations. The pitfalls of this behavioral attitude are discussed. Finally, various methods that psychology employs to enhance organizational decision making that are likely to benefit African organizations are discussed. Human relations as practiced in African organizations are that branch of organizational management whose focus is to minimize labor management conflict. Human relations are an inherited concept. It was a well-developed segment of management during the colonial era, and it continues to receive recognition today from African organizations and governments. This is because colonial organizations used human relations departments to stifle the demands of African workers. On the other hand, independent African governments perceived labor demands for fair wages to be antithetical to their desire for rapid economic development and industrialization, hence the recognition and use of labor relations as the colonial managers did.

Chapter 6 goes beyond the traditional conflict-avoidance attitude of contemporary African organizations to present a new conceptualization of conflict. This recent view insists that conflict, whenever it occurs, signifies neither bad interpersonal relations nor bad labor management relations. Rather, conflict, whether in interpersonal relations or in labor management relations usually teaches a lesson. Organizations are better off learning from conflicts. Emphasis is placed on learning to manage conflicts so as to benefit from the lessons they teach, rather than avoiding them.

The chapter further illustrates, with examples from African organizations, how easy it is to resort to the use of power and authority to force the apparently less powerful party in a conflict situation to give in to the wishes of the more powerful, which is usually the government or management. Other aspects of conflict in African organizations that are discussed in this chapter include significance of conflict, antecedent conditions in organizations that may predispose them to conflicts, costs and gains of organizational conflicts, and conflict resolution in organizations. The chapter closes with a brief discussion of bargaining in organizations during which social psychological models such as those of Morton Deutsch, John Magenau and Dean Pruitt's are considered. It is finally observed that since government is the largest employer of labor in these African countries, there is the tendency to regulate conflict by the institutionalization of conflict resolution mechanisms.

Chapter 7 states the obvious. African organizations from the moment of independence were in short supply of employees with adequate managerial, technical, and research skills required for the efficient and effective management and development of African organizations. Ironically, the development of such essential manpower skills was not a primary concern of the pre- and post-independence expatriate organizations that dominated the African enterprise environment. The chapter systematically reviews the African employment sectors and graphically details how the development of technical, managerial, and professional skills has been the preoccupation of African governments since independence. The evidence that these governments regard this issue as a priority responsibility is demonstrated by the level of African governments' involvement and investment in technical, vocational, industrial, and apprentice development and training. The chapter presents an example of a modern organizational model of human resources planning that is a regular part of major organizations in the industrialized, Western world. The model includes short-term, medium-, and long-term planning. It is argued that as a result of unpredictability of the African environment, such as economic and political instability, and unavailability of information or data, long-term human resources planning in African organizations is fraught with difficulties.

It is further contended that in well-integrated and developed organizations in industrialized countries, personnel recruitment and classification, job analysis, the utilization of psychotechnologies such as tests and interviews, and the control of assessment centers are some of the functions of the human resources department. Most of these procedures and their use are yet to reach many African organizations and are yet to be fully developed in expatriate organizations in Africa.

Chapter 8 examines the issue of employee performance evaluation. In organizations where appointment to managerial positions is based on patronage or political connection, performance is not usually considered of prime importance. Employee performance is an aspect of management that is carried out with all seriousness in the industrialized countries because of its impact on the performance of the organization as a whole. Many African organizations rarely carry out any regular employee performance evaluations. The annual evaluation of middle and junior staff that is often attempted is usually poorly carried out. There are several reasons for this. One of the reasons for the lack of seriousness of African managers toward ascertaining the performance of their workers is the traditional dependence on the government for annual subsidies, which sustain the life of their organizations. The second and most important reason is that many African managers do not know how to specify and quantify good performance. Third, even if they know, they do not have the appropriately reliable and valid psychological instruments for measuring performance, nor do they have the knowledge or skills for drawing the necessary inferences about good or adequate performance from scores obtained from such instruments.

The aim of the chapter is to X-ray the importance of periodic, systematic employee appraisal to African organizations with the hope that they will adopt and incorporate regular evaluation of their workers for purposes of bringing about some improvements in the performance of the organizations. A second purpose of the chapter is to remind a few expatriate and indigenous organizations that attempt annual evaluations that the available instruments are yet to be standardized for use with the African population. It is partly the responsibility of these organizations to collaborate with African psychologists in developing and validating organizational evaluation instruments that are appropriate for use in African organizations. In order to accomplish this instrument development and standardization, there must be job descriptions against which employees' performance is measured. Many African countries and their organizations do not have job descriptions. The chapter is expected to contribute to the intensification of the discussion and debate on how to measure the performance of African employees accurately and reliably so that employees are remunerated equitably in accordance with their contributions.

The book ends with Chapter 9, which focuses on the principles and methods of effective management training and personnel development. African organizations are realizing the importance of training and development for the acquisition of management skills and technical know-how for their managers. As a result, a mushrooming of numerous professional, company-based, and private management and development training programs offers various training courses oriented to management or technical skills acquisition. Among the problems that confront most of these training and development programs is the fact that many of the African organizations do not know how to systematically determine both their short-term and long-term training and development needs. Second, neither the training consultants nor the organizations make any efforts to evaluate the effectiveness of training and development in the organizations.

The chapter outlines the usual necessary procedure for the determination of effectiveness of training and development in the organizations, organizational training needs, the principles and methods of training and development of organizational personnel, and procedures for identifying training needs of the managers through personnel scores, surveys, interviews, and skills and knowledge tests. How to effectively utilize these procedures in the African organizational environment is said to be the task with which African organizations must deal. Emphasis is placed on the importance and the need for regular assessment of training and development program outcomes in Africa.

1

Colonial Management Legacy in Africa

The model of industrial and organizational management in Africa is colonial in character. African countries have been independent for several decades, yet most of their management theories and practices continue to reflect substantially early twentieth century colonial management models. Strong evidence for colonial management practices is witnessed in both the public and private sector organizations in Africa.

The structure of the colonial management model that was grafted onto African industrial and organizational management by the European powers was bureaucratic. This system of management is characterized by overcentralization of power. The European managers of the colonial era dictated the relation between their organizations and the African workers. Colonial African employees occupied a humiliating position. They were not involved in any major decision making in the organizations. Communication was one-way, from the parent companies in metropolitan Europe to their subsidiaries in Africa. Colonial managers made no attempts to improve managerial methods, nor did they undertake any research to improve efficiency or the welfare of their African employees.

There were, however, instances of some specific differences in management style between the colonial European countries in Africa. In the Portuguese colonies, organizations were hierarchically structured with unified administration. Channels of communication between the departments and top management were specified and clearly laid down. The functions of each department were minutely defined. The last decision in any matter rested with the manager. The supervision and control of all subordinate personnel and departments were the responsibility of the manager. The manager was the center and focus of the organization and coordinated the moral and material activities of the organization.

The colonial British bureaucratic machinery is illustrated by the organizational structure and the management of colonial government departments. At the top of the departments were the permanent undersecretaries. These were time-honored, knowledgeable, experienced, hardworking civil servants. They were firstline permanent staff. They participated in policy formulation and implementation. Permanent undersecretaries as heads of their departments reported to the governor general, who, in turn, reported to the Colonial Office. In spite of their elevated position in the hierarchy, they were responsible for the smooth working of the office routine. They were charged with the absolute responsibility of determining how the office work was to be divided and performed, including such matters as keeping minutes of meetings and other procedures and the employment of extra typists (Cell, 1970). They advised on the promotion and placement of junior clerks in the permanent establishment at the end of their probationary years. Their management style made them feel indispensable. They often refused to delegate a part of their workload to their subordinates.

The most fundamental weakness of the British colonial management and administrative system lay in the selection and training of employees (Cell, 1970; Onyemelukwe, 1966). Every employee became permanent after a probationary year or two. There was also the general belief that management could be learned only through conformity, hard work, and on-the-job experience. Instead of providing employees with the opportunity for appropriate, job-related education and training, the British colonial management model emphasized learning by experience (Onyemelukwe, 1966). The French model, on the on other hand, was centered on testing and selecting African employees by the use of psychological instruments developed for use in France.

In general, colonial European managers were reluctant to grant African supervisors and foremen and women the status commensurate with their responsibility. Quite often such supervisors and foremen and women were employed as stooges by colonial organizations to fend off African workers and their demand for equitable treatment. There was a markedly inefficient system of division of labor in the colonial management model. This resulted in management's inability to utilize employees' intellectual and mechanical skills. African workers were poorly remunerated, and the organizations did not provide them with much incentive. The system of meritocracy, which characterized the cultures of some African peoples, received no recognition from the colonial managers.

COLONIAL POLICY AND MANPOWER DEVELOPMENT

Colonial authorities in Africa were confronted with a major dilemma as to the issue of the education of Africans. This is because the encouragement of education, including management education, would defeat an important aspect of colonialism, which was to keep the colonial peoples dependent on European countries. Colonial countries were supposed to depend on these overseas nations for both their skilled and nonskilled manpower. The colonial managers who served in the private and public organizations in the colonies were highly remunerated, relative to their African counterpart, irrespective of whether they were qualified or not. There was also a high rate of turnover among such expatriate managers. The negative effects of these policies impacted on the development of modern organizations in Africa. A high turnover rate created instability in the development of these organizations. Second, the policy of paying the expatriate staff very high salaries relative to what the African workers were paid led some African employees to believe that modern organizations are characterized by injustice and the exploitation of the weak by the more powerful owners of the industrial organizations. This contributed to the development of strong labor unions in many African countries prior to independence.

A few primary and secondary schools were established by the colonial administrations in each of the colonial countries. These schools produced interpreters, clerks, supervisors, and foremen for use in colonial establishments. Later, a few universities were established where emphasis was put on literary education. The colonial universities specialized in the production of historians, lawyers, linguists, and Africans who were specialists in modern and classical European languages. Africans with expertise in these fields had the control of planning and policy formulation and implementation in the public and private sectors of these countries at independence. Some countries, like Angola and Namibia, had the misfortune of not having more than a total of five university-educated managers in the country at the time that colonial Portugal pulled out.

The European attitude toward manpower development in African colonies or what received emphasis is hardly surprising if one considers the status of management education in Europe at the time. Until the second half of the twentieth century Europe did not believe that the art of management could be formally taught. Management appointments in the public or private organizations in the home countries or posts in the colonies were based purely on an individual's distinguished career in politics or the armed forces (Onyemelukwe, 1966). Onyemelukwe cited an instance in 1945 when a joint committee of university professors and business executives, who were nominated by the Cambridge University Appointments and Board, recommended to the university that it should not establish courses in management. According to this report, the study of management "was not worth the status of Cambridge" (Onyemelukwe, 1966, p. 299). The bias that management as a discipline was "vocational" and lacking in any rigorous intellectual demands was communicated to the African colonial countries in various ways.

Effectiveness in management requires some knowledge of human behavior as embodied in psychology. Scientific psychology originated in Europe in 1879, when Wundt set up the first known psychology laboratory. Following World War II, the United States assumed leadership in the study of psychology. Until, now, North America has dominated the study, development, and practice of psychology. The European colonial powers, with the exception of France, lagged behind in the study and application of the science of psychology. The French government commissioned extensive psychological studies in their colonies in Africa, in addition to research activities of French social scientists, who conducted various psychological studies that utilized African subjects (see Wickert, 1967). Unlike the French, the little psychology that was exported by the British colonial power to its colonies in Africa during the second half of the twentieth century tended to emphasize only educational and developmental psychology. None of the higher educational institutions established by the colonial administration in Africa, including France, had any type of specialization in any area of psychology. There were no attempts made by these colonial powers to share their expertise in psychological knowledge and technology with the Africans, nor did most of them attempt to understand the behavior of the colonial African peoples at work. They did not give positions of trust and responsibility to members of the African population who worked for them. Such management policies were justified by the negative stereotypes held by these expatriate managers about the Africans.

African employees were perceived as being strange to modern industrial organizations. They were said to be preoccupied with religious beliefs and activities, lacking experience and modern organizational discipline, and too attached to the extended family tradition. Other stereotypes by which European managers characterized African workers included traditional habits, attitudes, and behavior that were said to be inappropriate for modern industrial labor. The expatriate managers held that African workers' rate of productivity was low, while their rate of absenteeism and turnover was high.

ORGANIZATIONAL MANAGEMENT AT INDEPENDENCE
Many African managers and their subordinates who assumed the responsibility of managing African private and public organizations and government departments at independence inherited no guidelines from the colonial managers and administrators. Since the outgoing managers did not involve them in any meaningful management, they lacked relevant background experience on which to draw. The African managers inherited departments already staffed by appointed officers who were responsible only for the rigid discharge of their prescribed duties. The departments where they worked were organized in offices whose spheres of competence and hierarchy of responsibility were clearly defined. Employees were permanent and were remunerated by fixed salaries. The rates of salary that officers received at each grade were a function of their seniority. The long-term goal of these officials was to make a life career out of their specified duties. Organizations had no stated, clear mission and lacked articulated objectives and goals.

The employees were also subjected to a meticulously spelled out code of conduct and discipline. Routine files on their incoming and outgoing baskets were boldly marked "confidential." Any evidence that the content of any file had been compromised was sufficient reason for a prompt termination of the appointment of the employee incharge. Management and administration were carried on in a rational way and in an orderly manner. Every aspect of administrative activity at every stage was recorded in detail in writing and authenticated by the manager's signature, even when oral communication was also involved. Any documentation whose correctness was not attested to by the signature of the top manager, as the head of the department, was rejected as not in conformity with laid-down procedure. The inherited colonial management operated impersonally on the basis of written and ascertainable rules, procedures, and precedence.

Often people were appointed to office positions not on the basis of proven qualifications or skills but on the basis of patronage. This practice resulted in some of the departments and ministries being staffed predominantly with people from one or two ethnic groups. Many of these senior appointees in government ministries and parastatals had what O'Connell (1962) called "literacy education" which was not balanced by any training in modern management. Consequently, in spite of over a century of colonial administration of European countries in Africa, there existed in each of these African countries at independence an acute shortage of trained manpower in the professional, management, and technical areas. Colonial organizations made no attempt to improve managerial methods. They conducted no surveys on consumer behavior and undertook no selection and placement research. The African managers inherited colonial, European assumptions that management techniques that were successfully applied in European countries were good enough for African organizations. There was no attempt to explore new ways that social, economic, psychological, and cultural conditions, and the technological level of the African countries could affect management effectiveness.

PSYCHOLOGY AND MANAGEMENT

The relevance of psychology to management in Africa was raised in a keynote address to participants at a bank management seminar (Ugwuegbu, 1991). The title of the address was: "Psychology and bank management" Psychology is defined as the scientific study of human behavior and mental processes. Management, on the other hand, is defined as the process of setting and achieving organizational goals through the basic functions that acquire and utilize human, financial, material, and informational resources. The interface of psychology and management is human behavior. Psychology studies people's actions, behaviors, attitudes, and mental processes. It has developed elaborate theories on how people learn, what motivates them, and how attitudes and behaviors can be changed. It has other theories and principles on how to understand and improve people's performance and how to increase their satisfaction and well-being. These are some of the goals that management processes are working hard to achieve in organizations. Of all the resources needed to optimize organizational objectives, the most complex and least understood by managers in the African subregion organizations is human behavior.

Effective, optimal utilization of people in organizations, including those in Africa, has been a pressing problem since the Industrial Revolution. Managers in an organization, whether large or small, face the following problems:

- how to organize work and allocate it to workers
- how to select, train, and effectively manage the people available to work
- how to program work conditions and reward and punishment systems to enable the employees to maintain high levels of effectiveness and sufficient motivation to remain effective over a long period of time
- how to adjust the organization to changing environmental conditions and technological innovations
- how to cope with competition or harassment from other organizations or groups within their own organizations
- how to motivate managers to persevere in discipline and the management ethic

Such questions attracted the attention of psychologists, as their theories and methodologies enabled them to get involved in finding solutions to these organizational problems.

The area of management that first attracted psychological interest and activities is *assessment and selection of individual workers.* The earliest successful efforts of management psychologists involved the testing of recruits in order to enhance the selection methods of organizations such as the U.S. army or large organizations in industrialized countries. Psychology improved selection in organizations by making the process more scientific. It measures individuals for those characteristics that the organization requires for improved performance and quick adjustment to the organizational environment by new recruits.

Aided by their improved scientific and systematic approach, psychologists are now involved in the process of designing and organizing work itself. This area is growing into a popular specialty called *ergonomics.* Here psychologists work closely with engineers to analyze the basic characteristics of work in order to give each individual worker a job that maximizes the worker's human abilities and limits. They also handle coordination and teamwork among employees and monitor overall efficiency.

Psychology also carries out time-and-motion studies to determine how competently workers actually perform on a given job task. Job analyses are carried out to standardize the work and to improve managers' selection and training of workers; physical surroundings, noise levels, fatigue, and monotony are studied to determine their effects on the quality and quantity of work.

From psychology studies in the laboratory, psychologists have generalized their findings on the *systems of rewards and punishments* to the management of behavior in organizations. These research findings demonstrate that rewards such as pay, promotion, and responsibility and punishments such as reprimands (Odumosu, 1994) can be manipulated to serve as motivators and as conditioners of learning. Knowledge that has been acquired in laboratories in learning experiments has been tested within the organizational context. The kind of incentives and incentive schemes used by management has been another area where psychology generated much knowledge and understanding.

As to the issue of the motivation of workers, no other area of study has contributed more to its understanding than psychology. The experiment of the Hawthorne studies (Mayo, 1933) shows that how hard workers work may depend much more on how hard their coworkers work and how important they value their relationship with their supervisor than on how much money they will make or how hard their supervisors drive them. It is clear, through psychological findings, that an organization has within it many groups that generate their own norms of what is right and proper working behavior and that such norms extend to the amount and type of work to be performed (Mayo, 1933).

According to Schein (1970), organizations as a total and complex system first began to come into focus during psychologists' studies of employee motivation, incentive systems, personnel policies, and intergroup relations. Psychologists recognize that for individual members, whether members of the rank and file or the management, an organization as a whole exists as a psychological entity to which they react on the basis of cognitive summation or mental analysis of what is going on in the interaction between the individuals and the organization and the individuals and the informal groups to which they belong with their patterns of cooperative, competitive, or different relations to one another. In other words, according to Schein (1970), the deeper that psychologists delved into their research about the behavior of individuals who work in organizations, the more they discovered that the organization is another complex social system that must be studied as a total system if individual and group behavior within it is to be truly understood and interpreted. This discovery created management psychology in its own right.

PSYCHOLOGY IN AFRICA

The benefits of scientific psychology to management are yet to be extended to organizations in Africa because Western psychology has only recently reached that subregion. Scientific psychology is the brainchild of Western culture. As a discipline of study, psychology arrived on the continent of Africa in the early 1960s, following the achievement of independent nationhood by many African countries. Writing about the difficulties of psychology in Africa, Abdi (1975) observed that the field of psychology is so alien to the people of Africa that the vocabularies of the various languages do not contain the concept.

Some years ago the author was confronted with a jocular inquiry. The occasion was an interview session for the Federal Republic of Nigeria post-secondary scholarship award. One of the interviewers, on learning that the young lad sitting before the panel wanted to study psychology in an American university, quipped, "You want to study American psychology? What are you going to do with it?" The interviewer later suggested that the author should go to Britain and study educational psychology "if you want a federal government scholarship." The candidate promptly turned down this offer.

The interviewer, in this brief episode, represents a large proportion of the educated population in Nigeria and other African countries, who are, unfortunately, unfamiliar with the discipline of psychology. For many students from the African subregion, psychology is a discipline that is concerned with the problems of America and other Western countries. Many of the university-bound students in Africa, for example, know practically nothing about psychology. The primary and secondary school syllabi on social science do not include any topic in psychology despite the overwhelming human, social, and economic problems being experienced by each of these countries and the continent of Africa in general.

The Growth of Psychology in Africa

Nigeria has the highest number of psychologists on the continent of Africa, followed by South Africa and Egypt. The Republic of South Africa has the best organized and the most efficient national psychology organization in Africa. The government of South Africa fully recognizes the Psychological Society of South Africa (PsySSA). Psychology in South Africa reached maturity during the sad history of apartheid in that country. Unfortunately, the apartheid government of South Africa employed psychological techniques in its racial wars against the blacks in Southern Africa.

The Nigerian Psychological Society (NPS) has over 1,000 registered members. Both the Psychological Society of South Africa and the Nigerian Psychological Society publish psychology journals, the *South African Journal of Psychology* and the *Nigerian Journal of Psychology,* respectively. The Psychological Society of South Africa also inherited the *Journal of Behavioral Sciences, Psychologia Africana, and South African Psychologist* from its apartheid past. Unfortunately, most of the articles in the *Nigerian Journal of Psychology* and the *South African Journal of Psychology* are biased toward educational and clinical psychology, respectively. There are also the *African Journal for the Psychological Study of Social Issues*, based at the University of Ibadan and *Ife Psychologia* at the Obafemi Awolowo University, Ile-Ife. As was indicated earlier, much of the progress in the development of psychology in South Africa occurred during the unfortunate apartheid period. Many universities in South Africa offer specialties in different concentrations of psychology. Another country that has relatively well developed psychology programs is Egypt. Like Nigeria, Egypt produces enough psychologists to meet its internal needs. Many universities, including teachers' colleges, offer psychology. Egypt has a national psychology organization that regulates the practice of psychology. In order to practice psychology in Egypt and South Africa, one is required to register with the government regulating body.

Although Nigeria may have the largest number of psychologists in Africa, their national association is not given the type of recognition that other societies, such as economics, enjoy. Government also does not regulate the practice of psychology in Nigeria. This may be partly accounted for by the fact that psychology is about the last social science discipline to be established in many Nigerian universities and psychologists have not succeeded in impressing government of their relevance.

The University of Nigeria, Nsukka, has the honor of first establishing a department of psychology in Nigeria (1963). This was followed by the Universities of Lagos (1965), Ibadan (1976), Jos (1976), Obafemi Awolowo Ile-Ife (1977), Ondo State (1981), Nnamdi Azikiwe (1985), and Enugu State (1992). The departments of psychology at Nsukka, Lagos, Ibadan, Jos, and Obafemi Awolowo Ile-Ife award B.Sc., M.Sc. and Ph.D. degrees. The department of psychology at Ibadan, responding to an environmental demand, developed a professional program called Master's in Managerial Psychology (MMP), which leads to a professional master's degree, in addition to the regular degree programs. The University of Benin admits students for advanced degrees in clinical psychology in the department of mental health within the faculty of medicine. Recently, too, some of the newly created federal universities of technology and some state universities introduced either departments of, or courses in, psychology. Most students who pursue advanced degrees in psychology in Nigeria major in either industrial/organizational, social, or clinical psychology. A few go into developmental and personality psychology. The concentrations in psychology that are most relevant to management of human behavior in African organizations are clinical, social and industrial/organizational psychology. Each of these areas is briefly discussed.

Clinical Psychology

This area deals with mental health, counseling, and psychotherapy in organizations. The complexity of life resulting from industrial and technological advancement in Western countries, especially in North America, created an increased demand for clinical psychologists. Organizations such as hospitals, industries, military establishments, and government agencies and institutions constantly demand people with training in clinical psychology to meet the mental health and adjustment needs of their workers. In the African countries, clinical psychology is yet to attain the professional status that the discipline has attained in the West. The services of clinical psychologists are barely available to the working masses because the few clinicians that are available are concentrated in the universities.

The history of the development of clinical psychology and the practice of psychotherapy in Africa cannot be complete without mention of Professor Lambo's contributions. Lambo, a social psychiatrist by profession, held, and rightly so, that the Western and African cultures produce divergent philosophical orientations to causation and the notions of cure.

First, unlike the Western world, Africans believe that both physical and mental illnesses are externally caused by the breach of taboos, or customs, disturbances in social relations, spirit possession, and other afflictions by ancestral spirits and the gods. They also believe in life after death and reincarnation. Lambo (1978) pointed out that the notion of spirit causation is still very prevalent, even among educated Africans. Odejide (1979) in a study of traditional healers and mental illness reported that the native healer's concept of causes of mental illness related mostly to supernatural forces. It must be observed here that Lambo's observation is very relevant to understanding interpersonal and intergroup interaction and relations among workers in African organizations. Instances of failure to secure promotion, sudden ill health, mental illness, or death of an employee is usually attributed to the evil machination of enemies (usually coworkers), often those from other ethnic groups. In addition to hearing people discussing such beliefs and attitudes, Ugwuegbu's (1983a) survey of major industrial organizations in Ibadan and Lagos showed significantly that 67 percent of the middle management people who participated in the study indicated that they would resign their position from their organization if they were transferred out of their geographical region of origin.

Second, Lambo (1978) also noted that the concept of cure that is prevalent in Western theories (i.e., the notion of individualism) is contrary to the African philosophy of human interdependence. According to Lambo:

African concepts of health and illness like those of life and death are intertwined. Health is not regarded as an isolated phenomenon but reflects the integration of the community. It is not the mere absence of disease but a sign that a person is living in peace and harmony with his neighbors, that he is keeping the laws of the gods and tribe. (p. 35)

Lambo implemented his understanding of the African philosophy of life and mental health by the establishment of the Aro Mental Hospital, a village like community where the patients live with their relatives while receiving treatment. He employed native healers and Western-trained therapists in the treatment teams.

The Aro Mental Hospital remains the largest institution for the application of clinical psychology in Africa. In Nigeria other institutions that provide psychiatric and psychological services include the university teaching hospitals at Enugu, Ibadan, Lagos, and Zaria and the psychiatric hospitals located in Lagos and several other centers. With the exception of the departments of psychology at the University of Nigeria, Nsukka, and its Enugu campus, where Professors Azubike Uzoka and Peter Ebigbo established consulting clinics, the departments of psychology in Nigeria are more research-oriented than treatment-oriented. Most of these facilities are in the urban areas and can attend to a highly limited number of Nigerians who are in need of psychological help On the whole, clinical psychology has not as yet succeeded in penetrating industrial organizations in Africa, partly due to a shortage of manpower in the area and partly because many managers in African organizations are still unaware of the mental health needs of the employees in their organizations.

Social Psychology

This is like clinical psychology in that it is also a recent event in Africa. The need to understand the social networking of formal and informal groups, problems of interethnic relations, perception, conflict, beliefs, attitude, attribution of causality, and motivation makes social psychology a good candidate that deserves important attention for the development of African organizations. The French colonial psychologists were aware of the relevance of social psychology to French colonies in Africa (see Wickert, 1967, pp.109-226). These scholars carried out several social psychological studies in French colonial organizations. These included studies aimed at verifying the problems of African workers in Gabon and the Congo; psychological factors that affect the productivity of employees in Dakar; factors that promote the commitment of Gabonese to the organization they work for; and studies related to the African notion of time.

Most African countries realized the relevance of social psychology long before it became necessary to establish a department of psychology in most African universities. For example, at the University of Ibadan, the premier University of Nigeria, social psychology was established as a subdepartment of the department of sociology four years before the establishment in 1976 of a department of psychology. Beyond university and classroom boundaries, the principles and theories of social psychology, such as the theory of contact hypothesis (Ugwuegbu, 1999), were being employed by some African governments in an effort to create a cohesive and ethnically tolerant society in their countries.

All these events were going on in Africa after independence, in spite of the fact that very little in the literature could be called a serious contribution to social psychology in Africa. Frederick Wickert's *Readings in African Psychology* (1967) summarized interesting French colonial research work in psychology, including social psychology. Mallory Wober's *Psychology in Africa* (1975) included chapters from which a careful reader gets a feeling of the nature and concerns of what might be called social psychology in Africa. Initially, the area attracted contributors from western European, white South African, and, later, American social anthropologists, educationalists, missionaries, and sociologists. Indeed, most of the contributors to the field were people whose educational backgrounds did not condition them to the rigid principles of experimental social psychological research. For example, Professor Armer, an anthropologist, wrote *African Social Psychology* (1974). The involvement in social psychology in Africa of researchers from different disciplines produced a retarding effect on the focus and progress of the area. First, with a few exceptions (LeVine, 1966), many of the contributions lacked any theoretical or practical relevance to the problems of Africa and the developing countries. Second, the area evidenced a total lack of concerted effort and continued contributions. Third, the methodologies employed by each research worker were influenced by the researcher's background, making the results difficult to compare or replicate. Finally, the results of studies conducted in one locality were often generalized to the entire African continent.

Social Psychological Research in Africa. The focus of the early social psychological research in Africa was very narrow. It covered attitude research concerning the social changes that were going on in Africa. Wober's (1975) summary indicates that researchers distinguished two structures of attitude. These were the traditional attitude (congruent with traditional forms of society) and the emergent, "modern" attitude. The modern attitude is said to correspond to Western social forms and is influenced by Western attitudes. A second area of research interest was the intergroup attitudes and ethnic relations. The central focus in this area was the question of tribalism and nationalism. Another area of interest was personality and identity, which utilized projective techniques and questionnaires to arrive at a definition of the African personality. Wober (1975) indicates that the approaches in this area have been psychoanalytic in development.

The reader should be aware of the following general problems with early attempts at social psychology studies of Africa. There was a lack of consensus in the definition of concepts. What is the Western attitude? Is it an English, American, or French attitude? Contemporary researchers in social psychology and anthropology are raising questions about the concept of "modernity." Contributions by research workers such as Doob (1960) and Dawson (1967) illustrate the type of confusion and waste of effort that a lack of precise definitions of a researcher's concepts can cause in any area of research.

The second problem is the "missionary model of orientation" of these research workers. This includes the general attitude exhibited by these researchers that what is African is "bad" and that what is Western or European is "good." Coupled with this is the erroneous belief that Western cultures should set the pattern to be followed by new attitudes in Africa. By implication this orientation denies the relative contribution of the African environment in the evolution of the cultures of African people. These research workers failed to acknowledge that cultural changes are a two-way process. Africa was portrayed by early social psychological researchers on Africa as merely receiving Western influences and giving nothing in return.

Other aspects of biases are evident in Western contributions to the social psychology of Africa. These include biases due to experimenter effect, statistical procedures, sampling and nonsampling errors, use of unreliable and invalid questionnaires, and ignorance of African languages and cultures. There were errors arising from the relationship between the white experimenters and their African subjects. Other errors emanated from a cultural response set, such as the African tendency to hospitality toward strangers, respect for elders, and general courtesy to other human beings. Such behavioral tendencies and set prevent African subjects in social studies from not disagreeing with the views of others, including strangers, even when they know that such views are wrong. Respect for elders results in ingratiation so that the respondent distorts answers in order to win the approval, attention, or favor of the interviewer. Finally, in "sucker bias" the interviewee makes deliberate efforts to mislead, deceive, or outwit the interviewer. These games go on in research interaction without the awareness of some researchers who are ignorant of the cultures and languages of the African peoples.

Earlier attempts made by American social psychologists to promote social psychology research in Africa resulted in an international conference that was held at the University of Ibadan in the last week of December, 1965 through the first week of January, 1966 (Smith, 1968). The conference objectives included the encouragement and promotion of social psychological research on the problems of developing countries and the fostering of more appropriate patterns of research collaboration and coordination, research training, and scientific communication based on international cooperation between African social scientists and their European and American counterparts (Smith, 1968). This one, short conference ended without achieving any of the objectives that it had for itself.

Like early social psychology in Africa, the conference did not extend to applying psychological knowledge to the understanding of human behavior in African organizations. A few research efforts that investigated some organizational behavior of the African workers made efforts to confirm the usual stereotypes held about the African employees. Exceptions among these are works by Berg (1963), Harbinson (1959), Kilby (1960), and Wells and Warmington (1962). Harbinson (1959) showed that Egyptian managers identified the principal organizational problem that reduced their productivity and commitment to industrial work to be lack of freedom to implement work. Kilby (1960), on the other hand, concluded following his study in Nigeria that Nigerian workers are capable of producing as much as their European counterparts. Wherever they have been found to be less productive, it has been discovered that such low productivity is accounted for by inadequate incentive, poor supervision, and lack of proper work organization.

Industrial Organizational Psychology

Development in Africa and its increasing impact on society seem to follow a process similar to that in the West. In other words, the need for industries to solve practical, day-to-day problems has led to the demand for people with some scientific knowledge of human behavior. Again, French psychologists and their colonial government were in the forefront of others in realizing the need for industrial and organizational psychology in Africa (see Wickert, 1967, pp. 49-106). Studies carried out in this area by these French psychologists include those classified by Wickert as psychological testing in personnel selection and training and job analysis in personnel work. While the African population served as subjects in these studies, the technology of conducting of these studies cannot be aid to have been transferred to the African population in any of the African French colonies.

In many African countries, the need to solve the problems associated with human behavior in organizations was intensified by the African governments' attempts to restructure the received colonial organizations. For example, in Nigeria two processes, the so-called oil boom of the mid-1970s and the Manpower Indigenization Decree of the Nigerian government (1972), intensified this need. The oil boom increased industrial and economic growth expectations in the country, while the provisions of the indigenization decree increased the level of managerial responsibilities of Nigerians in various private industries and organizations. According to Popoola (1983), the manpower implication of the decree was felt more by the multinational corporations that had, prior to the decree, relied heavily on foreign manpower and expertise. The large-scale promotion of Nigerians to senior management positions brought about the realization that unless those individuals so promoted were properly trained, they might not acquire the appropriate leadership attitudes and orientations required for the management of people in their various positions. Hence, there was a great need for industrial psychologists in Nigeria.

At the University of Ibadan, about 50 percent of the students who apply for the master's degree program elect to specialize in industrial psychology. Many of these are employed in industries after obtaining the master's degree. Ugwuegbu (1983b) lamented that the development of industrial and organizational psychology in Nigeria was an uphill task because those who obtain higher qualifications in this concentration usually prefer to work in industries, including the banking organizations, where the financial rewards are more attractive than in universities, where research and the development of strong theoretical aspects of the discipline are likely to take place. The tendency in such a situation is that Nigeria and other developing African countries will continue to depend on imported theories in the area.

Impediments to the Development of Psychology in Africa

Some of the most obvious obstacles, which are hindering the rapid development and application of psychology in African organizations, are as follows.

1. Shortage of manpower, resulting in lack of appropriately trained psychologists. Shortage of, and in most countries, a complete absence of people with sufficient psychological knowledge to train required personnel in some areas of psychology.
2. Limited financial resources, resulting in loss of highly educated psychologists to other sectors of the African economy where there are better financial opportunities. Poor remuneration of psychologists in African universities. This results in the phenomenon of brain drain, which benefits the Western industrialized countries. Shortage of funds to construct laboratories and equip them hinders the development of research in psychology in these countries.
3. Lack of skill in constructing simple laboratory equipment. Poor maintenance of available laboratory equipment caused by both lack of skill and shortage of spare parts and total absence of psychotechnology skills.
4. Limited psychological services. In Africa this fact leaves a large proportion of the population to the care of native or traditional medicine people called *dibia* or *babalawo* in some cultures.
5. Lack of advocacy for, or politicization of, psychology. This is attributable to failure on the part of psychologists and their respective national psychological societies to speak out for psychology and to make psychology relevant to the human, social, industrial, and economic development of Africa.

6. Uncritical acceptance of, and total reliance by African psychologists on, the principles, theories, and models of psychology developed by Western psychologists for the benefit of Western cultures.
7. Poor communication channels, resulting in dependence on a few willing Western journals as outlets for African research findings. Others are poor library facilities and the wide gap between scientific information and government social policies.

Currently, psychologists in Africa look upon the idea of adherence to a particular historical school of psychology with disfavor. Instead, emphasis is laid on the contributions that each area of psychology has made to the broadening of the views of psychology and to clarifying its scientific objectives relative to the problems of general development in Africa and Third World countries. With such objectives in view, applied areas of psychology such as industrial and organizational psychology, medical and health psychology, organizational behavior or managerial psychology, criminal psychology, social psychology, psychology and the law, and environmental psychology, to name but a few, are looked upon with greater favor in the developing countries of Africa.

SUMMARY

The structure and process of the colonial European management model that was grafted onto the African industrial and organizational sector were bureaucratic in nature. The management model is characterized by overcentralization of power and authority. The most fundamental weakness that characterized the colonial management and administrative system is its failure to recognize the importance of selection, training, and development for the employees. Every employee was made permanent after a brief period of probation. The system believed that effective management could develop only through conformity, hard work, and protracted, on-the-job experience.

The model made no attempt to understand the behavior of African workers. The European managers alone decided what African labor was worth and provided poor remuneration for African workers. They did not grant African supervisors and foremen and women the status commensurate with their responsibility. The system was marked by inefficient division of labor, resulting in management's inability to utilize African employees' intellectual, mechanical, and creative skills. Effective and efficient organizational management requires some knowledge of human behavior as embodied in the science of psychology. Psychology originated in Europe, but many of the colonial powers in Africa failed to see its relevance to understanding work in Africa and how it would have aided them to understand African workers. Consequently, none of the colonial powers' higher institutions of learning in Africa offered courses in psychology or attempted to solve Africa's dearth of managerial, professional, and technical manpower.

At independence countries such as Angola and Namibia had less than five university graduates to take over the management of those nations and their organizations. Africans who assumed the responsibility of managing Africa's private and public organizations and government departments and their parastatals inherited no guidelines from the colonial managers and administrators. Since they were not previously involved meaningfully in any decision making and other management aspects, they lacked relevant background experience to use as a frame of reference.

African countries embraced the study of the science of psychology in the second half of the 1960s after their independence. Egypt, Nigeria, and South Africa have developed the study of psychology more than the rest of the countries in Africa. Most of the departments of psychology in Africa emphasize clinical, industrial and organizational, and social psychology. These areas of psychology are relevant to the understanding, prediction, explanation, control, and management of human behavior in organizations. While psychology is the scientific study of human behavior and mental processes, management is the process of setting and achieving organizational goals and objectives through the basic functions that acquire and utilize human, financial, material, and informational resources. The interface of management and psychology is human behavior. Human behavior, whether through effective decision making or goal achievement orientation of the employees, moves organizations forward to the level of profitability. Psychology has developed elaborate theories on how people learn, what motivates them, how to improve employees' performance, and how to increase workers' satisfaction and well-being. These are some of the goals that management processes are trying to accomplish. Human behavior in organizations is the least understood of the resources needed for the optimization of organizational objectives in Africa.

2

Psychological Problems in the Management of African Organizations

STRUCTURE OF AFRICAN ORGANIZATIONS

A highly noticeable feature of organizations in Africa is the relative economic dominance of small industrial organizations and businesses such as mining, quarrying, and the processing of agricultural products. With the increasing cry for more African peoples' participation and quest for transfer of technology, there has been a corresponding increase in cottage industries, artisan industries, and small-sized industries, that specialize in various products. Modern artisan organizations that belong to this class include automobile repairing, radio and television services, electric machine repair shops, cabinetmaking, ironworks, brick and block making, garment manufacturing, manufacture of transport equipment, and fixtures. These organizations employ fewer than fifty workers. Most of these are individually owned and are characterized by the owner-manager management style. Others, in this category of organizations, are outposts of large expatriate organizations such as the United African Trading Company (UAC).

There are also medium-sized organizations. These employ more than between 50 and 100 employees. They include printing outfits, cabinetmaking and joinery, timber production, bakeries, chemical production and marketing (soap, pharmaceutical products, cosmetics, insecticides), food processing, including meat and dairy products, preservation and canning of fruits and vegetable and animal oils, and production of fat, textiles, clothing, and footwear, fisheries, and hotel services. Ownership of these organizations ranges from single individuals, families, cooperative groups, and government. The management model in these organizations is usually owner-manager or family manager, or it is entrusted to a few members of the group, or the government department under which the organization is located appoints a manager for the organization. Often the owner-manager or member of the family who is entrusted with the overall management has no expertise in professional management. Such family members are often selected on the basis of their being the person with some education in the family or because the individual is the eldest member of the family.

Large organizations are modern in nature. Some of these are inherited by the present African governments from the colonial administrations. These include railway corporations, postal service organizations, and government departments and their parastatals, such as hospitals, universities, schools, and prisons. Others were established by indigenous African governments since independence, such as airlines, cement companies, solid mineral mining companies, and print and electronic media organizations. There are also major nongovernment organizations such as breweries, soft drink companies, textiles, and tobacco companies, banks, tire manufacturing companies, and paint production and marketing organizations. Many of these organizations were previously "limited" liability companies with capital provided wholly by foreign sources, or they were built in partnership with government and/or private sources.

The multinational giants are another class of organizations that can be identified among African organizations. These employ over 1,000 to 5,000 workers. A list of major multinational organizations in Africa includes the following: Unilever, United Africa Company, Breweries Plc, John Holt Plc, SCAO, PZ, CFAO, Shell Petroleum, Mobil, Texas Oil, the big pharmaceutical companies, and the big gold, copper, diamond and other solid mineral mining companies in Angola, Namibia, Sierra Leone, the Republic of South Africa, Republic of Congo or Zaire. Others are refineries, automobile assembly plants, textile factories, timber and plywood, furniture companies, rubber processing companies, sugar manufacturing organizations, cotton, and farming businesses, and fisheries.

It is fitting to recall here that groups of African peoples came under the colonial, European countries as a result of international rivalries and these countries' ambition to create trading outposts for the exploitation of rich, raw materials in the African subregion. The need to appropriate more regions led to the scramble for Africa and the eventual partitioning of the continent in 1884/1885 among the nations of Europe. Until today, these multinational organizations have had their headquarters in Euro-American metropolitan centers, where most of their major decisions concerning planning and other management functions are made.

In addition to the multinationals that serve as outlets for manufactured products from their parent companies in Europe and America, there are medium-sized and small-scale organizations. These are owned in part or whole by either foreigners or Africans and their governments, or they are in joint ownerships. In countries such as Nigeria, the government's indigenization policy in 1972 removed small-scale organizations from those that are open to participation by foreigners. Both ownership and size of an organization have a bearing on management (Onyemelukwe, 1966). These characteristics also affect the type of management approach that is applied to the organization and the type of problems that it creates for modern management style. All organizations whether small, medium-sized, large, or multinational, and whether owned by one person, family or government, or a public liability, are relatively characterized by division of labor and the need for planning and coordination of human and material resources needed for a productive endeavor.

This must have influenced Edgar H. Schein (1970) when he defined a modern organization as "the rational co-ordination of the activities of a number of people for the achievement of some common explicit purpose or goal, through division of labor and function, and through a hierarchy of authority and responsibility."

Schein's definition is influenced by the popular classical theory of organizations. There are two types of organizations, formal and informal. Organizations such as business firms, companies, industrial organizations, hospitals, universities, prisons, labor unions, government ministries and their agencies, mining establishments, and agricultural enterprises are examples of *formal* organizations. These are run according to prescribed rules, policies, and procedures. They are best depicted by the organizational chart, the officially prescribed structure or framework of the organization as a formal system. Koontz and O'Donnell (1968) maintain that the structure of an organization involves not only the departmental framework but also the procedures for assigning formal activities to the departmental units. We define a *formal* organization as a group of people who possess different skills, attitudes, motivations, and perceptions but who are working together toward the achievement of common goals and are governed by some formal rules of behavior that are pertinent to their common objectives. In order, therefore, to effectively manage organizations, the manager or leader must be able to understand, describe, explain, predict, and control the group's differing organizational behavior characteristics.

Informal organizations, on the other hand, evolve from the ways in which the employees interact and work with each other. Many of the interactions and activities of an informal organization are not prescribed by the organization and are much more casual in nature. For example, two secretaries in an office are supposed to perform only their assigned job responsibilities. But they often do more than that. They may wish to talk to each other, and go out on a break together to have lunch. While waiting for their food, they may engage in conversation concerning the behavior of their boss and share some complaints about their job. They may, with time, even become friends and start engaging in an exchange of weekend visits. These two secretaries would have established relationships that are reaching far beyond those formally required by their job responsibilities. Relations such as these tend to arise in all formal organizations. They are designated as *informal* organizations. Formal and informal organizations as factors influencing human behavior in the work environment are quite inseparable. Psychology holds that formal and informal organizations, both exist simultaneously in workplaces and interact to influence the effectiveness or ineffectiveness of workers. Many of the psychological problems in the management of African organizations arise from the complex interaction of informal and formal organizations and between the formal organizations and their environments.

THE NATURE OF ORGANIZATIONS

There are several theories of organization. The classical, behavioral and open system theories are briefly discussed here. They are examined for possible problems that such theories raise for African organizations.

Classical Theories

Classical theories of management for a long time remained the most coherent and powerful explanation of organizations. The theories were derived from Fayol's (1949) analysis of management. The theories embody the classical principles of organizations as characterized by clearly defined objectives, division of labor, clearly spelled-out coordination of activities toward a common goal, unity of command, and responsibility. Fayol also listed the following additional principles as characterizing organizations: specialization, discipline, subordination of individual interest to general interest, fair remuneration, centralization, order, equity, stability of tenure of employees, initiative, and cohesiveness of the work group. According to classical theories of management, the functions of managers include planning, organizing, commanding, (tell subordinates what to do) coordinating, and controlling.

Organizations based on classical theories are bureaucratic in nature. The classical theories have been criticized on the grounds that they are too broad to provide much help in practice. The principle of specialization or division of labor, for example, does not tell the organizer how finely the tasks should be divided. Classical theories are too mechanistic and, as such, incompatible with human nature. This criticism points out a very serious deficiency if it is recalled that formal organizational structures are designed solely for the purpose of enabling workers to perform effectively to achieve organizational objectives. Many of the criticisms of classical theories have come from behavioral scientists. These theorists contend that classical theories fail to take into consideration human behaviors, especially motivation. However, African managers can benefit from the classical theories if they emphasize in their organization objectives that are clearly articulated and shared by the entire workforce, equitable remuneration, and cohesive work groups and if they create opportunity for their employees to express their creativity.

Behavioral Theories

These derive from the work of researchers such as Christ Argyris (1957), Wright Bakke (1953), Chester Barnard (1938), Mason Haire (1959), Rensis Likert (1959, 1961, 1967), Elton Mayo (1960), and Douglas McGregor (1960). The theories are concerned with examining the ways in which organizations and their subunits or systems actually behave, which may be different from the way that the formal structure of organizations would appear to dictate. Behavioral theorists are conscious of the psychological properties of human beings, such as perception, cognition, and motivation, and the complexity of relationships among these variables. They are aware that any attempt to alter any one of these cognitions is likely to start a chain reaction. During the interactions within an organization, management organizational orders or policies, no matter how plainly and clearly stated and communicated, are subject to reinterpretation according to the psychological *set* of those who transmit or implement them. The environment in which those down the line of authority find themselves and the conflicting pressures from the formal and informal organizations to which employees are subjected influence the degree to which company rules and responsibilities of workers are understood. Behavioral theorists know that workers in an organization are motivated by many forces that may be different from those factors that prompt a manager's decisions. Workers in an organization may also be seeking goals that are different from those assigned to them by the organization's manuals. For the behavioral theorists, work is a group activity (Mayo, 1960). Work also is seen to provide avenues for individuals to satisfy their needs for interpersonal relations.

Managers of African organizations have much to gain from behavioral theories. First, the acceptance of work as a group activity is culturally relevant to the African philosophy as life of human interdependence. The involvement of workers as individuals and as members of a group enhances workers performance. Second, the traditional perception of organizational employees in Africa as a *tabula rasa*, who should always conform to managers' orders must give way to the perception of employees as individuals with differing cognitions and social and psychological needs, that they expect to satisfy in their formal and informal interactions with the organization and its environment.

Open System

The open system theory is the best available conceptual framework for describing an organization. Katz and Kahn's (1966) theory likened organizations to living biological beings. They defined a system as the arrangement of relationships among component parts that operate together as a whole. Each component is said to be a subsystem that has some system properties of its own. The components of the system are integrally linked in an elaborate web of complexity to the extent that a change in one component sets off a chain of reactions in other components. As a result of the complexity and causal relationships, it is usually difficult to predict the eventual state of each component, including the one that was originally changed.

Wexley and Yukl (1984) summarized Katz and Kahn's (1966) nine common characteristics of open systems under the title of *Input-transformation–output cycle*. According to these authors, a system is open if it has reciprocal transactions with the environment in which it exists. Transactions between an organization and its environment involve inputs and outputs. For an organization, inputs are usually in the form of materials, money, information, personnel, equipment, and other forms of energy, which the organization takes in. These are received by the organization from its environment. The organization, in return, makes outputs, which can take many forms depending on the nature of the organization. Most of the outputs are derived from inputs that have been transformed by the organization. For example, breweries transform raw materials such as corn and millet into beer and malt drinks, while flourmills transform wheat into flour for making bread, and the refineries turn crude oil into petrol (gas) and kerosene. Other by-products that result from the process of refining crude oil include waste products that are of no other use. These are also treated as outputs. Equipment, energy, and money paid to suppliers for necessary materials and to the workers for their labor all play a role in the transformation process. The cycle of inputs, transformation, and outputs is continually repeated. Organizations that do not sell their products or services for profit, such as universities and government hospitals, for example, must rely on other sources, especially government, to come to their aid. Public service-oriented organizations in Africa, such as the railways, postal service system, state owned airlines, and some government parastatals, depend on government subsidy to complete the cycle.

Just like the biological organism on which Katz and Kahn's model is built, the survival and growth of any organization depend on the favorable balance between inputs and outputs of energies. In terms of funds, the organization must receive at least as much as it expends in the transformation process and the maintenance of itself (Wexley and Yukl, 1984). If the organization earns more money from its products than it expends, the excess can be used as a reserve that can be applied in the future for various programs such as expansion and further growth of the organization. Katz and Kahn (1966) call the process *steady state and dynamic homeostasis.* If the ratio of inputs to outputs is not favorable, the organization can survive only by finding some creditors to subsidize it. In addition to monetary inputs, the organization must be able to obtain adequate inputs of labor, energy, and supplies from the environment to maintain equilibrium.

Managers of African organizations, especially those owned by government, do not bother about survival. Organizations are not thought of in terms of living organisms that can survive or die. This is because government regularly subsidizes them by allocating annual budget to them for their day-to-day operations, including the salaries of their employees. Organizations are politically located rather than locating them in favorable environments with adequate supply of raw materials and skilled labor. An outstanding example is the case of the Iron and Steel Industry in Nigeria, where the federal government, instead of siting the organization at or near Onitsha (Igbo part of the country), where there are abundance of raw materials including energy, located it at Oshogbo (Yoruba part of the country) which has neither the raw materials nor the required infrastructure. The consequence is that raw materials for the Nigerian Iron and Steel Industry are being transported by trucks over several hundreds of miles from their sites to the industry. Physical distance and unnecessary cost of transportation of raw materials constitute survival problems for the organization.

ENVIRONMENTAL INFLUENCES

Organizations are influenced by cultural, economic, political, and scientific developments in the immediate and distant external environment. These can affect the goals of an organization, or they can both affect the goals and also disrupt the regular input–transformation–output cycle, as illustrated with the fate of the Nigerian Iron and Steel Industry. A catalog of major environmental factors that affect African organizations include, political and economic stability, government policies and actions, infrastructure (supply of water, electricity, roads, and telephone), the cultural subenvironment, suppliers of materials, energy (coal, fuel), equipment, and equipment parts; customers, consumers, labor unions, and competitors; and owners or shareholders.

Government directives and agencies set the stage for the type of economic policies in the environment in which the organization is located. Whether the economic environment is favorable or unfavorable depends on the government's economic, political, and social policies. Consumers and competitors, on the other hand, are the principal determinants of the market forces for the organization's output of products and services. Suppliers, cultural background, competitors for sources of supplies, and labor are principal determinants of whether the organization can obtain adequate amounts of these essential inputs. Labor unions, the owners of the organization, stockholders, creditors, and consumer groups make conflicting demands and exert conflicting pressures on the organization and influence its goals and activities. The values, beliefs, attitudes, and behavior of the workers in the organizations may be a consequence of their cultural background and level of education. These are some of the environmental factors that have an impact on organizations in Africa. Finally, the stability and predictability of the social, economic, and political environment of an organization influence its short-, medium-, and long-term planning. All of these impact organizations' input–transformation–output cycle, productivity, and survival.

The organization can also, on its own, as a consequence of its behavior, disrupt the steady state and dynamic homeostasis by its neglect of the environment. The quality of the product output determines how far the organization can sustain the pressure of competitors. Environmental concerns of the organization can generate positive or negative feelings and reactions toward it. If the organization is not concerned with environmental degradation and the health and education of the population within its immediate environment, the labor input into the input–transformation–output cycle is drastically affected. Organizational neglect of its environment can also lead to the disruption of the input–transformation–output cycle, as the experiences of Shell Oil Company in the Niger Delta regions of Nigeria have demonstrated.

CULTURAL INFLUENCE

Many researchers and authors have blamed African cultures for the inability of the African managers and workers to assimilate Western work and management models. These researchers hold that African managers and workers are basically different because of their cultural and belief orientations. They hold that African cultures and beliefs condition African managers and workers to poor attitudes to work, low motivation, low productivity, lack of initiative, and excessive religiosity.

According to Eze (1995, p. 147), Farmer and Richman (1965), and Osuji (1984), sociocultural factors are the real obstacle hindering the introduction of "advanced management practices and know-how into developing countries." Eze (1995) went further to enumerate other culture-associated factors such as ethnicity, heterogeneity of cultures and languages, authoritarianism, and extended family backgrounds as some of the barriers that prevent the creation of a conducive environment for the transfer of Western management models to African organizations. While Oloko (1977) attributes poor performance in African organizations to the inability of Africans to perceive the relation between good performance and reward, Ejiofor (1981) ascribed to culture what he called a "bad" attitude to work.

Another major contributor to the cultural explanation is Onyemelukwe (1973, 1983). Onyemelukwe argues that the African child is socialized into the belief that the norms and values of the group are supreme and should not be challenged; elders possess all wisdom and therefore should be respected. The African is socialized into affiliative behavior and expected to be loyal to the primary group. The results of this model of socialization, according to Onyemelukwe (1983) include individuals who lack initiative, are without problem-solving orientation, and usually do not accept personal responsibility. Above all, as managers, they find it difficult to delegate responsibility to their subordinates. Delegation (Onyemelukwe, 1983) assumes that the subordinate to whom the manager is delegating the task has the ability, skill, and initiative to handle the task as delegated.

Finally, other cultural explanations (Roberts, 1990) assume that African models of management and organizational characteristics emphasize a focus on internal, resource-linked issues rather than on policy. These explanations claim that African managers avoid change and innovation, and that they tend to favor consensus above individualism. Roberts' (1990) theory also maintains that Western management models, on the other hand, assume very different organizational characteristics and managerial incentives. The view further suggests that while analytical and quantitative methods can be transferred to Africa, strategic planning, motivation, human resource management, conflict resolution, and bargaining are deeply rooted in distinct, Western cultural values. These cannot transfer to African managers (Roberts, 1990). This author did not conduct any empirical research to support his claims but was just satisfied to make a barren observation that was simply anchored on a traditional, colonial stereotype.

Problems with the Cultural Explanation
The cultural explanation is the last vestige of the colonial, stereotypic view of Africans and African workers. The unfortunate thing about this is the extent to which some African intellectuals bought these untested, early, Western views. An understanding of the indigenous African attitude to work requires a thorough

grasp of the traditional African system of work. When the Europeans colonized African countries, they found that the African system of work was differently organized. It was unlike the early Industrial Revolution system of work with which they were familiar in Europe. Africans worked for self, parents, age group, or extended family members. A person was always a part owner of the work that the person did. Only slaves worked for other people. Since people were part owners of the work that they performed, they were not paid for working.

The implications of this were that workers were independent people. They made independent decisions about when to go to work, how long to work, and how hard to work. The location of the farm or trading post determined what time the workers left home for work. Distant farms or trading posts required an early start, such as long before sunrise. African workers achieved closure at work. They began and finished whatever they started and derived satisfaction from their finished products. People achieved recognition in their community through hard work. For example, the Igbo culture emphasizes achievement. In Igbo culture success is internally rather than externally attributed. Chinua Achebe (1958) described this cultural orientation when he said: "But the Ibo people have a proverb that when a man says yes his chi says yes also. Okonkwo said yes very strongly; so his chi agreed. And not only his chi but his clan too, because it judged a man by the work of his hands." (P. 19) The Igbo name "Ogbuji" means a person who achieved fame through hard labor, especially farming, while "Uzoma" signifies that the individual has been blessed through hard work in business away from his home. African people worked because they had physical and psychological needs to satisfy. People attained social prestige through work.

The European system of work, on the other hand, was slave labor because in that system people were forced to work. It made people lose their individual independence. African people were told when to come to work, as if there were anything special about reporting to work at seven in the morning as against five or nine or even noon. The European system of work introduced payment for work, and the European people alone decided how much African labor was worth.

African workers' reaction to an imposition of European system of work, that deprived people of their independence, is often confused by some uninformed researchers as the African attitude to work, which they generally blame on African culture. For one thing, culture is not static. It is dynamic. Even if this reaction has now attained a status of culture, it ought to change with the increasing African perception that the European system of work has equitable rewards that are worth working for. If the African has borrowed successfully some of the new, Western religions with their promises of a better life hereafter and has adapted their teachings to the African environment and demands, one would not think that the African managers are incapable of doing the same with Western management principles and techniques if they got appropriate rewards. Research has shown that where this has not been possible, the environment of work failed to provide adequate incentive or was due to poor supervision and lack of proper work organization (Kilby, 1960; Ugwuegbu, 1983a).

Other evidence is that countries with stronger cultural and family ties, such as China, Japan, Taiwan, India, and Brazil, have successfully absorbed and adapted Western management styles and work orientation. With the exception of Brazil, these countries have strong, indigenous religious beliefs and strong family ties to which they are loyal. These emerging economic markets and Asian tigers, as they were once called before their 1997 financial crises, have more than demonstrated that a cultural explanation of problems in the management of African organizations begs the question; therefore, it is time for researchers to start dealing with the problems that inhibit African workers' performance in African organizations, namely, reward system and leadership problems.

However, Ugwuegbu (1983a) has suggested that if cultural predispositions are the main barriers preventing African managers from acquiring Western management models and work attitudes, attempts should be made to protect the organizations by eliminating applicants high on negative cultural predisposition through the use of psychological tests and structured interviews during selection processes. Managers who escape detection through interview screening should be desensitized through training and development programs. Finally, attempts should be made to redesign African organizations to adjust to the major functional cultural predisposition of the people. Japan has provided a model of how some functional cultural predispositions could be incorporated into the organizational management to enhance productivity of workers.

A third argument against the cultural explanation is what Ugwuegbu calls a theory of two Nigerian personalities, the Nigerians who work for themselves, private companies, or foreign international organization such as the International Institute of Tropical Agriculture. The second Nigerian personalities are those who work for the Nigerian government, its parastatals, universities, hospitals, and other agencies. Assessed in terms of work attitude, motivation, productivity, commitment, and satisfaction, Nigerians who work for themselves, international organizations, and private companies are more committed, productive, and efficient than those that work for government and its departments and parastatals. These two groups of Nigerians are products of the same culture and possess similar values and beliefs, so one must look elsewhere for causes of the differences in either their management style or work performance.

African managers and workers in African organizations are responding to organizational arrangements rather than to cultural predispositions. Human behavior in organizations does not occur in isolation. Behavior in organizations can be understood only in context. That is, human behavior is highly influenced by the design of the organization and the nature and way in which information and work flow through the organization, the behavior and management style of the managers, the way and manner that incentives are scheduled and distributed, and the way that work is organized.

A series of researches by Ugwuegbu (1983a) supports the hypothesis that African managers and employees may be responding more to organizational management styles and the problems associated with the specific and general organizational climate, especially to systems of reward and opportunity for growth, than to any cultural stimulus. Several studies support this position. In a correctional study on the effects of cultural predisposition on job satisfaction, Ugwuegbu (1983a) showed that the more satisfied that employees are with perceived opportunities for advancement based on merit, the more likely they are to accept the attitudes and beliefs that are in agreement with the white, Anglo-Saxon, Protestant ethic predisposition to work. He also found that when workers are dissatisfied with the level of authority they have, retirement provisions, information on organizational development, and future plans, they tend to judge companies harshly on issues of discipline and the termination of employees' appointments.

Finally, Ugwuegbu (1983a) showed that employees prefer to work under managers and supervisors from their own part of the country (a cultural predisposition) when they perceive:

- their manager as lacking in fairness, good sense, and good intentions;
- the present position that they hold as lacking in economic advantages;
- the present position as lacking in opportunities for advancement based on merit;
- the cooperation and group efforts provided by fellow workers as low; and
- the management as lacking in foresight and planning.

RECRUITMENT, SELECTION, TRAINING, AND PLACEMENT

Work is a group activity. But the groups do not assemble to perform organizational tasks until individuals have been recruited and placed. A major psychological problem for managers in African organizations is how to recruit employees from a population of low skilled and poorly educated people available for employment, how to select and train them, and how to place them in jobs for the most effective role performance. In small or owner-manager organizations in Africa, recruitment, selection, training, and placement are not systematized. There is no requirement for any specific aptitude, education, or experience. The recruitment of relatives is preferred over hiring strangers. Often members of the extended family are attached early in life to the owner-manager, who may provide these relatives with accommodations, food, and medical needs. There is usually no formal training. Skills are acquired through experience on the job. Onyemeluke (1966) noted that as some of these business owners become successful, they tend to expand into other areas, such as banking, estate management, export-import business, electronics, transportation, or hotel organizations, and they begin to recruit educated and qualified managers.

The large industrial organizations irrespective of ownership, are structured and managed as are Western formal organizations. They have departments such as production, marketing, accounts, and personnel with distinct functions. In both small and large organizations in Africa many managers are unaware of the negative consequences of a haphazard employee selection and placement system and lack of training about organizational productivity. Organizational management in Africa requires the development of recruitment, selection, training, and placement policies in order to obtain the best performance from employees.

Evidence from Western countries indicates that the existence of a systematized selection and placement policy does not usually completely ensure that the psychological and material needs of the individual workers that they bring to the place of their employment and that they expect to fulfill through membership in the organization will, in fact, be met. It thus remains a major problem in organizations that management policies and practices, where they exist and are facilitative of organizational effectiveness, often do not satisfy the needs of individual employees. In some instances they may even aggravate the individual problems that the workers brought with them on joining the organization. According to several authors (Howell and Dipboye, 1982; Schein, 1970), sometimes it happens that employees' reaction to the failure to fulfill security, growth, and self-esteem needs is manifested in alienation, a feeling of insecurity, and bitterness. These psychological conditions may further degenerate into overt antisocial or antimanagement behaviors such as physical aggression and antagonism.

Organizations face two aspects of problems with regard to recruitment, selection, training, and placement: first, how to develop organizational policies and practices that facilitate organizational effectiveness and, at the same time, meet the needs of employees and, second, how to balance the testing and selection approach with the ergonomics and job design approach in order to maximize the employee potentials available to organizations.

The testing and selection approach lays emphasis on selecting the best available individuals from a pool of applicants and fitting them to the jobs. If such a match is not available, the next best available person can be selected and trained. The other approach, which is associated with the engineering psychology approach, lays emphasis on redesigning the job and its physical environment to fit the limitations and capacities of the humans. The task would be designed in such a way that any person could perform it. Of these two approaches, the test and selection approach is more common, as exemplified by the emphasis that colonial France put on testing and selection in Africa. Because of the absence of reliable and valid test instruments, the selection process in most African organizations is limited to personal data and interviews, which by themselves are a very unreliable selection process. Recently, multinational and some indigenous organizations, especially banks have been using aptitude tests that are designed for Western populations to recruit their African workers. The reliability, validity, and culture-free characteristics of these tests are yet to be demonstrated.

PSYCHOLOGICAL CONTRACT

Motivation to work at a high level of performance or to continue such high performance is a crucial problem for African organizations. Earlier studies on motivation tended to catalog the motives and needs of employees and then to relate these to the incentives and rewards offered by the organization. With more and better-designed research studies, it is now realized that the problem is more complex than was thought. A recent conceptualization is in terms of *psychological contract* (Argyris, 1960; Kolb, Rubin, and McIntyre, 1971; Schein, 1970).

In the developed and industrialized world the notion of psychological contract implies that the individual upon being employed has a variety of expectations of the organization and that the organization, on the other hand, has a variety of expectations of the employee. These expectations cover how much work is to be performed for how much pay; they also involve the whole pattern of rights, privileges, and obligations between employee and organization. The psychological contract is unlike a legal contract in that it defines a dynamic, changing relationship that is continually being renegotiated. Often important aspects of the contract are not formally agreed upon, and key organizational and individual expectations are sometimes unstated, as well as implicit premises about the relationship. For example, an employee of the Nigerian Breweries would expect the company not to fire him after he has worked there for a certain number of years, and the company may expect that the employee will not run down the organization's public image or betray the company by giving away its secrets to competitors. Such expectations are usually not written into any formal agreement between employee and organization, yet they operate powerfully as determinants of behavior (Argyris, 1960).

In many African organizations the balance of expectations in terms of responsibility tends to tilt in favor of organizations rather than employees. While employees are expected to be loyal, perform their duties, and conform to other employee obligations, the organizations tend not to be conscious of the rights and privileges of employees. The principle of perceiving the relationship between employees and organization in terms of a contract is a psychological reality that has implications for efficiency and productivity as well as employee satisfaction.

As Kolb, Rubin, and McIntyre (1971) indicate, the dynamic quality of the psychological contract means that individual and company expectations and individual and company contributions mutually influence one another. High expectations on the part of the organization can produce increased employee contributions, and great contributions will likewise raise expectations. From the company's point of view, the issue becomes how to manage available human resources so as to maximize individual contributions and how to socialize employees to accept organizational expectations and norms as legitimate. For the individual, on the other hand, the issue is how to gain satisfaction and rewards from the organization and how to manage one's career so that one's socialization takes places in organizational settings that encourage personal growth and development.

Support for the importance of the psychological contract between an individual employee and an organization comes from a growing body of research evidence from developed countries. This demonstrates the importance of early organizational experiences to the future performance of individual managers. Berlew and Hall (1966), in a study of managerial performance in a large public utility, report a very strong and consistent relationship between the company's initial expectations of the managers and their future performance. Company expectations focused on the type and quality of contributions expected of the managers, and performance was measured by rate of salary growth. In other words, the managers for whom the organization had high initial job expectations were found to be among the highest performers five years later. We must add, however, that the organization, on its own part, must have fulfilled the expectations that the tested managers had for it. If an organization fails to meet the expectations of the employees and, at the same time, cannot *coerce* them to remain as members, the employees will most likely leave. If the employees fail to leave, they become problem workers.

As Schein (1970) maintains, problems of motivation and organizational incentive or reward are best thought of as a complex bargaining situation between the organization and the employee. It involves the decision of an individual to accept an offer of a job, how hard to work, and how long. It implies, in turn, feelings of loyalty and commitment, an expectation of being taken care of, now and at retirement, and of finding a sense of identity through the organizational role. These are more intense psychological problems in organizational environments where authority and power may be perceived as not legitimate, where reward and promotion are not contingent upon performance, and where workers' remuneration is low and their expectations are not met by organizations, as happens in many African organizations.

SURVIVAL, GROWTH, AND DEVELOPMENT

Organizations come into existence to fulfill certain objectives, be they services or products. In order to survive, they must serve some useful function. If they fail in this regard, they cease to exist.

But when organizational growth and development are considered, one discovers some psychological problems. Normally, organizational growth and development in a business concern need an environment conducive to the development of new products and new processes for making products that improve the competitive edge of the company. New ideas for products come from people. African organizations, therefore, face the problem of how to create an environment and a set of management policies that will not only get the primary task performed effectively but, in addition, stimulate creative thinking and innovation among managers.

The problems of growth and development of organizations relate to problems of managing change and adaptation. African organizations find themselves in a very difficult and dynamic environment. These include technological changes elsewhere, which have practically left them years behind, creating problems of obsolescence. An unstable political environment that has created problems of unpredictability, unavailability of foreign exchange, low-capacity utilization, downsizing, and the changing tastes of the African population thus reduces the competitive ability of the African organizations.

For African organizations to grow and develop in the global market environment, members of the organizations must show creative thinking. The crucial psychological problem that African organizations face, if they are to survive, grow, and develop, is how to develop in their managers the kind of flexibility and adaptability that may well be needed for survival in the face of a changing, harsh environment. One way of doing this is to develop to the utmost the capacities of employees and the skills of managers as leaders, whether these are needed now or may be relevant later. Finally, some key African managers must develop attitudes and skills that permit them to employ social science data as well as the findings of industrial and organizational psychology in decision making in organizations. As the contributions of psychology to organizational management grow, it is becoming clear that organizational growth and development in Africa will depend on the ability of each organization to diagnose its own problems and to develop solutions for them. Managers, especially key managers in each organization, will be the agents of such planned change. These managers will have to take a systems view of their organization, diagnose the complexities of organizational problems, and learn to utilize third-party expertise intervention where necessary in order to aid in the diagnosis and facilitation of growth and development. All organizations in Africa face this problem of how to develop such attitudes, skills, and orientations in their key managers and other personnel.

Difficulties in leadership, decision making, conflict resolution, performance evaluation, and communication are some of the important process problems faced by African organizations. Others are problems of accountability and lack of clarity of mission, objectives, and goals.

FUTURE TRENDS FOR AFRICAN MANAGERS

In addition to their need for appropriate attitudes and skills, African managers of the future have two very important problems to deal with. These are the unpredictable and turbulent political environment under which African organizations operate and the expectations of African workers and consumers.

African managers of tomorrow must learn to solve organizational problems through negotiation rather than the use of power and authority. The traditional hierarchical structure of an organization with its autocratic and exclusive tendencies, which Africans inherited from European colonial powers, should be allowed to disintegrate and disappear. Structurally flat organizations are the future. African managers should replace management layers with team management. By so doing, they will work more closely with people over whom they have no apparent authority. Without authority, managers must achieve their aims by balancing the organization's needs with those of team members or the outsiders with whom they are trying to reach agreement. Managers can do this by being empathic, by being honest in handling disagreements, and by persuading others to agree rather than through exercise of power and force.

The workforce in Africa includes women and people of different ethnic and religious groups. Most conflicts in Africa result from intolerance of other ethnic and religious groups, and bias against women. In order to work effectively with such a diverse population managers must be open to new ways of thinking and relating to employees irrespective of their gender, ethnic, and religious affiliation. Stereotypic and egocentric thinking should be avoided.

Until recently, managers who rose from the ranks were afraid of applicants or employees with talent. African managers must always bear in mind that they are as successful as the talent they surround themselves. Identifying potential workers and providing them with challenging work will continue to be a key ingredient of productive management. Developing people while motivating them to contribute their best is one way to build a successful and efficient organization. African managers have not succeeded in reverting to the traditional methods of solving organizational problems through a team approach. Previously authors tended to condemn the extended family system and its collectivist approach to problem solving. Recently, other studies have demonstrated that modern organizational problems are better handled by collaborative rather, than individualistic, efforts. African managers of the future should intensify efforts to integrate collective problem-solving approach into their management style. African managers of the future have to tap the creative power of every employee. In order to achieve this, managers must give their subordinates responsibilities and the necessary information and authority to make decisions. Managers must trust their employees and be worthy of their trust, be good listeners, and reward creative and innovative thinking.

One of the measures of the effectiveness of an organization, department, or work unit is the quality of its product or service. African managers must incorporate the philosophy of continuous performance improvement. This implies that every employee believes that improvement is possible in whatever the worker does. Managers and other employees alike must always anticipate product and production process changes.

SUMMARY
There are two types of organizations. The organizational chart best depicts formal organizations. Formal organizations are run according to prescribed rules, policies, and procedures. Informal organizations evolve from the interactions between and among employees. Both informal and formal organizations interact to influence the effectiveness of employees. Many of the psychological problems in the management of African organizations arise from the complex interaction among formal and informal organizations and their environments.

For a long time, classical theories of management remained the most coherent and powerful explanations of organizations. Classical theories of organizations have been criticized as being bureaucratic in nature, and too broad and mechanistic, as well as ignoring human motivation. Social and behavioral scientists proposed the behavioral theories of organizational management. These theories emphasize motivation. In behavioral theories work is a group activity. The open system proposed by Katz and Kahn provides the best available conceptual framework for describing an organization. The theory is built on the input–transformation–output cycle model. The survival and growth of any organization depend on the favorable ratio of input and output of energies and other resources. African managers benefit from these theories by gaining insight into how others perceive organizations.

Researchers and authors in the past have attributed to African cultures the failure of African managers and workers to imbibe the Western work ethic and management models. This belief is questioned here, and other explanations are offered, such as the failure of rewards scheduling and rewards allocation. Other management difficulties are problems associated with recruitment, selection, training, and placement, psychological contract problems, and problems associated with survival, growth, and development. Finally, there are problems of management leadership, decision making, communication, and performance evaluation. Suggestions are also made about what is expected of future African managers.

3

Employee Work Motivation

Individuals differ in their work performance. This is true whether they consist of tobacco farm employees, assembly plant workers, technicians, salespeople, or managers. Two important variables are implicated namely, differences in skills or abilities on the part of the individual employees and differences in the employees' level of motivation.

It is important to indicate that the mere possession of the necessary skills or abilities is not an adequate guarantee of satisfactory work performance. Managers are often disappointed to see that some employees, in spite of demonstrated abilities in the past, are not able to perform satisfactorily at assigned tasks following employment. Such employees may have performed well for the first six months and then decline in task performance; or the decline in performance may have occur immediately after, or at the same time as, some changes in the employees' work environment, for example, transfer to another department, or reduction or enlargement of work responsibilities.

People have different amounts and kinds of experiences. They also vary in the degree to which they possess the necessary intellectual abilities required for satisfactory performance on a given job. These differences contribute to the differences in work performance that we observe. However, given similarity of ability and experience, the level of the individual employees' motivation is the principal determinant of their level of work performance. This chapter brings together major theories, research, applications, and criticisms of the subject of motivation for work performance. The chapter also discusses some strategies for fostering work motivation in African organizations.

THE CONCEPT OF MOTIVATION

Motivation is an important psychological construct. Katzell and Thompson (1990) define work motivation as a broad, hypothetical construct pertaining to the conditions and processes that account for the arousal, direction, magnitude, and maintenance of effort in a person's job. This definition implies that motivation is a major determinant of human behavior. One would expect a highly motivated person to do a given job better, more quickly, and with fewer errors than a person who is poorly motivated (Eysenck, 1963).

It is easy to have the notion that performance is a good index of motivation. This notion is not correct, because performance depends not only on motivation but also on innate ability, eye-hand coordination, experience, habits in performing the task, the nature of the task, and the suitability of the available instruments, materials, or equipment for performing the task.

THEORIES OF WORK MOTIVATION

The earliest theories of work motivation were very simplistic. These include the so-called scientific management (Taylor, 1911) and the human-oriented approaches. The tenet of the scientific management approach is that people should be paid for being good workers and punished or fired for being otherwise. The theory advocates that if one wants to motivate workers, one should increase their salaries and other incentives to a level high enough for them to experience monetary gain. The earn-as-you-produce (piecework rate) approach, which requires that, following job analysis, job elements should be given monetary values, is an example. Employees are paid in accordance with the number of such elements that they produce in a given period of time.

In contrast to Taylor's theory are the human-oriented approaches, which base their appeal on practicality rather than altruism. These approaches try to sell to managers the idea that good human relations make for happy workers, that happy workers are productive workers, and that organizations should be concerned about the well-being of their employees because it increases profitability.

There are, however, some problems with these positions. It is acceptable that appropriate remuneration can motivate and foster more compliance with organizational goals and objectives. According to Ugwuegbu (1990b), however, the experience from Nigeria as to the effect of salary increases and other monetary incentives is that, although money is important, especially when one does not have it, its effects on work motivation are inhibitory and, at best, short-lived. Monetary incentives are essentially motivators for some grades of workers but not for the majority of employees in most companies. Workers are propelled sometimes by other needs.

The validity of the scientific management and human-oriented approaches is furthermore questioned by empirical findings. Current research has not established any clear relationship between employees' feelings of satisfaction in their job and their productivity. Evidence also exists to show that happy workers are not necessarily productive workers. Herzberg, Mausner, and Snyderman (1959) and Roethlisberger and Dickson (1939) have demonstrated that workers respond to incentives and disincentives rather than to monetary rewards. Finally, the correlation between job satisfaction and job performance is generally low, thus voiding the major assumption of the human relations movement.

Deficiencies in these early theories of work motivation led to a variety of other theoretical approaches. Katzell and Thompson (1990) summarized these theories under two broad headings, as dealing either with *exogenous causes* or with *endogenous processes*. According to these authors, exogenous theories focus on motivationally relevant independent variables that can be changed by external agents. Variables such as organizational incentives and rewards and social factors such as leader and group behavior are exogenous variables, according to Katzell and Thompson (1990). They serve as handles that can be used by managers or policymakers to change the motivation of workers.

Endogenous theories, in turn, deal with process or mediating variables such as expectancies, attitudes that are amenable to modification only indirectly in response to a variation in one or more exogenous variables. Some of these motivation theories are discussed next in this chapter. In doing so, Katzell and Thompson's (1990) approach has been adopted because it seems to impose an acceptable grouping order into an area that is otherwise very disorganized due to the multiplicity of views that characterize the area.

Exogenous Theories

Motive or Need Theory. This insists that people have certain innate or acquired propensities to seek out or avoid certain kinds of stimuli. These propensities, called motives or needs, influence behavior and are major determinants of performance. Various theories differ in content regarding the number of basic needs or sets of needs proposed and in whether needs are arranged in some hierarchical order.

Of the theories in this category, the best known among African managers is Maslow's need hierarchy. Maslow (1954) advocated five needs, which are regulated by their potency and arousal levels: physiological needs (hunger, thirst, and recovery from fatigue), safety needs (freedom from pain), belongingness (love, affection, and friendship), esteem needs (prestige, achievement states, dominance), and self-actualization (expression of creative capacity). Maslow's approach advocates that people are motivated to satisfy these basic needs before the higher order ones.

The implication of the need theory for organizational management, according to Ugwuegbu (1989a, 1990b), is that:

- It is important for managers to discover where on the hierarchy an employee's need satisfaction has stopped so that they can manipulate the reinforcement system to move the worker to the next higher level of motivation.
- Satisfying all the employees' lower needs liberates them to pursue creative achievement and self-actualization needs.
- Knowledge of workers' needs level should determine their selection and placement level and the type and content of a training program suitable for the workers.

Incentive or Reward Theory. At employment, a company may offer an employee a package which may include growth opportunity, free medical, retirement benefits, and life insurance. Such incentives consist of features of the work situation that lead the workers to associate certain forms of behavior with certain types of rewards. On the other hand, disincentives are job characteristics or stimuli that, conversely, evoke avoidance or restraint, such as a company policy that deducts from a worker's pay when that employee is absent. Incentives are therefore important in attracting and holding employees and in directing behavior. Rewards are job characteristics or stimuli that satisfy one or more motives and therefore arouse positive psychological states that serve to encourage and maintain the behavior that produces them.

Reinforcement Theory. This postulates that workers are motivated to perform well when there have been positive consequences of good performance. It advocates that ineffective work behavior should not be positively reinforced or should be punished. It insists that the occurrence of good work behavior be rewarded immediately. This will strengthen the association between the behavior and its reinforcement. This is because the effects of reinforcement depend heavily on the schedule according to which reinforcers are delivered. The closer reinforcement follows good work behavior the more effective it is in promoting such behavior. The theory thus emphasizes the importance of close schedule between performance and reinforcement rather than the properties of the reinforcers.

Goal Theory. This emanated from Locke's (1968) proposition that conscious goals affect performance. But before this happens, it is necessary for a goal to be set, understood, and accepted. This can be seen as an example of the arousal of motivation or as making salient the link between performance and rewards. Several studies support the positive effects of goal setting on performance for a wide variety of jobs.

Tubbs (1986) carried out an analysis of several studies and found agreement that setting goal has less effect on job satisfaction than when no goals are set. Goal setting is most effective when specific production targets are set instead of when workers are only encouraged to do their best and when goals are difficult than when they are easy. Feedback or knowledge of results (KR) tends to increase the level of performance if workers find they are lagging behind. Tubbs' review further showed that studies tend to agree that a combination of goal setting and feedback is more effective than either alone and that workers need feedback to continue to perform at high levels. Commitment to a goal may be increased by money or another concrete reward or by participating in setting the task goals. Results on the effects of participation in setting goals have been most inconsistent. While a number of field studies have shown a positive effect of participation by groups of subordinates, the overall results of some other studies show that participation has very little effect. Some authors (e.g., Argyle, 1990) reasoned that this may be because participation results in higher goals being set; but with goals held constant, Tubbs (1986) found only six studies that showed an effect of participation.

Personal and Material Resources Theory. This holds that constraints on workers' abilities or opportunities to attain their task goals are demotivating. If such constraints are dragged to extremes, they can lead to apathy, learned helplessness, absenteeism, and high turnover rate. On the other hand, conditions and organizational environments that facilitate goal attainment are positively motivating. Katzell and Thompson (1990) maintain that constraints and facilitators can be personal, such as ability and skill level, or material, such as equipment and the totality of the environment, including the general infrastructure, such as availability of the power and water supply.

Group and Norm Theory. This maintains that workers are motivated to perform well when their formal and informal work groups facilitate and approve of such performance. The dynamics of formal and informal work groups often includes the development of cohesiveness and norms that regulate behavior, how much work is appropriate, and the conformity of individual members to these norms. Through the use of social rewards and sanctions, the work group develops and regulates adherence to group norms. According to Katzell and Thompson (1990), working in the presence of other group members is itself a source of arousal, especially if the other members are perceived as monitoring or evaluating one's task performance.

Sociotechnical System Theory. This postulates that people are motivated to perform well when the work system is designed so that conditions for effective personal, social, and technological functioning are harmonized. When the task is meaningful, challenging, and diversified and when workers possess the skills, autonomy, and resources to do the work well, workers are motivated.

Endogenous Theories
According to Katzell and Thompson (1990), these theories focus on internal processes that mediate the effects of conditions of work on performance. Physiological and affective states are the two types of mediators that have received the attention of researchers. Motivation theories classified under this heading by these authors are briefly discussed.

Expectancy–Valence Theory. This assumes rational behavior by the worker. It holds that the workers believe that their level of effort will yield a certain number of positively, valued outcomes. The emphasis is that reward should be contingent upon performance, that is, in order to maintain motivation, reward should be based on good performance. If this is properly implemented, workers will be motivated to work because they derive satisfaction from performance.

Equity Theory. This advocates that people are motivated by their need for fair treatment. Justice consists of a balance between a worker's input in a given situation and its outcomes. A worker's input consists, for example, in ability, seniority, and level of education, while the outcomes may include salary, promotions, and authority. Equity exists when output over input ratios for the individual worker and those of the comparison group are equal.

Inequity, on the other hand, exists whenever some workers (Group A) compare the ratio of their own outcomes to their inputs with that of other workers (Group B) and perceive that the ratios are unequal. This may happen either (1) when person A and person B are in a direct-exchange relationship or (2) when both are in an exchange relationship with a third party and person A compares self to person B (Adams, 1965). Social comparison occurs in organizations, but the problem for managers is that they do not know with whom the employees compare the ratio of their outcomes.

Attitude Theory. This maintains that people who have positive attitudes toward their jobs, work, and organizations are more highly motivated to remain in, and perform, their jobs. Katzell and Thompson (1990) indicate that the principle of cognitive consistency also implies that people act in ways that accord with their attitudes. Two major work-related attitudes are job satisfaction (i.e., the affect associated with a person's job) and job involvement (i.e., how important the job is to the job incumbent.)

ACHIEVEMENT MOTIVATION

In many areas of life one could point to standards that define excellence, achievement, and success, whether in academics, sports, management, politics, or business. A person's motivation to achieve these standards or to excel has been designated need achievement motivation (n'Ach). Murray (1938) defined need achievement as:

The desire or tendency to do things as rapidly and or as well as possible... to accomplish something difficult. To master, manipulate and organize physical objects, human beings, or ideas. To do this as rapidly, and as independently as possible. To overcome obstacles and attain a high standard. To excel one's self. To rival and surpass others. To increase self-regard by the successful exercise of talent. (p. 184)

Maehr and Sjogren (1971) maintain that an achievement situation may be "self-competitive" or "other-competitive." On the one hand, the standard of excellence imposed on, or associated with, the situation may be socially normative, involving comparison or competition with others. On the other hand, it may be structured so as to involve comparison or competition with idiosyncratically defined standards. Situations tend to determine the type of behavior, which is presumed to be indicative of achievement motivation.

Basic achievement behaviors may be routines or behavioral patterns, which are normally developed in most persons through the course of socialization, ready to be elicited under the "right conditions." According to Ugwuegbu (1995a), the need for achievement is established through the process of socialization between 6 and 12 years of age. As a result of exhortations from parents, teachers, and other socializing agents in the extended family, plus imitation of successful models and rewards for achievement, a child acquires the drive to carry out home and school or age-group tasks with persistence and to do well at them. Neff (1985) asserts that at school the child learns the difference between work and play and acquires a work personality. Ugwuegbu (1995a) maintains that in Africa, however, this learning takes place simultaneously in the family and in the school.

According to this line of reasoning (Neff, 1985; Ugwuegbu, 1995a), the work personality that the school and the home impart on a child is characterized by the following basic components: (1) the ability to concentrate on a task for an extended period of time, (2) the development of emotional response patterns to supervisory authority, (3) the limits of cooperation and competition with peers or siblings, (4) the meanings and values associated with work, and (5) the rewards and sanctions for achievement and non-achievement, that is, the effects, positive or negative, that become associated with being productive.

Achievement theory is a cognitive theory. It assumes that a person's beliefs about the likelihood of attaining a goal mediate between the perception of the task stimulus and the final achievement-related response. One of the pioneers of research in the area of achievement motivation was David McClelland (1961, 1965a, 1965b, 1965c, 1971a, 1971b). He was the first to demonstrate that people's hidden or unconscious reserves of need achievement could be reliably measured by looking at their fantasy life under certain controlled conditions. By employing a personality test called the Thematic Apperception Test (TAT), McClelland found that he could score the subject's stories for the number of achievement-related themes in them. The scores derived from such measures were reliable enough to differentiate low n'Ach people and high n'Ach people. The scores also had validity; that is, they were, to a certain degree, able to predict real differences in "striving" behavior in real contexts.

The Dynamics of Achievement Motivation

Psychologists study the dynamics of achievement motivation by comparing entrepreneurial tendencies with nonentrepreneurial ones. Their studies conclude that entrepreneurs are very special people with special needs. They want to be on their own, taking responsibility for their success or failure. They like situations in which they get immediate, concrete feedback on their performance. They do not bet on anything over which they have no control, and they take moderate, realistic risks in their own performance. They score high on a particular TAT. McClelland (1961) in his book *The Achieving Society* maintains that the need to achieve makes entrepreneurs what they are and that economic development in a culture or society is highly dependent on the number of such men and women in the culture. He maintains that n'Ach is the motive most associated with business and economic success. From studies that he conducted across countries such as the United States, Britain, Japan, Germany, and France, he concluded that the rate of economic growth of the country has been positively correlated with an increased level of n'Ach in the inhabitants. McClelland also showed relationships between high need achievement scores and (1) entrepreneurial behavior and (2) preference for business occupations when they represent a moderately high level of aspiration for a boy and occupational status as a business executive versus specialist or professional in the United States, Italy, and Poland. McClelland interpreted these findings to mean that high n'Ach predisposes a young man to seek out an entrepreneurial position in which he can normally attain more achievement satisfactions than he can in other types of positions.

Many of McClelland's cross-cultural investigations of achievement motivation assume motivational inferiority, namely, that the developed cultures are developed because they are populated by a majority of people who are high on n'Ach, while the developing cultures are so because they are inhabited by people who are low on n-Ach. This line of reasoning seems to have influenced Eze (1995), who hypothesized that "Nigerian managers would be driven more by lower-order motivators than by higher-order motivators in their performance." (p. 47). Eze's hypothesis was not supported by the facts of the results of his study. He also failed to show that spiritual world, religion, ancestral concerns, and so on rank higher than science and technology as motivators for the Nigerian populations that he studied.

Nwachukwu (1994) showed that 48.3 percent of the workers whom he studied in Nigeria indicated that a manager who has the ability to place and assess subordinates accurately, who assists subordinates in problem solving, and who understands employee needs and aspirations would motivate them more than a manager who is characterized differently.

Obi-Keguna (1994) provided results from two companies that showed that among the factors that cause low motivation and dissatisfaction among the Nigerian workers whom he surveyed were lack of opportunity for promotion, meager remuneration, denial of promotion because one has no "god-father," and management's nonchalant attitude toward workers. Finally, LeVine's (1966) *Dreams and Deeds: Achievement Motivation in Nigeria* vividly illustrates that n'Ach exists in the major cultures of Nigeria, even if at different magnitudes.Such findings under score the position that is taken here, contrary to my African colleagues, that no culture is inferior in n'Ach. Achievement motivation is universal, perhaps also evenly distributed. A researcher has to identify what a culture considers achievement criteria, and then establish the appropriate cues or context for eliciting these behaviors.

Maehr (1974) has leveled several criticisms against culture-based achievement motivation interpretations. He maintains:

- McClelland's work has given limited attention to the situational contexts that affect achievement.
- The possibility that achievement may take a variety of forms and be pursued to differing ends has really not been fully explored.
- Since different cultures do provide different contexts for social learning, it is likely that members of these cultures will hold varying orientations toward achievement and that such orientations will determine when and how achievement motivation will be exhibited.

- Finally, the current assessment procedures for achievement motivation are so culture-bound that they sample instances of achievement motivation associated only with a Western culture.

MOTIVES RELEVANT TO WORK BEHAVIOR IN ORGANIZATIONS

A number of authors emphasize six social needs that are relevant to work behavior in organizations. These are useful in understanding motivation in work organizations. Following consideration of these six motives, we consider the three most important motives that best predict managerial motivation.

Need for Achievement

Wexley and Yukl (1984) maintain that a worker with high n'Ach obtains satisfaction from experiencing success in accomplishing a difficult task, attaining a standard of excellence, or creating a better way or method of doing a job. N'Ach employees seek out and enjoy challenging tasks that test their competence. They derive satisfaction from performing their job well. Such workers do not always rely on external cues for reinforcement or recognition but tend to rely more on internally generated reinforcement. In other words, they are aware when they are performing well. They prefer tasks in which success depends on their own effort and ability rather than on chance factors beyond their control. They desire concrete and frequent feedback about how well they are performing so they can enjoy the experience of making progress and accomplishing objectives. They enjoy competition with other people (other-competitive) or with their own record (self-competitive). They appreciate a job in which they can exercise initiative in solving problems.

Need for Affiliation

The need for affiliation is one of the innate needs of humans. Children best express this need. It is the desire for companionship and friendly interpersonal relationships in which affection and nurturance are given and received. This need is expected to be very strong in cultures of African societies with their human inter-dependence relationships and extended family structure. The strength of the need for affiliation, like other needs, varies from person to person even in African societies. A person with a strong need for affiliation is concerned, especially, with being liked and accepted and responds negatively to cues indicative of rejection or hostility from others. Such a person likes to work with others as long as they are friendly and cooperative.

According to Wexley and Yukl (1984), a person who has a strong need for affiliation is usually unwilling to let the work interfere with harmonious relationships. The chief concern of a person high on need for affiliation is the maintenance of good relationships rather than moving up the organizational ladder. Occasions for conflict are usually avoided. When conflict occurs, however, the individual tries to smooth things over rather than confront genuine differences. A person with strong affiliation needs, if placed in a position of authority, avoids making unpopular demands on subordinates. According to McClelland and Burnham (1976), this kind of person is likely to permit exceptions to rules and dispense rewards as a means of winning and keeping friends.

Need for Esteem

This is a desire to be respected and appreciated. Those who have a strong need for esteem judge their self-worth from the feedback they get from the environment, especially what others say of them. Other people satisfy the individual's need for esteem through the provision of praise, formal recognition of the person's accomplishments, and awards of status symbols. Among nonprofessional people in Africa, especially traders and business people, the need for esteem is met by taking traditional titles, the purchase of honorary doctoral degrees from church schools in America, and the ownership of big houses and luxurious cars. Sometimes they satisfy this need by remote association with people in power in government, and the military or, with those who are rich by claiming that they know such people or are related to them.

The need for esteem is sometimes referred to as an ego need. People with strong ego needs expect subordinates and other people to adhere to protocols of behavior or suffer punishment consequences. They are sensitive to cues that are indicative of possible disrespect or criticism. They are likely to be upset and even exhibit aggressive behaviors if they believe that they have not been given appropriate symbols for their position in the status hierarchy of the organization. They crave praise and tend to be upset if praise is not forthcoming when they believe it is justified.

People with strong ego needs tend to satisfy these needs by gaining fame or pretending to be popular, by aspiring to prestigious social positions and membership in social clubs or organizations, and by pursuing high-status occupations. Public speaking, acting, singing, and performing in front of live audiences are also ways of satisfying esteem needs, provided the audience shows appreciation. If the environment fails to show appreciation, individuals with high esteem needs resort to aggressive and hostile behaviors to force the environment to acknowledge their social esteem.

Need for Autonomy

Parents usually take care of their infants and children until they reach adulthood. The need for autonomy theory holds that at adulthood most parents expect these formerly helpless infants to be independent. Research in psychology and anthropology indicates, however, that some cultures socialize their young ones for independence or autonomy, while others socialize them for dependence. There are, therefore, cultural and individual differences in the extent to which people desire freedom and in the way that their socialization processes condition them to react to authority figures.

People who have a high need for autonomy want to have and exercise a great deal of freedom and independence. They critically evaluate figures of authority and feel uneasy when these figures attempt to impose restraints and restrictions on their behavior. On the job, these people are not comfortable with close supervision or frequent interference in their work by superiors. They resist any work environment that makes them dependent on others for resources and support. These people are usually their own boss and entrepreneurs and managers of their own businesses.

People who have a low need for autonomy depend on others to tell them what to do next. They feel most comfortable when there is a parent substitute to tell them what to do and to provide coaching and close supervision. Although psychological theories blame some cultures for bringing up men and women who are obedient to parents and figures of authority while others foster values of freedom, rugged individualism, and a skeptical attitude toward authority, our position indicates that no culture produces mainly people with a low need for autonomy while another produces those with a high need for autonomy.

Need for Power

The instability in the African polity has demonstrated how widespread the need for power is in the African subregion. People high in need for power find great satisfaction in influencing others and arousing strong emotions in them. They employ fear, awe, pleasure, anger, and surprise as tactics of relationship with subordinates and others. The exercise of influence over the attitudes and behavior of others gratifies power needs. People with high n'Power enjoy winning arguments, defeating opponents, eliminating enemies, and directing the activities of others. They are very sensitive to power politics in an organization and will attempt to develop their own power by building alliances that are often based on organizationally irrelevant factors such as gender, race, ethnicity, or religion. Through such illegitimate and unholy alliances they may gain control over budgets, information channels, resources, and projects or even the organization itself. People with strong power needs usually seek positions of authority such as manager, administrator, public official, police officer, military officer, and politician in which they can exercise influence more readily (McClelland, 1965a).

Wexley and Yukl (1984) indicate that most people probably have only a moderate need for power. People with low power needs tend to avoid positions of authority and feel very uncomfortable exercising influence over others. They are not usually very assertive and are reluctant to tell others what to do. These people may not rise to management position in organizations. If they do, they will prove to be very ineffective.

Need for Security

People have the need to avoid physical harm and economic disaster, but some people are emotionally more concerned about this than others. Psychology maintains that people with a strong need for security are more likely to worry about such things as illness, accidents, crimes, wars, armed robbers, and economic conditions. They are very strongly concerned about job security and loss of income. Such people are likely to seek a secure job where there is little chance of layoff, dismissal, downsizing, or mergers and acquisitions, that may threaten their position. Those with a strong need for security find the following features of a job especially attractive, (1) that it is confirmed until retirement or

(2) that there is a long-term employment contract with guaranteed salary, health, and disability insurance and a comprehensive pension plan.

In a job in which an individual could be dismissed for incompetence, people with security needs worry about losing their jobs; they are very slow and reluctant to make decisions, especially when they are aware that the outcome could affect the security of their jobs. They do not show any leadership or initiative but prefer to follow rules and regulations rather rigidly. They will avoid tasks and assignments that involve risk of failure.

In contrast to people with a high need for security, those with a low need for security will seek out dangerous and risky activities just to experience the excitement that these activities provide. They have little regard for their own health and safety and tend to believe that economic disaster and serious accidents are "for the other guy" (Ugwuegbu, 1977).

INTERACTIVE VIEW OF MANAGERS' MOTIVES

The six social motives just discussed are distributed randomly in varying degrees among any population of workers that can be found in organizations in Africa. But for people in management positions, emphasis is laid on three of these social needs, namely, need for achievement (n'Ach), need for power (n'Power), and need for Affiliation (n'Affil), because these needs appear to be central to managers' organizational life. The need for achievement governs the individual managers' orientation to tasks that they face in the organization. Managers who have a high need for achievement are concerned about doing their job well. Needs for affiliation and power govern workers' interpersonal relationships. Such managers exhibit warm and friendly characteristics.

Need for Power (n'Power)

Many managers have a high need for power. Results of research (Wainer and Rubin, 1969) indicate that a manager needs a reasonably high n'Power in order to function as a leader. Whether such a manager uses it well depends, in large, part on the other personality values and motives that the manager holds. Being high in n'Power does not entail being autocratic or authoritarian. Effective management may, indeed, depend on the managers' ability to understand their own need for power and to enjoy using it in creative, satisfying ways.

Need for Affiliation (n'Affil)

Managers who are high in n'Affil alone focus their concerns more on warm, friendly relationships. Such managers are likely to end up at the supervisory job level, where maintaining relationships is more important than participation in hard decision making. Kolb and Boyatzis (1970) showed that people high in n'Affil alone are seen as ineffective helpers, probably because they fear disrupting relationships by forthrightness and confrontation. They have also shown, however, that people who are seen by others as effective helpers tend to have relatively even motive strengths across the three motives, not being extremely high or low on any of the three. Although strong n'Affil does not seem to be central to leadership and management performance, some concern with the feelings of others is necessary. Managers' show of some concern with affiliation is important in understanding the needs of those who work under them so as to generate an organizational climate that takes those needs into consideration.

Noujaim (1968) has demonstrated that high n'Affil managers spend more time communicating and relating with subordinates than high n'Ach, or high n'Power managers. Communicating with others in warm, friendly ways is of real importance to the achievement of organizational goals. When people can relate, collaborate and communicate on task accomplishment, the climate of the organization tends to improve. It has now been proposed that managerial motivation is better predicted from a combination of high power motivation and low affiliation motivation. Evidence also exists that a combination of high power motivation and low affiliation motivation predicts managerial success for nontechnical managers (McClelland and Boyatzis, 1982).

Need for Achievement (n'Ach)

Whereas a high need for achievement seems absolutely necessary for an entrepreneur it is not necessary for a manager as a facilitator of an organization's climate, to be extremely high in this motive. Research shows that executives who are high in n'Ach tend to schedule and hold fewer meetings than other executives hold and tend to want to work alone, despite the fact that many organizational problems would be better solved by collaborative effort. As with executives high in n'Power, the effectiveness of executives high in n'Ach as managers depends more on their other values than on their motivation alone. For example, for senior management personnel and for managers in large firms, success and promotion may depend not on individual achievement but on the capacity to influence others.

People high in n'Ach want to take responsibility for success or failure, like to take calculated risks, and like situations in which they receive immediate, concrete feedback or knowledge of results on how well they are doing. The need for feedback keeps the managers from getting too involved in open-ended, exploratory situations with no concrete goal and no benchmarks along the way. As a result of the managers' sense of personal responsibility, they do not delegate authority unless such managers hold values that allow them to see developing a viable organization as a legitimate achievement goal. High n'Ach managers are task-oriented, but the kind of climate that they create in an organization will be healthier if the n'Ach is balanced by moderate needs for power and affiliation, provided such managers are committed to building an achievement-oriented organization that is capable of taking responsibility and calculated risks and that enjoys knowing how it is doing each step of the way.

STRATEGIES FOR FOSTERING WORK MOTIVATION

The review of the theoretical contributions of different schools of motivation as well as some of the empirical data presented in this chapter indicate that perhaps there is no single best way to motivate workers. There are differences in the needs and expectations of workers. Differences among organizations are distinctive as to tasks to be performed by workers, organizational climate, and leadership style of the management team. The question that follows is, How does an organization use all the knowledge that psychology has made available about work motivation? How do the organization and their management teams go about fostering high motivation among their workers? While endogenous theories of motivation help to explain what is going on in motivation, the exogenous theories of motivation provide managers with a handle that they can employ to open the door to the benefits of work motivation.

Katzell and Thompson (1990) in their excellent analysis extracted seven key strategies from exogenous theories for improving work motivation. Here we consider each of the motives discussed under exogenous theories to see how a manager can employ them practically to enhance work motivation in African organizations.

Motive or Need Theory

The lesson that a manager learns from motive or need theory is that every employee comes to an organization with a set of motives and values that may not conform to organizational objectives, goals, and values. It becomes very important, therefore, to ensure that employees have motives and values that are relevant to the type of organization and to the jobs in which they are placed. There are two main strategies for improving work motivation among those workers with diverse motives and values. These are *selecting* workers whose motives match the situation during personnel section and developing the appropriate values and motives in workers through *training*.

Personnel Selection. This provides the organization with the opportunity to select new workers or, at interviews for promotion, elevate managers who emphasize managerial potential and personal characteristics that correlate positively with motives that the organization is promoting. The selection program should look for such important qualities as motivation to perform well, desire for rapid advancement, independence of the approval of others, and reduced concern with security, in addition to candidates' having the requisite intellectual, administrative, and social abilities. Bray and Grant (1966) found these qualities to be essential to managerial success. Howard and Bray (1988) also found that motivational dimensions, especially the dimensions of advancement or achievement motivation, and work involvement are prominent in predicting career advancement and success.

Job Preview. This technique is designed to implement the motivational imperative of fitting workers' motives to the job. This program ensures that candidates are provided with realistic job previews during selection. The results of research indicate that when organizations provide candidates with realistic previews of what their jobs would be like through the provision of brochures, films, and even reports of previous employee attitude surveys, there tends to be a reduction in the rate of employee turnover compared to when applicants are not provided with job previews.

Motive Training. This is based on the principles that some values and motives workers bring to the organization are learned and, therefore, are subject to change. McClelland and Winter (1969) showed that achievement motivation can be strengthened through training with positive consequences for job success. During such training, acceptance of responsibility for success and failure and the consequences of good and poor performance are emphasized.

Incentives and Rewards

The lesson that we learn from incentive or reward theory is that jobs and their associated factors must be designed so as to be attractive, interesting, and satisfying to workers. When the Survey Research Center, University of Michigan, (1971), asked a national sample of 1,500 workers about the importance to them of various features of a job, the highest ratings were assigned to the rewards of interesting work, good pay, availability of needed resources, having sufficient authority, and friendly and cooperative coworkers. Etuk (1983) employed executive officers of some parastatals and government ministries in the old Cross River State of Nigeria. His study showed that employees are motivated, in the following decreasing order of importance, by rewards of (1) responsibility associated with the job; (2) opportunity to grow on the job (3) feelings of achievement, (4) congenial coworkers, (5) salary, (6) participation in decision making, and (7) feeling of security. A study by Ugwuegbu (1983) showed that Nigerian workers are motivated to perform in companies where they are rewarded according to their individual merit and not on seniority or on an emotional basis.

Employees and their unions support conditions and policies that provide rewards and incentives in organizations. In administering rewards and policies, equity should be the guiding principle. If equity were undermined, the effects of rewards and incentives on enhancing motivation in organization would be distorted or obliterated. Another important principle in the administration of rewards is that the system of rewards should be made contingent upon good performance.

The structural and physical aspects of a job that act as incentives to employees are *job enrichment.* This innovative program is designed to fulfill the imperative of making jobs attractive, interesting, and satisfying. Job enrichment is based on the hypothesis that diversified, challenging jobs are more satisfying and intrinsically motivating than simpler, more routine jobs (Hackman and Oldham, 1975, 1980; Herzberg, 1966). A number of attempts to implement job enrichment programs have been reported. Many of the reports show that the effects of job enrichment on attitude are usually favorable, while the effects on performance, although often positive, are less consistent (Stone, 1986).

We must recall that, due to differences in attribution style, what one employee regards as reward may not be so regarded by another employee. There are various incentives and rewards in different organizations. Examples, in addition to job enrichment, include financial compensation, promotion, merit rating, benefit programs, considerate supervision, and recognition awards. Because of individual differences in what people regard as desirable, Lawler (1987) advocated the "cafeteria" plan, that is, a company should present its package of rewards and benefits from which individual workers would choose the combination most suitable for them. Cohn (1988) confirmed that cafeteria plans have been found to be workable and useful in industry.

Reinforcement

Managers should learn from this strategy that effective performance should be positively reinforced in order to be maintained in the future. In the same vein, ineffective behavior should not be rewarded; instead, such behavior should be judiciously punished. The emphasis here is on reinforcers and their linkage to performance, not on the nature of the reinforcer as in the reward and incentive theory.

Financial Reinforcement Programs. These are the most common organizational reward system. Often financial reinforcements are ineffectively administered. In most African countries, financial compensation is often administered in a noncontingent manner, or the contingency involves just coming to work regularly enough and performing well enough to avoid being removed. In some organizations the appropriate contingent rewards are administered, but their contingency is not clearly understood. Another problem is that very frequently poor performance is reinforced as good performance. When an organization makes workers aware that rewards are contingent upon good performance, it appears to contribute to workers' effectiveness (Feder and Ferris, 1981). A number of systems have been devised by organizations to tie financial remuneration more directly to performance. These include an incentive pay system that links the workers' remuneration to some concrete measure of output, such as units sold or parts completed. Research data support the beneficial effects of such techniques on performance (Locke, Feren, McCaleb, Shaw, and Denny, 1980). Research, however, has found wide variations in those effects, from excellent to negligible. Possible causes of these variations, according to Katzell and Thompson (1990), include:

- differences in coping with such problems as measuring performance and providing a sufficiently large pay supplement and
- institutional differences that have been occurring that make incentive plans based on individual or small group performance less congruent with contemporary social values (Lawler, 1987).

There are also plans that are based on the concept that employees are influential participants in the organization and therefore that their compensation should be related to their performance at their level of organization or its major subdivisions. These plans includes profit sharing, employee stock ownership, and gain sharing, in which supplemental payments depend on production improvements, not on profits. The advantages of gain sharing are that changes in production are more directly attributable to employee performance and can be calculated more regularly.

Nonfinancial Reinforcer. These include praise and feedback, time off, opportunity to obtain additional vacation time, posting of individual performance data, and best worker of the week or month, which may earn the employee a trophy. These must also be made contingent on performance. Self management is another type of nonfinancial motivator. It is a system of intrinsic reinforcement by which individual workers learn the responsibility of setting targets for themselves, monitoring their own pace, and obtaining feedback without depending on their manager or supervisor.

Goal Theory

The lessons that managers learn from goal theory are that performance goals for workers should be specific, clear, attractive, and difficult but attainable. Knowledge of results or feedback of goal attainment is essential for maintaining the motivational force of goals. (Locke, Cartledge, and Koepl, 1968). There has been quite some disagreement on whether goals should be assigned or participatively set. Reviews by Locke, Shaw, Saari, and Latham, (1981) and Tubbs (1986) show that studies have revealed positive results when goals are assigned or set on an individual basis and when formal feedback follows, rather than precedes, goal setting. In Nigeria, Akinola (1986) demonstrated that the combination of individual goal setting and feedback significantly improved bank workers' performance more than feedback or goal setting alone.

Management by Objectives (MBO). This incorporates goal setting. It entails elements of participatory negotiation where the supervisor and the subordinate collaborate in setting the work goals and together consider and implement the necessary environmental and material requirements essential for the attainment of the set objectives. It also entails feedback, which can come in the form of praise or criticism. In management by objectives it is crucial that the worker be committed to the goals, a condition that is enhanced by ensuring that the goals are acceptable. The participatory nature of MBO helps to accomplish this acceptability requirement (Locke, Latham, and Erez, 1988).

Several other human resources management practices incorporate goals, even though such practices are not usually embarked upon as goal setting techniques. These practices include total quality management, job description, training, performance appraisal, participatory management, quality circles, and incentive pay plans.

Personal and Material Resources

The lesson that we derive from this theory is that inadequate resources such as skills and materials for work can adversely affect workers' attitudes and their emotions. Katzell and Thompson (1986) maintain that inadequate resources affect the morale and work effort of employees. For workers to be motivated, they need the personal, social, and material resources that facilitate their goals. One strategy for improving personal resources is through training and other psychological interventions. The organization should provide workers with the appropriate training and adequate materials to carry out their job responsibilities.

Social and Group Factors

The lesson that derives from social and group factors theory is that the social environment, including interpersonal and group processes, must support members' goal attainment. An example of a program for improving the motivational climate promoted by work groups is division of labor, which involves reorganizing employees into work teams that are given the responsibility and necessary information that they need to manage their work. The regrouping must be based on members who are more likely to work well together. The group should be charged with setting group goals and group norm building, group problem solving, and interpersonal and intergroup relations management, as well as the responsibility of clarifying and improving the allocation of tasks among group members. Finally, the group should select and develop its own leadership. This usually improves the performance and attitude of the group members. Good leaders selected by the group can help create the climate that enhances workers' motivation.

Socio-technical Systems

According to Katzell and Thompson (1986), these are systemwide interventions that result in improvement in the performance and attitude of workers. These include interventions that have features such as increased training, improved internal communication, shared responsibility for decisions among managers, job rotation, and incentive pay. The objective of sociotechnical systems is to develop a system of exogenous variables that harmonize the individual, social, and technical parameters of the organization in order to create a conducive environment for the enhancement of workers' motivation.

SUMMARY

Motivation can be defined as the conditions and processes that account for the arousal, direction, magnitude, and maintenance of effort in a person's job. The earliest theories of work motivation, such as the scientific management and the human-oriented approaches, were very simplistic. The deficiencies in these theories led to a variety of other theoretical approaches.

A recent proposition grouped the theories into exogenous and endogenous theories. The exogenous theories focus on motivationally relevant independent variables that managers can easily change in order to bring about increased motivation in workers, while the endogenous theories deal with process or mediating variables that are amenable to modification only indirectly in response to a variation in one or more exogenous variables.

A person's motivation to achieve high standards or to excel is called need achievement motivation (n'Ach). It is believed that n'Ach is the motive that distinguishes entrepreneurs from nonentrepreneurs. It is associated with business and economic success as well as with the level of economic development in a given culture.

The implied motivational inferiority in non-Western cultures is rejected. Achievement motivation is universal and also evenly distributed. It is only a question of establishing the appropriate cues or contexts for eliciting need achievement behaviors. Culture-based achievement motivation has problems of instrumentation and conceptualization.

There are social motives that are relevant to African organizations. For those in management positions the most relevant motives for effectiveness are a mixture of need achievement (n'Ach), need for power (n'Power), and need for affiliation (n'Affil). These needs are central to organizational life. The need for achievement governs the individual managers' orientation to tasks that they face in the organization. Needs for affiliation and power govern the workers' interpersonal relationships. If high n'Ach is balanced by moderate n'Power and n'Affil, the manager creates a healthier organizational climate for good performance, provided the manager is committed to building an achievement-oriented organization that is capable of taking responsibility and calculated risks and that enjoys regular feedback on performance.

Enhancing the level of motivation in African organizations and those who work in them is crucial for the overall development of Africa. Exogenous theories of motivation can easily be programmed to provide the needed environment for the promotion of motivation. Programs that organizations should institute to bring about increased motivation include proper personnel selection, job preview, motive training, job enrichment, financial reinforcement, nonfinancial reinforcement, self-management, MBO, and division of labor and group composition. Through systematic analysis, organizations should come to select the programs that are feasible for the organization and those who work in them.

4

Leadership and Power in Organizations

Traditional African hamlets, villages, communities, or city-states always had leaders if such societies wished to survive for a period of time. Leadership may be earned, as among the Igbo and Tiv nations of Nigeria, and the San and Khoikhoi of Zimbabwe, or it may be inherited, as among many other ethnic groups or societies in Africa. Societies in Africa where leadership is inherited have centralized autocratic leaders, while those with an earned leadership system have a republican, collectivist system of authority in which leadership is invested in the council of elders of the community. Leadership in human affairs has always been very important. Ironically, one important area in which modern African organizations are experiencing critical difficulty is effective leadership. Problems of leadership in African organizations are responsible for the underdevelopment of organizations in many African countries.

Locke (1991) states Warren Bennis and Burt Nanus' case for organizational leadership when he opined, "A business short on capital can borrow money, and one with a poor location can move. But a business short on leadership has little chance for survival" (Bennis and Nanus, 1985, p. 20). Many cogent explanations are offered when organizations fail. These explanations may include that the organization lacked strategic alignment between it and its competing environment or that market changes or the introduction of new technologies, global competition, corruption, and financial troubles were responsible for the failure. However, the one answer that everyone thinks about and most identify is that the executive leadership of the failed organization was not up to the management challenge. The reverse is also true, namely, when an organization is doing well, the executive team is usually identified as the central reason for success.

The contemporary state of decay of African organizations, the failed banks in most African countries, the failed private companies, including most private and government-owned airlines, parastatals, and corporate organizations, the poor performance of Africa's postal and telecommunications systems, and the poor power and water supply infrastructure are all due to inept leadership of these governments and corporate bodies.

Failures of corporate private and publicly owned organizations in African countries are on the increase. At the peak of the Structural Adjustment Program, (SAP) which was grafted onto African countries by the World Bank and the International Monetary Fund, over 80 percent of Africa's commercial and mortgage banks failed. Over 87 percent of private and public organizations failed in Africa as a whole. This may reflect a combination of two major factors: incompetent management leadership, including inability to predict and adapt to a changing environment, and changes in the attitude of the developed Western countries toward African markets and Africa's quest for industrialization.

For most experienced and effective managers the concept of leadership is very important. In their everyday work, leaders of these organizations are continually faced with the major issues of leadership responsibility and authority delegation, target setting, control, performance evaluation, team building, productivity, and management of conflict.

THE CONCEPT OF LEADERSHIP

Locke (1991) defines leadership as the process of inducing others to take action towards a goal. Ugwuegbu (1989a) defines it as a process of influencing the activities of an organized group in its efforts toward the achievement of a set mission and its goals and objectives. It involves influencing people and bringing about changes in group members' behavior to exert more effort in agreed-upon tasks. Psychology has always held that leadership is an influence process. A good leader is one who, among other things, helps subordinates to strengthen their beliefs in themselves, who makes them feel strong and responsible, who rewards them properly for good performance, and who sees that things are organized in such a way that subordinates feel a part of the process and know what they should be doing (McClelland, 1975).

Leadership differs from supervision in that supervision is influencing subordinates to do nothing more than simply fulfill the minimum requirements of their jobs to avoid negative consequences, while leadership is influencing them to participate actively in the group's activity. Effective leaders get more commitment and the best efforts out of their followers and in so doing produce positive outcomes for both the organization and the group members. Some authors refer to leadership as a system of relationships with some constraints and opportunities. System constraints include not only task demands but also the expectations and commitments of subordinates. Leadership is not about self-actualization but about organizational effectiveness. That is why McClelland and Burnham (1976) say that a leader's job seems to call more for someone who can influence people than for one who does things better on his or her own.

Earlier attempts tried to distinguish between transformational leadership and transactional leadership, but the efforts have not been very successful. According to the distinction, *transformational* leadership involves changing the organization through motivating subordinates to work for higher-level goals that transcend their immediate self-interest (Bass, 1985; Burns, 1978; Locke, 1991;

Tichy and Devanna, 1986). *Transactional* leadership, on the other hand, maintains or continues the *status quo*. It involves an exchange process whereby followers get immediate rewards for complying with the leader's orders. Locke (1991) regards all leadership as transactional in nature.

The concept of leadership cannot be successfully treated without a discussion of the concept of followership. In organizations the subordinates or the employees are the followers. If there were no employees or subordinates, there would not be managers or leaders. Effective organizational leadership depends on responsive employees in a process involving the direction and maintenance of collective activity called work. In organizations some employees want strong, dominant leaders; others want leaders who allow independence and innovation. The recent shift in emphasis from a leader-dominant view to consideration of followership is a result of greater attention being given to groups and team effort in the workplace. The shift is attributable, in part, to Japanese management practices (see Ouchi, 1981).

LEADERSHIP IN AFRICAN ORGANIZATIONS

In small and medium-sized owner-manager organizations the owner is the leader of his or her company. The owner makes all the decisions without consulting anybody. The owner decides what the line of business will be at any stage, how much of the goods to purchase, and the retail price. When there is need for expansion, the owner decides the new venture. If the owner-manager retires or dies, leadership passes to the eldest son, who has often been prepared by the owner-manager to take over the leadership of the organization.

Leadership in government departments, parastatals, and public organizations is by appointment, often by the government-of-the-day in each country. The process of appointing these leaders is usually devoid of the rigorous procedures that organizations use during selection and placement. The countries' leaders who make the appointments often do not know, personally, the individuals whom they elevate to these leadership positions. They usually rely on the recommendations of friends or close associates, fellow politicians, or trusted bureaucrats. Another thing that guides government appointment of leaders in these organizations in some African countries is an effort to achieve some level of national diversity; that is, government in its effort to appoint leaders for these organizations tries to make sure that different ethnic groups, and gender and religious interests are represented in these appointments. Sometimes emphasis is placed on membership in the bureaucratic ruling class over professional and technical expertise.

Multinational and international organizations get their leaders from American and European capitals. Often every young executive managers who have never before been to Africa are shipped to lead branches of these organizations in the continent of Africa. This happens when there are older, African personnel with better education and longer experience in these organizations than the young, fresh polytechnic or liberal arts college graduate from Europe or North America.

The process by which people assume leadership positions in organizations affects the way and manner in which they perform leadership functions in the organizations. Yukl, Wall, and Lepsinger (1990) identified several categories of leader behavior in organizations. These include planning and organizing, problem solving, clarifying, informing, monitoring, motivating, consulting, recognizing, supporting, managing conflict and team building, networking, delegating, developing, and rewarding. No studies have evaluated how the process used in appointing organizational leaders in Africa affects the leaders' performance of their leadership functions and the consequences of such process on organizational climate.

IMPORTANCE OF LEADERSHIP

For any group or organization to survive, it must have a leader, someone or a subgroup that exercises leadership powers. For example, in some African societies before the colonial, European powers imposed a single leadership system on most communities, social groups such as the Igbo and Tiv of Nigeria, and the San and Khoikhoi of Zimbabwe, among others, entrusted leadership to the elders of the communities. These elders exercised power of leadership based on consensus. The colonial powers tried to discourage this system of leadership through the appointment and imposition of chiefs and centralized authorities, whose main leadership function was not to create a more effective leadership system but to protect the interests of colonial European powers, including the collection of taxes for the imperial authority. The importance of effective leadership, either in the polity or in organizations, differentiates the contemporary, poverty-stricken, underdeveloped countries of Africa from the rest of the world. Political instability with its consequent interethnic conflicts, wars, poverty, and high rate of infant mortality is clear evidence of the ineffectiveness of today's borrowed political and organizational leadership style in Africa. In business and organizations, including government parastatals and departments, leaders lack accountability, honesty, and integrity, leading to mass failure, closures, and downsizing of public and private organizations and government agencies. Leaders are important in these institutions and organizations because they are the transmitters and upholders of organizational visions, objectives, goals, and values. Effective leadership makes a significant difference in important organizational outcomes. Effective leaders in organizations move their respective organizations to the upper levels of profitability and improved material well-being for their workers.

While persons in an organization ranging from the supervisors to the chief executive officer are all regarded as leaders and are expected to carry out these leadership functions, the relative importance of the functions differs by organizational level. Hogan, Curphy, and Hogan (1994) maintain that only a very few studies have been directed to the evaluation of the impact of leadership on the organization's rank and file. Some of the best studies that these authors cited were the performance of flight crews (Chidester, Helmreich, Gregorich, and Geis, 1991), military units (Curphy, 1991, 1993), and U.S. presidents (House, Spangler, and Woycke, 1991). The results of these studies show that when the appropriate indices of effective leadership are studied, certain leader characteristics are associated with enhanced team performance.

A second way of properly identifying the importance of leadership is through the examination of the contemporary history of African organizations and by comparing the development of African organizations with the development of East Asian organizations, whose colonial and, to some extent, cultural experiences are similar to those of African organizations. The surprising thing is that organizations in both democratic and totalitarian regimes in Asia have imbibed Western management techniques, while those of African countries have not.

A third way of assessing the importance of leadership is to investigate the effect of leadership on subordinates' performance and satisfaction. Studies have demonstrated that several patterns of effective leadership behavior are associated with workers' high performance and job satisfaction (Bass, 1990; Yukl, 1989). On the other hand, workers' reactions to ineffective leadership include low productivity, turnover and absenteeism, insubordination, industrial sabotage, malingering, and possibly industrial conflict.

Inept leaders create the worst stress in their subordinates. The most frustrating and stressful aspect of incompetent managers is their unwillingness to exercise authority; that is, the managers are unwilling to confront problems and conflict, or they are not as self-confident as competent managers are. They are unwilling to give up power or to share power and are threatened by the presence of subordinates with better education, talent, and skill. Such managers adopt defense mechanisms that interfere with effective management. Second, workers resent the managers' tyranny of managing those under them too closely and the way they treat workers as if they were stupid. These styles of incompetent management lead to corporate failures, which have been on the increase among African organizations in recent times.

For example, Hogan, Raskin, and Fazzini (1990) maintain that the base rate for managerial incompetence in America is estimated at between 60 and 75 percent. DeVries (1992) estimates that, for a period of ten years, the failure rate among senior executives in corporate America has been at least 50 percent. If these figures reflect the base rates of managerial incompetence in the world's most industrialized and technologically superpower, what would one hypothesize to be the base rate of incompetence for Nigeria, Ghana, South Africa, or the whole of Africa? A reasonable hypothesis would be a base rate of 90–95 percent managerial incompetence, while the failure rate among senior executives in corporate Africa may be at least 85 percent.

THEORIES OF LEADERSHIP
Psychology has contributed much research to the understanding of leadership. These efforts have resulted in several theories, some of which we now review.

The Trait Theory of Leadership

The trait approach of leadership is a popular, naïve, traditional understanding of leadership. It holds that leaders are born and not made. The conception was founded on the major assumption that leaders possessed universal characteristics that made them leaders. These leadership characteristics were seen to be fixed, largely inborn, and likely to occur irrespective of the characteristics of the situation where these leaders may find themselves. In essence, this was the "Great Man" theory of Galton (1869) and his followers. An organization in Africa that subscribes to the "leaders are born and not made theory" would look for the sons and daughters of great politicians and traditional rulers for appointment as leaders. The problem with the trait theory of leadership was that it failed to take into consideration the characteristics and nature of the employees, the nature of the situation faced by the leader, and the quality of the leader's performance.

Style of Leadership Approach

This approach seems to have been rooted in practical observations by U. S. psychologists following the horrific consequences of the leadership of Adolf Hitler in Germany and Joseph Stalin in Russia. Hitler's leadership, which was characterized by dictatorial and overcentralized power and authority, led to World War II and its horrible consequences for humanity, at the end of which the issue of leadership style became an intellectual curiosity. According to Ugwuegbu (1989a), a style of leadership is the totality of the mutual relations of the leader and the subordinates that are most characteristic of a given group or organization. Research identified three principal styles. These are *authoritarian, conniving,* and *consultative.* The theory holds that leaders adopt one of these tendencies as a function of their personal inclinations and the situation in which they have to perform their leadership roles, that is, as a function of their personalities and the leadership situations. It further holds that the styles are leader-specific; as a rule, a leader who adopts one of the styles usually finds it difficult to switch to others.

The Authoritarian Style of Leadership. This is usually based on rigid and one-sided actions of the leaders toward those under them. On a personal plane, the leaders do not share responsibilities or delegate work responsibility to subordinates. They make all the decisions for the operation of the organization, dictate all the steps and techniques for attaining the group goals, assign tasks and task partners, and remain distant from employees, including immediate subordinates. Authoritarian leaders make decisions and repeal them on their own. If this proves impossible owing to the democratic nature of the organization, the authoritarian leaders use roundabout ways to attain their goals of absolute rule.

The colonial history of African organizations oriented them to the authoritarian style of leadership with overcentralized authority and power in the office of the manager or the chief executive officer, who makes all the important organizational decisions. Most leaders in African organizations worked their way up from the lower grades. Such leaders feel threatened and tend to resist the views and opinions of the younger, more educated and talented members of their workforce. The African cultural set of deference and respect for elders and those in authority helps to compound the autocratic leaders' monopoly over leadership, power, and authority. Occasional incursion of the military into the governments of some African countries has tended to legitimize authoritarian leadership style in most African organizations. There is a great tendency for leaders in African organizations to adopt the authoritarian management style whenever a military regime in power is dictatorial.

Studies show that leaders who employ the authoritarian style of leadership usually choose their deputies from consideration not of professional ability but of their ability to conform. When they have such deputies, the leaders do not wish to delegate a part of their functions to them. Consequently, the leaders are psychologically alienated from the employees, their subordinates, and the labor union. They are often guilty of tactlessness and personal despotism. The direct effects of the authoritarian style of leadership upon the members of that organization include lack of initiative caused by alienation, apathy because of lack of general interest in the organizational goals, and general dissatisfaction among members of the organization.

The authoritarian style of management in African organizations by colonial administrations led to a faster growth of radical labor unions in these colonies. Labor union activities are often the only instrument for fighting authoritarian regimes in African countries and their organizations. Although there is a general dislike for the authoritarian style of management, some authors favor it in time of crisis. This is because when leadership is concentrated in a few hands or a single hand, leaders can swiftly intervene to put things in order. Second, conditions may arise in organizations that warrant recourse to the authoritarian style. These include general lack of discipline or order in the organization, disregard of authority of a newly appointed leader by the group or part of it, or a sharp change in a situation to which everyone has grown accustomed. In cases like these, the authoritarian style of leadership may be justified. Third, some leaders strive to be authoritarian because of their personality. Such leaders are motivated to acquire more and more power.

The Conniving Style of Leadership (laissez-faire). This consists in the leaders' indifference toward the affairs of the group (Sherkovin, 1985). Conniving style of leadership gives members complete freedom, gives up leadership, and avoids all responsibility for the course of affairs. Some prevailing environmental and cultural reasons may dispose leaders in organizations in Africa toward the conniving leadership style. These include situations where the majority of the subordinates seize upon religious, ethnic, and gender differences between them and their leader to create problems for the leader. The objective of such unfortunate manipulation is to cause the removal of a leader and his or her eventual replacement with a person from the subordinates' ethnic or religious group.

Leaders' conniving style in their relations with the workers in this regard may be born out of fear manifested by their disinclination for disagreement with anyone. Subordinates, on the other hand, will insist on gaining privileges, which the leadership will continue to grant until it runs out of privileges. This may result in the leader handing over part of the leadership functions to other members of the group, letting them make those decisions that the leaders themselves are bound to make. In an organization where the leadership style is conniving, an atmosphere of excusing one another's defects and mutual cover-up prevails. This type of leadership is ineffective, and the level of performance in the group as a rule is very low. It is the worst type of leadership style. Members of an organization who are interested in setting the goals and working toward goal attainment look to the leader for help and advice, not inaction. The conniving style, which, in turn, encourages inactivity, in the final analysis corrupts the group. If proper corrective action is not taken in time to rectify the leadership problem, the organization may disintegrate.

The Consultative Style of Leadership. This is a far cry from the type of leadership that operates in contemporary African organizations. It is the direct opposite of the authoritarian and conniving styles of leadership. The consultative leadership style, sometimes called democratic style, assures active participation of the subordinates in decision making through consultation or a committee system. It permits criticism of the leader. It is usually called the participatory style of leadership. The outstanding quality of consultative leaders is their ability to use power without "pluming" themselves on their high position. They have the last word in making decisions, for they bear personal responsibility for making and implementing them, but they do so after due consultation.

The consultative leadership style is based on the principles of consultation "from top to bottom" and from "bottom to top" (Sherkovin, 1985). Leaders who adopt this style do so from their understanding of people and their behavior. They have a gift for selecting as assistants people whose abilities, to some extent, complement their own. That means that, in some instances and on some issues, the subordinates inevitably have their own opinion, which is different from that of the leaders.

The consultative style of leadership, as opposed to the authoritarian style, encourages personal or group initiative by the members of an organization. Members of the group or organization have individual opportunities for demonstrating their independent ability, opinions, and skills. Leaders who adopt the consultative style of leadership are more concerned with the professional abilities of their subordinates than with their personal qualities. They have regard for the opinions of their more experienced group members and strive to create a feeling of *esprit de corps* among the members of management, employees, and labor union members. Another advantage of the committee system that the consultative style of leadership employs is that it is an aspect of the culture of some African peoples. The consultative style is best suited for the development of a creative atmosphere in organizations. The ability to use the style effectively requires thorough training, experience, delicacy, and a high level of psychological knowledge of group members and their culture.

Culture and the cultural expectations of a leader and subordinates become relevant in the African environment, where the process of socialization of children is autocratic, and they are expected to totally conform and respect the leadership elders. In such a culture the members of the group may expect their leader to tell them how to do everything. If the leader does not assume total leadership, he or she may be perceived as weak or lacking knowledge and the necessary skill to lead. In African organizations the extent to which subordinates are willing to point out contrary views and opinions is limited by their cultural set and the cultural expectations of the leader. While due consultation may be possible, meaningful participation by all may not be. This may be the problem of the consultative style of leadership in the African polity and organizations, thus reinforcing the point made earlier that the adoption of the idealistic democratic leadership style in African organizations requires an understanding of the cultural expectations that regulate interpersonal interaction between Africans of differing social status and background.

It must be emphasized that a particular style of leadership is not sufficient by itself to make an effective leader. The degree to which leaders possess good personal relations with their coworkers, how far they are perceived as being legitimate, and exercise legitimate powers, and the extent to which they have clear goals play an important role in the determination of the leaders' effectiveness.

The Situational Approach to Leadership

The situational approach to analyzing leadership came on the scene and largely displaced the dominant trait approach. Its primary thrust was that situations varied in the qualities demanded of leaders and that some qualities were appropriate to a particular task and interpersonal context and others were not. This development marked a change from the traditional trait conception and was reinforced by research at Ohio State University that focused on leader behavior. According to the findings of the university, two qualities distinguished leaders: initiating action and consideration.

- Initiating action means that effective leaders are involved in the coordination of the efforts of employees, and the ways and means of attaining group or organizational goals. Leaders take into consideration the possibilities and consequences of certain decisions and reduce to a minimum the conflicts within the groups that they lead.
- Consideration is the second behavior of a leader that is considered very important by the situational approach. Consideration represents the extent to which the leader shows "behavior that is indicative of friendship, mutual trust, respect and warmth" (Wrightsman, 1972).

Others have shown that one symbolic, important interaction that indicates an individual's consideration for another is the creation of opportunity for effective communication between them. Such communication is significantly important when it occurs between the leader and a subordinate. Effective leadership in organizations can be measured by the level of upward and downward communication that goes on in the organization. Organizational leaders must also be aware that for communication to produce the effect that is intended, it must be processed, assimilated, and retained, and the recipient must be motivated to act on the communication.

Another aspect of consideration is a leader's recognition of a subordinate's performance. Recognition is a kind of reinforcement, feedback, or knowledge of results, as mentioned in the previous chapter. Its function is to inform individuals on how they are performing. Approval of a group member's action, praise for a task well performed, and the confirmation of the significance of their performance by the leaders are essential for continued increased effort by members of the organization. Those aspects of consideration raise the status and self-esteem of the recipient of such recognition and arouse various favorable emotions such as pride and happiness in the followership. According to Hollander and Offermann (1990), a direct outcome of interest in leadership studies was the development of assessment centers to evaluate leader skills.

Many more situational variables are now recognized as having an impact on the process of leadership, in addition to the characteristics of the leader and the subordinates. Among these variables are the nature of the task or activity, its history, the availability of human and material resources, and the quality of leader and subordinate relations (Hollander and Offermann, 1990). All of these variables and more can play major roles in shaping followers' perceptions of, and responses to, their leaders. This link between perceptions and behavior is very relevant to leaders in multiethnic and multireligious societies like Africa, and their organizations. It is also relevant in multiracial states such as the Republic of South Africa or the United States. Studies in Nigeria (Ugwuegbu (1983a), show that subordinates judge leaders from minority ethnic groups by their perceived stereotypic beliefs about the leaders' groups rather than on the basis of leaders' actual performance. The link between perceptions and behavior has aroused interest in leader attributes as perceived by followers and the followers' implicit leadership theories (ILTs) (e.g., Calder, 1977; Hollander and Offermann, 1990; Rush, Thomas, and Lord, 1977). According to Hollander and Offermann (1990), implicit leadership theories are the followers' preconceptions of what a leader ought to be like, such as competent and considerate. Such preconceptions are derived from the stereotypic images held about the members of those ethnic groups. Bias is the principal problem with the use of ILTs in multiethnic countries if they adopt it as the basis for rating leaders rather than the leaders' actual behavior.

Contingency Model Approaches to Leadership

Fiedler (1967) first introduced the contingency model, named the least preferred coworker (LPC) model. The path-goal model (Evans, 1970; House, 1971) and the normative model of leadership and decision making (Vroom and Yetton, 1973) followed later. These theories considered leadership effectiveness to be a joint function of leader qualities and situational demands as contingencies that interact to make leader qualities variously appropriate to the task at hand.

Using the LPC model, Fiedler (1967) distinguishes between two leadership styles, namely leaders, who are task-oriented and those who are relationship-oriented. The LPC measure asks the respondents to rate the person in their lives with whom they could work least well. High LPC scores are associated with favorable or positive ratings and relationship orientation, while low LPC scores are associated with unfavorable ratings and task orientation. According to Fiedler and his colleagues, such orientations are associated with more or less effectiveness depending on three situational contingencies: leader member relations, task structure, and leader position power. Fiedler (1967) maintains that when the factors are either all favorable or all unfavorable, task-oriented leaders should perform best. When they are mixed or intermediate, relationship-oriented leaders should perform best. As the first and most researched contingency model, the LPC is not without controversy in spite of the interest and volume of research results that it has generated (see Fiedler, 1977; Rice and Kastenbaum, 1983; Schriesheim and Kerr, 1977).

The Path-Goal Theory

House (1971) and House and Mitchell (1974) maintain that the path-goal theory is a contingency model based on the leader's effectiveness in increasing subordinates' motivation along a path leading to a goal. The three contingencies that the leader faces are the task, the characteristics of the subordinates, and the nature of the subordinates' group. The emphasis, according to Hollander and Offermann (1990), is on the leader's behavior as a source of satisfaction to subordinates. Prominent among the predictions of this model are that (1) leader consideration behavior will be more effective when there is low role ambiguity for subordinates, whereas initiating structure will be superior under conditions of high role ambiguity and high job complexity and (2) that subordinates will respond better to a leader's directive behavior when the task is unstructured and less well when it is structured.

The Normative Contingency Model

Vroom and Yetton's (1973) model of leadership is more of a guide for decision making in organizations than a style of leadership. It emphasizes increased follower involvement in decision making, ranging from the autocratic, to the consultative, to the group leadership styles. It advocates that the choice of style is a function of situational factors, including the importance of decision quality, availability of information to the leader and followers, clarity of the problem, and the degree to which followers' acceptance is necessary to implementing the decision. Baker (1980) maintains that studying the Vroom and Yetton normative model may give leaders an awareness of how they make decisions, what goes into them, and how to improve that process. The general problems that confront consultative leaders in African organizations also apply to the normative contingency model of leadership.

In his criticisms of the trait and contingency theories, Locke (1991) maintains that these theories are not totally wrong but that they are not adequate as theories of leadership. This is because, according to Locke, they assume that the possession of certain traits appears to be a necessary precondition for effective leadership. For example, "leaders must be energetic and honest, and they must want to lead." (P. 10) The possession of such traits is necessary but not sufficient for effective leadership. As for the contingency theories, Locke (1991) indicates that "the contingencies might involve such factors as the volatility of the environment, the size of the organization, the amount of authority given the leader, and the complexity of the task or technology. Because most of these contingency theories deal with supervision rather than real leadership, it has been very difficult to evaluate the validity of their claims." (p. 10) Locke then introduces his own model of leadership, discussed next.

Locke's Leadership Model

This model of leadership was developed from research work that Locke (1991) and his students carried out in industries with executives and managers of different companies. He claims that the model deals more with effective leadership than with simply leadership. The model consists of four key parts (see Locke, 1991 p. 7), namely, motives and traits that are characteristic of effective leaders and that are different from those of nonleaders; knowledge, skills, and ability that are associated with effective leadership; vision; and, finally, implementation of vision.

According to Locke (1991), *motives and traits* of effective leaders are different from those of people who are not effective leaders. The characteristics of effective leaders are drive, energy, and ambition. Effective leaders are tenacious and proactive in pursuing their goals, want to lead, are honest, and have integrity. They generate mutual trust among subordinates and between them and the leadership. They have a very high degree of self-confidence. The second part of Locke's (1991) model includes *knowledge, skills, and ability*. The leader must have extensive knowledge of the industry, technology, and organizational environment in which the leader operates. The effective leader must possess a variety of skills. Because of the relational nature of the leadership, "people skills" are essential, according to Locke. The "people skills" that the leader must possess include ability to listen and communicate orally, network building, conflict management, and the assessment of self and others, and skills in problem solving, decision making, and goal setting. The effective leader must also possess cognitive ability such as enough intelligence to process a large amount of information, integrate it, and draw logical and objective conclusions from it.

Vision is the third part of Locke's model. According to this model, the leaders' motivation, drive, experience, and intellectual capacity provide effective leaders with the capacity to define the mission of their organization, what it should strive to be and to do and to set the objectives and goals to achieve this mission in the set time period. They have the capacity to articulate that vision precisely, formulate the strategic vision that specifies how the vision will be attained, and promote commitment from their followers by a style of communication that is both clear and compelling (Locke, 1991).

The fourth part of the model is *implementation of the vision.* Locke (1991, Pp. 63-99) holds that "a vision that is not implemented remains a dream." According to the model, effectively implementing the critical action contained in the dream requires six major steps.

- *Structuring,* which allows for innovation and rapid response to market conditions without interference from those higher in the organization.
- *Selection, training, and socialization* of personnel, which ensure that only individuals considered capable of performing effectively are selected, placed, or promoted. Focused training and resocialization into the organizational culture ensure that employees understand and accept the organizational vision.
- *Motivating subordinates,* which derives from the use of legitimate authority, serving as a role model, building subordinates' self-confidence, setting specific and challenging goals, delegating responsibility and authority, and using positive rewards for those who accept the vision of the organization and are working to accomplish it.
- *Managing information,* which is another essential characteristic of an effective leader plays a role in vision implementation. Effective leaders are good in gathering information, which they do from listening to their subordinates and customers. They also read and develop wide information networks. They share and disseminate information appropriately within the organization.
- *Team building,* which is an essential aspect of vision implementation that takes place at the top management level and is encouraged at all lower levels in an organization run by an effective leader.
- *Promoting change*, which indicates that the organization wishes to survive. Effective leaders communicate the need for change and innovation constantly to all employees. Goals for positive change are set, and rewards are given when they are accomplished.

With Locke's (1991) model, some aspects are said to be equally crucial for all leaders if they are to be effective, irrespective of the situation and the nature of the task. These are desire to lead, honesty and integrity, people skills, and creating and communicating a vision. Much of Locke's effective leadership model is yet to be empirically tested. On an impressionistic level the building blocks employed in the model are sound management principles, which are actually not new by any means.

Other theories or approaches not dealt with here are the transactional approaches that develop out of a social exchange or transaction over time that exists between the leaders and followers, including reciprocal influence and interpersonal perception (see Hollander, 1964, 1978; Hollander and Julian, 1969; Homans, 1961). We also do not deal with an old, trait-based concept popularly called the charismatic leadership hypothesis. Those interested in charismatic leadership should see Bass (1985), Bennis and Nanus (1985), and House (1977) for further information on the transformational value of such leaders in organizations.

LEADERSHIP EFFECTIVENESS

The issue of when to consider a leader in an African organization effective or ineffective is a persistent controversy. Impressionistic evaluation of a leader is always biased by emotional involvement. In multiethnic and multireligious societies in most African countries, one needs to go beyond impressionistic evaluation to assess the effectiveness of a leader. Psychology has, however, made significant contributions in this area by introducing some measure of reliability in the way leadership effectiveness is assessed. The appropriate use of these measures in African organizations will reduce the controversy over who has served effectively and who has not.

Measuring Leadership Effectiveness

The question of the effectiveness of a given leader requires an empirical and objective answer. We also agree with McClelland and Burnham (1976) that measuring leadership effectiveness in the real world is difficult, whether the measure is applied to leadership effectiveness in production, marketing, finance, or research and development. The most often used measure of leadership effectiveness is the extent to which the leader's group or organizational group or unit performs its task and achieves its objectives. In other words, team performance must always be kept in mind when one evaluates a manager or other person's leadership ability.

Hogan, Curphy, and Hogan (1994) reviewed and organized studies on leadership effectiveness in terms of five categories. According to them, we can gain accurate knowledge of how effective leaders are by evaluating the actual performance of their department, team, or unit. The problem with this approach is that some areas of performance such as sales and production lend themselves to a more quantifiable evaluation than others, such as the work that higher-level managers do.

Another way of assessing leadership effectiveness is peer rating. With this approach the manager's effectiveness is evaluated by the ratings of performance obtained from the manager's subordinates, peers, and superiors. An implication of this approach is that while subordinates are often in a unique position to evaluate their leadership's effectiveness, the approach may not produce a reliable assessment of the leaders in multiethnic or multiracial societies because of bias and the cultural set and orientation of some African societies that are characterized by deference and respect to elders and people in authority positions.

A review of managerial productivity by Sweetland (1978) concluded that effective leadership and increased group output were a function of the interaction between managers and their subordinates. A study by Murphy and Cleveland (1991) indicated that the assessment of a leader's performance depends partly on the relationships that exist between the leaders and subordinates. The question of leadership characteristics that influence subordinates' rating of their managers as effective has been raised and answered by Campbell (1991), Harris and Hogan (1992), and Lombardo, Ruderman, and McCauley (1988), who showed in separate studies that the leaders' credibility or trustworthiness is the single most important factor in subordinates' judgment of the leaders' effectiveness. The most important factor that determines superiors' ratings of managers' effectiveness is technical competence of the managers, while the rating by managers of superiors is mediated by judgment of the supervisors' integrity.

Effectiveness of managers is also assessed through a *performance interview.* This involves evaluation of the leadership potential of unfamiliar managers on the basis of their performance in interviews, simulations, and assessment centers. Leaderless group research tells us what a person must do to be perceived, in the short run as leaderlike. It provides no information on the effectiveness of leaders. However, assessment center research often uses organizational advancement as a criterion, and it tells us about the characteristics related to getting ahead in large, complex organizations in societies, such as the United States. It is difficult to generalize the results of these studies to African organizations, where leadership is often arbitrarily imposed by an outside authority like government, or the metropolitan headquarters in London and New York without any African workers' input.

After-the-fact evaluation or what Hogan, Curphy, and Hogan (1994) termed a *career in jeopardy or derailment* can be a direct measure of how effective the managers have been. Peterson (1993) and Peterson and Hicks (1993) studied managers whose careers were in trouble, using a wide variety of assessment techniques and psychological tests to identify different jeopardy and derailment factors. The results of the studies revealed managerial incompetence to be associated with untrustworthiness, excessive controlling of others, exploitation, micromanagement, irritability, unwillingness to use discipline, and an inability to select and place personnel or make business decisions.

One can also gain knowledge of how effective managers are by asking them to rate themselves. However, self-rating tells us little about leadership effectiveness. Above all, one would expect such ratings to lack objectivity. Authors, however, seem to indicate that the value of self-rating is that managers' routine over evaluation of their performance is seen as an evidence of poor leadership.

On a broader sphere, Ugwuegbu (1989a) outlined the following as measures of effective leadership in organizations: survival of the organization (i.e., the organization has not been liquidated and does not depend on government subsidy or bank loans to stay in operation), group preparedness, group capacity to deal with crisis, leader's concern for power, subordinates' satisfaction with the leader, subordinates' commitment, psychological well-being and personal growth of the employees, and the leader's retention of authority in the organization or among subordinates.

Personality and Leader Effectiveness
It is difficult to conclude a discussion of leadership without mentioning how the personality structure of leaders influences their effectiveness or lack of it. Personality is an organization of stable structures within people that disposes them to act in certain ways. A few of the observable personality structures of

workers in organizations include aggressiveness, the tendency to dominate others, a strong desire to be liked, talkativeness, shyness, argumentativeness, defensiveness, and externalization of faults, to name but a few. The definition of personality as consisting of stable structures implies the existence of some "factors" inside people that explain their observable behavior. Hogan, Hogan, and Roberts (1996) indicate these factors include temperaments or genetically controlled dispositions that determine the fundamental pace and behavior mood of a person's action. These include interpersonal strategies that people have developed to cope with the environment in which they find themselves. These factors inside people dictate their social behavior, including energy output, level of effort, and performance in leadership positions. The key structures that explain a person's social behavior, according to Hogan (1994), are the person's identity or the views that one holds regarding one's own competence and how others in the social environment usually regard the individual as a person. Others are, the person's goals, (or what the individual is trying or striving to achieve) and the individual's methods of interacting with others (how the person normally relates to other people in the person's day-to-day interaction).

MacKinnon (1944) maintains that personality refers to people's distinctive interpersonal characteristics, especially as described by those who have seen them in a variety of situations. This aspect of personality is functionally equivalent to what the author calls "individuals' reputation" among people who interact or deal with them. Such aspects of personality are usually portrayed in novels and plays and other literary works. For example, Julius Caesar warning Mark Antony against Cassius describes Cassius as wearing a lean and hungry look and says that such men are dangerous. Chinua Achebe (1958) in *Things Fall Apart* describes Okonkwo as a muscular, energetic, industrious, and successful man who is also characterized by "brusqueness in dealing with less successful men" (p. 19).

Psychologists take these generalizations and characterizations of individuals very seriously and have used them as bases for deriving personality profiles from the observer's perspective according to Hogan, Hogan, and Roberts (1996). The observer's characterizations are bases for deriving accurate information about people's personality. For example, Hofstee (1994) argued that the best way to obtain a good definition of personality structure as well as to obtain a valid assessment of an individual is to aggregate the views of those who know and interact with the person. Reputation, according to Hofstee (1994), is always built on a person's past actions and behavior. Past actions and behavior serve as a vehicle for predicting what to expect from an individual: thus, past behavior is very important in understanding workers' personalities in an organization.

Hogan (1994) points out four noteworthy and important issues about personality from the perspective of the observer:

- This aspect of personality is essentially equivalent to a person's reputation, and reputations are both stable and consequential. In organizations, people are often hired on the basis of their reputation.

- A person's reputation will reflect the amount of status and social acceptance that the person enjoys in the group. Effective leaders of organizations pay attention to how they are being evaluated.
- Past reputation predicts how a leader will behave in the future.
- Personality from the perspective of the observer has developed a well-defined and acceptable taxonomy. This taxonomy is the so-called five-factor model (FFM) (Goldberg, 1993).

The FFM maintains that each person's reputation can be profiled in terms of five dimensions of interpersonal evaluation called adjustment, ascendance, agreeableness, conscientiousness, and intellectance, that is, culture or openness. *Adjustment* concerns a person's apparent self-confidence and ability to handle stress. *Ascendance* reflects a person's social impact. People who are high on ascendance are outgoing and assertive; persons low on it are quiet and withdrawn. *Agreeableness* reflects the degree to which a person seems pleasant and friendly, as opposed to tough and critical. *Conscientiousness* is related to the level of a person's trustworthiness and integrity. Finally, *intellectance,* culture, or openness is a dimension of reputation that concerns a profile of creativity at the high end and inability to form abstract ideas at the low end. Hogan (1994) maintains that the five-factor model describes the bright side of personality, that is, the aspect of personality that is often seen in an interview session or in scores on a measure of normal personality, such as the psychological test called the California Psychological Inventory (CPI).

Interface of Personality and Leadership Effectiveness
That personality structure influences leadership behavior has been demonstrated in several psychological studies as summarized by Hogan (1994) and Hogan, Curphy, and Hogan (1994). The first piece of evidence comes from Stogdill's (1974) review, in which he found that *surgency* (which comprises dominance, assertiveness, energy or activity level, speech fluency, sociability, and social participation), emotional stability (i.e., adjustment, emotional balance, independence, and self-confidence), conscientiousness (i.e., responsibility, achievement, initiative, personal integrity, and ethical conduct), and agreeableness (i.e., friendliness, social nearness, and support) were positively related to rated leadership effectiveness.

Bentz (1985, 1987, 1990) reported similar findings from his research on executive selection at Sears, a distributive and service-oriented corporation in U.S.A. The results of his study, in which he used the Guilford-Martin Personality Inventory, showed that executives promoted to the highest levels at Sears were articulate and active (i.e., surgency), independent, self-confident, emotionally balanced (i.e., emotional stability), and hardworking and responsible (i.e., conscientiousness).

Bray and Howard (1983), working with executives of American Telephone and Telegraph (AT&T), found results similar to those of Stogdill's (1974) review summaries. Those personality traits that most predicted managerial advancement were the desire for advancement (desire to lead), energy-activity level and the readiness to make decisions (i.e., surgency), resistance to stress and tolerance for uncertainty (i.e., emotional stability), inner work standards (i.e., conscientiousness), and range of interests (i.e., intellectance) (Bray, Campbell, and Grant, 1974; Howard, and Bray 1990). Again, the processes of appointing leaders in these American organizations differ from those of most African organizations, thus barring generalization.

An interesting piece of evidence cited by Hogan (1994) is a study by House, Spangler, and Woycke (1991) that compared the personality characteristics of successful and less successful U.S. presidents. Success was defined by the researchers in terms of a president's evaluations by his cabinet members, his legislative accomplishments, and historians' ratings of his greatness. House and his associates conceptualized personality in terms of McClelland's needs; consequently, effective presidents as contrasted to less effective presidents were characterized by strong needs for power and achievement, and they were highly energetic and socially assertive. Using the FFM model, the profile of the effective presidents consisted of high adjustment, ascendance, and, additionally, prudence. Finally, personality characteristics such as arrogance, hostile attitude, boastfulness, egotism, passive aggressiveness, and authoritarianism are associated with ineffective leaders. These personality characteristics are often impressionistically associated with successful leadership in African organizations.

Principal Tasks of Effective Leaders

The key function of effective leaders is to serve as a model for the subordinates or employees whom they lead. Hogan (1994) listed four other functions. According to him, it is the function of effective leaders to recruit talented personnel to the team, work group, or organization. Initially, managers inherit their personnel and their teams. But with time they may have the opportunity to recruit new members. At this juncture the managers would know the type of talent they need to achieve specified goals and objectives. Hogan (1994) maintains that it is a major mistake for the people in charge to delegate this recruitment process to others if they wish to control the process.

As mentors, effective leaders motivate, energize, and inspire the members of their team or department. Since they develop and articulate a vision for their organization or group and understand the vision more than anyone else, it is their responsibility to make the vision "interesting, engaging, and compelling or worth working for" (Hogan, 1994). Often the goal is developed by the group and may include a determination to perform better than the group has done in the past or to accomplish more or better things so that the team members or department can benefit materially or psychologically more than they benefited in the past.

Such leaders serve as skill and material resources for their department or team to achieve their set goal. Leaders must possess the necessary technical and administrative skills for the accomplishment of their group goals. When their work groups run into difficulties, effective leaders provide solutions. They must also be in a position to acquire the materials needed to carry out the work in their groups. They develop intergroup coalitions with members of other groups.

According to Hogan (1994), leaders are the strategic planners; they identify the specific steps through which the organization's vision can be attained. Finally, effective leaders monitor how the team, department, or group is doing in its work activities, including the recruitment of talented personnel, in motivating, energizing, and inspiring members and in serving as resources for group work performance. These are done for necessary feedback and new programming for direction. Also evaluated are the talent and skills of the new recruits and the group's morale to know where efforts are to be intensified or modified.

SOCIAL POWER

Leadership, power, and authority are associated. The role of a leader requires the exercise of power and authority. The concept of power has been entrenched in everyday, nonscientific vocabulary, and because of this it has acquired a rich heritage of connotative and denotative meanings that have sometimes been associated with behaviors that can be described as antisocial. For example, we describe an individual's behavior as being "power-hungry" and talk of "power tactics" and "power politics." Leavitt and Bahrami (1988) define power by treating it as "influence that worked." Power is not the same as leadership, but several authors indicate that it is often seen as a feature of leadership (see Maccoby, 1976, 1981; McClelland, 1975; Zaleznik and Kets de Vries, 1975).

Power relations are best illustrated by the dynamic relationship between the chief executive officer of a company and the general manager, or between the general manager and the linesupervisors or between teachers and pupils in classrooms. The chief executive officer's power over the general manager or the general manager's over the linesupervisors or the teachers' over pupils is not absolute. In order for the chief executive or the general manager to be able to evoke compliance or enforce conformity, the act must have some significance for the subordinate; it must conform in some way to the subordinate's motive base. Schopler (1965) maintains that the magnitude of the inducing force on the subordinates is a joint function of the strength of the manager's act and the motive base to which it is relevant.

Another concept related to power is authority. Leavitt and Bahrami (1988) refer to authority as one of many kinds of potential power. It is an extra power given by a third party (the organization) to some of its members in order to guarantee an unequal distribution of power. Authority is that process by which an organization makes sure that those different positions with their roles carry more power than others do. Authority in organizations includes potential power over other people, power to restrict or punish, and power to reward. The higher the leaders' authority and the more effective they are in exercising power of reward and punishment, the more effective they are perceived as leaders. The nature of the leaders' influence and the extent of their effectiveness, to an extent, depend on the leaders' personal relationships and the leaders' legitimate power. The nature of the relationships is partially determined by the leaders' personality.

Hollander and Offermann (1990) identified power in organizations as having three distinguishable forms, which often coexist as a result of people's positions in time and place as well as their personal qualities. These are listed as *power over,* which is explicit or implicit dominance. Leadership in organizations involves such power in varying degrees. African leaders in organizations psychologically and physically feel that they possess a high degree of power over the employees. Quite often these leaders do not realize that their dependence on power over the employees undermines their relationship with the followers and their work environment. It also tends to undermine goal achievement (Kipnis, 1976). A second form of influence that leaders in organizations exercise according to this classification is *power to.* This type of power gives managers the opportunity to act more freely within some realms of organizational operations, through power sharing or *empowerment;* that is, they empower their employees to meaningfully participate in the process of managing the organization and workflow. A third form of influence is *power from,* which is the ability to resist the power of others by effectively fending off their unwanted demands. Leaders with high status in organizations have the potential for all of these power forms, while lower-status people may have one or two of the latter forms available to them. Leaders command greater attention and influence in organizations, but it would not be correct to say that the role of the subordinates is that of passive observers. Their group behavior through their union and their individual expectations, perceptions, and attitudes affect the process of leadership and power in organizations.

Bases of Leaders' Power

In any relationship any need or desire of the subordinate serves as a source for exercise of a manager's power. For example, demands for improved conditions of service or requests to go on leave, to be late or absent from work, or to go to the hospital are all instances for the leader or manager to exercise power. In organizations, including institutions of higher learning in Africa, one can see the bases of sexual harassment of secretaries and other subordinates by their managers or those in positions of power over employees. Studies by French and Raven (1959) identified five types of bases of power: legitimate, reward, coercive, referent, and expert power.

The Leader's Legitimate Power. This, sometimes referred to as position power, is conferred by the organizational chart. How legitimate a leader is perceived to be by subordinates is an important component in a leader's effectiveness. Legitimate power is a result of value internalization of norms in an organization through socialization of subordinates that gives subordinates the feeling that the management or their superiors should exert or have a right to exert influence and that they, the subordinates, have an obligation to conform or at least comply with such influences.

In an organization the source of legitimate power is the organizational structure and the hierarchy of authority as exhibited by the organizational chart. A leader's legitimacy influences subordinate's task behavior. Subordinates who work under leaders they perceive to be legitimate tend to internalize organizational values and norms more than those under illegitimate leaders.

They also perform their task responsibilities without being closely monitored or supervised. Legitimacy is often an important characteristic of reward and coercive power and is capable of changing the meaning of these power bases. For example, a bribe is illegitimate reward power. In Africa where leadership in an organization may be imposed by governments and their agencies, legitimacy is often difficult to attain. Such a leader may be perceived by the subordinates as not meriting the position and as an outsider who occupies a leadership position either because he or she is a government crony, has a godfather in government, or just used to satisfy federal government character requirements. This perception affects employee morale, discipline, motivation, productivity, and job satisfaction. Sometimes it leads to industrial conflict if the organization has a strong union.

At this juncture the appointed leader who experiences some difficulties in gaining acceptance may resort to other types of authorities to achieve legitimacy.

- The leader may adopt *authority of suppression* tactics in which the leaders show off their superiority, as far as their rights and powers are concerned, to keep the members of the organization or department in constant fear of possible punishment or uncertainty about the future. The leadership may decide to retire the departmental managers and single-handedly replace them with new managers. Authority of suppression causes feelings of humility or cowardice in subordinates, at the same time generating disrespect for the leader and further resistance in the members of the group.
- The leader may adopt *authority of distance,* which is based on leaders' tendency to adopt a system of administration that regulates the leaders' contact with subordinates. Leaders create extended social distance between their offices and the members of the organization and other departments. This device is used by the leadership to avoid possible criticism and feedback and to elevate formal influence at the expense of informal influences. These leaders assume a purely official attitude toward their former friends, restrict personal contacts with them to official occasions only, and endeavor to be as inaccessible to the group members as they can. The "Oga is very busy; he cannot see anybody today. You can check next week" syndrome that one contends with in many African organizations is a dramatic illustration of a leader who has adopted authority of distance. Some observers in Africa maintain that these leaders create social distance to allow them to hide their management and personal incompetence and deficiencies and to protect themselves from possible pressure groups.
- A third tactic that illegitimate leaders adopt is *authority of pedantism.* This allows the leader to overemphasize unnecessary conventions and petty traditions and regard the observance of these barren rules as the essence of mutual relations within the organization.
- A fourth manifest behavior of illegitimate leaders is *authority of the meddler.* Here the leader adopts false authority. Meddlers attempt to appear omniscient and annoy the subordinates by their constant lectures and exhortations, even when the subordinates possess better knowledge of issues than their leaders. Some leaders may endeavor to win the sympathies of the group members by unnecessarily exaggerated attention to their needs, thus setting the stage in such an organization or department for the authority of bribery and corruption.

The Leader's Reward Power. This resides in the subordinates' belief that the manager has the ability to mediate positive outcomes such as rewards, promotion, and favorable recommendations for the subordinates. The manager's use of reward power rests on the manager's possession of some resources that the subordinates value and desire and that the subordinates can obtain by conforming to the manager's act or directive. According to a well-known psychological explanation, the strength of reward power increases as the amount of reward increases and with the subordinates' estimate of the probability of attaining rewards if they conform. Because the subordinates' conformity or compliance is based on the prospect of being rewarded, the use of reward power depends on the manager's ability to observe the subordinates' behavior. Reward power is also likely to increase the attraction of the subordinates to the manager and, over time, to shade into referent power.

The Leader's Coercive Power. This is the third base of a manager's power. It does not create a conducive organizational environment for the employee and management relationship. Managers' coercive power emanates from the employees' belief that the manager can mediate punishments such as poor annual evaluations, refusal to recommend them for promotion, denial of rewards and incentive, and punishment, such as removal from office. The strength of coercive power depends on the magnitude of the negative valences controlled by the manager or supervisor and the subordinates' estimate of the likelihood of avoiding them by conforming with, or complying with, the manager's directives. The use of coercive power requires the manager to maintain surveillance over subordinates, who, in turn, maintain changes only as long as the manager's power is salient. The effects of constant use of coercive power include lowering of the subordinates' attraction to the manager, generalization of negative valences to other regions of life space, and the setting up restraints to prevent the subordinates from withdrawing.

The Leader's Referent Power. This arises from the attraction or liking that the employees have for the managers, which arouses in the employees compliance with prescribed organizational goals and objectives and the prescribed means of accomplishing them because they admire the leaders and want to gain their approval.

The Leader's Expert Power. This is triggered when the employees perceive the manager as somebody who, first and foremost can lead and second, possesses knowledge and skills in a particularly, relevant area(s). The subordinates must also believe that the manager is sincere and is acting in good faith.

According to French and Raven (1959), the five bases of power are conceptually distinct; however, they often occur in combination with each other. Reward power and referent power tend to occur in combination more than the rest. Finally, the effective leader's use of any of these influence approaches is to get the subordinates committed to the group goal. In order to be successful, the leader must possess the ability both to diagnose the situation and to determine which influence strategy is the appropriate form of power to enlist subordinates' commitment. The strategy employed depends on the personality of the leader, the nature of the task, the leader and member relationship, the leader's position power, and the situational factors.

WHY LEADERS FAIL

Leaders in organizations fail for a variety of reasons. Most leaders in African organizations achieve their position through political patronage, ethnic or religious dominance, or influence. These characteristics predispose them to failure. A manager's failure could also result from reduced interest in the company's product line by customers, drastic decline in demand in services that are no longer required, or reorganization, downsizing, or totally going out of business. Another view of failure by a number of leaders in all aspects of life, family, politics, or organizational management is that it is mostly caused by personal, rather than structural or economic, reasons. Such leaders may be skilled in a particular area, such as accounting, engineering, management, or sales. They fail when they can no longer rely solely on their own skills and effort. The author recalls a group of five Nigerians who were very successful as used car salespeople. They prospered and made considerable profit. They later decided to sell their business and go into computer marketing. They established ten major shops and several branches. Within a year they went out of business. Dramatic failure may occur when people change from their previous occupation or receive promotion to positions that require them to work through other people to be successful (Peter Principle). When they have no skills in building a team or communicating with subordinates; their management careers come to a halt. Such an abrupt end to a manager's career is identified as derailment. Social scientists in Africa have yet to pay attention to studies dealing with derailment in order to understand how frequently it occurs in African organizations.

Reports of research from some of the industrialized countries show that among the managers with the appropriate positive characteristics such as intelligence, confidence, and ambition, some of them fail. They fail because they are characterized by an overriding personality defect or "character flaw that alienates their subordinates and prevents them from building a team" (Bentz, 1985). Others fail because they are dishonest, arrogant, and overcontrolling or play ethnic or gender politics.

Research on managerial or leadership incompetence at the Center for Creative Leadership, Greensboro, North Carolina, has drawn similar conclusions. The observation of the center is that many managers who are bright, hardworking, ambitious, and technically competent fail because they are characterized by traits perceived as arrogant, vindictive, untrustworthy, selfish, emotional, compulsive, overcontrolling, insensitive, abrasive, aloof, too ambitious, or unable to lead, that is, unable to delegate authority or make effective decisions (Hazucha, 1991; Kaplan, Drath, and Kofodimos, 1991;

McCall and Lombardo, 1983; Peterson and Hicks, 1993). These qualities erode a person's ability to recruit and motivate a team.

One question that may be asked is, How did a man or woman so characterized reach a leadership or top management position in the first place? In African organizations the answer is not far-fetched. People there become managers through ethnic connections, membership in cults, godfatherism, economic and political connections, or corruption. Another reason is that in African organizations such as the universities, getting into a top administrative, leadership position is not based on the individual's leadership qualities and skills but on academic achievement or other emotional factors. The posts of vice-chancellorship (president) and dean are prerogatives of academicians who are professors as a result of academic "excellence," not management know-how. Their academic colleagues, whose assessment of the candidates' suitability for the office is most often based on ethnic considerations, also elect them into those positions. It is not surprising why the regimes of some of these vice-chancellors are ridden with conflict and confusion. The Nigerian federal civil service resolves this problem by the recommendations of the *Implementation Guidelines on the Civil Service Reforms,* section III, subsection (7), where it says:

The principle of Federal Character shall be faithfully adhered to at the point of entry, i.e., Grade Level 07–10, while thereafter, from grade 11 and above (that) ... experience, performance on the job, length of service, good conduct, relevant qualification, training, performance at interview and relevant examination where appropriate (shall be the basis of promotion). (1988, p. 9)

Unfortunately, this recommendation is not adhered to when the president at his pleasure appoints ministers or permanent secretaries, the two most senior leaders of each ministry, who are supposed to provide leadership in these departments.

Flawed managers rise to the top because, according to Hogan (1994), characteristics such as arrogance, insensitivity, vindictiveness, selfishness, and dishonesty coexist with well-developed social skills. These negative characteristics are extensions of normal personality. They are hard to detect in an interview or with a psychological measure of normal personality, and they are associated with the derailment of managers.

Organizations and Failed Managers

Managers are usually evaluated by their superiors or chief executive officers and psychologists who are brought into the organization as consultants. One talent that characterizes many incompetent managers is the ability to ingratiate themselves with their bosses. In spite of this, employees know who the bad managers are, if one cares to ask them. Under the right situation, employees will tell you, because bad or ineffective managers are insensitive, suspicious, and self-centered. Various subordinate ratings have consistently confirmed this assessment. Organizations often do not know what to do with failed managers or "dead woods." Generally, people have the tendency to confuse how fast individuals climb the organizational ladder with leadership effectiveness. Hogan (1994) raised this issue first. He warns that people should not do so. People should not confuse talent for self-promotion with characteristics of future effective leadership. Most people at the top of large organizations, even presidents of countries usually have a talent for self-promotion, but only a few have appreciable talent for leadership, according to Hogan (1994).

Second, a person may have the talent for leadership but fail to develop the appropriate leadership skills. Thus, the evaluation of a person's managerial performance requires more information than is usually obtained from an interview or an assessment center. Third, in order to separate failed managers from an organization, it can use a combination of managerial assessment procedures, which may include:

- Upward appraisals, which involve asking the people who work for the managers to evaluate them.
- Self-evaluation, which involves asking the managers to complete an inventory on normal personality and an inventory on personality disorders. This reveals the managers' positive and negative characteristics.
- Evaluation of the performance of the managers' units or teams relative to other comparable units in that or other organizations.
- Obtaining from employees under the managers some critical incidents of notably good or poor performance behavior by these managers.

When these four sources of information are put together, the organization has a good picture of the individuals' talents and shortcomings as managers or leaders.

According to Hogan (1994), since narcissism, dishonesty, insensitivity, paranoia, and externalization of faults characterize ineffective managers, these managers do not benefit from feedback. Hogan (1994) insists that the more ineffective the managers, the more difficult it is to persuade them to correct their management style through feedback. The only successful approach that psychologists use is direct evaluation of poor managers' performance either through role-playing or by videotaping and then critiquing their performance. A second method is to follow a manager around for a day or so. In this way the consultant can provide feedback regarding specific actions and behaviors. The intervention agents' task must be to provide flawed managers with alternative ways of conceptualizing managerial performance, give them specific examples of their own good and poor performance, and then develop a regular system of performance evaluation and feedback.

LEADERSHIP IN FUTURE AFRICAN ORGANIZATIONS

The leadership models inherited by most African organizations are colonial in character and process. The colonial leadership model is largely a master and servant relationship. This leadership model must change if African organizations are to meet the management challenges of the twenty-first century and protect their organizations from becoming extinct.

Since independence, African organizations have gone from periods of buoyancy to depression, characterized by mass unemployment and overwhelming poverty of the population. Although opportunities for higher education have increased for the youth in countries such as Nigeria, South Africa, Ghana, and Egypt, the leadership in these educational institutions has not been visionary enough to orient the courses and contents of the courses to the needs of African organizations in the twenty-first century. Leaders of organizations consequently will inherit a fairly educated and unskilled unemployed population of young men and women from whom they will select those who will work for their organizations. The labor market for skilled workers will tighten, and there will be increased competition for talented personnel. Survival in the African environment will be more difficult because of international competition from Asian markets. As major organizations cannot compete, they shrink or downsize, fewer middle managers will be needed, and the responsibilities of top managers will expand.

The implications of these trends for leaders of African organizations include the following:

1. Because competition for skilled and talented employees will increase, with the consequent expansion of managerial responsibilities, the overall quality of management will need to improve. The mass failure of banks, government parastatals, and private organizations in most African countries can be attributed mostly to incompetent leadership. This point is exemplified by the folding of many commercial and mortgage banks in Nigeria in the early 1990s. As a result of growth in the financial sector in Nigeria owing to the liberalization of the banking system, many unskilled and ill-qualified employees were promoted to leadership positions. The direct consequence was the collapse of most of those organizations. The same misfortune befell indigenized organizations in Nigeria between 1972 and 1990.

2. There will be an increased emphasis on productivity in African organizations as these organizations change from government ownership and limited liability companies to commercialized, privatized, and public liability organizations. This will lead to close scrutiny of the performance of senior managers. The intensity of the scrutiny will vary with whether the organization is government, private, or a public liability company, with the last two being most closely monitored by owners or shareholders. Since incompetent managers are not easily detected, African organizations should adopt a multiple perspective appraisal in evaluating the effectiveness of their future managers. Psychologists in North America and Asia play key roles in the development and refinement of psychological assessment instruments in these countries. African organizations should collaboratively work with African psychologists in an effort to develop culture-suitable psychological instruments for the selection of managers in the twenty-first century. Once these instruments are available, more African organizations should be encouraged to adopt them.

3. The present African management practices that are still influenced by early colonial models have to change as we move toward a service-oriented and more internationally competitive economy. African organizational leaders have to ask questions. How do we manage employees who are educated but without much skill? How do we manage more women in the workforce? How do we manage a population of young workers who are predisposed to consumption rather than production and a delay of gratification? These are questions that psychologists are

uniquely qualified to answer. African organizations should depend more on African psychologists.

4. Successful African organizations of the future will have to increasingly rely on innovation and the development of new products and services. How to manage creativity is one of the most important problems of the future (Hogan, 1994). Here again, psychologists can provide input in the resolution of that problem.

5. African managers will manage in an environment with reduced labor union activities. There are two reasons for this. The East and West ideological battle has declined. Many African organizations are going public, where the shares now largely belong to members of the public including the workers. As employees are gradually becoming part owners of the organizations for which they work, the previous feelings of being exploited and working for others will give way to greater commitment to the goals and objectives of the organizations and a feeling of being part owner of those organizations. Competition among organizations for available manpower will lead to a rise in earnings of employees, thereby reducing poverty and material want among African workers.

SUMMARY

Leadership is central to the survival of any group or organization. Leadership is a process of influencing the behavior and direction of others. Leaders in African organizations are looked up to by the employees. They are central to the management of the organizations. They usually see themselves as bureaucrats who are there to administer the rules and regulations governing the establishment of the organizations rather than to develop and manage the organizations. Leaders of organizations in the developed countries usually have dreams that they articulate so well that other members of management and employees are willing to team up with them for the purpose of actualizing the dreams. In most African organizations there are no defined mission, goals, and objectives. Wherever they exist, these mission statements, goals, and objectives are neither well articulated nor shared by the rank and file. It would be of great interest to know what percentage of employees of major companies in Africa know the missions, objectives, and goals of the organizations for which they work.

Contrary to the procedure in Europe and the United States, African governments play a major role in dictating who leads government departments, parastatals, and public liability companies where government has shares. Governments exercise this prerogative by appointing the chief executive officers of such organizations. Often government puts into consideration management-irrelevant variables such as gender and ethnic and religious backgrounds of the appointees rather than management and technical expertise. Leadership positions in international and multinational organizations in Africa are still reserved for employees with European and American background, who are often sent to African branches from the metropolitan headquarters. These young executives are sent to manage indigenous African employees who are better educated and more experienced than the executives.

An engaging aspect of leaders in organizations is how their personalities interact with their leadership style to determine the level of their effectiveness.

Studies show that surgency, emotional stability, and conscientiousness are positively related to leadership effectiveness in organizations. The personality traits that some studies found that predict advancement of managers in organizations were desire to lead, high energy-activity level, and readiness to make decisions.

In African organizations leadership, authority, and power are highly correlated. The organizational chart illustrates the hierarchy of leadership, power, and authority associated with a given leadership position. Leaders possess different kinds of power (legitimate, reward, coercive, referent, and expert). When leaders, as a result of how they attained leadership, fail to gain legitimate power, they employ other methods such as coercive power to force legitimacy. Leaders in African organizations fail due to several reasons. Some fail because of the way they obtained their position. Some derail, and others fail as a result of some flaws in their character that alienate their subordinates and prevent them from building a cohesive team. Still others fail because of dishonesty, arrogance, bribery and corruption, overcontrolling of their subordinates, and engagement in ethnic, religious, and gender politics.

If African organizations are to prosper in the twenty-first century, African managers as leaders of their organizations should look forward to increased managerial responsibilities and increased demand for higher productivity as governments commercialize and privatize most African organizations that formerly belonged to them. They should look forward to a more service-oriented management, and a more internationally competitive economy that relies more on innovation and development of new products and services. In order to be effective in such an organizational environment, leadership in African organizations should move from overcentralization of power and authority to consultative and team management systems of leadership.

5

Decision Making in Organizations

Decision making is vital and pervasive in life. The complex web of living is constituted of decision making. People make individual decisions and are often called upon to make decisions about other people and for other people. Decisions range from the routine and trivial to the profound and historic. Should I visit my neighbor today or not? Should Nike study economics or law at the university? Decision making is a cognitive process characterized by the limitations of human understanding.

This chapter examines what is known about human behavioral decision making in organizations. The focus is decision making in contemporary African organizations, followed by a review of research and theory describing how decisions are typically made. We also examine some of the literature on how decisions should be made. Single individuals make decisions. Individuals or groups also make some organizational decisions. The chapter briefly discusses decision making by individuals, organizations, and groups. Dealt with, also, are suggestions on how to enhance effective individual, organizational, and group decision making in the African environment.

DECISION MAKING IN THE AFRICAN ENVIRONMENT

Decision making is defined as a process by which an individual or group deliberates, evaluates alternatives, and consciously chooses a particular course of action or behavior to effect an intended action. In traditional African societies with centralized authority, group decision making was entrusted to such centralized authorities and their councils. Where there was no central authority, as among the Igbo and the Tiv of Nigeria and the San and Khoikhoi of the present Zimbabwe, group decision making was carried out by the elders of the communities. These elders would assemble in the compound of the oldest of these elders or at a designated traditional site, sit under a tree, "break cola" and pour a libation, and deliberate on the problem until they reached a consensus or decision. Ratification and the binding nature of the decision so reached were symbolized by an oath sworn by each member of the team before each other. In these societies group decisions are usually reached by consensus.

Colonial legal procedures were not sufficient for decision making in some African colonies. In order to handle this, the British colonial power introduced the customary courts where the tradition and customs of such African peoples provided the framework for decision making, but colonial courts were still not sufficient to handle decisions involving ownership of lands or land boundaries. Customary courts and other colonial institutions always referred decisions concerning such issues in Igbo communities to the elders of the communities for decision.

As for individual problems that required decisions, the eldest in the extended family was consulted, or the individual might seek an explanation and choice from those who held the realms of the supernatural world such as the *dibia*, the fortune-teller, or the *babalawo*. They would provide deeper understanding for the supposed causes of the individual's problems to enable the person reach a decision about course of action. These were the data bank of the community, whose views were sought for reliable and valid decision making. Gray hair symbolized wisdom, and elders played that role.

As has been pointed out (Ugwuegbu, 1987), decision making in traditional African societies was guided by intuition, common sense, precedence, reliance on the authority of elders, and revelations by those associated with the spirit world. Through the latter, the hidden mysteries of the world around people were rendered knowable and their visions manifested to enable people make proper and reliable decisions.

African researchers have not produced much knowledge in the area of decision making in African organizations. Random observations, however, show that in contemporary African organizations decision making is intuitive, probabilistic, utilitarian, and sometimes based purely on chance or luck. It is decision making without facts. Most of the organizations in Africa do not have departments of research and statistics. Wherever they do exist, their personnel may lack the skill required for the collection of valid and reliable data relevant to effective organizational decision making. Often managers in some organizations do not see the relationship between research data and decision making.

Ugwuegbu (1987) sounded a note of warning that the importance of objective and reliable data in the day-to-day management of government and other organizations' affairs cannot be overemphasized. This is so because management has become a scientific endeavor that involves decision making. Effective decision making is impossible if it is not guided by reliable and valid data. Very often problem-solving and decision-making approaches in Africa are philosophically handled, partly because of the absence of reliable and valid data and partly because decision makers are not familiar with how to relate research results to decision making. Because of this, quite often the technical conference approach of making decisions is preferred. It is not uncommon, according to Ugwuegbu (1987), for government to appoint a commission headed by a judge to decide questions of drug trafficking, examination malpractice in secondary schools, or the causes of traffic accidents. A government white paper and a subsequent promulgation of a decree would follow. The problem with such a decision-making approach is that decisions arising from it are usually based on the impressionistic expressions of a few outspoken members of society. Such expressions lack reliability and validity and do not allow general conclusions to be drawn.

Soyibo (1996) made similar observations when he considered policy making decisions in Nigeria. He indicated that there are three types of policy making practices in Nigeria. First, policy decisions are taken from "technocratic position papers" without any research input. Second, policy decisions are based on recommendations derived from government commissions of inquiry or investigations, the so-called special national conferences, seminars, and workshops. Finally, policy decisions are derived from consultancies, contributions from research institutes, or policy research sponsored by government agencies.

Another general observation about the contemporary decision-making process among Africans is exemplified by thousands of Nigerian youths who seek admission each year to universities. Every year, thousands of these youths apply to read medicine, economics, and law. Such decisions are often based on the subjective expected utility (SEU) of these disciplines. While medicine and law are professional careers, economics forms a base for a possible career in accountancy or an opportunity to work in banks. All of these disciplines have a broader base for possible employment in lucrative organizations. They are also socially highly regarded, thus positively correlated with high social self-esteem. In deciding to pursue these socially highly regarded courses, neither the parents of these youths nor the youths consider what it takes intellectually to reach such goals. They overestimate their abilities and relegate to the background any realistic assessment of the probability of their competing favorably against others in the Joint Admission and Matriculation Board (JAMB) examination, which is the university entry examination. They gather information neither from the university about their interest nor from JAMB about the probability of their gaining admission to the university of their choice. Some of these youths that have resource people in their families do not even discuss their problems with them, who are in a good position to advise the youths.

These youths and their parents are simply SEU-driven. They assume that, irrespective of their intellectual ability or social power to influence the environment, they will gain admission. Year in and year out, a large number of these youths' and their parents' empty assumptions prove them wrong, and year in, and year out, more boys and girls and their parents continue to make decisions based on intuition, luck, hopes, and prayers, and SEU without data and without information. Sanusi (1992) summarized individual and organizational decision making in Nigeria when he said that the picture that it presents is of a chaotic and unstructured decision process.

Information or data for making decisions in organizations are the number one crucial factor in decision making. Unlike decision making in developed countries of Europe and North America, it is very difficult to obtain the necessary information to make organizational decisions in Africa. Most organizations in Africa do not have a department of research and statistics. They do not collect or store information that could aid decision making. There is no national or organizational central place where available information on any aspect of organizational management could be obtained. In the Western, industrialized world most organizations have their own research and development departments, and essential information is also codified in great detail, published, and made available to the public. Such information is continuously updated. With the exception of the Republic of South Africa, organizational management-relevant information such as available manpower in each of the African countries, government legislation and policies on organizational development, and other essential management information are usually scattered about. In most African countries essential statistics that are nationally collected are often significantly different from World Bank estimates.

In order to remedy this chaotic situation, the author organized several workshops for some ministries of the Nigerian government and several organizations in that country between 1985 and 1990. The workshops and seminars were organized under the theme of Social Research and Information Gathering and National Public Opinion Poll. As a result of these efforts and input from other quarters, the Nigerian government created the Department of Research and Statistics in all the ministries and their parastatals. The Ministry of Information, Youth, and Culture also embarked on a program of establishing a data bank for the country, to collect; store; and disseminate information for the country. The establishment of the National Opinion Poll, for which the author served as the chief consultant, followed later. These programs came to an abrupt end with the beginning of Major General Sani Abacha's dictatorship regime. Prior to Sani Abacha's regime, the Ministry of Information, Youth, Sports, and Culture under PrinceTony Momoh, as honorable minister and Ason Bur, as permanent secretary, was setting the stage for other organizations to emulate government efforts in improving the collection, storage, and dissemination of information necessary and relevant for decision making in organizations.

Organizations in Africa still behave as if, and believe that, what is good for European organizations is good enough for Africa. Neither the multinational nor the indigenous African organizations gather and store data or have any links with the universities in Africa for provision of reliable data for decision making. They do not apply indigenous data for decisions on product development, marketing, or product tracking or for the understanding of consumer behavior and attitudes. Decisions about these are usually taken in Europe or America based on data collected from populations from those regions. These organizations are yet to heed to Onyemelukwe's (1966) advice that these expatriate organizations should try to attain a "happy blend" in which these organizations invest a part of their profit fortunes in research and data gathering to improve leadership and management of their organizations in these African countries.

PSYCHOLOGICAL CHARACTERISTICS OF DECISION ISSUES

Each decision issue is characterized by decision alternatives. A decision maker is expected to choose one alternative, either A1 or A2. Both A1 and A2 are characterized by a number of positive or plus (+) and negative or minus (–) aspects (signs). If these characteristics are absent from either A1 or A2, there is no choice, and, therefore, such a situation does not require decision making. If a decision maker chooses A1, all the positive and negative aspects of A1 would have been chosen (e.g., A1 + + –), and all the positive and negative aspects of A2, (e.g., A2 + – –), the nonchosen alternative, would have been forgone. The psychological consequence of the negative characteristics of the chosen A1 and the positive aspects of the rejected A2 cause postdecision regrets. These are feelings of regrets following decision making.

Given the psychological characteristics of decision issues, some decision situations have been characterized as:

- *Approach-approach. Decision.* Decision makers are presented with equally attractive alternatives. Alternative A1 is equally as attractive as alternative A2, and the decision makers are expected to choose between the equally attractive alternatives because they are not able to achieve both goals.
- *Approach-avoidance.* Decision makers have two choices, one of which A1 is attractive, and A2 is repulsive. Here decision making is not as stressful, and a choice is easily reached.
- *Avoidance-avoidance.* Decision makers have alternatives (A1 and A2) that are unattractive and disadvantageous or, at worst, harmful, but the decision makers must decide on a course of action. An example of such a situation occurs when the management is faced with a choice between downsizing or allowing an organization with a strong union to be acquired by another, bigger organization or going out of business.

The approach-approach and avoidance-avoidance decision situations generate more stress in decision makers than approach-avoidance. In order to make an approach-approach or avoidance-avoidance decision, effective managers must follow a rigorous decision-making process. These decision-making situations also generate the most prolonged vacillation in decision makers, especially when the goals are very similar in strength.

MANAGERIAL DECISION MAKING

Any organization or institution, irrespective of its size or location, is established for the purpose of achieving certain objectives or goals, and the management group within it is inevitably charged with the responsibility of achieving the stated vision, goals, and objectives. Building a cohesive work group is, however, a challenge that has often defied managerial talent and imagination (Sirippi, 1979). Decision making is a basic organizational behavior.

Organizational and institutional survival often depends on managerial or leadership decisions.

The decisions that managers make profoundly influence the lives of many people within and sometimes outside the organization, for example, decisions to pay only the minimum wage, to expand production of a particular line of production, to reduce production, to eliminate a product line, to downsize an operation, to refuse to pay workers on strike for several months, and to lay off workers. Sometimes managers in African organizations delay and avoid taking decisions that they should have taken. Making decisions is a rational behavioral process that can be learned and mastered. Two keys to management success in decision making are required, namely, that African managers require decision-making skills and the confidence to tackle even avoidance avoidance and approach approach decisions at the right time. Lack of decision-making confidence and skill is responsible for the famed bureaucratic nature of African organizations, where it takes months and sometimes years before some of these African managers could make a simple decision.

Toffler (1990) testifies to the importance of decision making at the right time when he insists that the speed of progress in a wealth-making system in any country can be measured in terms of machine processes, business transactions, communication flows, the speed with which laboratory knowledge is translated into commercial products, the length of time needed to make certain decisions, and lead time for delivery. He identifies slow decision making, failure to meet deadlines, and difference in pace of economic life between the developed and developing countries as the principal reasons that many deals collapse (see p. 390-401). For example, banks in Africa take months to reach decisions on customers' requests for loans, thus creating opportunities for corruption and other illegal practices. A bank can cut the time needed to make a decision on a loan from several weeks and months to thirty minutes by presenting the necessary information simultaneously to a group of loan specialists, rather than by routing it in sequence from one specialist to the next. The importance of time required to make decisions by an effective manager cannot be overemphasized.

In all organizations, management problems are the stimuli that arouse decision-making behavior. Problem solving is, therefore, another name for decision making. While not all decisions are made to solve problems, the existence of problems within the organization or its environment triggers the motivation to make decisions.

In organizations in Europe and North America decision making is shared among different management levels. In these organizations top managers make apex decisions that deal with the mission of the organization and strategies for achieving it. Such decisions affect the whole organization. Middle-level management personnel focuses its decision making on implementing the strategies and on budget and resource allocations. The supervisors make the day-to-day operational decisions. In African organizations decision making is highly centralized. Often it is the prerogative of the chief executive to make the decisions. I recall a female manager who used to tell her subordinates, "I like your suggestions, but you must remember that in the final analysis I am responsible to the authorities on how this assignment is carried out." In other words, thank you for your views but the decision is mine to make.

Managers, irrespective of where they work and the nature of their organizations, make planning, structural, and activation decisions. A large percentage of a manager's life is spent making decisions. Often the process of decision making is so much a part of the routine that managers do it without taking special note of it. According to Koontz and O'Donnell (1968), managers engage in *planning* decisions, which give purposeful directions to ensure orderly system operations. Such decisions help to set goals, formulate policies, develop procedures, establish rules, and provide long-range as well as short-range plans. They also engage in *structural* decision, which help to create the mechanism for operations by spelling out in detail specific activities that will lead to the achievement of the main objectives, the type and volume of resources needed, and the formal links of authority and responsibility. Structural decisions are executive organizing decisions.

Activating and *control* decisions (Koontz and O'Donnell, 1968) are the second group of decisions that managers make in organizations. Activating decisions arise from the managers' leadership role. Managers make these decisions at a time and place to guide, instruct, inspire, and motivate subordinates into an efficient working team. In these decisions they demonstrate their human skills. Control decisions, on the other hand, are those that managers make to enable them to effect meaningful evaluation and timely adjustments and corrective measures to ensure efficient attainment of organizational objectives. Such decisions facilitate organizational management and increase sensitivity to effectiveness and efficiency. Sirippi (1979) maintains that since the manager's decisions affect people in an organization, decision-making behavior "assumes a unique social significance, demanding the utmost in discretion, judgment, and integrity."

Opportunity Decision Making

Plunkett and Attner (1994) observed that not all decisions are made to solve problems in an organization. Some decisions are made by managers to seize opportunities. The authors define opportunity as a chance for progress or advancement whose realization requires that a decision be made. Opportunity decisions are the most important decision-making situations for managers and entrepreneurs. They include innovation, creativity, profitable venture identification, an emphasis on effectiveness rather than efficiency, and conscious, voluntary decision making in nonprogrammed situations.

Much of an entrepreneur's time and energy is devoted to identifying opportunities and implementing ideas in the marketplace. Becoming aware of opportunities requires insight, creativity, and the ability to generate and recognize a new idea whose implementation will yield positive results (Olson, 1986). In business and organizations, instances abound of managers or entrepreneurs who saw opportunities in their environment and seized them. Observations show that many small and medium-sized owner-manager organizations in Africa engage in more opportunity decision making than the bureaucratic government departments, parastatals, and large, international organizations. For example, more owner-manager business-people more than other managers, saw the opportunities that government's negative Structural Adjustment Program (SAP) policies created in the Nigerian market for used cars, used car parts, and refrigerators and freezers. Owner-manager business-people and entrepreneurs who saw the opportunities seized them and enriched themselves with the profits. The introduction of "luxurious" passenger buses by Ekene Dili Chukwu from Onitsha to Lagos and other parts of Nigeria are another example of opportunities that create situations for decision making. Such decisions are triggered not by problems per *se* in the organization but by problems within the organizational environment that, in turn, create needs yearning to be satisfied. Such problems in the larger society create opportunities for decision making in organizations.

The Environment of Managerial Decision Making

Decision making can be likened to a statement of a null hypothesis because it is related to a future state of events. It, therefore, has elements of uncertainty. It is also characterized by consequent riskiness caused by the dynamic nature of the decision environment. The incidence of choice from given alternatives implies the use of discretion. But, according to Sirippi (1979), the sphere of discretion within which managers exercise their judgment is characterized by a number of constraints that dictate the criteria of choice. Most significant among these constraints that impinge on African managers' decision-making ability are company and government policies, the political environment, and pressure groups. Other factors that impinge on managers' decisions are low technological development, poor physical infrastructure, poor communication network, economic dependence, and lack of necessary information for making decisions. Finally, psychological properties of the managers such as their personality including attitudes, values, beliefs, and cognitive ability affect managers' decision making.

Government policies in African countries create either a favorable or an unfavorable environment for operation of organizations and therefore what type of decisions the organizations can make and not make. Often government policies and legislative acts of government determine the nature of the products, the type of relationship that the organizations should have with labor unions, and where to buy and sell the manufactured products of a given organization.

Policies of an organization put constraints on decision making within it because it is these policies that put a ceiling on the type and extent of decisions that are acceptable. Decisions are made in keeping with organizational goals and with departmental objectives in view. Policies, says Sirippi (1979), "symbolize the conscience of an organization and as such have tremendous influence on the executive decision-making behavior."

Africa as a whole not only is technologically backward but has difficulty maintaining the borrowed technology it has acquired. African organizations are characterized by constant breakdown in equipment and have difficulties finding replacement parts. Technology available jointly with quality of personnel in terms of technical expertise sets limits for what managers and their departments can plan for and efficiently achieve. The managers' decisions can bring good management results only to the extent that the organization has adequate and effective resources to make them feasible.

Physical factors aid the successful execution of what the managers decide through physical input. Thus, the managers' decisions can be meaningful if they call for actions within the capacity or biological and psychological competence of their work teams. Actions required must be possible within the physical setting in terms of facilities, temperature of the workplace, lighting, and noise.

Economy determines the limit of decisions in organizations. The decision makers must accommodate themselves within the economic limitations of the organization. Given the available resources, the managers make their decisions with a view to optimizing favorable outcomes to the extent that this can be made possible in the light of current market conditions and future prospects. This amounts to intelligent budgeting, budget monitoring, and an efficient use of resources.

An information feedback system characterizes every efficient organization. Sirippi (1979) describes an organization as a network of communication and activities, "an information decision activity system." Forrester (1961) defines management as "a process of acquiring or assembling information and converting it into action." A proper and efficient flow of information helps to maintain organizational equilibrium. Events, conditions, or states are converted into information and they form the basis of decisions for action. The input and output characteristics of organizations underscore the importance of the communication structure in the complex, interconnected system. Information is the "lifeblood" of any organization. The communication structure ensures the proper flow, so that decision-making centers will be adequately fed with timely data to facilitate timely decisions. African managers are limited in their decision-making effectiveness due to lack of available information for decision making and problems of organizational communication.

Psychological properties of managers, such as their attitudes, values, and cognitive limitations, are constraints to the type, frequency, and kind of decisions that African managers can make and may wish to make. Other personality factors that may impede their decision making include overconfidence, familiarity, and emotional involvement.

A major environmental factor that may affect how managers make decisions in organizations in Africa is pressure groups. These are sectors of African society that may, from time to time, demand favors from organizations Among these sectors are government agencies, including the military, customs and immigration, police, ethnic group associations and relatives, and professional associations such as engineering associations and employers' associations.

Types of Managerial Decisions
Just as problems and opportunities that trigger decision making vary, so also do managers' approaches to decision making. Simple and recurring

problems are usually resolved by following prior patterns of decision making, namely, reliance on precedence. For complex and/or uncertain problems, managers rely on a formal decision-making process.

There are two major types of decisions in African organizations. These are *programmed* and nonprogrammed decisions. According to Simon (1977), the two are not really distinct but can be placed on a continuum with highly programmed decisions and highly nonprogrammed decisions at each extreme Programmed decisions apply to problems or situations that have been experienced repeatedly by the organization. The circumstances and solutions of such decision tasks are predictable. The manager's identification, analysis, selection, and implementation responses will be routine. That is, such a task will call for the use of particular patterns or procedures developed in the past to reach decisions on similar tasks. Such situations call for little cognitive processing. Identification of a similar problem will arouse a programmed response in the minimum length of time. There is usually precedence, and the decision in the case is to follow a standard procedure.

Decisions that are made in response to problems and opportunities that are characterized by unusual circumstances and unpredictable result, and that have important consequences are *nonprogrammed*. Such decisions are handled in an individualistic, nonroutine manner (Olson, 1986). Here the manager may not have specific procedures available to respond to the stimulus or the challenging situation, because the situation is novel, or because it is important enough to deserve special treatment. Sirippi (1979) says that here the manager needs to demonstrate considerable insight, good judgment, and creativity.

DECISION MAKING PROCESS

Decision making is a cognitive process. The real act of choice is the climax of a mental process involving definition of the problem, analysis, and evaluation of alternatives. Scholars of decision making have outlined some steps to decision making. Some of the scholars list five steps, and others list more, but the essence is that decision makers follow some identifiable, systematic steps in arriving at a final choice of course of action for implementation.

Awareness

Decision making, whether for an individual or for an organization, begins with awareness of a problem that demands some action. Sirippi (1979) indicates that in order to manage effectively, executives must be sensitive to problems as well as opportunities. They must be able to sense changes in the environment and be aware of problems that call for timely measures. Only awareness arouses the managers to seek action to solve the problem or seize opportunities. Managers differ in their awareness threshold for problems and opportunities that will arouse their decision-making tendencies.

Awareness demands specific identification and definition of a problem, which arouse in management the need to seek information on the specific problem; that is, the manager must gather information about the problem in order to solve it. For example, if an organization wants to prevent competitors from reducing its majority hold on the soft drink market in Africa, it has to gather information on its competitors, what changes these competitors have effected in the quality of their products, their bulk and retailing prices, and recent strategies adopted by these competitors to cut into the dominant organization's monopoly of the local market. Such information could be gathered through reading and discussions with experts and trusted friends. Time, effort, environment, and resources limit the search efforts. In order to be useful, the collected information must be adequate, valid, and reliable. As Sirippi (1979) states, management is essentially a process of converting information into action; the efficiency of the process is contingent upon the kind of information available and how the conversion is carried out. From the various sources of information the manager selects the source and type of information on which to rely in order to solve the problem at hand. Such information can provide the necessary background to the issue as well as offer potential leads to the right solution.

The collection of reliable and valid data or information helps in the definition of the problem. According to Ugwuegbu (1990b), problem definitions are based on assumptions about the causes and location of the problem. These assumptions, by their very nature may suggest certain solutions. If the assumptions are wrong or narrow or lack a comprehensive grasp of technical and human behavior, the approach to decision making for problem solution will be inadequate and inappropriate, and the decision will be unsatisfactory and not lead to the solution of the problem. Managers should question assumptions and examine alternative definitions of the problem as well as consequent approaches; by so doing they will expand and validate or invalidate current thinking about the problem. Unless the real problem in a decision-making process is well defined, the tendency is to deal with the symptoms rather than the root causes.

Thus, at the awareness, identification, and definition stage, the gathering of information, data, and evidence and the application of reason and policy or goal analyses are crucial. Since most organizations in Africa do not gather and store information, they are limited in their definition of various problems. Inappropriate identification and description of organizational problems result in making incorrect and inappropriate decisions and the prescription of wrong remedies.

Search for Potential Alternatives

Following the diagnosis of the real causes and definition of the required solution, the decision maker next searches for, and develops, all the possible means of reaching the desired goal. Sirippi (1979) indicates that this includes conceptualizing within the limits of time and resources the possible lines of action that will best lead to the right solution; what new conditions to introduce to interact with the current situation; how and when to restructure the coordination of solutions to achieve the most effective measures in the long-term interest of the organization.

Sources of alternatives that a manager will consider as suggested by Plunkett and Attner (1994) include the manager's past experience, other persons whose opinions and judgments the decision maker respects, group opinions obtained through the use of task forces, committees, focus groups, and opinion polls. The quality of executive decisions is positively correlated with the number of good alternatives that can be searched for and from which the choice of decision can finally be made. The goal in developing alternatives is to be as creative and wide-ranging as possible. Sirippi (1979) has warned that if one course of action is deemed the only way to solve a problem, that course may probably be wrong, while Plunkett and Attner (1994) insist that any action for which only one alternative has been found is by definition not a decision. "With only one choice, a bad decision is likely."

Identify Limiting Factors
The third step is that the decision maker must systematically identify the limiting factors or constraints that rule out certain solutions. One group of such factors includes time, company and government policies, and pressure groups. Another includes availability of resources such as personnel, money, facilities, equipment, and equipment parts. These factors tend to narrow the range of possible alternatives and, as a result, tend to limit the type of decision that a manager may consider in African organizations.

Analyze and Evaluate Alternatives
This step is an assessment process in an ongoing decision process. It involves a critical analysis of each alternative in terms of possible advantages and disadvantages. It is a deliberate effort to identify all the possible consequences that can emanate from a particular course of action. This helps the decision maker to assess the total cost involved if a decision on a particular course of action is taken. This includes the assessment of some likely unintended consequences. From this "cost-benefit" analysis, a process of weighing and balancing, the decision maker is put in a position to determine which course of action will effectively serve the desired goal of solving the problem.

Selection of the Best Alternatives
A deliberate choice in the decision-making process is the climax. The manager after considering the pros and cons of generated alternatives, selects the one that most appropriately meets the demands of the organization. Sirippi (1979) advises that here the criterion of efficiency should become the rationale of executive behavior and that the "decision rule" should be based on the total systems concept. He further suggests that under normal circumstances the executive should be guided by three factors in selecting a given decision over others. These include:

- Contribution of the chosen alternatives to the objective in view, that is, to what extent the course helps to achieve the desired end. This is said to be the primary condition that lends validity to the chosen course of action.
- Maximum degree of economic effectiveness, that is, the degree to which the decision will permit the efficient use of available resources. This is the economic feasibility of the selected course of action.
- Probability of implementation of the chosen decision. The course of action must be logical as well as have a high probability of being executed. Once the course of action is so characterized, employees will understand, accept, and get committed to management decisions.

Implementation of Decisions

This is a critical stage in the process of decision making. Here the decision is put into action. A decision that is not implemented becomes useless and is nothing but an intention. A decision becomes effective if the "action commitment" element is built into it from the start. The outcome of a chosen course of action is invariably determined by how it is implemented.

If a decision is made at the top of an organization, it has to be carried out by everybody in the organization. Therefore, a well thought-out plan is needed for effectively communicating the decision to those affected by it in terms of what to communicate, and when and how to communicate it. If this is done effectively, proper understanding, cooperation, and commitment for successful operations will be ensured.

Evaluation

The final step in the decision-making process is to create a control and evaluation system. This system should provide feedback on how well the decision is being implemented, what the positive and negative results are, and what adjustments are necessary to obtain the results desired. The implementation of a decision often generates new problems or opportunities that in themselves require decisions. An evaluation system can help identify those outcomes. The creation of a control system helps to assure the organization that the decision is effectively implemented and that the subsequent outcomes are channeled to good advantage.

The discussion on the steps that decision makers take shows that individuals or managers in making decisions are, in effect, concerned with a continuation of processes and relationships in a time-binding sequence. The extent to which the managers are successful depends largely on the way each step is efficiently and effectively carried out to sequentially lead to the next step.

THEORIES OF DECISION MAKING

In the practical, day-to-day decision making in African organizations, managers do not approach it from any theoretical perspective. There are no systematic studies and documentation on decision-making processes among African managers. Since decision making is a cognitive activity, it is assumed that the rules that guide the process of decision making in the West can be generalized to Africans and African managers.

Many disciplines have made major contributions to the theories of decision making. Economics, mathematics, philosophy, and psychology have all contributed to this area. Because of the differing orientations of these disciplines, it is often quite difficult to synthesize the research contributions on decision making. Attempts are made here to review some of the basic theoretical contributions of economics, mathematics, and psychology.

Rationality Model

This is a traditional economics theory of decision making. The theory holds that rationality is basic to all acts of choice and enables the "executive to choose the best option as a means of optimizing the value of the situation" (Sirippi, 1979). It further postulates that organizations always seek to maximize their profits and that business decision makers always choose the most profitable course from all alternatives open to them.

The rationality model also proffers a method of determining when an organization should stop the investment of extra resources of one type or another in its operations in the hope of producing extra profit. Dale (1969) called this type of theory *marginal productivity.* As it is commonly known from our knowledge of economics, this theory states that as extra inputs of any one type, such as labor or equipment, are added, profits increase, but each new increment of profit is smaller than the last one, and at some point the cost of the extra input will exactly equal the extra revenue that it will bring in. At the marginal point the wise decision should be for the organization to stop. Marginal analysis is used to determine decisions on hiring workers, purchasing new machinery, and pricing products. Finally, it is used as a guide to decision making in many cases. However, marginal theory cannot be used to avoid all risks and so make decision making merely a routine.

Another criticism against rationality, according to Toffler (1990), is that executives of organizations are often exposed to unique and uncommon situations arising from the interaction between the environment and the organization or arising from unexpected turbulence in the organization itself. Such situations are sudden changes in government policies, markets, or disasters. About 1975 fire broke out at the headquarters of Johnson Wax in Lagos, Nigeria. Some of its managers were killed, and some suffered third-degree burns. In 1996 a section of the Ikeja area of NEPA burned down. The insurance coverage for the installation was not comprehensive. Such events often hurl managers into situations for which nothing has adequately prepared them or their bureaucracies.

According to Toffler (1990), "when situations" such as these or others similar to them "arise that can't easily be assigned to predesignated informational cubbyholes, bureaucracies get nasty." Rationality is thrown overboard and managers begin "to fight over turf, money, people—and the control of information." This unleashes tremendous amounts of energy and raw emotion. Instead of solving problems, however, all this human output is burned up in the struggle. "What's still worse," Toffler continues, is that "these fratricidal battles make the organization behave irrationally," and "the vaunted rationality of bureaucracy goes out of the window. Power, always a factor, now replaces reason as the basis for decision" (p.169).

Another unrealistic assumption of the rationality model is that complete information about alternatives and their consequences is available to the decision maker. The proposers of rationality choice and their disciples later realized how unrealistic this assumption is and have since relaxed it. They now assume that all solutions can be discovered through a process of search.

A further unrealistic assumption of the rationality model is that all relevant consequences of each alternative are known. This assumption, however, has recently been modified to assume that the decision maker can make a reasonably accurate estimate of the probability of each outcome.

Sirippi (1979), in defense of the rationality model, insists that the fact that these drawbacks exist and work against the executive's efforts to be totally rational does not necessarily render the concept of rationality invalid. Rather, executives who recognize these limitations will be in a better position "to lift the quality of (their) decision making to the highest level possible within available cost and time constraints" (McFarland, 1974, p. 266).

Mathematical Decision Theory

This is concerned with the best way to make decisions under conditions of risk or uncertainty. Conditions of "risk" are those in which the probability of various outcomes is known or can be estimated. For example, if an unbiased coin is tossed once, the probability of getting either a head or a tail is known. It either comes up head or comes up tail. If the coin is thrown 100 times, the probability is that 50 percent of the time heads will be obtained and for 50 percent of the time tails will be obtained. Under uncertainty, on the other hand, the decision maker is completely ignorant of the odds.

The mathematical decision theory, therefore, provides a systematic way of laying out the possible outcomes of different decisions when the decision makers face complicated problems in which many of the factors that will affect results are completely beyond their control. Game theories, which are very popular in psychology, are models of mathematical decision theory. According to Dale (1969), factors within the decision makers' control are called "acts," and those outside their control are called "events."

Again, the problem of decision making based on the marginal economics and mathematical theories is that all these theories assume that all managers or executives are, as far as their organizational decisions are concerned, an "economic people" whose motivation is to maximize their organization's profits to the level of their ability, within the law of the country, and to the extent of ethical standards. Practical experience shows that managers and executives attempt to optimize their organizations' profits, not to maximize them.

Psychological Decision Theories

Psychological decision theory has two interrelated facets, namely normative and descriptive. The descriptive facet, which includes studies on choice, is of interest here. Choice model concentrates on psychological aspects of individual judgment and decision making. Various approaches of this model are discussed.

Elimination-by-Aspects (EBA). This is a major choice theory proposed by Tversky (1972a, 1972b). The model describes decision making as a covert, sequential, elimination process. It assumes that in making a choice or decision, the individual decision maker views the alternatives as sets of aspects. For example, when purchasing a television set, one would consider the price, model, make, and color. At each stage in the choice process an aspect is selected with probability proportional to its importance; alternatives that are unsatisfactory regarding the selected aspect are eliminated.

Studies on choice methods show that managers use many rules and strategies in making a decision. These include conjunctive, disjunctive, lexicographic, and compensatory rules and the principle of dominance. A typical choice may end up involving several stages and employing different rules at different junctures. At the initial stage, managers tend to compare a number of alternatives on the same attribute and employ conjunctive rules to reject some alternatives from further consideration. After reducing the alternatives, decision makers employ compensatory weighting of advantages and disadvantages on the reduced set of alternatives in order to reach a decision.

Slovic, Fischhoff, and Lichtenstein (1977) maintain that features of the task that complicate the decision making, such as incomplete data, incommensurable data dimensions, information overload, and time pressures, tend to encourage strain-reducing, noncompensatory strategies. In some instances, managers tend to reduce memory load by comparing two alternatives at a time and then retaining only the better one for later comparisons (Svenson, 1974; Russo and Rosen, 1975). On the whole, managers appear to prefer strategies that are easy to justify. They do not rely on relative weights, trade-off functions, or other numerical computations, according to this theory. Faced with a choice of two alternatives that are equal in value for them, managers do not choose randomly. They usually follow the easy and defensible strategy of selecting the alternative that is superior on a more important dimension.

Script Processing. This is based on the concept of a "cognitive script," which is a coherent sequence of events expected by the individuals on the basis of prior learning or experience (Abelson, 1976). The model holds that when individuals are faced with decision making, they are said to bring into play relevant scripts or experiences. Such scripts help individuals to make a choice or reach a decision fast. When there are no such scripts, the decision maker reverts to other means of making choices.

Consumer Choice Model. This uses multiple regression, conjoint measurement, and analysis of variance to describe consumers' values in choice decisions. Some researchers have investigated basic psychological questions such as the effect of amount and display of information on the optimality of choice or decision making. Jacoby (1975, 1976) has argued that more information is not necessarily helpful in a choice decision because it can overload consumers and lead them to select suboptimal products. It also leads to a protracted decision-making time span. Many of the studies on choice have been done within the domain of consumer psychology.

Risky Choice. This involves decision making under conditions of risk. Decision making under conditions of risk has been of interest to psychologists. This is probably due to the availability of appealing research paradigms such as choice in gambling, and the dominant normative theory, and the SEU model, against which behavior can be compared. The SEU model assumes that people behave as though they maximized the sum of the products of utility and probability. Studies in the area of risky choice do not produce consistent results but show that situational arrangements and the nature of the task have very strong effects on the SEU model.

Regression Approaches. These employ analysis of variance, conjoint measurement, and multiple regression techniques to develop algebraic models that describe the method by which individuals weigh and combine information in order to reach a decision. Among these approaches are *integration theory* which results from Anderson's (1974a, 1974b) information integration theory Anderson illustrated that simple algebraic models describe information use quite well in an impressive variety of judgmental, decision-making, attitudinal, and perceptual tasks. These models have revealed that people tend to engage in stimulus averaging. Particularly relevant to decision making are studies of risk taking and inference (Shanteau, 1975), such as card games or football pool forecasting.

The second approach is the *policy capturing theory*, which assumes that most judgments depend on a mode of thought that is quasi-rational, that is, a synthesis of analytic and intuitive processes. The elements of quasi-rational thought are cues, their weights, and their functional relations to both the environment and the judge's responses. Operationalization of the theory employs multiple regression analysis to derive equations representing the judge's cue utilization policy, while judgmental performance is analyzed into knowledge and "cognitive control," that is, the ability to employ one's knowledge consistently (Hammond and Summers, 1972). Several studies have demonstrated that linear models have been used with similar success to analyze complex real-world decisions. Subjects in the studies have included business managers (Hamner and Carter, 1975; Moskowitz, 1974). The findings have been replicated for decision making in other instances.

Satisficing Model

The theory of satisficing rather than maximization of profit was postulated by Herbert A. Simon (1957). The theory holds that a decision maker simplifies the decision and selects a satisfactory solution rather than the optimal one. Business decision makers do not generally seek the highest profit possible. Instead, their efforts are toward "satisficing." Simon explains this by insisting that while the economic person seeks and selects the best decision that will yield the maximum profit from among those decisions available, the manager "satisfices," that is, looks for the decision that is satisfactory or "good enough" or that will yield a satisfactory result. Adequate profit is the aim rather than maximum profit, as is "fair price" rather than maximum price.

According to Simon's theory, only when the attainment falls short of what the managers consider satisficing or adequate do they embark on a further search for more profitable courses of action. Wexley and Yukl (1984) maintain that satisficing simplifies a decision problem and allows the manager to make decisions without the need to consider numerous alternatives.

Critics of the satisficing model of decision making maintain that the problem with it is that it is difficult to distinguish its real meaning from profit maximization. What may look like efforts to satisfice in the meantime, they say, may become profit-maximizing in the long run. Satisficing may result from fear of violating the law, of attracting other potential competitors, or of losing the goodwill of the public (Dale, 1969). These may be the real reasons that keep an organization from pursuing courses of action that would lead to profit maximization. Dale went on to say that many organizations tend to satisfice, because such organizations confuse means and ends. Sometimes an organization may concentrate on volume of sales or share of the market rather than on profit. Second, profits grow with sales, and managers are accustomed to thinking of the two as directly related. Thus, to an organization that has traditionally increased its profits by increasing its sales, any cutback in sales appears to be a retreat. This need not be so. Conversely, tradition can operate to keep sales down when an increase in volume would produce a higher profit. A company that specializes in making high-quality products for a small market and has prospered may be slow to see possibilities in expansion. Sometimes management inherits a set of traditions, "almost insensitive beliefs" (Lloyd, 1949). Lloyd's contribution arises from the fact that he was among the first to call attention to the importance of personality and tradition in the decision-making process. According to Lloyd, the importance of these psychological variables has always been grossly underestimated.

Vroom and Yetton Decision Tree

This model is a guide to managers in selecting the factors that are most important in a given decision, especially when both decision acceptance and quality of decision are crucial. The model provides managers with a series of questions that serve as a guide to the appropriate style. As each question is asked and answered, the manager becomes more aware and learns more about the nature of the decision. The circled number at the end of the relevant series of questions designates the most effective decision-making method and corresponds to the numbers of Vroom's (1973) subordinate involvement styles.

Vroom maintains that subordinates affect a manager's decision-making environment in significant ways. For managers to perform effectively, they need their subordinates' support, input, and understanding of decisions that these managers make. The manager must evaluate the level of subordinates' involvement, which can range from zero input to full participation.

Vroom (1973) describes five levels or styles of subordinates' involvement:

1. Managers make decisions that have no input or assistance from subordinates, because the decisions are routine, or the managers have the information necessary for such decisions.
2. Managers get the necessary information from subordinates and then make the decision. During the process of obtaining the information, the managers may or may not reveal the real problem under consideration. The subordinates merely provide the information.
3. Managers discuss the problem and solution with subordinates, ask for inputs on an individual basis, and make the decision, which may or may not reflect the subordinates' input.
4. Managers involve the subordinates as a group, obtain their collective ideas, and make a decision, which may or may not reflect the subordinates' influence.
5. Managers review the problem with the subordinates as a group. Together, they collect the necessary information, formulate the information into alternatives, and try to reach consensus on the best solution. Here the managers act as the leaders of the teams; they do not try to influence the choices of the committee. The managers finally accept and implement any reasonable decision that receives the support of the entire group.

As an example of how the Vroom and Yetton guide works, consider how a department manager who is developing work schedules goes about these decisions. The manager begins by asking these questions (see Figure 5.1):

A. Is there a quality requirement that might make one solution more rational than another? Since the answer is no, the manager moves to D.
D. Is acceptance of the decision by subordinates critical to effective implementation? Since the answer is yes, the manager moves to E.
E. If the manager makes the decision alone, will subordinates accept it? Since the answer is no, the manager should use style number 5.

The tree branch that is followed at any juncture depends on the answer to questions asked.

We can see that by applying the Vroom and Yetton decision tree, the department manager learns that the problem should be shared with the subordinates as a group. As a team they will generate and evaluate alternatives and attempt to reach a solution.

Figure 5.1
Vroom and Yetton Decision Tree for Choosing a Decision-Making Style

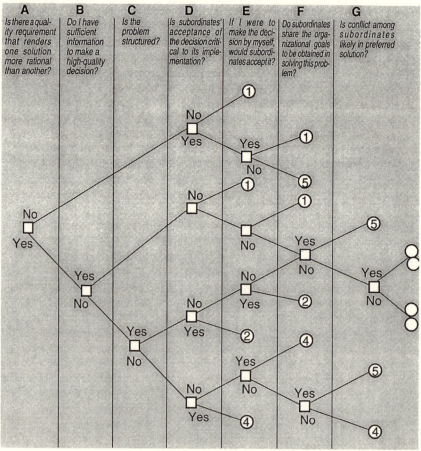

Source: W. R. Plunkett and R. F. Attner (1994, p. 171).

An array of theories of decision making has been presented. Some of them apply to individual decision making; others are relevant to organizational decision making. None of them can explain all decision making in every organization all the time. How far African managers involve these theories in their everyday decision making is yet to be studied and demonstrated. The next section considers group decision making.

GROUP DECISION MAKING

Many of the decisions in modern organizations are made by groups or teams rather than by individuals. In some organizations, groups are established to make organizational decisions. These decision-making groups may be permanent management teams and committees whose membership changes periodically, for example, an appointments and promotions committee, a finance committee, or temporary teams and committees set up to deal with a particular problem in an organization. The psychological principle involved in participatory decision making is that human beings take pride in being involved and in taking responsibility. Participation is, therefore, likely to produce more compliance and conformity with the decisions of the team or committee than nonparticipation.

The concept of group decision making in modern organizations is yet to become popular in the African management environment. The African colonial heritage with its bureaucratic distances between the hierarchies and the rigidity of African bureaucrats have yet to permit an effective program of group decision making in government organizations and many private and public companies to take root. Another cause is that, unfortunately, in Africa since independence those having power want to keep out rivals. When groups or committees are instituted to help make decisions, the reports and recommendations of such committees are often not acted upon. At the government and other organizational levels committees and teams are window dressing whose reports and recommendations are often not utilized in organizational decision making. For African organizations to compete effectively in the global market of today, rank-and-file employees must become partners with the managers in decision making for the well-being of the organization.

There are some advantages to group decision making. Recall the old adage, that maintains that two good heads are better than one. It speaks to the positive value of group decision making. Groups are more appropriate than individuals in making complex and technical decisions that require a pooling of expert knowledge and ideas by several people. Committees facilitate the making of difficult and unpopular decisions. By using committees and teams, the responsibility for unpopular decisions is diffused among several persons. A member of a committee or other decision group feels involved provided the group is perceived as representative of all. Membership in a committee results in better understanding of decisions and increased commitment to implement group decisions more effectively by participating members than if the decision was just received from above.

Managers and leaders should also understand some of the disadvantages of using groups, committees, and teams to make decisions in organizations. Committees and groups usually take much longer to make a decision than a single manager would take. In an emergency situation where a decision has to be taken immediately, it may not be feasible to assemble a representative committee or group to find a solution for a pressing problem. The best that the chief executive can do is to assemble the managers or heads of departments to deliberate and find a solution for the problem.

A decision from a group or committee may not necessarily be better than a decision made by a single manager who can assemble all necessary information and who has the expertise needed to make the decision. This is more so in gender-biased, multiethnic, and multireligious societies and where such teams or committees are not balanced with respect to these factors. Groups have been shown by studies in social psychology to take riskier decisions than do individuals. This phenomenon is known as "risky-shift" (Stoner, 1961) or the tendency for a person's risk-taking behavior to increase following participation in a group discussion of a problem.

When members of a team disagree sharply about the objectives of a decision, the compromise they settle upon is usually very poor and unsatisfactory. Group decisions are strongly affected by a number of group characteristics such as size, composition of the group, member traits, status differentials, group cohesiveness (Wexley and Yukl, 1984), and levels of psychological involvement with the issue in question or with the department, unit, or persons who are the object of the decision.

Group Size

Many people always complain when Government sets up committees or groups to help solve some problems. In Nigeria when the Constitutional Drafting Committee and Vision 2010 Committee, made up of 170 members, were set up by government, many felt very uncomfortable due to the number of people included in each of these committees. There are some advantages to be gained from a large group, if one discounts the hidden ploy of the Sani Abacha dictatorial regime. A large group has the advantage of more collective knowledge and expert, provided the group is selected with particular attention to ensure wide dispersion of relevant information and ideas among many people with different backgrounds and technical specialties. However, as a group grows larger, it becomes more difficult to regulate discussion and ensure equal participation. It often happens that a few extrovert, talkative, and aggressive individuals hijack the discussion. This produces inhibition in some members, who then refuse to make any contributions. A majority of the members feel isolated, intimidated, and left out. The quality of the decisions taken by such a committee is lower than it would otherwise have been if members participated on an equal basis. When a large group is assembled like that, after the initial discussion of the issues, the group should be broken up into committees of experts to review decisions in their area of expertise. Managers should accommodate procedures that will yield the best decision making.

Group Composition

The importance has been already mentioned of the composition of members of committees or groups, especially in the African subregion with its characteristics of differences among its peoples with respect to gender, ethnic background, language, culture, and religious affiliation. These characteristics have to be respected when a team or committee is composed, not only at the national level but also in every organization if the decisions of such committees are to be acceptable to all those whom the decisions are likely to affect.

The findings of research are that heterogeneous groups tend to produce better solutions to complex problems than homogenous ones. Groups composed of people with differing technical and professional specialties tend to define a problem more broadly and more appropriately and are more likely to generate more creative solutions (Dearborn and Simon, 1958; Wexley and Yukl, 1984).

Status Gap

Groups and committees should not be composed of people whose social and professional status is widely diverse, such as messengers, typists, managers, and general managers. The discussion among such a group would be inhibited by the wide gap in status in the organization. Low-status members, such as typists and messengers in this instance, tend to defer to the ideas and opinions of the high-status members, the managers and general managers. They also do not like to criticize them, even when they find their views to be incorrect. In composing a committee or a team, care must be taken to avoid wide status differences among group members.

Personality of Members

The values and attitudes held by different people affect any group decision on equal opportunity for women in an organization. Personality traits such as authoritarianism can affect decisions made by a group. Research in psychology has demonstrated that compatible groups, where the individuals can agree with each other, produce superior decisions under conditions of time pressure than groups that are not compatible (Liddell and Slocum, 1976; Shutz, 1955). Groups with highly competitive and aggressive members are more conflict-oriented, while groups with immature and emotionally unstable members have more disruptive, self-oriented behavior (Wexley and Yukl, 1984).

Group Cohesiveness

If a group is too cohesive, it tends to come to agreement too quickly without exhausting consideration of all available alternatives. Individual members of a cohesive group are usually less willing to risk social rejection by questioning a majority point of view or their leader's position or presenting an opinion contradictory to a group stand. The critical evaluation of ideas is inhibited during decision making, and creativity is thrown out the window during problem solving. Member's motivation in such a group is to show how much they are committed to the group goal.

Groupthink

Sometimes highly cohesive country, ethnic, or religious groups, teams, or committees experience a phenomenon that psychologists call *groupthink*. Groupthink is a behavioral tendency that results from group members being noncritical over commitment to group goals and objectives to the extent that these members rationalize the correctness of the course of their action and exaggerate their ability and power and underrate those of their opponents. The unrealistic evaluation of the facts of the course of the group's action leads the group to adopt psychological defense mechanisms to protect the group and justify the group's poor decisions. A careful examination of the civil wars and political conflicts in Africa indicates that most of these are characterized, to a certain degree by groupthink.

In a series of case studies Janis (1972) showed that cohesive groups are characterized by groupthink that distort their decision making. This often leads them to make decisions that have disastrous social, political, and economic consequences that were not foreseen. Janis (1972) held that groupthink is characterized by *illusion of invulnerability*. This implies that members of highly cohesive groups tend to overemphasize the strength and virtues of their group and over-estimate the group's capacity to successfully carry out a risky course of action. Examples abound in the African environment. The Igbo people and the Nigerian civil war and the Yoruba people and June 12, 1993, the meeting of the Association of University Teachers (ASUU) in Nigeria and the 1996 strike are concrete examples of groups riding on the roller coaster of groupthink.

Another characteristic is *rationalization of negative information*. This is the tendency for the group members to collectively discount and rationalize warnings of imminent danger and to discount indications of likely losses, which, if properly considered, could have persuaded them from pursuing a certain course of action.

A group characterized by groupthink has the tendency to *stereotype opposing outgroups*. Group members collectively share a distorted perception of competitors, opponents, rivals, and enemies as too weak, ignorant and stupid and as lacking the knowledge and skill to be a threat. A labor union and management in conflict may see each other as too untrustworthy to negotiate with or too weak to be a significant threat. During the 1996 ASUU strike, members of ASUU saw the military regime in power as ignorant, stupid, and weak. "If they don't grant our demands, other military boys will overthrow them and grant our request." "Parents will revolt against the military boys and side with us." Indeed, none of those expectations took place.

Another characteristic of groupthink is a *holy than thou attitude*. Group members believe that the inherent morality of their group and its objectives justify the methods employed by the group to attain its objectives. In order to maintain the cohesiveness of the group, members engage in *suppression of dissenting views*. Group members are not encouraged to speak out about their doubts and misgivings regarding the course of action chosen by the group. The resulting unanimity is, in turn, incorrectly interpreted among members as a sign that they are in agreement with the course of action.

Since information that is contradictory to the course of the group's action is psychologically stressful, group members take it upon themselves to protect the group from information that is not positive to their course by discounting or suppressing such information. Information that is positive is overexaggerated. Members also adopt different tactics of direct *social pressure,* including social isolation, and sometimes physical attack of dissenting members to discourage any expression of doubt or criticism about the group's illusions, stereotypes, or judgments concerning the group's course of action.

A group characterized by groupthink suffers from lack of critical thinking and lacks rationality in the decision-making process. The group's consideration is too narrow to guarantee consideration of a wide variety of alternatives. The group seeks information supportive of the preferred alternative and ignores unfavorable information. It neither seeks nor obtains information from experts. The leaders of such a group claim and convince the members that they possess the most reliable information. Wexley and Yukl (1984) maintain that the group's decision is likely to be very poor because of narrow and biased evaluation of alternatives.

The decision made by ASUU in 1996 to go on strike is a good example of a groupthink decision. The membership of ASUU includes great intellectuals in Nigeria, professors who advise government at all levels, economists who are aware of the government's economic policy, and labor management experts who should have learned from history what the government's record was like in relating to labor unions at the time in that country. Yet they overestimated the power of ASUU in confrontation with the dictatorial regime. They also overestimated parents' sensitivity to their children's need for a university education. Moreover, they overestimated the support that their union expected from the nation's newspapers, parents, and the public at large. They failed to consider carefully the risks involved in calling their members out on an indefinite strike. None of the group members considered what unsuccessful ASUU demands would mean for ASUU, the members, and the entire educational system in Nigeria.

Psychologically, groups characterized by groupthink engage in these illusions to insulate the group from excessive anxiety and psychological breakdown. In order to accomplish this, the group unconsciously employs defense mechanisms such as repression, projection, reaction formation, displacement, denial, and rationalization.

Protecting a Group from Groupthink

Organizations need to be protected from groupthink if they are to survive. Wexley and Yukl (1984) recounted procedures proposed by Janis (1972) for avoiding grouphink in decision groups. In order to avoid groupthink, groups and teams should insist on democratic leadership, which subjects group decisions, actions and choice of actions to a group's open discussion, debate, and choice. Often the leadership in groups tends to talk more in meetings and committees, leaving members few moments to participate in the discussions. This is a strategy used by the leadership to limit opposing voices. The leadership also selects members of committees whenever they are set up. The tendency is to fill such committees and teams with members who share the leader's course of action or views. This tendency perpetuates groupthink.

These types of manipulation must be avoided. Policy decisions vital to an organization must be assigned to more than one decision group, whose members should be made up of core and peripheral group members. This is more easily said than done, given the motive of the group leadership, namely, to prove itself to be correct and to maintain the cohesiveness of the group. The leadership will not risk sharing vital decision making with individuals of whose position it is not quite sure.

When an organization sets up a committee or a team with members from different departments or units, the manager should require the team or committee members to get periodic reactions and views from their colleagues in their departments and units. The representatives should periodically brief their coworkers in their respective departments and units as to what the committee is doing and, the difficulties with which they are dealing, and listen to the information, ideas, and criticisms of their colleagues from their units and departments.

The group should utilize third-party intervention. Experts or consultants from outside the organization who are not emotionally involved in the group's course of action should be invited to attend some of the group's meetings where important decisions are to be taken so that the experts can listen and comment on the views of the group members. When the group is assessing alternative course of action, subcommittees composed of members with differing views should be used. After reaching an initial agreement regarding the best alternative action, an enlarged group should be formed to hold a review meeting to allow members to reconsider the evidence and express any doubts before a final decision.

Rigid adoption of all these procedures is not necessary for a group to avoid groupthink. In some cases, a particular procedure may be feasible, and in others it may not. The leader and the group or the consultant psychologist should select a subset of appropriate procedures that, when taken together, are likely to prevent members from ignoring critical judgment during group decision making.

AIDS FOR IMPROVING DECISION MAKING IN AFRICAN ORGANIZATIONS

The importance of decision making in organizations prompted the introduction of many different kinds of decision aids to improve the quality of decisions made by individuals and groups. Some aids help a person or group interpret confusing data and help the decision maker to determine the relevance of data or information available. Some aids help the individual to comprehend the causes and critical elements of a problem. Others help to generate a series of alternative ideas and information about possible solutions to a problem and the likely consequences of a particular decision. Still others actually make decisions based on stated preferences and expectations (Bass, 1983; MacCrimmon and Taylor, 1976; Wexley and Yukl, 1984). In this last section of the chapter, several of the most useful types of decision aids already in use in the West that can be applied to African organizations are discussed.

The Computer

Computers are the latest decision aids. Computers can generate the needed information and millions of alternatives and help select the best one. Computers can help make decisions based on stated objectives, preferences, and expectations.

However, according to Toffler (1990), "Politics is about power, not truth." Organizational decisions are not always based on "objective" findings or profound understanding, but on a conflict of forces, each pursuing its perceived self-interest. Computers cannot eliminate this necessary parry, thrust, and power struggle. Computers raise it, instead, to a higher level.

Another problem is that most managers in African organizations rarely have the time, inclination, or skill to understand the hidden issues in any case. Lacking these and the training needed to cut through the barrage of facts and pseudofacts themselves, decision-makers in African organizations are forced to rely more on the computer specialists and their overseas headquarters. The monitoring of more variables, plus the enormous jump in data availability and processing capacity made possible by computers, changes the problem facing the decision-making manager from information underload to information overload. Finally, since the necessary data for decision making may not be available in African organizations, the use of the computer for decision making may be limited.

Structured Association Technique

This is a technique for increasing the number of innovative solutions to a problem. It encourages a decision maker to systematically associate the many elements of a complex problem. In a procedure introduced by Zwicky (1969) called *morphology,* the key dimensions and elements of a problem are first identified, and then all possible pairs or combinations of several elements are considered. A few of the combinations may prove insightful for a novel solution that might otherwise have been overlooked. Wexley and Yukl (1984) suggested a simple example of the technique for a construction firm that is searching for ways to build low-cost housing. Two of the key dimensions of the problem are type of dwelling and type of construction material. The various types of dwelling (e.g., duplex, barracks-type of house, high-rise apartments, single-family house) are listed as the column headings of a matrix, and the construction materials (e.g., brick, wood, stucco, aluminum, glass, cement blocks) are listed as the row headings. The feasibility of each combination of method and material (i.e., the matrix cells) is then considered. Other techniques broaden the range of possible changes considered for an object, product, or procedure involved in a problem. The decision maker then uses a checklist to systematically consider all of the possible changes in the hope of discovering good solutions that might not have been considered otherwise.

The Delphi Technique

This is a group decision-making technique developed by the Rand Corporation of America. The Delphi technique provides structure to group discussion. It leads to consensus and emphasizes equal participation. Unlike other group decision-making techniques, Delphi participants do not assemble. Instead, decision making is conducted by a group leader through questionnaires. The five steps of the Delphi technique are:

- A questionnaire puts a problem before a group of experts who do not interact face-to-face. Each expert is asked to provide a solution.
- Each expert completes and returns a questionnaire, that is, provides a solution.
- A summary of opinions is developed from the answers received from the experts. This summary is distributed along with a second questionnaire.
- Experts complete the second questionnaire. At this stage, experts have the benefit of others' opinions and may change their suggestions to reflect them.
- The process continues until the experts reach consensus. According to *Small Business Reports* (1988), the Delphi technique works especially well for solving ambiguous problems in spite of its expense and time-consuming nature. It is not a feasible decision-making technique when a rapid decision is needed.

Nominal Group Technique

Group discussion sessions can be rendered ineffective when a few people dominate the conversation. The nominal group technique helps eliminate such a problem by creating a structure that encourages equal participation by all members. The steps are as follows (Plunkett and Attner, 1994, p. 176):

- *Problem definition.* When the group is assembled, the group leader defines the problem, with no discussion.
- *Development of ideas.* All members write down their ideas about the problem, with no discussion.
- *Round-robin presentation.* Members individually present their ideas to the group. The leader records the ideas on a blackboard. The process continues without discussion until all ideas are recorded.
- *Clarification of ideas.* The group conducts an open discussion of the ideas, with members explaining their ideas as needed.
- *Initial voting.* By secret ballot, members individually rank the recorded solutions. The solutions with the lowest average rankings are eliminated.
- *Evaluation of the revised list.* Members question each other about the remaining solutions.
- *Final voting.* In another secret ballot, all ideas are ranked. The idea that receives the highest total vote is adopted. It can be seen that the second function of the nominal group technique is that it encourages individual creativity. The technique requires a fair amount of time.

Brainstorming

This is a method of shared problem solving in which all members of a group spontaneously contribute ideas focused on the subject problem. An advertising executive named Alex Osborn in the late 1940s first formalized the technique. The technique works most effectively when basic guidelines are followed. The procedure for effective brainstorming is as follows:

- Sessions are usually held in a comfortable setting for a specific time and free from outside interruptions.
- Participants must be made aware that they are in a leaderless group and that they are free to speak openly, free from constraints of status or position. They must be made aware that the organization has sanctioned their participation in the group.

- Group members must understand that no idea or suggestion is too silly or far-fetched to be voiced.
- Every member should be encouraged to build upon the contributions of others, until all opinions have been presented.

During the session all ideas voiced should be written down on a blackboard. Later, ideas are sorted, and the best ones are examined in detail, either by the manager or by another group. Brainstorming generates enthusiasm and stimulates participants to think creatively. According to Osborn (1957), "the proof of a good brainstorming session is the number of ideas produced and the way participants feel afterwards." Brainstorming works well with a straightforward, well-defined problem in a supportive atmosphere.

Outcome Psychodrama
This is a decision aid developed to help decision makers become more aware of emotionally charged outcomes that are likely to have an important influence on eventual satisfaction with a decision (Janis and Mann, 1977; Wexley and Yukl, 1984). The decision makers are made to imagine or project themselves into the future, say a year or two or five years ahead, to visualize what has happened as a result of choosing the most attractive alternative. The decision makers do this by creating an imaginary scenario of events and describing how they would feel about them. The decision makers may be asked to create two scenarios, in one instance, they assume that things went well, and in the other, that things did not turn out well. The procedure can be repeated for all the other principal alternatives being considered. When there are several alternatives, proponents suggest that it is best to enact only unfavorable scenarios in order to save time. Outcome psychodrama helps people to develop a more realistic "balance sheet" of costs and benefits for each alternative choice decision.

SUMMARY
This chapter examined individual and organizational decision making in the African environment and came to the conclusion that decision making by individuals has not been systematically studied, but evidence from practical observations shows that decision making in organizations in Africa is chaotic. It is also largely based on precedence, while decision making by individuals is intuitive and based on subjective expected utility (SEU). Decision making is a basic organizational behavior. It is so vital that sometimes the survival of an individual or an organization may depend on it. Managers make planning, structural, activating, and control decisions. Managers and entrepreneurs spend much of their time making opportunity decisions.

Decision making follows some identifiable steps in arriving at a final choice of course of action for implementation. These steps include awareness, identification, and definition of the problem; a search for possible alternatives; identification of limiting factors; analysis of alternatives; choice; implementation; and evaluation. These seven steps are not rigidly followed in every instance of decision making. While nonprogrammed decisions may follow these steps, programmed decisions and situations that have been already experienced and are repeated may not follow them.

Decision making is a cognitive process, and it is assumed that the process and theories that account for the process in Western cultures may be generalized to contemporary processes of decision making in African organizations. These models include rationality, mathematical decision theory, and psychological theories and models. Since African organizations are bureaucratic in character, with their overcentralization of decision making, Vroom and Yetton's model of decision making would suffer the same disadvantages as those of the consultative system of leadership in African organizations. The satisficing model explains the decision-making strategies that most owner-managers of small and medium-sized organizations in Africa use.

The use of groups, committees, and team systems to make decisions has not taken very strong root in many African organizations. It is better to utilize groups, committees, or teams to help make more complex and technical decisions. The advantages of such a decision-making approach is that the decision reached may be a better-quality decision. Another benefit is that the consequence of the decision outcome is shared by all the members of the committee, not by the manager, as would be the case if the manager made the decision alone. Members of the organization feel more committed when they or their representatives are involved in making organizational decisions that they would be called upon later to help implement in their respective departments. Implementation of such decisions is easier for the organizations. Whether decisions are made by an individual manager, groups, or committees, such decisions should be guided by relevant data or information.

When utilizing teams or committees to make decisions, organizations should watch out for the psychological phenomenon known as groupthink. In order to avoid groupthink, membership in teams and committees should be rotated from time to time. Groups and committees should not be allowed to become too cohesive. Management techniques for aiding decision making are gaining acceptance in some African organizations. Wider adoption of these techniques should be encouraged by the organizations.

6

Conflict and Conflict Management in Organizations

Competition over the use of a toy between two siblings or a wife's misperception of the role of her husband's secretary in the office may result in disagreement at home and subsequent conflict. According to Deutsch (1980), conflict is a basic and inherent feature of relationships, be it the relationship between husband and wife, between employees and their supervisors, or between the workers and an organization. Historically, conflict has been part and parcel of industrialization, if one considers the industrial development of European countries or that of the United States and the behaviors of the employees in their organizations. History also demonstrates that in countries where conflicts are radicalized, as has been the case in some African countries, they may constitute a problem for industrial growth and development. Radicalization of organizational conflicts in Africa has led many African governments to the belief that organizational conflict is antithetical to the goals of rapid industrial growth and development, which African countries so desperately need.

Conflicts are common among factory workers, but with the deteriorating economic and increasing military dictatorship in Africa, it has extended to professional groups. It has now become frequent in industries and organizations with strong unions. These strong unions include those covering universities, teaching hospitals, primary and secondary school systems, railway corporations, public transportation systems, ports authorities, and banks. Some of these organizations have a long history of unionism.

This chapter examines types of conflict, the antecedent conditions for conflict, causes of organizational conflict, paralyzing costs of conflict in Africa, conflict resolution and collective bargaining, and institutionalization of conflict resolution systems in Africa.

TYPES OF CONFLICT

A conflict exists whenever incompatible activities occur (Deutsch, 1973). An action that is incompatible with another action tends to prevent or block the latter and makes it less likely or less effective. Incompatible actions may have their origin in one person, group, or nation. If conflict has its origin in one person, it is called intrapersonal conflict. Psychologists provide the expertise for dealing with individuals suffering from intrapersonal conflict. If the conflict occurs in a group, it is called intragroup conflict, it is intranational conflict if it originates in a nation. Conflicts may also reflect incompatible actions that originate in two or more people, groups, or nations. Such conflicts are designated interpersonal, intergroup, or international. Supervisor and subordinate conflict is an example of interpersonal conflict, while management and labor union conflict and United States-Cuba conflict are intergroup and international conflicts, respectively.

Other types of conflict are joint-venture conflict and labor-management conflict. Open war or manifest aggression and hostility are the climax of a conflict episode. This discussion does not deal with intrapersonal or intrapsychic conflict such as postulated by Freud or Kurt Lewin's field theory with its dynamic concepts of tension system. It also does not deal with intranational and international conflict.

SIGNIFICANCE OF CONFLICT

The basis of conflict in society lies in perceived and actual relative inequity. Differing interests receive unequal recognition in society and organizations. Such reward allocation is not based on the full recognition of the needs and interests of all. Rather, there exists a systematic domination of some by others that is supported by very little, if any, generally espoused rationale (Batstone, 1979). Because of this, conflict is usually regarded as bad interpersonal relations or "bad labor relations" by some authors. For these authors "co-operation is good" (Stagner, 1956). Individuals and groups learn from conflict situations. Industrial conflict has led to the improvement of working conditions and changes that are desirable from the point of view of broad social policy. Parties in conflict have interdependent interests; their fates are woven together (Deutsch, 1980); that is, competitive and cooperative interests are intertwined in conflict.

Conflict is not bad or good. One must always examine it from different perspectives. Often the occurrence of overt conflict between individuals or employers and employees is a disruptive affair that causes inconvenience to many people, including individuals not directly involved in the conflict. Conflict causes disruption of communication between the conflicting parties; it affects the cohesiveness of a group as well as its cooperation. It reduces the productive activity of the conflicting parties by causing them to divert time and energy to fighting conflict. Individuals and groups involved in open conflict experience stress, frustration, and anxiety. Such emotional reactions, in turn, reduce job satisfaction and commitment, impair concentration on tasks, create apathy, and encourage displacement of aggression and hostility. Finally, conflict results in avoidance behavior known as absenteeism and turnover. Prolonged conflict may also result in impairment of the conflicting parties' health, due to anxiety, depression, and other physiological and psychological reactions.

FACTORS THAT FOSTER CONFLICT

The behavior basis of conflict is that conflicts result from people's event perception, beliefs, motivation, attitudes, and values of the conflicting parties as well as their activities, which may or may not correspond with veridical social realities. Other major antecedent conditions, according to Robins (1974), Walton and Dutton (1969), and Wexley and Yukl (1984), include task interdependence, role ambiguity, status problems, communication barriers, and personality characteristics of people. Many conflicts are caused by a combination of these antecedent factors, and the categories are not mutually exclusive.

Motivation

Graduate secondary school teachers in one of the former regions (Western State) of Nigeria in 1975 demanded from the state government automatic grants of car loans. They threatened to strike if the Western State government failed to meet their demand. A survey conducted by the author among these graduate teachers showed that there was a general feeling of deprivation. Second, the teachers were resisting their participation in compulsory, long-vacation remedial school imposed on them by the State Schools Board. It is evident that conflict, whether interpersonal or industrial conflict, springs from the whole, broad range of aspirations and ungratified needs that compel workers to struggle relentlessly toward what they think will be a more satisfying life for themselves. A search for the psychological causes of conflict cannot be divorced from questions about the "wants" or "needs" and frustrations of the present-day African industrial and organizational man and woman over perceived or real deprivation.

Problem of Perception

Human behavior is not governed by "objective" facts as perceived by individuals. Uniformity of behavior of a group depends on uniformity in perception. An individual (a supervisor or an employee) or members of a group (perhaps union members) see the "facts" in one way; members of management see them differently (Stagner, 1956). Studies in industrial psychology show that company executives and workers differ sharply as to the facts regarding many industrial situations and issues that affect industrial conflict. Executives and union officers likewise differ. Other variables such as emotional involvement, selective perception, and social roles also tend to influence labor and management perception of expected work behavior and job-related issues. The differences in perceived realities often precipitate conflict between husband and wife, children and their parents, employees and their supervisor, and labor unions and management.

Problem of Attitude

The attitude that workers and employers have toward each other can serve as an antecedent cause of conflict. Recall an incident that happened in Nigeria in the colonial days in one organization when the African employees went on strike because the white supervisor told one of them that he, the supervisor, spent more money to feed his dog in a day than the company spent on the African employee in a month. As indicated early, the colonial managers in African organizations kept African workers in a subordinate and humiliating position. They worked practically without participating in organization they are employed. They made no serious decisions and were paid poor salaries, and their growth in the organization depended wholly on the whims and caprice of the colonial managers. Any evidence of a colonial manager's negative attitude or offensive language was enough to trigger a conflict because that was seen as adding insult to injury and served as a convenient vehicle for the African employees to hit back at the colonial supervisors and the management they represented. An attitude is simply a learned tendency or readiness to react to a specific object or person in a predictable manner and direction. For example, a hostile attitude toward an organization implies readiness to engage in behaviors and activities that may injure, harm, or weaken the interests of the company. The best way that labor usually expresses hostility is by engaging in conflict. Knowledge of the attitude of labor union members through an empirical survey can provide management with not only a basis for predicting the possible development of labor unrest but also a vehicle through which needed changes can be monitored and identified and action initiated to avert conflict.

Frustration

Frustrations on the job can be arbitrary, and they can also arise as a function of job dissatisfaction or from watching others in the same organizations or other organizations who are no better than one is or who work no harder than one does but have better returns for their efforts than one is getting.

Arbitrary Frustration. This emanates from what workers perceive as a denial or breach of their rights. An arbitrary frustration elicits much more anger than one that is perceived as reasonable. Arbitrary frustrations may arise from issues associated with promotions, award of annual increments, or implementation of individual conditions of employment. Others are the system of grading as used in Nigeria by the Udoji Public Service Review Commission, which lumped together workers with differing experience onto one type of scale. Workers who were negatively affected and their labor unions saw the lack of distinctiveness as arbitrary. So also was the two-step differential between members of the Academic Staff Union (ASUU) and the Non-Academic Staff Union in the Nigerian university system.

Most often workers who experience feelings of arbitrary frustration cannot verbalize the causes of their frustration. This is because some of the causes of workers' feelings of frustration are psychological and may even be located outside their work environment. For example, Ubeku (1983) narrated two cases of arbitrary frustration that were located outside the workers' work situation but were perceived by the employees as organizationally associated problems. One involved an employee who insisted on being paid during a period of casual leave. His demand was against the company rule that employees were to be paid casual leave granted on compassionate grounds only for illness or death of a relative. Management did not understand why the employee was insisting on being paid. But the employee insisted that he was entitled to be paid for the period of his absence. Prolonged discussion with the worker revealed the nature of the employee's frustration. "He was his mother's only child, his father was dead, and their land was being taken away by an apparently stronger man" (p. 158). This employee felt helpless. His poor monthly salary was not sufficient for him to meet the demands that were being made of him. The loss of face in his community arising from his inability to successfully challenge the man who usurped the piece of land bequeathed to him by his father generalized to a feeling that even the company he worked for could not come to his aid at his hour of need.

In the second case an employee wanted his company to buy him a pair of spectacles, when they were not covered by the employee's health plan. The employee's attention was drawn to the relevant sections on medical coverage, yet the employee could not be persuaded. During the discussion the employee complained about "company procedures for promotions and discipline and stated how he was earmarked for promotion for foreman but was later passed over" (Ubeku, 1983, p. 159). Thus, the apparent conflict over the provision of eyeglasses ended up being a manifestation of frustration over company promotion practices.

Job Dissatisfaction. In African organizations this arises principally from poor remuneration, lack of growth opportunities, poor work organization, and leadership problems. Usually, all these and more produce frustration on the job. Workers need increased income for different reasons. Any threat to workers' income arouses feelings of frustrations. They also need to participate in a meaningful way in their work. If employees are not finding any fulfillment in their work, or lack the necessary skills and material resources to perform their work they are frustrated and dissatisfied.

Comparison Level and Frustration. Workers are always comparing themselves with others who work in the same or different organizations on the bases of output, investment, and returns. They compare themselves with those individuals or groups to assess how poorly or how well they are doing. The standard of comparison for housewives, husbands, workers, and unions plays an important part in creating frustration. Workers compare their input and output in terms of income and incentives with those of others at their level, either in the same or similar companies.

Employers who know that their fringe benefit payments are less than those of their competitors may offer less resistance than would be expected when the union demands an increase in fringe benefits. One also expects workers who receive low pay in a high-paying industrial area to be more frustrated and more prone to labor conflict than workers who receive the same pay but work in an area with low-average pay. The problem for managers is that they cannot successfully predict the comparison persons or groups for their employees at any particular time.

Incompatible Priorities
When two individuals, groups or departments depend on each other in some way for the successful performance of their tasks, conflict is likely to occur if the two parties have different goals or priorities. In organizations, priority incompatibility may involve provision of supplies, information, assistance, or direction, as well as coordination of the activities of the two parties. The greater the differences in goal orientation for the parties, the more likely that conflict will develop (Wexley and Yukl, 1984). Such conflict is commonly found among interdependent departments that are highly specialized, such as research and production or sales and production.

Unclear Roles
When role boundaries are unclear, and responsibilities overlap, people are not usually sure or clear whose responsibilities the tasks and responsibilities in the gray area are. Such gaps are sure to create conflict between the two individuals, groups, or departments. Such conflicts arise because one person or party attempts to take control of the good outcome of the responsibilities and give up the negative outcomes or aspects. When one person or party also attempts to take credit for success or to avoid blame for failure in joint activities, conflict is also likely to develop.

Struggle for Power
This occurs when a low-status person or department in an organization tries to take over the leadership and dictate the pace by initiating activities and schedule changes over and above a high-status person or department. The high-status person or department usually resents the attempt by the low-status person or department to "steal" (Wexley and Yukl, 1984) what the high-status person or department perceives as a leadership role. Usually, departments do not give up their leadership role in organizations. Any attempt by low-status departments or individuals to strip them of their authority is resisted because such attempts are seen as a threat to the high-status person's position in the status hierarchy.

Another type of status conflict is caused by perceived inequity in rewards, job assignments, supply of material resources, and recognition of status symbols. If individuals or departments believe that they are not receiving the equitable benefits or opportunities that they deserve, frustration and resentment can develop into conflict with the manager perceived to be responsible for the administration of the rewards and supplies or with the persons perceived to be receiving better outcomes.

Communication Problems

Insufficient communication or lack of communication between two individuals, between departments, or between labor union and management contributes to development of conflict by preventing one party from gaining insight, knowledge, and understanding about the reasons the other person, department, or party made a particular decision or failed to take a particular action. Communication when sent must be decoded, read, and comprehended by the receiver before carrying out its directive. Problems of decoding and understanding communications received, selective interpretation of information and symbols, and or, the wrong choice of medium for sending communications encourage perpetual, mutual distrust and conflict.

Wexley and Yukl (1984) indicate that there are situations in which too much open communication creates conflict that would not otherwise have occurred. Good communication, according these authors, tends to reveal inequalities, value differences, biases, and prejudices between individuals and parties.

Personality Traits

Conflicts between two individuals or two groups are partially determined by the personality traits of the parties. Antiauthoritarianism, displacement of aggression, and ethnic and gender prejudice are functions of personality traits These are all traceable to the socializing processes of the individual or group They are personality traits that are likely to create conflict between individuals or groups. Conflict behavior is more likely when the individuals or parties in interaction are high in dogmatism and authoritarianism and low in self-esteem Low self-esteem on the part of interacting individuals promotes the use of defense mechanisms such as scapegoating, and biased perception of the authority figure as oppressive and dictatorial or tribalistic. Finally, conflict is more likely between persons or groups with different orientations, such as social, political, moral, or religious values, than between persons with more homogeneous values and orientations.

PEOPLE'S REACTION TO CONFLICT SITUATION

Individuals, groups, and units involved in conflict deal with conflict situations in a variety of ways. Many authors have previously discussed these (Ackelsberg and Yukl, 1979; Blake and Mouton, 1964; Pruitt, 1972; Walton and Mckersie, 1965; and Wexley and Yukl, 1984). The reactions are briefly discussed.

Excitement

Some individuals, because of their personality structure, are excited by, and enjoy, conflict situations. They are never happy unless they are involved in one conflict or another. Families with such a husband or wife never know any peace, love, and happiness. Communities with retired policemen in Africa have also noticed that some of these ex-officers enjoy controversy and conflict. They benefit, materially from conflict. They usually collude with their colleagues on active duty to exploit the communities and groups that the retiree pretends to belong to or care for.

Other groups that enjoy and welcome conflicts are student union executives and some of the labor union executive organizations, including those in African universities. For these groups, conflict is welcome because, through conflict, they test and demonstrate their importance to their followers. They employ conflict to maintain cohesion in the group. Any successfully concluded conflict is beneficial and positively rewarding to the members. The status of each executive is directly linked to the successful prosecution of each conflict episode. The higher the rewards or outcomes of each conflict episode for the members, the higher the status of the leaders.

Accommodation

This occurs in a conflict situation when one of the individuals or parties, guided by the African adage that maintains that "two people do not run mad at the same time," yields to the requests or demands of the other. Wexley and Yukl (1984) maintain that accommodation is most likely when the issue is relatively unimportant to a party in comparison with maintaining a harmonious relationship, when the perceived power of the opponent is overwhelming, and when the yielding party sees no opportunity for avoidance or compromise. A peace-loving individual or group that values human relations may also react to conflict by accommodation not because it is weak but because it feels that the time and energy for conflict are better invested in more productive ventures than in conflict.

Wexley and Yukl (1984) insist that the problem with accommodation is that the "winning" party will see the other person or party as weak and will press for additional concessions. This, however, would not work in the case of a peace-loving party that accommodated not because it is weak but because it wanted to maintain peace.

Leaving the Scene

Conflict is one of the top causes of people's leaving organizations. Conflict is an aversive stimulus. The physiological reaction is emotional, usually including reactions such as anger, frustration, helplessness, and other negative emotions, against the object, person, or party in conflict. In order to avoid these negative emotional reactions, the parties to a conflict tend to withdraw from the relationship and even physically avoid the presence of each other. In some instances, one party may end up leaving the organization.

Wexley and Yukl (1984) recommended that mutual avoidance can be an effective means of coping with the conflict if the two individuals or parties have no need to interact in performing their organizational roles. This is not possible in an organization. Avoidance does not resolve the issues in conflict. If the relationship is that of a manager and subordinate, staff and line relationship, or head of department and staff where they have interdependent task roles that require coordination, mutual avoidance will seriously impair their department's performance.

Conciliation
One or both parties may react by ignoring their difference and attempt to "smooth over" the conflict (Wexley and Yukl, 1984). One party to the conflict refusing to engage in a confrontational attitude can achieve this. The party or individual would instead adopt a more conciliatory approach such as noncombatant, cooperative, and agreeable relationships accompanied by respectful approach of the other person. Other attitudes may include a refusal to trade accusations, threats, or disparaging remarks, readiness to reciprocate favors and good gesture, by offering assistance, avoiding emphasis on differences in values or beliefs, and emphasizing common characteristics and things that bind the two individuals together. Generally, conciliation involves a positive approach and positive reinforcement of the actions and behavior of the party in conflict.

Wexley and Yukl (1984) say that conciliatory moves may be an effective way for preventing an escalation of open hostility and the disruption of work relationships provided the source of the conflict is not directly related to task performance. We noted earlier that ineffective leaders refuse to confront conflicts. Smoothing, therefore, will not be an effective way to handle conflict if it is used to avoid confronting disagreements involving problems of coordination and joint performance. Such problems are not likely to go away because they were swept under the carpet; instead, they are likely to grow worse. The party that chose conciliation may end up ruining its pride and self-esteem.

Communication
One approach to confronting conflict is an attempt to open up communication with the other individual, groups, or parties, during which an attempt is made to persuade them to change their position. This means winning them over by providing insight and factual evidence that support your position, discredit wrong and biased perception, information, and ideas, and point out the benefits of your position and the costs and disadvantages of their position. Finally, you should show how your position would better promote the goals and objectives of the organization than their position. You should also listen to their position and examine their evidence. You must be willing to accommodate their view points that will contribute to the goals that the organization wants to achieve. While persuading them to move toward your position, be ready to accommodate other views that are reasonable.

The success of this encounter depends on the credibility of the person making the persuasive appeal and the willingness of the other party to open up and consider factual information relevant to the disagreement. If both parties are committed to incompatible goals, such an encounter is likely to be ignored or discounted. The persuasive session should not be judgmental. Its essence is to open up communication and help the other party gain insight and increase self-esteem.

Power and Authority

Another reaction to conflict is to resort to power and authority to force the less powerful party or individual to give in. For example, in the case of a boss and subordinates, force is often employed by the boss to resolve a disagreement. Attempts to force the other party to capitulate or make concessions can also be used in conflicts in which no authority and power differential is present, such as in conflicts between two departments or between union and management. The major types of pressure tactics available to the powerful and those with authority include threats, punishment sequences, and positional commitments.

When conflict breaks out, the more powerful and authoritative party may issue a threat, an explicit or implicit warning that an action with negative consequences will be carried out unless the less powerful party complies with certain demands. For example, when conflict breaks out between labor and management, management may threaten labor with a lockout if its members do not stop their wildcat strike. Labor, on the other hand, may also threaten management with a full-scale strike if it does not meet its demands. The extent to which a threat works is a function of the perceived credibility of the party issuing the threat. If the party making the threat is perceived to have the capacity and willingness to carry out the threat, then a threat is effective. Otherwise, a threat will be ignored.

A punishment sequence according to Wexley and Yukl (1984), is one method of showing the other party that aggressive actions can be taken to punish it if it does not behave. In the 1996 ASUU strike, the government, first of all, applied its small amount of coercive power by stopping salaries of ASUU members to demonstrate "a taste of what will happen" if members did not call off the strike and go back to work. Finally, government applied the full dose of punishment by proscribing ASUU and terminating the appointments of ASUU members.

The ASUU and government conflict of 1996 demonstrates that threats and punishment sequences do not necessarily produce the desired effects. People usually resist intimidation. When both parties have threat capacity, threats from one party are met with threats from the other party. The same is true of punishment sequences. Such exchanges can easily lead the conflicting parties to aggressive, open conflict with its consequences.

A positional commitment is another kind of threat in which one party has taken a position not to concede further and states that the other party must give in or face the consequences of a deadlocked negotiation. Examples of this approach are "nonnegotiable demands" or "take it or leave it" final offers. The use of positional commitment requires that the party find out how far the other party is willing to concede; otherwise, positional commitment is not an effective way to react to conflict. In general, forcing is seldom the best way to resolve a conflict (Burk, 1970). Forcing often creates considerable resentment in the weaker, less powerful party and tends to damage the relationship between the parties for the future.

ORGANIZATIONAL CONFLICT

Organizational conflict, sometimes referred to as industrial conflict, has attracted the attention of several African writers. Among these are Adewumi (1997), Ijewere (1958), Oyemakinde (1970), Otobo (1995), Tamuno (1964), Ubeku (1994, 1983), and Yusufu (1962). Others have considered labor laws in some African countries (e.g., Uvieghara, 1987). This attraction is probably due to the frequency with which organizational conflict occurs in the African continent as illustrated by conflicts in the university system in Ghana, Kenya, and Nigeria in the 1980s and 1990s; the railway strike in Nigeria in 1945; the general strike of 1964; the wave of industrial conflict that followed the publication of the Nigerian government's white paper apparently based on the Udoji Public Service Review Commission; and the promulgation by the Nigerian federal military government of decree number 7 (1976) and number 23 (1976) on labor unions, to name but a few. In Africa a national strike can paralyze the economy of a nation.

CAUSES OF ORGANIZATIONAL CONFLICTS

The system of government in a particular country influences the frequencies of organizational conflict. Autocratic military regimes in Africa, limit the freedom of labor unions. This arouses workers' resistance, as witnesses in Nigeria under the dictatorial governments of Major Generals Ibrahim Babangida and Sani Abacha. Opinions also differ on the role of the size of an organization as the principal cause for the frequency of strikes (see Howells, 1972). Conflicts may increase in number as a function of the organizational structure. Conflicts are also affected by economic influences, although, as Stagner and Rosen (1965) maintain, there is no economic formula to determine a "fair day's work" or "a fair day's pay." Organizational conflicts are also affected by the labor market, by perceived wage levels elsewhere, and by customary profit ratios. On the other hand, increases in the frequency of conflicts have been recorded when companies are making huge profits as well as in periods of very low profits.

Psychologists recognize the importance of these variables. However, they assume that organizational conflict is human conflict. At the center of the conflict are people (e.g., individuals or groups and members of a union) with given perceptions and motivations characterized by certain interests, needs, desires, and goals that are incompatible with those of the other party, that is, management. Conflicts between labor unions and management constitute over 75 percent of the all organizational conflicts recorded in Africa, 15 percent are due to interunion conflict, and 10 percent are due to other causes. Most of these arise from conflict over disagreement over a reward system and collective disputes.

Reward System

The reward system in an organization, such as promotion, benefits, and wages, is central to the problem of organizational management in Africa. The reward system and its implementation in organizations generate more controversies, conflicts, dissatisfaction, and low morale than does any other subject in African organizations. This is because wages are generally low. Wages and promotions in many organizations are not often based on performance but on seniority. Workers, on their own part, perceive fair wages and benefits as their own legitimate right and/or share of the organization's annual profits. Since the true performance of the organization is not communicated down the line, employees usually believe that the organization is making huge profits. Workers in organizations in Africa distrust management and believe that management is out to exploit cheap labor and Africa's natural resources.

For example, in a training session for employees of oil companies in Nigeria in 1996, when the world crude oil price was at its lowest, the author was not successful in persuading the participants at the workshop that it was a wrong time for the employees to ask for increased wages. The participants argued that the intentions of the multinational oil companies were to exploit both the labor of the people and the nation's natural resources. They insisted that the indigenous managers who worked for the Nigeria National Petroleum Corporation (NNPC) were corrupt and were siphoning away the NNPC oil money into their private, overseas accounts. Employees of international oil companies in Nigeria, who were present, argued that private oil companies in Nigeria were exploiting their workers and that they "are in the habit of transferring large amounts of profits to their home countries." The participants maintained that "if these malpractices stopped, both indigenous and expatriate companies can pay workers decent wages and still make huge profits."

The principle that workers should be rewarded contingent upon their level of productivity is generally accepted in the industrialized parts of the world (Onyemeluke, 1966). This implies that full-time employees have the right to expect that their remuneration should be enough to enable them to meet at least reasonably essential, basic needs. The minimum wage, which is not strictly enforced in many African countries, requires each country to set a "basic standard of living below which no workers should fall" (Onyemelukwe, 1966). It is generally believed that a standard of living below that provided by the minimum wage would harm the health of the population and subject it to malnutrition, low productivity, and inefficiency.

The apparent economic principle, often cited in some African countries, that increasing workers' salary will result in inflation, is a ploy used by these governments to hide the inhuman practice of freezing workers' wages for years in a row. Workers do not like government or management to impose freezes on their wages in the interest of long-term growth. Protracted wage freezes lead to frustration, poverty of the employees and their families, and subsequent conflict.

In the developed countries of the West wage policies are usually aimed at encouraging the development of skills, and knowledge, and increased productivity. Wages and salaries are used as a thrust for increasing workers' commitment and feelings of being a part of the organizations for which they work. In Africa poor remuneration results in frustration, and helplessness, which lead to conflict. As a result, employees, with professional, managerial, and technical skills are forced to leave the African labor force and migrate to Europe and the United States. The yet-unmentioned consequence of this present trend, which is often referred to as "brain drain," is that it tends to leave Africa with a bulk of second-rate of professional, managerial, and technical labor.

Collective Disputes

In organizations, management's refusal to grant demands made by the union or refusal to recognize a union or, bargain with a union or its representatives often leads to conflict in organizations. Sometimes a union may regard an issue as important and worthy of consideration by management, such as wages, salaries, housing allowance, and other fringe benefits. Management, on its part, may not regard these issues as requiring fresh consideration. Such disagreement usually leads to open conflict. Some governments, including military dictatorships in Africa, sometimes adopt an antiunion stance and may tend to victimize and discriminate against active antimanagement or antigovernment individuals, groups, or unions. Finally, individual or union perception that management is in violation of a legislation or rule of condition of employment or is misinterpreting and misapplying the provisions of collective agreement leads to conflict in many organizations.

Interunion Relations

Relationships between unions or within the same union in an organization can be a cause of conflict. Interunion conflicts may occur when a large organization has subunions or associations that are more or less loosely unified. This type of structural organization among workers characterizes most of Nigeria's public and private industrial establishments. For example, junior workers and intermediate workers in institutional organizations tend to belong to different unions. In university institutions there are three different unions, the Academic Staff Union of Universities (ASUU), the Non-Academic Staff Union of Universities, and the Senior Staff Association of Teaching Hospitals, Universities, Research Institutes, and Allied Institutions (SAIURAI). This is also the situation for the skilled and the nonskilled workers in private and public organizations. It is thus clear why the multiplicity of union organizations in Nigeria and other African countries explains the frequency of industrial conflicts.

Intraunion conflict may occur as a result of a split of one union from its mother union and its splinter parts engaging in conflict with each other rather than with management. It is necessary, however, to recall that, among others, intra-and interunion conflicts may lead to serious organizational conflicts. Intraunion disputes may occasionally precipitate a union-management controversy because the leaders of union factions vie with each other to demonstrate to rank-and-file union members the leader's ability to win better concessions for members from management. A checklist of the ways in which workers and their unions express organizational conflict includes strikes, overtime bans, working-to-rule, absenteeism of staff, turnover, and sabotage. Between the extremes of collective sanctions and individual retreat from the work situation there exists a host of other actions that reflect or imply worker awareness of conflict in the organization. In some organizations, theft, either from the organization or from customers, is of importance. In others relationships are marked by emotional outburst and violence.

COSTS AND BENEFITS OF ORGANIZATIONAL CONFLICT

Concerning the question that rocks one's mind immediately—the issue of the cost of organizational conflict—is it possible to realistically estimate the costs and benefits of conflicts? Take, for example, conflicts in the Nigerian university system, which have reached monumental proportions. In the past five to ten years, universities in Nigeria with a total student enrollment of over 300,000 students, were shut down for a total of over thirty months. Many students caught up in this vicious circle spent seven years in the universities for a normal four-year program, while others have spent eight years for a five-year program. The ASUU took the federal government or the Ministry of Education and/or the vice chancellors of universities to court several times, while some members of ASUU were arrested and jailed overnight. Many lost their jobs, while hundreds of these lecturers left the country and migrated to South Africa, America, and Europe, thus depriving Nigeria (and Africa) of essential, skilled manpower, which Africa needs for development. Many of the lecturers who remained went for several months without salary. Academic productivity came to a halt. The conditions in the nation's universities were so bad that a constitutional drafting committee set up by government recommended that the federal universities be handed over to state governments where such institutions are situated. If government had accepted the recommendation, it would have been the deathblow to the university education system in Nigeria.

How does one quantify in costs and benefits the scars that the conflicts in Nigerian universities have left in the lives of thousands of Nigerian youths caught in this vicious circle? What of the psychological impact on the lecturers and the effects on the nation's developmental efforts? Researchers in the area of conflict maintain that conflict is neither bad nor good but that the focus should be on how well conflict is managed. Conflicts should be managed in such a way that the benefits are retained and the adverse effects are minimized (Thomas, 1976). Judging from this standpoint, one would come to the conclusion that conflicts in the Nigerian universities, teaching hospital, and other organization are very poorly managed. It is hoped that the crippling costs of these poorly managed events in universities and other organizations in this type of situation will stimulate such organizations, including government, to reevaluate the way that conflict is being managed.

Costs

Scholars agree that it is very difficult to calculate the total cost of any conflict. Organizational conflict in a developing country like Africa has dramatic effects on the whole country. For example, any open conflict between the government and members of the Road Transport Workers, Tanker Drivers,

Bank Workers, Electricity and Water Supply Employees Unions would paralyze the entire country. Because of the poor state of the essential infrastructure in most African countries, there would be no alternative to which to turn in times of open conflict between the workers and government or management. Consequently, an open conflict of a few days' duration in any essential or key organization would bring the national economy to a standstill in most African countries.

Brett, Goldberg, and Ury (1990) in their discussion of costs of conflict suggested that conflicts could be assessed as to their transaction costs, satisfaction with outcomes, effect on relationships, and probability of recurrence of same or other conflicts.

Transaction Costs. These refer to the time, money, and emotional energy expended in disputing, the resources consumed and destroyed, and the opportunities lost (Brett, Goldberg, and Ury, 1990). Again it is not easy to quantify transaction costs into monetary or statistical values.

Satisfaction with Outcomes. This depends primarily on the degree to which the outcomes of the conflict meet the disputants' interests, needs, desires, and concern, and whether or not the parties to the conflict believe that the process used in resolving the dispute is fair. In the ASUU strike, the government refused to yield; any ground in addition, members of ASUU lost months of salary. Thus, the lecturers got nothing from their seven-month strike except an opportunity to vent their frustration. Conflict management procedures that allow the disputing parties to vent their emotions, voice their concerns, and participate in determining the final decision are perceived as providing fairer outcomes than procedures that allow the disputants less involvement (Brett, 1986; Lind and Tyler, 1988; Brett, Goldberg, and Ury, 1990).

Effect on the Relationship. This is usually observable no matter how much the parties involved in the conflict try to cover it up. It includes avoidance and conciliatory attitude, stress, and anxiety. Conflicts destroy interpersonal and intergroup relationships, irrespective of their outcomes. They destroy trust and make the parties unable to work together again on a day-to-day basis. The long-term effects on the relationship are a third criterion for evaluating the effectiveness of a dispute resolution system.

Recurrence of Dispute. This is another important criterion for measuring the costs of conflict. According to Brett, Goldberg, and Ury (1990), recurrence is a measure of whether a dispute stays resolved or whether it recurs. These authors maintain that recurrence can take three forms, namely, the same dispute that involves the same parties; a different dispute that involves the same parties; and the same dispute but among different parties. All three types of recurrence could result from the same situation or in the same organization.

Benefits of Conflict

Organizations that avoid conflict have no opportunities for incremental changes, which are some of the benefits associated with managing conflict. The resolution of conflict is a major factor driving incremental change in an organization or in a relationship. Brett, Goldberg, and Ury (1990) proposed that from the long-term perspective of the organization or interorganizational relationship, reconciling conflicting interests is generally a less costly way to resolve conflicts than determining who is right or who is more powerful.

Interests. The interests of the conflicting parties should be the focus of resolving the conflict rather than the "who is right" and "who is wrong" approach. Reconciling interests often involves identifying underlying concerns, prioritizing them, and devising a trade-off in which parties in conflict concede on low-priority interests in order to receive satisfaction of higher-priority interests (Raiffa, 1982). Trade-off is a particularly effective means of resolving conflicts when the interests of disputing parties overlap. This happens when the interests of high priority to one party are of low priority to the other party, and vice versa (Fisher and Ury, 1981).

Brett, Goldberg, and Ury (1990) indicated that "bridging" is another technique for reconciling interests. Bridging involves devising creative solutions that serve the disputants' primary interests. It is like a trade-off in that both parties are likely to have to make concessions on low-priority interests. Three other techniques for reconciling interests and reaping the benefits of conflicts rely on the creative use of resources. The first is cost cutting, in which some disputants get what they want in return for acting to reduce or eliminate costs likely to be incurred by others.

The second is nonspecific compensation. This technique allows some disputants to get what they want, and others to receive some type of substitute compensation. Finally, when a dispute is about resources, and new resources sufficient to satisfy all disputants can be made available, the conflict can be resolved, at least until resources again become scarce. Resolving a conflict through this interest-based approach tends to yield greater benefits to an organization than through other approaches that are based on who is right and who is more powerful.

In the law and in contracts the procedure for resolving conflict is investigating who is right. Sometimes labor and management employ this technique for resolving organizational conflict. With this approach the focus is to determine who is right in accordance with some independent standard of perceived legitimacy or fairness. Laws, contracts, and social norms, such as reciprocity and precedent, are all potential rights standards, according to Brett, Goldberg, and Ury (1990). The difficulty with this approach lies in choosing a standard and then determining what it implies with respect to the conflict.

Determining "who is more powerful" (Brett, Goldberg, and Ury, 1990) is yet another way to resolve disputes. The authors maintain that the trouble with this approach is that without a decisive contest, such as a fight, strike, or war in which power is put to the test and costs imposed, it is often difficult to determine which of the conflicting parties is more powerful. This is because, according to Emerson (1962), power is interdependent, and each party's perceptions of its own and the other party's alternatives to resolving the conflict may not coincide. It is therefore difficult to predict at what point each party will prefer its own alternatives to continuing to deal with the other party.

A comparative analysis of conflicts handled by focusing on interests as against pursuing who is right shows that reconciling interests tends to produce a higher satisfaction with outcomes, better working relationships, and less recurrence of conflicts and may incur lower transaction costs than procedures that try to determine who is right. This conclusion has been reached based on several research findings that compared mediation (an interest-based dispute resolution procedure) with arbitration (a rights-based procedure).

Disputants prefer mediation to arbitration or the court, for example, in simulated management decision making (Karambayy and Brett, 1989), in the context of labor grievances (Brett and Goldberg, 1983), and in small claims (McEwen and Maiman, 1981). This preference is due to the fact that agreements reconciling interests often provide all parties with much of what they wanted. The information shared in the process of searching for a resolution tends to increase mutual understanding, which benefits the relationship. Above all, recurrence is low following interest-based conflict reconciliation.

Determining who is right or who is more powerful does not bring about a peaceful resolution of conflict because it does not protect the conflicting parties' self-esteem. It often becomes a contest distinguished primarily by transaction costs. Violence costs more than litigation. Power contests often create new injuries and disputes and leave a residue of anger, distrust, and a desire for revenge, as the Nigerian government's show of power in its dispute with ASUU has vividly demonstrated.

Optimizing the Benefits of Conflict

Brett, Goldberg, and Ury (1990) outlined some guidelines for maximizing the benefits of conflicts in organizations and industries. In order to derive the benefits of organizational conflicts, managers must be ready to effectively manage conflicts before, during, and after conflicts occur. Brett, Goldberg, and Ury (1990) suggest the steps that should be employed in order to accomplish this.

Consultation and Feedback. These involve consulting with the grieving parties before the stage of conflict is reached and providing feedback to the parties at the end of conflict. Conflict is inevitable in organizations and is often an early warning of a need for change, implying that organizations should make significant efforts to discuss issues that may cause conflicts and to learn from those conflicts that do occur. Consultation before disputes erupt can minimize the occurrence of unnecessary disputes. Feedback after a dispute has occurred helps heal the wounds and prepares managers to take action to prevent any recurrence.

Focus on Interests. This means focusing on the interests of both parties rather than resorting to the determination of who is right and who is wrong. Negotiation that is always available to disputing parties may not always reconcile interests. Framing negotiations as a cooperative, rather than competitive, exercise facilitates interest-based resolutions (Pruitt, 1981), as does an exchange of information about interests, either directly by sharing information or indirectly through the exchange of proposals (Pruitt and Carnevale, 1982). Providing training in negotiation skills that focuses on techniques for reconciling interests not only may increase skills but also may establish norms about how disputes are to be handled within an organization (Fisher and Ury, 1981; Lax and Sebenius, 1986; Brett, Goldberg, and Ury, 1990). Interest-based negotiations are not always successful. This is because the disputants are so emotionally involved with the dispute that they need to vent their emotions before they can engage in any meaningful, successful negotiation. In such a case, a third-party mediation may be effective in reconciling interests. A mediation may provide a controlled environment in which one or both parties may express emotions and feelings and acknowledge those of the other. Mediation may also help the parties understand their interests as well as the other party's interests, induce them to evaluate their alternatives if no resolution is reached, and encourage each to think about an agreement that both can accept.

Rights Negotiation. Here the parties are concerned with the letter of the law, legislative rights, or the correctness of the interpretation of contracts. Often negotiations fail because the parties' perceptions of who is right or who is more powerful are incompatible so that they fail to establish a range in which to negotiate. Information about how rights standards have been applied in other disputes can serve to narrow the gap between the parties' expectations of the outcome of a rights contest and thus make agreement possible. For interorganizational disputes, advisory arbitration (a nonbinding decision concerning how a case would be resolved in court) may be the simplest procedure for acquiring rights information (Goldberg, Green, and Sanders, 1985). Intraorganizational disputes may fall back on information about corporate norms (what was done in the past) to help them establish a bargaining range. Loop-back procedures or a cooling-off period helps disputing parties to avoid power contests. A cooling-off period is a specified time period during which the disputants refrain from a power contest. This period occurs before the strike when the disputants are called upon to "sleep on" a decision or it is a period for talking it over with an uninvolved third party before any of the disputing parties take action. "Loop-back" and "sleeping on" are practical rules of thumb that allow emotions to cool and rationality to regain control.

Provide Necessary Negotiation Resources. These resources include skills for negotiation, coaching, and motivation. Brett, Goldberg, and Ury (1990) indicate that negotiators are better at distributive bargaining (i.e., maximizing their own gains) than integrative bargaining (maximizing joint gains). They also know how to compromise by splitting the difference between their positions.

What they do not do well is find agreements that integrate interests, agreements by which they receive more than they would have if they had simply compromised on each issue (Bazerman, 1983). Negotiators are often subject to several cognitive biases, of which cognitive set is one. Cognitive biases tend to prevent people from finding integration. Parties tend to approach a negotiation with the perspective that the task is solely one of distribution. It is cognitively simpler for people to deal with each issue separately rather than perceiving it holistically. This produces trade-off between issues rather than among issues.

In general, coaching helps negotiators to increase the benefits of interest based negotiation procedures. Several experiments carried out to teach negotiators how to overcome their cognitive biases have been very successful (Bazerman, Magliozzi, and Neale, 1985; Thompson, 1988; Brett, Goldberg, and Ury, 1990). Subjects after coaching have also been shown to perform better than subjects without coaching on an integrative negotiation task when specific goals are given on how many points they should try to score. Lectures on problem-solving negotiation have also been found to produce beneficial effects (Neale, Northcraft, and Earley, 1988).

COLLECTIVE BARGAINING

Collective bargaining is a process through which disputing parties—union and management—attempt to reach an agreement on issues about which they disagree. Deutsch (1980), on the other hand, refers to bargaining as an agreement between parties in a dispute, settling what each party will get and what it will give in transaction between them. When a conflict or strike breaks out in an organization, one way of achieving peace is through collective bargaining between the two parties, labor union and management. In some instances in Africa the government acts as the referee. In most African countries government is the largest employer of labor. Often the observation is that the bargaining is conducted between government representatives and the labor unions. This often complicates and compromises the power of the unions in seeking fair wages for their members.

In the United Kingdom the government attitude toward collective bargaining is based on *laissez-faire* doctrine, where labor and employers are left to determine the scope of the relations between them. That implies, according to Ubeku (1983), that Great Britain's system of collective bargaining places priority on "voluntary over compulsory procedural rules of collective bargaining."

In the United States the process of collective bargaining is apparently a private system of labor-management democracy. The many rights of employers, unions, employees, and individuals that arise by virtue of collective agreement are respectively covered by core democratic values of the nation. Sometimes these may require litigation in the courts to resolve conflicts. The law occupies a prominent place in the labor-management relations in the United States.

Earlier, the collective bargaining process was formally recognized. Later, acts of the National Assembly such as the Taft-Hartley Act of 1947 was enacted to protect the rights of individual workers from the negative behaviors and actions of union members. The Taft-Hartley Act identified some unfair labor practices on the part of labor unions and their members and placed certain limits on these excessive behaviors and practices. It reduced the power of the union over the individuals and left the union as the only effective means by which the employee could be represented in the workplace.

The Landrum-Griffin Act of 1959 further gave every union member equal right to participate in union meetings and elections. It protected the core democratic rights of union members by protecting their freedom of speech and association with other members in discussing union affairs both in and out of union meetings. It provided that members were subject to disciplinary measures only if they failed to pay their dues, not for exercising their freedom. In the United States the labor laws regulate both the relationships between the union and the employers and those between the union and its members. In spite of these laws and acts, collective bargaining in the United States continues to be voluntary. Bargaining and the interpretation of collective contracts continue to be conducted without recourse to legal proceedings and without the involvement of the courts or government.

In Africa the colonial governments and their agencies did not grant African workers any active participation in their organizations. They did not consider it necessary to encourage labor unions or unionism as a channel for dealing with workers' needs, demands, and conflicts. They preferred to fix workers' remuneration and conditions of employment in industry by statutory authority rather than by any system of collective bargaining (Ubcku, 1983). Any organizational conflict that erupted in most organizations was met with colonial management violence. This was the case in many of the mining companies in Southern Africa. The case of the Iva Valley Coal Mine in Enugu, Nigeria, is fresh in mind. When the coal miners went on strike over conditions of employment, the colonial manager called police, who shot to death twenty-one of the miners. The first strike called by the Trade Union Congress of Gold Coast (present Ghana) was harshly repressed by the colonial government. The colonial government employed various measures, including imprisonment of the striking union leaders and the Convention People's Party leader, Dr. Kwame Nkrumah, to suppress workers' demand for labor democracy.

Following independence, the low tolerance threshold for labor-management conflict and the neglect of workers' rights continued in many African countries. The national governments in many African countries did not institute the principle of free, voluntary collective bargaining through legislation. Military regimes in some countries such as Nigeria and the Congo Republic and civilian governments in Tanzania and Ghana eroded the independence of trade unions. These governments enacted laws, decrees, and other legislative acts that brought unthinkable changes in the way conflicts between labor and management were handled. Some of the laws, decrees, and legislative acts banned strikes, and lockouts and declared some industries and organizations as *essential services* where unions have no rights to exercise their strike prerogatives. These organizations were removed from the list of organizations in which conflicts and work stoppage due to strikes could occur. Arbitration of conflict was made compulsory in many African countries.

In Ghana under Kwame Nkrumah and Tanzania under Julius Nyerere, the central labor union was placed under the control of the Ministry of Labor. This put the national government in a position to regulate the labor unions and control conflict and collective bargaining processes between workers and their employers. In Senegal and other French-speaking African countries, as well as Nigeria, government institutionalized conflict resolution procedures, and labor and management were bound to employ the procedures for settlement of conflicts.

SOCIAL PSYCHOLOGICAL MODELS OF BARGAINING

Four basic questions usually asked by social psychology with respect to collective bargaining include:

- What factors determine the likelihood that the parties in dispute will reach agreement?
- What accounts for the speed at which the disputing parties will reach agreement?
- What circumstances guarantee to one party a better outcome than to the other?
- Under what circumstances will the disputing parties be able to find and adopt an interest-based negotiating procedure rather than a rights and power procedure?

Research has also focused attention on the types of behavioral strategy that a negotiator or a negotiating team can adopt at any time during the negotiation. These include:

- The negotiator or negotiating team can break off negotiations.
- The negotiator can concede, that is, make a new proposal that is worth less to the proposing side than the original proposal.
- The negotiator can try to persuade the other party to concede. Magenau and Pruitt (1979) call the group of tactics employed in this persuasive process "distributive tactics." They include threats, persuasive arguments, and positional commitments.
- The negotiator can seek a coordinated movement toward a mutually satisfactory outcome, which may involve the parties in an exchange of concessions along some understandable dimension, or an integrated solution, which reconciles the needs of both parties. This is similar to what Brett, Goldberg, and Ury (1990) call an interest-based negotiation procedure.

Social psychology has provided some models of the collective bargaining process to give some answers to these questions and issues. Some of these models aim to provide answers to the four basic questions   regarding negotiation. A few of these contributions come from Deutsch (1980) and Magenau and Pruitt (1979).

Morton Deutsch's Model

Deutsch (1980) in his review of fifty years of conflict dealt with three relevant issues. One was condition, which gives rise to a constructive or destructive process of conflict resolution. This aspect of the model is based on the assumption that if the parties to a conflict have a cooperative, rather than competitive, orientation toward one another, they are more likely to engage in a constructive process of conflict resolution. Deutsch (1980) reasoned that a cooperative process is more productive in dealing with a problem that the parties face than a competitive process. He indicates that cooperation induces, and is induced, by a perceived similarity in beliefs and attitudes; a readiness to be helpful; an openness in communication; trusting and friendly attitudes; a sensitivity to common interests and de-emphasis on differences between the parties; and an orientation toward the enhancement of mutual power rather than power differences.

Similarly, according to this model, competition induces, and is, in turn, induced by, the use of tactics of coercion, threats, or deception; attempts to enhance the power differences between one party and the other; poor communication; and an increased awareness of opposed interests. These tactics increase suspicion and hostile attitudes.

Deutsch (1980) concludes that if one has a systematic knowledge of the effects of cooperative and competitive processes, one has a systematic knowledge of the conditions that typically give rise to such processes and, by extension, to the conditions that affect whether a conflict will take a constructive or destructive course.

The second point emphasized tactics for winning conflicts. This aspect of Deutsch's (1980) model deals with the issue of circumstances, strategies, and tactics that lead one party to do better than another in a conflict situation. The bargaining strategy and tactics discussed by Deutsch include "being ignorant," being tough, "being belligerent," and "having bargaining power."

Being Ignorant. This idea advanced by Schelling (1960), appears incompatible with common sense. Schelling (1960) proposed that in a collective bargaining situation it is sometimes advantageous for a party to be in a position of ignorance of the other party's preferences. Schelling's idea has been supported by research findings (Harnett, Cummings and Hughes, 1968; Cummings and Harnett, 1969). Several items of research involving bargaining demonstrated that a bargaining party without complete information about the bargaining schedule of the other party began bargaining with higher initial bids, made fewer concessions, and earned higher profits than bargainers with complete information of the other party's position.

Being Tough. This has been defined experimentally in terms of setting a high level of aspiration, making high demands, and offering fewer concessions or smaller concessions than does one's opponent. Bargaining scholars agree, and research findings support the complex notion that toughness plays a double role and has contradictory consequences. Toughness decreases the likelihood that the parties will reach an agreement. It increases the payoff of those who survive the possibility of deadlocked negotiation. A relentlessly tough posture throughout bargaining tends to result in worse outcomes if the parties reach agreement at all, compared to a more conciliatory approach. There is, however, evidence that initial toughness, namely, high opening demands coupled with readiness to reciprocate concessions, may lead to an agreement that maximizes outcomes for the parties.

Belligerence. This includes the use of threat, coercion, and power in a collective bargaining situation. Research findings on the effect of belligerence on bargaining outcomes show that the use of threats seldom improves and almost always decreases a bargainer's outcomes if the other party is similarly armed and if the values are important to both of them.Threats have the tendency to lower the reputation of the party that employs them as a strategy. They are viewed much more negatively and are less likely to get compliance from the other party. When the power of the conflicting parties is unequal, coercion can be successful if it is employed by the more powerful party.

Bargaining Power. This is assessed by examining the relative power of the bargaining parties to inflict pain or harm upon one another, the relative desirability of the alternative routes to bargaining that are available to each of the bargainers, and the relative time pressure on each bargainer to reach an agreement.

Deutsch (1980) discussed the research findings regarding bargaining power. The findings indicate that when bargaining power is relatively equal, agreement is relatively easy to reach, and the outcomes to the parties are high. When bargainers have unequal bargaining power, a power struggle often ensues, as the bargainer with more power tries to assert superior claims. The behavior of the bargainer with less power could resist the claims of the more powerful opponent. The consequence of this struggle is that agreement is difficult to reach, and the parties have low bargaining outcomes. When bargaining power is markedly unequal, the differences in power are more likely to be accepted as legitimate, and, as a consequence, agreement is quickly reached, with the advantage going to the more powerful bargainer. Having higher power than one's collective bargaining opponent may be less advantageous than having equal power if the low-power bargainer is motivated to resist any heavier claims that the high-power opponent might make as a result of having more power.

Collective Agreement

Deutsch (1980) dealt with factors that determine the nature of the agreement between conflicting parties. According to him, two variables, "perceptual prominence" and "distributive justice," determine the nature of an agreement for settlement in conflict. Deutsch's position is influenced by that of Schelling (1960), who suggested that perceptually prominent alternatives serve a key function in permitting bargainers to come to an agreement. He insisted that most bargaining situations involve some range of possible outcomes, from those most acceptable to those most unacceptable. Within such a range bargaining parties make their concessions in order to avoid failed negotiation. "The final outcome," Schelling continues, "must be a point from which neither expects the other to retreat, yet the main ingredient of this expectation is what one thinks the other expects the first to expect."

A win-win, that is, equal concessions, would be a perceptually prominent agreement. Such a split would provide a place of safe convergence where each party would be expected to stop making or expecting further concessions (Deutsch, 1980; see Magenau and Pruitt, 1979). Deutsch (1980) further indicates that Homans' sense of distributive justice (1961, 1974) would play a role in the determination of the nature of agreement between parties in dispute. According to Homans' "proportionality" or "equity" rule, people expect rewards to be distributed among individuals in proportion to their contributions. J. S. Adams (1963, 1965a; Adams and Freedman, 1976) and Walster, Walster, and Berscheid (1978) in their equity theories continued Homans' emphasis on the rule of proportionality. Research in the areas has demonstrated that if the rule of proportionality is violated, it tends to arouse psychological resistance and emotional distress in the parties less favored.

Deutsch (1980) concludes that "if a conflict is experienced as having been resolved unjustly, it is not likely that the conflict has been adequately resolved." Similarly, a bargaining agreement that is viewed as unjust is not apt to be a stable one. "Justice" and "conflict" are intimately intertwined; the sense of injustice can give rise to conflict, and conflict can produce injustice, according to Deutsch (1980).

John Magenau-Dean Pruitt's Model
Magenau and Pruitt (1979) employ concepts such as limit, level of aspiration, and demand to help them answer the four basic questions usually asked by researchers with respect to negotiation.

Limit, Aspiration, and Demand. This principle maintains that during negotiation, each party to the conflict endorses an alternative known as its *demand.* For example, in a negotiation over a wage raise, labor's current demand may be $5 increase per hour, while management offers $2. Underlying a demand is usually some sort of target or desired outcome. The value of the target to the person or party holding it is the *level of aspiration.* For example, labor's current demand of $5 per hour may be part of a strategy to achieve the aspiration of $2.50 per hour. A bargainer's *limit* is the smallest level of value acceptable in the foreseeable future. That is the level below which the party would rather break off negotiations than reach agreement. According to Magenau and Pruitt (1979), a limit is not always necessary. In some negotiations, limits develop only at the point where the negotiator must first make a decision about whether or not to continue negotiations.

The negotiators' level of aspiration is always greater than, or equal to, their limits, and their demands are usually greater than the level of aspiration. The first reason for this, according to the theory, is due to what Magenau and Pruitt (1979) call a norm of "good faith" in bargaining. This norm requires negotiators to concede occasionally and not to withdraw a concession once it is on the table. Thus, to reach an agreement that is compatible with a party's level of aspiration, one must start well above the level of aspiration and move down toward it. The second reason is that high demands are a device for protecting the level of aspiration and thus preventing one's opponent from underestimating one's level of aspiration and limits. If a party to a negotiation concedes too rapidly, the opponent may well become committed to a position that is incompatible with these goals.

Experienced negotiators tend to start with higher demands. Several research works suggest that the levels of aspiration and limits, where they exist, play an important role in determining the level of demand. The higher these goals, the larger a bargaining party's demands. The levels of aspiration and limits appear to interact, in that limits have more of an effect on demand the lower the aspiration level (Holmes, Throop, and Strickland, 1971). This is because demand approaches limit as the level of aspiration diminishes (Magenau and Pruitt, 1979). The levels of aspiration and limit are also causally related (Yukl, 1974a, 1974b). Studies have also shown that during negotiation, demands change more often than the levels of aspiration, which, in turn, are more subject to change than limits, where limits exist.

Strength of Limits, Level of Aspiration, and Demand. These concepts theoretically allowed the authors to define location and strength. According to the model, location refers to the value of the entity as perceived by the bargainer. Strength, on the other hand, refers to the ease with which limits can be changed. The strength of the current demand is called "motivation to maintain demand." When a negotiator's demand is weak, the bargainer is prone to make concessions. When it is strong, on the other hand, bargainers are more likely to defend their bargaining demand by means of distributive tactics. When motivation to maintain demand is very strong, a bargainer may prefer to break off negotiations rather than make a concession.

Effects of Limits, Aspiration, and Demand on Bargaining Outcome. All of these have similar effects on the outcome of negotiation, which shows that when agreement is reached, an individual or group of negotiators who maintained strong and high limits, high aspiration, and high demands tend to achieve more favorable outcomes than negotiators who did not. Second, agreement takes longer to reach if one or both bargainers' limits, aspirations, and demands are strong or set high.

Finally, there is a U-shaped relationship between a bargainer's typical limits, aspiration, or demand and the typical outcome over a series of negotiations. If a bargainer demands little, agreement usually is reached faster, but the returns will be little. If too much is demanded, agreement will not be reached, with a poor outcome. But if demands are moderate, agreement is often reached at a good level of profit for both parties.

Limits and Level of Aspiration. These are differently determined. Kelley (1966) proposed that a bargainer's level of aspiration depends on (1) the estimate of the outcome that can be obtained in the present circumstances and (2) the perception of the outcome obtained in the past under similar conditions.

Magenau and Pruitt (1979) elaborated on these conditions by saying that negotiators who think they are powerful have a higher level of aspiration than do those who perceive themselves as weak. Limits are, in part, a function of the perceived value of failing to reach agreement. Hence, limits will be higher (1) the greater the outcomes that can be achieved in an alternative relationship and (2) the lower the cost of failing to reach agreement in terms of punishment from the other party or deterioration of the relationship. Other variables of importance considered by this model include motivation, the need to project an image, and urgency of agreement, trust and coordination, and integrative solutions. As might be expected, higher time pressure produces lower negotiation demands (Pruitt and Drews, 1969), faster concessions, and poorer outcomes (Balogun and Daodu, 1994).

INSTITUTIONALIZATION OF COLLECTIVE BARGAINING PROCESS

Governments in Africa consider it a part of their responsibility to maintain industrial peace and harmony between labor and management. Some of the governments also assume quite often that labor and management require a third-party intervention to help them reach agreement whenever there is any conflict between them. Most often government is an employer and cannot legitimately pretend to be an impartial mediator or arbitrator between labor and management. These reasons have led to the institutionalization of the bargaining processes.

Institutionalization involves setting up organizations and procedures to handle conflict through means such as collective bargaining or codetermination (Batstone, 1979). It is argued that institutionalization provides workers with a degree of industrial "citizenship." It also serves to isolate industrial conflict from other types of conflict. Some writers maintain that for conflict to become institutionalized, each party to the conflict (labor and management) has to recognize the legitimacy of the other's existence. Second, institutionalization involves some agreement or acceptance of certain rules and regulations as a framework for relationships. Such rules and regulations may cover a range of issues and frequently impose limitations upon the use of sanctions such as strikes or lockouts (Batstone, 1979). These factors may serve to encourage further the growth of organizations representing both labor and management. This, in turn, strengthens the institutions of collective bargaining, as does the achievement of perceived successes through negotiation. Experience from Africa, however, has shown that in setting out the rules and regulations that govern the relationship between labor and management, government often consults neither labor nor management and their views are not sought about these laws and regulations. Government proclaims or decrees these conditions that are usually in favor of management as a law.

Institutionalization of Collective Bargaining Process in Africa

National labor unions in Africa lacked unity. There were many unions in some countries. These often disagreed among themselves resulting in frequent inter- and intraunion conflicts. Some unions were also radical in their behavior. While a majority of them were affiliated with the Western bloc during the Cold War, some were affiliated to the communist-socialist bloc. Each country tried to apply some control over its labor unions to prevent them from being used by external forces to destabilize the country.

Tanzania

Under the leadership of President Julius Nyerere the labor union was made a part of government and placed under the Ministry of Labor. Government took over the determination of wages and wage policies as well as the outcomes of collective bargaining. Government played a primary role in enforcement of collective agreements, awards, and disciplinary code.

Ghana

Kwame Nkrumah's government in Ghana was eager for industrial peace to allow Ghana to implement its economic development plans. His government took steps to control the labor unions and their activities in organizations. Government reorganized trade unions into a controllable number. Unions were allowed autonomy as long as they operated in accordance with the overall policy regulating the Trade Union Congress (TUC), which is an umbrella union to which every other union in Ghana was required to belong. The TUC was controlled and guided by the political party that was in government. Government placed bans on strikes and lockouts, and the Ministry of Labor was empowered to call off or suspend any strike or lockout that the minister considered to be endangering the economy and safety of the nation. Institutionalization in Ghana and Tanzania usurped the functions of unions and management and restricted labor unions from exercising their freedom of association and the freedom to speak for the workers in collective bargaining with management.

Senegal

The position of trade unions in Senegal reflected the situation in the French former African colonies. Almost all labor unions in these countries were affiliated with the French *Confederation Generale de Travailleurs* (CGT). The affiliated unions received subsidies and aids from their metropolitan partner and the French government. In Senegal and its sisters, the former French colonial territories, the institutionalized procedure for handling collective bargaining is similar to that of Nigeria. The instituted procedure for these countries included conciliation and arbitration (Ubeku, 1983).

Nigeria

The *institutionalization* of the procedures for the resolution of organizational conflict was achieved by the Trade Disputes Act of 1976. This law, which institutionalized bargaining in Nigeria, stipulates that if the parties to the conflict write to the minister of labor that they are in a conflict and that they have failed to arrive at agreement about the issue or issues on which they disagree, the minister of labor may then take the following steps:

- Appoint a fit person to act as conciliator who may attempt to effect a settlement of the dispute.
- Constitute a Board of Inquiry if there are some difficulties with conciliation and arbitration and if the minister considers that the public interest is involved.
- Where conciliatory means fail, the minister refers the matter to the Industrial Arbitration Panel.
- Certain disputes may also be referred directly to the National Industrial Court; otherwise, that court acts as the final court of appeal for all industrial disputes.

Thus, in Nigeria there is a legally recognized, comprehensive institution for the resolution of conflicts, namely, conciliation, arbitration, and Board of Inquiry (Ubeku, 1994).

Conciliation

The Trade Disputes Act of 1976 requires that before a dispute is referred to the minister of labor, the conflicting parties must have made efforts to settle the dispute on their own by employing the grievance procedure, which exists or should exist in the organization. If, however, the attempt to settle fails, or if no such machinery for internal negotiation exists in such an organization, the parties are mandated within seven days of the failure to agree to meet together under the chairmanship of a mediator mutually agreed upon and appointed by, or on behalf of, the parties, with a view to the amicable settlement of the conflict.

Ubeku (1994) maintains that the operationalization of the conciliation aspect of the Trade Disputes Act is that those who have retired from the Ministry of Labor or well-known personnel practitioners from companies are usually invited as mediators. For example, according to Ubeku (1994), Van Leer, company and its house union invited the director of personnel of British Petroleum (BP) Nigeria Limited (now African Petroleum) to mediate in their dispute. Ubeku (1994) maintains that quite a number of disputes have been resolved at the stage of the conciliation procedure. He also indicated that while employers are happy to have disputes resolved at this stage, the unions are not so well disposed toward it unless the ruling is in their favor. In other words, unions are not usually happy when their demands are settled at the conciliation level unless they get all their demands from management through this procedure. Unions prefer to carry their demands up to conciliation and arbitration levels, where the panels are composed of different individuals, including those with sympathies for the unions. Furthermore, union members do not like their disputes to terminate at the stage of conciliation, when, according to them, "tempers are high." Ubeku (1994) insists that no matter what the arguments are against mediation, the advantages include (1) confining the dispute to the workplace and between the parties and (2) helping to reduce the workload on the few senior labor officers who are normally appointed conciliators.

The Trade Disputes Act of 1976 stipulates that if, within fourteen days of the appointment of a mediator, the dispute is not settled, the dispute shall be reported to the minister of labor by, or on behalf of, either of the parties. The report is expected to be in writing and should describe steps already taken by the parties to reach a settlement. The minister, after studying the report, may decide to refer the matter back to the parties if the minister is not satisfied that the parties to the conflict have exhausted all avenues to enable them to reach agreement. If, on the other hand, the minister is satisfied that the parties have exhausted all reasonable steps to settle the matter but have failed, the minister may refer the matter either to a conciliator or, in appropriate cases, to arbitration.

In the case of conciliation, the act empowers the minister of labor to appoint a "fit person" to act as a conciliator for the purpose of settling the dispute. The duties of the conciliator include inquiring into the causes and circumstances of the dispute and, by negotiation with the parties concerned, endeavoring to bring about a settlement. The Ministry of Labor provides conciliators with a guide covering the behavioral approach to handling conciliation between two conflicting parties. The three-part guide covers basic attitude and approach, meetings, and the search for agreement. With respect to basic attitude, conciliators are advised to always maintain a strictly impartial and neutral attitude toward the parties to the disputes. They have to establish their acceptability to the disputants. As the chairmen of the meetings, the conciliators must not be critical of any of the parties to the disputes in joint meetings or in the presence of the other parties. They must be impartial in action and utterance in the search for agreement. The conciliators must be patient and systematically guide the parties over the issues involved in the disputes. They should not formally make their proposals at a joint meeting without having first obtained the agreement of each of the parties separately.

Ubeku (1994) maintains that a number of conciliators, either as a result of lack of experience or in anxiety to achieve results, tend to break all or most of the guidelines during conciliation meetings. In spite of this, a reasonable number of disputes are settled at the conciliation stage. Where settlements are achieved within fourteen days of their appointments, the conciliators must report the fact to the minister of labor by sending a report of the terms of settlement signed by representatives of both of the conflicting parties. Such terms as agreed are binding on both parties effective from the date when the agreement is signed.

If, however, settlement of the dispute is not reached within fourteen days of their appointment, and the conciliators, after attempting negotiation with the parties, are satisfied that they will not be able to bring about a settlement, the conciliators send reports to the minister of labor. Within fourteen days of the receipt of such a report, the minister is obliged by law to refer the dispute to arbitration.

Arbitration
Arbitration of industrial conflicts and disputes in Nigeria is taken at two levels by two bodies, the Industrial Arbitration Panel (IAP) and the National Industrial Court (NIC). The Industrial Arbitration Panel is a standing body

whose function is to arbitrate a matter that failed to be resolved at the conciliation stage. It is made up of a chairman, vice-chairman, and at least ten other members, two of whom are nominated by the employers' association and two by the workers' organizations. The arbitrative process may consist of a sole arbitrator selected from among the members of the panel by the chairman; or a single arbitrator selected from among the members of the panel by the chairman and assisted by assessors appointed by the minister of labor; or one or more arbitrators nominated by, or on behalf of, the workers concerned from among the members of the panel and presided over by the chairman or vice-chairman.

An Arbitration Tribunal, no matter how it is constituted, must make its award within forty-two days of its constitution, with the exception of rare cases where the minister may allow a longer period. After receiving the tribunal's award, the minister must publish the details of the award and allow some specified time within which any of the parties to the dispute that is not satisfied with the award to raise objections. If no notice of objection is given to the minister within the time limit and in the manner specified in the original publication, the minister then publishes in the *Government Gazette* a notice confirming the award, and the award shall be binding on the two parties. If, however, a party to the dispute raises an objection to the award made by the tribunal, the minister refers the dispute for determination to the National Industrial Court.

The National Industrial Court is composed of a president and four other members. All members are appointed by the Federal Executive Council after consultation with the Advisory Judicial Committee. The president must have been a judge of the high court or a practicing lawyer for at least ten years. The other members are known as "ordinary members" and need not be lawyers. In addition to the five members of the court, the law empowers the minister of labor to draw up a list of assessors, made up of employers' and workers' representatives. From among the assessors, the president of the court may appoint four of them to assist the court in dealing with any matter. Of these four, two shall be persons nominated by, or on behalf of, the employers and two by, or on behalf of, workers' organizations. The assessors are drawn upon in cases where the president of the court or members feel that a specialist opinion or evidence by both employers and workers' representatives would be helpful to the court in arbitrating the dispute. The court has exclusive jurisdiction to make awards for the purpose of settling trade disputes and to determine questions as to the interpretation of any collective agreement previously reached by the parties or by the court itself or the terms of settlement of any trade disputes.

Ubeku (1994) maintains that the court's jurisdiction is appellate, namely, that issues, that cannot be resolved by the Industrial Arbitration Panel are referred to it for ruling. The court has original jurisdiction in two situations: (1) disputes in which workers in any essential services are a party and (2) those in which the minister feels that referring the case to the Arbitration Tribunal is inappropriate. In these two instances, the minister of labor may, within seven days of the receipt of such report, refer the dispute directly to the NIC. The NIC is the final court of appeal on all industrial disputes, and there is no appeal of any determination of the court.

The practice and procedure of the court are governed by the National Industrial Court Rules of 1979 and the Supplementary Provisions in part IV of the Trade Disputes Act of 1976. Both the provisions and the rules provide a mere skeleton for practice and procedure, as these are largely determined as the court proceeds and are always informal (Ubeku, 1994).

Inquiry and Investigation

The Trade Dispute Act empowers the minister of labor to set up a Board of Inquiry to look into, or investigate, disputes and other employment problems. Without the formal consent of the parties, the minister may do this where any trade dispute or threat of dispute exists. The power to do so derives from section 23 of the Trade Disputes Act of 1976 which provides:

- Where any trade dispute actually exists or is threatened, the minister may cause inquiry to be made into the causes and circumstances of the dispute and, if minister thinks fit, may refer any matter appearing to the minister to be connected with, or relevant to, the dispute to a Board of Inquiry appointed for the purpose by the minister; and the board shall inquire into the matter referred to it and report thereon to the minister.
- A Board of Inquiry appointed under this section shall consist of a chairman and such other persons as the minister thinks fit to appoint or may, if the minister thinks fit, consist of one person only. The supplementary provisions in Part IV of the Trade Disputes Act of 1976 that govern the National Industrial Court and Arbitration Tribunals also apply to the Boards of Inquiry. The procedure for Boards of Inquiry is informal. The boards are free to regulate their own procedures and practices. Parties to the dispute may either appear personally by themselves or have legal representation. Boards of Inquiry are not used often.

The picture just presented indicates that the process of resolving conflict between labor unions and employers has been completely institutionalized, yet it has not been effective in reducing the rate of strikes and other types of labor and management conflicts in African countries with such institutions. This supports what Batstone (1979) said, that institutionalization merely regulates conflict; it does not resolve it. In other words, the potential for "disruption" is ever-present, and there is no guarantee that government's structuring of institutions and the creation of channels can eradicate worker-employer conflicts. The notion of institutionalization is concerned primarily with means rather than with substantive results. It does not specify what sorts of agreements on wages will be reached. The willingness to use the institutions of arbitration or reconciliation is dependent on the goodwill of labor and management to maintain peace and preserve the relationship between them. The more radical labor unions always refuse to use these institutionalized procedures. Finally, the successful institutionalization of conflict resolution is dependent on their substantive effectiveness. This effectiveness is far from guaranteed, because it is easy for the initial success of such a body to lead ultimately to failure due to the nature of the agreement that it reaches between labor and management.

SUMMARY

Conflicts are common among factory workers, but with the recent deterioration in the standard of living in Africa, conflict has extended to professional, managerial, and technical groups in different organizations, including banks and other financial institutions, universities, teaching hospitals, and primary and secondary schools. The contemporary attitude toward conflict is that it is neither good nor bad. Conflict must be assessed from different perspectives. Management should focus on the management of conflict rather than try to avoid it. Organizational conflict is caused by a host of psychological and job-related factors such as arbitrary frustration, job dissatisfaction, incompetent management of organizational reward systems, violation of collective agreement, and misinterpretation and misapplication of labor legislation or law. Poor interunion and intraunion relationships also cause labor conflict in African organizations.

Organizational conflict is instructive as well as costly. Its cost includes time and energy diverted from work to engage in conflict. It is, however, difficult to quantify the cost of any conflict. Researchers are agreed that conflicts should be managed in such a way as to minimize the cost and increase the benefits for the individuals or groups in conflict and for the organization. This can be done by focusing on interests of the conflicting parties at the bargaining stage rather than emphasizing who is right and who is more powerful.

Unlike some countries in Europe, such as Britain and France, or the United States African governments have tended to impose some measure of control on the behavior of labor unions. This was caused partly by the behaviors of the union organizations in Africa and partly by the dictatorial posture of many of the African governments in places like Ghana and Tanzania, where the National Labor Union was made a department of the Ministry of Labor. In Senegal and other French-speaking African countries and Nigeria the relationship between the labor unions and the employers was legalized and institutionalized by government, with government as the final authority in this relationship.

Some authors see some advantages in the process of institutionalization of conflict resolution in that it provides workers with a degree of industrial citizenship. Second, it isolates industrial conflicts from other types of conflict, and third, it confers on labor and management some legitimacy of existence. The problem with institutionalization is that it merely regulates conflicts; it does not resolve them. It does not specify what sorts of agreements on wages labor and management will reach.

7

Human Resources Planning and Development

Until recently the contributions of psychology to human resources planning have been limited to personnel selection and classification. This is partly due to two reasons. Psychology developed powerful tests that aided selection and placement, and the emergence of human resources planning as a separate discipline.

The Human Resource Society appeared in 1978, with its own journal, called *Human Resource Planning*. This chapter reviews human resources development in Africa, human resources planning in organizations, and personnel recruitment and classification in African organizations. It is assumed that personnel selection and placement, the oldest functions of psychology in organizations, are aspects of the functions of a well-integrated and developed human resources program.

HUMAN RESOURCES DEVELOPMENT IN AFRICA

Large international and indigenous organizations in Africa have either a department or a unit usually designated as a human relations section. In many of the countries human relations is accorded the status of a management profession. Universities teach it as a discipline. Again this tradition was the way it was handed down by the European colonial countries. Personnel management as it is practiced in the United States has a short history in Africa. Human resources development as a management approach, because of its late emergence even in the Western industrialized countries, is barely known or practiced in most African organizations.

The industrial relations manager in African organizations handles collective bargaining, contract administration, and administratives hearings in personnel matters. Flander (1965) defined industrial relations as a study of institutions of job regulations. Ubeku (1983) added that "the rules of the industrial relations system are either procedural or substantive." The rules "are determined through the rule-making process of collective bargaining, which is regarded as a political institution involving a power relation between employers and employees," according to Ubeku, (p.5). This view maintains that the principal actors in industrial relations are the trade unions, employers' associations and government and its agencies. The role of the industrial relations officers in organizations is to manage the interaction process that goes on among these actors and to manage the conflict that results from such interaction. The industrial relations officers also administer or implement the rules and regulations that result from collective bargaining. They engage in conflict resolution and monitor the role that each actor plays and should play in this relationship.

What is striking as one reads the definition and functions of industrial relations officers in organizations is the narrowness of the field when applied to today's competitive, technoglobal society. According to the definition and the functions, human or industrial relations does not concern itself with the needs, growth, and development of the individual workers in the organization. It is legalistic and principally concerned with the maintenance of industrial peace at the expense of industrial democracy. The latter would include the worker and the employer as the principal actors in the interaction that the industrial relations officers manage.

The recent trends in developed countries such as the United States and Japan are that human resources development as a discipline and a profession is an umbrella for both personnel management and human relations. These are practiced within the framework of human resources development. Human resources planning in organizations includes the short- and long-term forecasting, planning, provision, and management of personnel; development of services in classification, compensation, labor relations, staff development, and training; improvement of the welfare of the workers in industrial organizations.

In Africa the general managers of the organizations perform the functions of human resources managers in addition to their specific management duties. Unlike in the United States, there are no human resources specialists to handle the short-term and long-term planning of the human resources needs of the organizations or to consult with employees, employers, and employers' associations on organizational policies and practices.

The lack of established human resources development policies in African organizations has important implications for organizational management in general. One implication is that even after independence African organizations have continued the colonial benign neglect of African workers by paying little or no attention to the workers' welfare. Second, where efforts were made to recognize the needs of employees, they were made by those who possess neither the expertise nor the appropriate knowledge in the field. Finally, international and large organizations left African governments with the responsibility of developing Africa's human resources instead of joining government and its agencies in their efforts to produce the manpower needed for work in Africa.

This situation should be reconsidered if Africa is to produce the appropriate and adequate managerial, analytical, technical, and research skills that it requires for development. School-linked human resources development in Africa does not often satisfy these professional levels. Human resources development in Africa that is provided by schools, polytechnics, universities, and other vocational education is aimed at formal employment. Roberts (1990) indicated that the present experience in Africa is that these sectors of the economy tend to overproduce skills for a stagnant labor market and nonexpanding public sector. Observers are, therefore, forecasting that essential changes are required in human resources development in Africa if the continent is to provide the needed manpower for self-employment and the market economy.

Employment Sectors in Africa
The major sources of employment for almost all African countries are the government and its agencies or parastatals, industries, agriculture, commerce and financial sectors, and the informal sector.

Government and the Parastatals. The state is the major employer of labor in all African countries. Estimates in some countries indicate that 60 - 68 percent of those who are employed work for government and its agencies. Government provides employment at two levels. On first level are those who are classified as civil servants. These include professional, managerial, and technically skilled bureaucrats as well as semiskilled and unskilled workers. Government agencies or the parastatals constitute the second level employment providers. These are organizations that manage the nation's infrastructures, electricity and water supply, telecommunications, postal system, railways, airways, print and electronic media organizations and other government-owned organizations such as banks, refineries, breweries, and agricultural and mining companies. The state also pays for social service employees who are involved in education, public health, agricultural extension, and community development services and in the maintenance of state security, including the military, police, and prison workers.

Roberts (1990) maintains that the public sector in Africa has grown more rapidly than the economy, resulting in huge human resources development investments to upgrade the caliber of public service and provide careers for the rising elite. Overpopulation and rising unemployment in most African countries have resulted in overstaffing in most government departments. This has resulted in what Roberts (1990) calls "bloated and inefficient civil service administration. Many of the state enterprises and parastatals run at a huge loss due to poor management skills and lack of know-how. Some countries, such as Benin, Cameroon, Congo or the former Zaire, Guinea, Ghana, Kenya, Mali, Nigeria, Senegal, and Togo, are responding to calls for commercialization and privatization of some of these enterprises and parastatals.

Industry. The 1980 Lagos Plan of Action (LPA) declared 1980 to 1990 the Industrial Development Decade for Africa. The period was to foster industries based on local resources and skills, enterprise, and self-reliance and to meet the basic needs of the wider population. The magic year 2000 has come; and yet the Lagos objectives remain largely unattained. Roberts (1990) asserts that observers think that the objectives of the Lagos Plan of Action were too "optimistic," plus the fact that many African countries and their governments were not committed to the objectives of the Lagos Plan of Action, which they had signed. Other obstacles to the attainment of the Lagos objectives are the internal economic weakness of many African states and instability in international financial and trading markets.

Industries contribute 10 percent to Africa's gross domestic product; this figure rises to about 20-25 percent in oil-exporting countries such as Nigeria, Angola, and Côte d' Ivoire. Much of the industrial production in many African states relies on imported raw materials, technology, and even skills. Almost all African countries rely on export-oriented industries that employ labor-intensive methods and limited technology to engage in processing of local natural resources and agricultural products.

Agriculture. Authoritative sources maintain African agriculture is in crisis. Agriculture provides the basic work and livelihood for a majority of Africans. According to Roberts (1990), the Food and Agriculture Organization (FAO) study called *Agriculture towards 2000* forecasts that food demand in Africa would expand by 3.4 percent per year up to 2000 (Roberts, 1990), while production would reach only 2.6 percent. Sufficiency in cereals would drop from 83 percent in 1980 to 56 percent by the present century if conditions did not change. Agricultural methods in most of the African countries lag behind those of the developed countries of Europe and America. As the population of Africa rises, and engagement in traditional farming becomes less rewarding, youths leave the rural areas and migrate to the urban areas in search of jobs, leaving aged men and women in the farms. These old men and women cannot produce sufficient food to feed Africa's expanding population. There is, therefore, a major need to attract to Africa large-scale farming methods with improved system of production. This will impact directly human resources development in agriculture through the introduction of improved skills, technology, and advanced methods.

Commerce and Finance. The commercial and financial sector of most African countries is expanding rapidly. Nigeria, Kenya, South Africa, and Côte d'Ivoire have fairly well developed banking, insurance, and financial service companies, computer bureaus, export-import agencies, and retail stores. In all, the sector employs a large percentage of Africans skilled in commercial, financial, computer, and managerial disciplines. The crisis in the banking sector in Nigeria in the second half of the 1990s was blamed on rapid expansion in this sector, which led to the employment as managers of people without the necessary managerial, professional, and technical skills and knowledge. Human resource, development in this sector becomes very important if these companies are to have a competitive edge for the future. Indigenization policies that transfer control and management responsibilities of commercial enterprises from expatriate managers to indigenous African personnel require a major leap in the development of professional and managerial skills.

Informal Sector. The informal sector of the African economy contains those economic activities that lie beyond the control of government. The informal sector is in the hands of millions of small- and medium-sized manufacturers, traders, business people, and other service providers who are self-employed. This sector, which is little known, produces Africa's new entrepreneurs. In Nigeria, although policymakers have not reckoned with it, the sector exercises significant power in the economy through its influence on price and supply of essential commodities. When the World Bank and other international agencies estimate the wealth of African nations, they usually fail to include the wealth that this sector controls. The indigenous African governments, too, because of a dearth of information, have no idea of the amount of goods and services that change hands in these numerous centers in Africa.

Many persons in the sector are self-employed. They rely on their own capital, and many have little or no formal education. Recently, many of the new entrants into the informal sector have been well-educated youths, some with university education. They pass their skills down to their family through the apprenticeship system. Roberts (1990) suggests that human resources development has the challenge of building essential business, marketing, and technical skills, including record keeping and accounting for this sector.

AFRICAN GOVERNMENTS AND HUMAN RESOURCES DEVELOPMENT

Governments in Africa give high priority to skills development for the workplace because they realize the importance of professional, managerial, technical, and human skills to nation building and development. This realization placed human resources development squarely in the lap of government following independence. Thus, the history of human resources development (HRD) in Africa has been what Roberts (1990) calls "centrally managed HRD by the Government." The government discharges this function through primary, secondary, and tertiary education. In other words, the government discharges the responsibility of developing human resources through the educational system.

The need for African governments to increase the literacy level of their citizens and broaden the base for participatory government by their people led to the expansion of primary education. Some of the governments introduced free education at the primary level. This increased the number of pupils who left primary school but had no opportunities for employment. Consequently, governments increased the rate of expansion of secondary schools to motivate those leaving primary school to continue their education. This, in turn, led to the creation of more tertiary institutions in many African countries, such as polytechnics, colleges of education, universities and universities of technology, which are presently all government-owned and-maintained. Roberts (1990) indicates that the trend now in most countries is a call for expanded human resources development schemes that emphasize entrepreneurship, self-employment, and entry into the informal sector. Indeed the slogan now in many African countries including Nigeria is "job creation" rather than "job seeking."

STRUCTURE OF HUMAN RESOURCES DEVELOPMENT IN AFRICA

Roberts's (1990) review of HRD structure in Africa lists the following as agencies that share in the production of human resources in Africa:

- Government-managed HRD
- Vocational education within the school system
- Technical skills institutions
- Nonformal human resources development (HRD)
- Human resources development (HRD) in agricultural skills
- Human resources development (HRD) role of employers
- Management development institutions
- Private human resources development (HRD) organizations

Government-Managed Human Resources Development

All African governments participate actively in the function of developing the human resources of each nation. In each of the African countries the Ministry of Education is in complete control of the formal HRD system. Some countries, such as Kenya, Côte d' Ivoire, and Senegal, have national training systems in which central agencies coordinate all job-related HRD. Other countries created special agencies that coordinate their central HRD systems.

For example, Zimbabwe has the Directorate of Industrial Training, Nigeria has the National Board for Technical Education, and Ghana has the Technical and Vocational Division, while Sudan has the Directorate of Technical Education. The Governments of Côte d'Ivoire, Nigeria, Zimbabwe, Malawi, Cameroon, and others encourage employers to train employees by charging a minimum levy of 1.0 percent of the payroll of organizations, and, in return, government refunds the costs of training. Governments also influence HRD by coordinating apprenticeship recruitment and controlling standards through trades examinations and certification.

Vocational Education in the School System

Many African countries subscribed to the 1976 Lagos Conference of Education Ministers, which recommended the incorporation of "productive work into education by integrating vocational education in educational systems from primary to secondary schools." The objective was to provide pupils in these schools with work-related skills and prepare them for effective transition to work and self-sufficiency through self-employment on leaving school. Tanzania is a country that introduced this type of HRD earlier by incorporating the practice of farming or agriculture into the school curriculum. Nigeria's 6-3-3-4 system of education (students spend 6 years in primary school, 3 years in junior secondary school, 3 years in senior secondary, and 4 years in university) is another such system. However, lack of equipment and appropriately prepared teachers, especially technical teachers for the junior secondary classes, have hindered the attainment of the objectives of the system.

In some countries the "new school system" included emphasis on agriculture and animal husbandry. The overall expectation from such integrated schools is that their graduates will enter the informal sector as self-employed or casual workers.

Technical Skills Institutions

In order to develop Africa's industrial sector, human resources planners must aim at the development of sufficient technical skills. Experience in Europe, Japan and the United States indicates that one important factor that promotes national development and industrial productivity is technical knowledge African countries have an inadequate supply of engineers, scientists, technicians, and professional managers. In Africa these skills are obtained in colleges and polytechnics in countries such as Nigeria and other English-speaking countries or in *écoles techniques* and *écoles d'études superieures* in the French-speaking African countries. These institutions offer instruction that produces middle-level manpower in the areas of professional, administrative, and craft skills.

Some of the countries with larger capacity have specialized centers run by the ministries and parastatals such as railway and transport schools, building and construction centers, engineering centers, telecommunication centers, and, recently, media and film production centers. In spite of all these efforts, technical education has not succeeded in achieving the goals of making Africa self-reliant and self-sustaining in technically skilled personnel.

Onyemelukwe (1966) discussed the problems of developing technical skills in Nigeria, while Roberts (1990) deliberated on some of the problems with technical skill centers in human resources development in Africa. Roberts (1990) maintained that performance at the centers is not uniform and that many of the centers are poorly conceptualized and funded. Most of them depend on foreign teachers due to lack of indigenous manpower, as well as isolated with little or no contact with the workplace. Their training is often based on inappropriate or obsolete teaching equipment and technology that are usually supplied by donor countries. Employers often view off-the-job human resource development as merely generalized preparation for in-company training, as a result they have negative attitudes toward the use of products of the centers.

Nonformal Human Resources Development

These are the initiatives to prepare young people and adults for the workplace that are undertaken by nongovernmental organizations (NGOS), communities, churches, age group associations, and labor unions. Nonformal human resources development programs are usually characterized by local community involvement in funding and management. The community sees the project as an aspect of self-help community development. Instruction is usually combined with production so that the participant is productive while learning. The projects have close links to local enterprises. Emphasis is on both citizenship training and community service. Such programs focus on target groups that the more formal human resources programs of the school does not cover, such as unemployed primary school leavers, adults, the nonformally educated, and rural women.

Nonformal HRD is an important source of skills acquisition for the growing informal sector. The are some problems with the nonformal HRD. Since government is not involved in the sector the overall system is poorly coordinated and managed. The type of labor that it supplies is not coordinated and monitored. This leads to oversupply of some traditional skills such as sewing, catering, carpentry, driving, and a total neglect of others. Poor management also leads to its being very costly, relying on support from church groups, wealthy individuals, nongovernmental organizations, and other agencies. Finally, many of them suffer from underfunding.

Well-known examples of nonformal HRD centers in Africa include the Botswana Brigades, which is a national movement of community-based skills and production centers that develop and help primary school leavers, school dropouts, and other unemployed persons to find employment in rural communities. Kenya's Village Polytechnics, whose philosophy is based on *harambee* (self-help), is another. These comprise about 200 low-cost, village-managed centers, which teach practical skills for self-reliance to primary-school leavers and educational dropouts. Others are Tanzania's Folk Development Colleges, based on *Uhuru* ideology, Nigeria's Craft Centers, Cameroon's Youth Centers, and Zambia's *Huanshya* Youth Self-Help project. These offer useful models of HRD that respond to the realities of African development.

Human Resources Development for Small Entrepreneurs

These include men and women who make their livelihood in self-employment by working in small family businesses, either in towns or rural areas. These people need technical skills and skills in bookkeeping, marketing, and accounting. At present many in this class are not receiving any HRD attention.

Human Resources Development in Agricultural Skills

Agriculture remains the main form of livelihood for the African people. In spite of that, Africa has found it difficult to feed its teeming population because of its failure to transform its agricultural practices from traditional methods of farming to modern, mechanized system. Human resources development in agriculture is examined for agricultural professionals and managers, for technical officers, and for farmers.

Professionals and Managers. The main centers for the development of agricultural professionals and managers are the universities and specialized agricultural management centers such as Agricultural Management Center, Swaziland; Agricultural and Rural Management Training Institute, Nigeria; and Pan-African Institute for Development, Cameroon, Burkina Faso, and Zambia. There are also a few international centers for livestock in Ethiopia. The International Institute of Tropical Agriculture (IITA) with its headquarters in Nigeria and the International Center for Research in Agro-forestry (ICRAF) in Kenya emphasize the production of agricultural professionals and managers.

Almost every university in most African countries awards degrees in agriculture. Countries with larger population and economic capacity such as Nigeria have established several universities of agriculture, including agricultural engineering. Roberts (1990) indicated that the 1984 survey of the FAO of the United Nations showed that, with the exception of Nigeria, demand for agricultural professionals and managers far exceeds supply in most African countries.

Technical Officers. Production of this level of agricultural officers takes place in colleges of agriculture, agric-polytechnics, and units run by Ministries of Agriculture. The supply of manpower here falls far short of demand in most African countries.

Farmers. Nonformal HRD centers provide some instruction in farming and animal husbandry skills. The system of extension agents and model farms that reach farmers in both urban and rural areas and give on-the-spot coaching, information, and advice is a very important HRD approach. Other HRD approaches that influence rural farmers are demonstration farms, films that are usually shown by extension officers in rural localities, and subsidized agricultural equipment, seeds, and fertilizer that are provided by the states and local governments. Roberts (1990) pointed out that a World Bank expert, Daniel Benor, developed the *training and visit system* in Asia. The system has proved to be effective and has shown great promise as a basic form of HRD that can reach a large population of productive African farmers.

Employers and HRD in Africa

Most large organizations in Africa such as government, public enterprises, and the multinational companies and organizations compete for university graduates whom they expect to develop to managerial and professional class. They also tend to send some of these skilled and semiskilled employees to different commercial and technical institutions. Different types of employers take different approaches to HRD.

Civil Service. In most countries in Africa the public service absorbs a large proportion of postsecondary and university graduates who go into the world of work. The civil service guarantees training and continuing education for its employees. This includes local and overseas training and education. Following independence, African governments established institutes for civil service HRD. In the former British colonies these became the National Institute of Public Administration (NIPAS), modeled on the British Royal Institute of Public Administration. The French counterpart centers were given names based on the French *Ecole Nationale d' Administration.* Roberts (1990) maintains that these institutes often are given ambitious mandates to develop all levels of public officials from senior civil servants, to secretarial staff. In practice, they actually focus at the middle and junior levels of personnel, where they provide basic courses designed around complex civil service procedures and rules. While the

Kenya Institute of Administration and the Ghana Institute of Management and Public Administration have succeeded in attracting higher-level managers and expanded their roles beyond the civil service, the Administrative Staff College of Nigeria (ASCON) has not.

Many of the civil service systems have in-service training or management services units either in a central ministry or in the cabinet office. The types of functions provided by such units for the civil service include management auditing and consulting, identification of training and education needs, arrangement of attendance at external courses, and the conduct of basic, off-the-job programs. The units have also the responsibility to ensure that civil service HRD is planned, coordinated, and assessed.

Most governments in Africa take seriously the development of senior managers through overseas or special in-country programs. These activities build useful skills but have done little to improve managerial practices and behavior because the civil service in Africa is a conservative bureaucracy. Roberts's (1990) observation is a noteworthy conclusion.

African bureaucracies like most cannot be changed by HRD aimed at individuals because knowledge, skills, and techniques are only part of the picture. African governments are run by small groups of skilled managers who centralize power. ...Despite much civil service HRD activity, important skills are lacking at many levels, especially policy analytical skills needed to guide programs of structural and sector reform. (25. 15)

In many African countries the civil service suffers from a dearth of skilled planners, financial specialists, and project managers to prepare and monitor development programs and projects. There are no information specialists to guide the generation and utilization of reliable and valid information for management and development.

Public Enterprises (PES). State-run enterprises have played very important roles in HRD, particularly in industrial management, manufacturing and technical skills, and entrepreneurship. The extension of the civil service reward system into public enterprises acts as a disincentive, that drives these good managers into the private sector. Often bureaucratic procedures prevent the dismissal of poor managers, leading to a system of rotation of managers as a method of dealing with performance problems.

Public enterprises such as railway boards, telecommunications, parastatals, national power authorities, and mining and oil exploration companies have their own HRD centers, institutes or colleges. On-the-job learning is the most important method of skill transfer, combined with occasional, off-the-job, short courses. Roberts (1990) maintains that in spite of these efforts, public enterprises lack skills in business management, strategic planning, marketing, project management, and public investment.

Private Sector. The major role of the private sector in HRD can be discussed under the apprenticeship system, employers' organizations, and multinational enterprises.

Apprenticeship systems vary from one country to another. In Côte d'Ivoire, apprenticeship caters mainly to people in rural areas, where it prepares people without formal educational qualifications for jobs in the informal sector. In other countries, such as Nigeria and Zimbabwe, it covers a wide spectrum from unskilled, to highly skilled, educated artisans and technicians for manufacturing. Apprenticeship systems in Africa play a very important HRD role.

Employers' organizations such as the Employers' Consultative Association in Nigeria play a vital HRD role. Such associations play intermediary roles between members and outside HRD providers. Some employers' organizations have HRD activities. For example, the Federation of Kenya Employers runs courses in applied management and labor management, the Ethiopian Chamber of Commerce runs courses in "effective mobilization of exportable products" (Roberts, 1990), and the Zambian Federation of Employers offers courses in financial management, industrial relations, and development planning. All these activities are important for HRD.

Multinational enterprises and foreign-owned companies are predominant in some African countries, such as Botswana, Côte d' Ivoire, Liberia, Cameroon, and Sierra Leone. Their HRD efforts are targeted at the development of middle-level managers. Their top management groups are usually sent overseas, where the courses and training programs may often be insensitive to the environmental, cultural, and personality factors that impinge on African management. In spite of these, the oil companies, banks, mining companies, insurance companies, and agricultural estates make major HRD investments.

Management Development Institutions

Africa has many national and regional management development institutions that generally serve public sector managers. Managers served by regional institutes are at a somewhat higher level than those usually served by the average national institutes of public administration. In the French-speaking African countries these institutions serve the private sector to some extent. They may also provide consulting services. Examples of the stronger national management development institutes include Nigeria's Center for Management Development (CMD), the Ethiopian Management Institute, and the Republic of the Congo's (former Zaire) *Centre de perfectionnement aux techniques de développement.*

Regional management development institutes have broader mandates than the national management development institutes. They also specialize in certain sectors and development management needs that may lie outside the capacity of the national development institutes. Examples are the Eastern and Southern Africa Management Institute (ESAMI) which is located in Arusha, Tanzania, and the Pan-African Institute for Development located in Douala, Cameroon.

Management development institutes play a very important role in the development of management skills. In order to consolidate their impact, management development institutes in Africa need to achieve greater autonomy from government and become more self-reliant. They also need to reduce their dependence on donors by developing indigenous HRD and performance improvement methods that attract the patronage of both expatriate and indigenous organizations. Efforts should made to reduce their reliance on imported HRD models and theories. They should develop a program of reaching higher-level managers as well as acting as effective agents in strengthening government policy skills.

Private HRD Organizations

Numerous private enterprises specialize in HRD services in most African countries. Some of these private management institutions are owned by groups of specialists, management associations, or solo management consultants. In a country such as Nigeria numerous solo or local consultants or small HRD firms offer personalized services to management clients. Many universities and polytechnics in Nigeria too, have private HRD units that are often independent of any faculty. All these make tremendous contributions to the development of management skills.

HUMAN RESOURCES PLANNING IN ORGANIZATIONS

Having examined the African employment sector and the structure of human resources development, the next question is how an organization utilizes these environmental facts to program its human resources planning.

Human Resources Management by Dr. Nwagbo Eze (1995) is probably the first textbook by an African to bear that name. This is an indication of the level of expertise on the topic possessed by African managers. Eze defined human resources management as "creating systems and institutions in which human beings in an organization can make their best contributions to achieve their individual goals and to develop the enterprise" (p. 2). The definition does not convey vividly the meaning and function of human resources planning as illustrated by Vetter's (1967) definition, which states that human resources planning is:

the process by which management determines how the organization should move from its current manpower position to its desired position. Through planning, management strives to have the right number and the right kind of people, at the right place, at the right time, doing things which result in both the organization and the individual receiving maximum long-run benefits. (cited in Jackson and Schuler, 1990)

In the developed economies, human resources planning occurs within the broad context of organizational and strategic business planning. It involves forecasting the organization's immediate, intermediate, and long-term manpower needs, as well as mapping how these needs will be met for the organization. Jackson and Schuler (1990) maintain that it involves defining objectives and then developing and implementing programs such as staffing (recruitment and placement), appraising, compensating, and training to ensure that the needed manpower is available with appropriate attitudes, knowledge, skills, and other characteristics when and where the organization needs them. It may include developing training programs to improve or update employee performance or to increase employee satisfaction, motivation, and involvement in order to facilitate organizational productivity and innovation (Mills, 1985). Finally, human resources planning includes the collection of necessary data that can be used for program and personnel evaluation and adjustment.

A good human resources plan must be integrated with the organization's short-term and long-term business objectives and plans. This is very important because "human resources represent a major competitive advantage" (Planning with People, 1984) that, if managed properly, can lead to increased profitability.

PROBLEMS OF HUMAN RESOURCES PLANNING IN AFRICAN ORGANIZATIONS

African countries are undergoing a crisis of unemployment and poverty engendered by a crisis in national human resources planning. Education was the preoccupation of each of the governments in Africa following independence The countries did not give any serious consideration as to where graduates of the school systems would be employed and whether or not the type of education these school-leavers were receiving provided them with the necessary skills to effectively work in the industries. Educational planning was thus marked by lack of planning and adequate attention to the industrial sector. Capacity for full employment in any nation requires that the planning and development of the industrial sector receive as much attention as the educational sector. Educational institutions should not just produce educated people without paying attention to the short- and long-term professional, managerial, and technical needs of the nation.

Formulation of short-term and long-term objectives is the backbone of human resources planning in any country. The development of long-term human resources planning is not feasible in many African countries because of the absence of the necessary data, as already discussed in Chapter 5. Human resources planning therefore tends to be confined to a short-term range. A three-stage set of human resources planning is usually recommended in the industrialized, developed countries of the West: short-, medium- and long-term plans.

Many African organizations do not have research and data collection and storage units. So the necessary information that can be used for long-term planning is not usually available. Furthermore, political and social instability make long-term organizational planning a real "dream." It is usually very difficult to predict whether the necessary resources such as equipment, personnel, spare parts, money, and motivation will be available when the time comes for the implementation of a long-term plan. At best African organizations are limited to short-term human resources planning.

In order to achieve the objectives of any human resources planning, correct analysis of the existing situations is important. With the exception of perhaps the Republic of South Africa, it would be difficult to assemble the necessary information to help a human resources planner in Africa to complete a meaningful plan. How many university graduates does a given country expect in a particular year, in the next five years, or in the next ten years? What percentage of these is graduating from technical institutions and with what type of skills? How many job openings is the country expecting next year and in the next five and ten years? What percentage of the expected job openings are technical, administrative, professional, semiskilled and skilled? Answers to these questions, while they are very easy to obtain in Britain, Japan, and the United States are very difficult to obtain in most African countries. There is a dearth of statistics on human resources demand, supply, and utilization in each of the African countries.

This is so in spite of the fact that each African country has a National Manpower Board or its equivalent (Onyemelukwe, 1966). The board has the responsibility of assessing the current and projected manpower needs of each country. It is also responsible for collecting information or statistical data to facilitate human resources planning and development. Finally, each nation's Manpower Board is charged with the responsibility for developing measures for combating unemployment and ensuring full employment for the country.

MODEL OF HUMAN RESOURCES PLANNING

Jackson and Schuler (1990) presented a theoretical model for describing human resources planning. The model is conceptualized as a dynamic linkage among components of a fully integrated system of organization and human resources planning. The model incorporates the activities engaged in by human resources planners, the four phases of human resources planning, and the three different time horizons. The four phases of human resources planning are as follows:

- gathering and analyzing data to forecast expected human resources demand, based on the organizational plans for the future, and to predict future human resources supply;
- setting objectives for human resources;
- designing and implementing plans and programs that facilitate the organization's actualization of its human resources objectives; and
- monitoring and evaluation of such programs. (Burack, 1988; Odiorne, 1981)

According to the model, activities related to these four phases of human resources planning are described for three different time horizons: short-term (up to one year), intermediate-term (two to three years), and long-term (more than three years). The time periods are designed to correspond to time horizons for organization planning. Employing the same time horizons enables human resource planning to correspond with organizational planning.

Jackson and Schuler (1990) maintain that the separation of human resources planning activities into four phases and into three time horizons should not be seen as suggesting that organizations segregate their planning activities. The reality, they maintain, is that organizations integrate their activities across the four planning phases as well as across all three time horizons; as illustrated by Figure 7.1.

Figure 7.1 shows the feed-forward and feedback arrows that connect the four phases of planning and planning activities within time horizons that are linked together into a dynamic system. Early phases such as demand and supply forecasts serve as inputs to later phases, such as setting objectives.

In addition to the arrows linking the four phases of planning within each time frame, Jackson and Schuler's (1990) model includes arrows to demonstrate:

- how longer-term objectives can influence shorter-term planning (dotted-line arrows);
- how shorter-term evaluation results can influence projections about future human resources and programs designed to meet future demands; and
- how the results achieved through the implementation of human resources programs can influence organizational plans.

Figure 7.1
Dynamic Linkages among Components of a Fully Integrated System of Business and Human Resources Planning

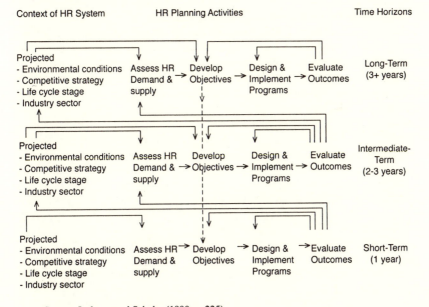

Source: Jackson, and Schuler (1990, p. 225).

Thus, planning for one time horizon typically has implications for others. For example, long-term planning usually prompts the development of programs that need to be implemented in the short term and intermediate term, according to Jackson and Schuler (1990). Also, the outcome of the evaluation of short-term programs always generates the need to reevaluate longer-term projections about the availability of manpower, which, in turn, may prompt adjustments in programs designed to meet longer-term needs. The goal is integration among all types of human resources planning activities as well as integration between human resources and organizational planning (Walker, 1988).

Short-Term Human Resources Planning

Organizations engage in activities related to the design and implementation of short-term programs such as recruitment, selection, and training to meet short-term organizational needs. Such activities generally involve some element of planning in that they are future-oriented activities. No matter how short-term these activities are, their overall objectives are usually linked to the achievement of long-term organizational objectives. For such a clear linkage to exist between human resources planning and strategic organizational planning, it is essential that an organization's top executives have a clearly articulated vision for the future. Such a vision should be clearly communicated to, and accepted by, managers throughout the organization.

Predicting Short-Term Demand and Supply. Manpower supply in the short-term horizon in an organization can be predicted with a high level of certainty. Jackson and Schuler (1990) define *demand* as the number and characteristics (e.g., skills, abilities, pay levels, or experience) of people needed for particular jobs at a given time and at a particular place. *Supply,* on the other hand, refers to the number and characteristics of people available for those particular jobs. The crucial demand-and-supply issue for human resources planners to deal with is to determine the number of jobs that will be vacated and filled in the next twelve months and where and how the organization gets the right people to fill those vacancies.

In order to resolve the demand issue, the human resources planner needs to predict who will leave jobs and create vacancies, which jobs will be eliminated, and which new jobs will be created. Jackson and Schuler (1990) suggest that one method of predicting both vacancies and job growth is to project the organization's historical trends into the future. What has been the trend in the past? What are the economic growth prospects for the organization? Is the organization affected by cyclical fluctuations in demand for its products or services? Such a historical and futuristic assessment, plus occasional employee surveys designed to assess the attitude and job satisfaction of employees, facilitates the prediction of which jobs need to be filled and vacated. Finally, predictions about how many and what types of jobs will be eliminated or created in the short term follow directly from organizational plans submitted by line managers of different departments.

The first step in answering the supply question (how and where will the organization get people to fill vacated jobs?) involves the determination of the desired characteristics of employees who fill or vacate the jobs of interest. The human resources planner has to determine the availability of such desirable characteristics in the organization's current workforce and the external labor force available in the population. The particular characteristics of current and potential employees that are inventoried and tracked by the human resources planners are a function of the nature of the organization and the external environment in which the organization operates.

It is thus important for the human resources planner to know the business needs and characteristics of the organization. The human resources planner gains this knowledge from meetings with the line managers, during which their business plans and human resources needs are shared. The process of discussion that increases the predictive accuracy of supply and demand, and this, in turn, facilitates the establishment of human resources objectives (Jackson and Schuler, 1990).

Setting Short-Term Objectives. These, according to Jackson and Schuler (1990), should include the development of strategies to increase the number of people in the population who are attracted and are willing to apply to the organization for jobs. The greater the number, the better the selection ratio for the organization. The strategies should include attracting a fair mix of applicants so as to secure those with different skills in different job locations; attracting those with improved qualifications; improving the qualifications of newly hired staff through training and workshops; reducing the turnover of desirable employees and increasing the turnover of undesirable ones in the organization; aiding employees who are recently hired to develop the skills and attitudes required by the organization through training orientation programs. Short-term objectives are straightforward and can easily be achieved by working collaboratively with line managers to ensure consensus on the program objectives.

Implementation of Short-Term Objectives. These objectives are achieved through recruiting policy, which determines the size and quality of the applicant pool in the population. Selection programs are developed for making selection decisions. The human resources department also installs performance appraisal systems through which performance deficiencies in the workforce are corrected and competencies to be rewarded are revealed. Training programs for the development of appropriate skills for use in the near future are developed. Attractive compensation systems are designed to attract skilled new employees, to motivate people to perform well, and to retain good employees. These programs are designed to achieve short-term objectives according to Jackson and Schuler (1990). They are also expected to have an immediate payoff, yet they can help an organization to achieve its longer-term objectives.

The high rate of unemployment in many countries in Africa, including Nigeria, means a large population of entrants into the labor force. This is good for human resources planners, because the activities of human resources planning are aimed at improving the ability of organizations to select employees on the basis of their job-related skills, abilities, and know-how, this is best accomplished when the organizations have a large pool of applicants from which to select. That is, organizations are able to make the best selection through tests when the selection ratio is low rather than when it is large. As the labor pool shrinks, selection ratios became larger. If a small selection ratio cannot be maintained, then organizations' resources are better invested in training the new entrants to upgrade their skills.

Evaluation of Short-Term Human Resources Programs. In organizations, every program, whether short-term or long-term, must of necessity undergo some evaluation to assess how well the objectives of the program are being attained. Again it is the responsibility of the human resources department to evaluate the organization's short-term human resources planning. Since the short-term program objectives are usually stated in easily quantifiable terms, such as the number of applicants, number to be hired, and expected number of employees expected to retire, and overall performance level. It is easy to assess how far such objectives have been attained. The evaluation may require the organization to conduct validity studies to verify to what degree they have the right people in the right job, how far their training programs have actually improved the deficiencies in the employees, and how far they have increased the workers' motivation and job satisfaction.

Intermediate-Term Human Resources Planning

A human resources program for recruitment, selection, training, and motivation of employees is aimed at reducing uncertainty by making sure that the right workers are available for the organization at the right time. At the level of short-term planning, there is very little uncertainty about how many persons and what types of skills are needed.

Jackson and Schuler (1990) maintain that as planning moves from short-term to intermediate-term, the questions of what the organization will need and what will be available become more complex and difficult to answer, thus requiring the human resources planner to pay more technical attention to the problem of forecasting or predicting. As in short-term human resources planning, the problems of predicting demand and supply must first be dealt with before objectives can be developed and before programs can be developed and evaluated. Since intermediate-term human resources planning is characterized by increased uncertainty, Jackson and Schuler (1990) maintain that collaboration between the manager in charge of human resources planning and line managers becomes more critical if accurate demand and supply are to be articulated.

Predicting Intermediate-Term Demand. This deals with the determination of how many new people and what skills they should possess to perform the jobs that will exist in the organizations in the next two to three years. In order to predict this, human resources planners must have existing data in the organization that will be useful in the prediction of organizational outputs, such as expected production volume, volume of sales, the total output that an organization intends to produce or deliver, and the technology that the organization intends to use to generate the output.

Jackson and Schuler (1990) outlined the factors that are usually considered when predicting output. According to these authors, they include the determination of future demands for the products and services that the organization provides, the percentage of the market that the organization is likely to be able to serve, the nature and availability of the type of technologies that may affect the amount and types of products or service that can be offered, and the different outpost countries with their political systems in which the organization expects to operate (Dumaine, 1989; Jackson and Schuler, 1990).

The middle-level line managers in an organization formulate output plans, while human resources planners translate these objectives for output into forecasts about the number and nature of jobs that employees need to perform in order to produce the desired output. For human resources planners to predict accurately the future manpower demand in an organization, they must develop an accurate picture of the factors that determine demand and supply as well as the ability to forecast the state of all the necessary variables in the model so developed. This in itself requires a stable environment; otherwise, forecasts for three years may be very difficult to predict accurately by reliance on historical trends and data.

Some of the methods employed by organizations to forecast their demands include statistical techniques such as regression analysis, managerial estimation, the Delphi technique, and job analysis, by which employee characteristics are matched to the existing jobs.

Predicting Intermediate-Term Supply. This is based on two sources internal and external information. Several authors (Bechet and Maki, 1987; Jackson and Schuler, 1990; Miller, 1980) maintain that internal sources are generally more crucial and more readily available in organizations than external sources. Similarly, there are two basic techniques for predicting internal supply, judgmental and statistical. One judgmental method for forecasting supply is called "replacement planning."

Replacement charts show the names of those occupying current positions and the names of likely replacements. This provides what Jackson and Schuler (1990) call a rough estimate of the "bench strength" of the organization. On the replacement chart, incumbents are listed directly under the job title. Those individuals who are most likely to fill the potential vacancies are listed under the incumbents. Such a list provides the organization with a reasonable estimate of which positions are likely to become vacant and who could replace whom if the situation arises. It also indicates whether or not there is a replacement for the vacancy (Walker and Armes, 1979). Present performance levels, ages, and information about the loyalty of current employees are used to predict future vacancies caused by retirement, turnover of top talent, and employee-initiated job changes.

The statistical technique for predicting manpower supply is less common. It involves the use of a computer to predict both internal and external supply. Two basic steps are required, no matter which statistical model is involved. The first step is to generate an inventory of current supply, that is, the number of people and their skills and abilities. The second is to predict how the supply is likely to change over time. Both steps usually consider internal and external supply sources.

Setting Intermediate-Term Objectives. These objectives are most likely to include training. Recall that short-term objectives include attracting new employees and assessing and assigning them to jobs. Training then follows to readjust employees' skills, attitudes, and behaviors to fit major changes in the needs of the organization, as well as to adjust human resources practices to fit changes in the needs of employees.

Implementation of Intermediate-Term Objectives. These objectives are achieved through training and retraining. The nature of training needed to meet the needs that will exist in two or three years can vary greatly. Programs provide basic skills training to newly hired workers, advanced education for existing employees and internships, work-study programs, and workshops.

Factors prompting organizations to engage in these training programs are many. They include changes in technology; a shift from a manufacturing-based, to a service-based, economy; and the failure of the African educational system to produce graduates who are competent to join the contemporary workforce; and, finally, the economic conditions that have forced on the economy the downsizing of many organizations and the workforce reductions that often follow.

The evaluation of intermediate-term human resources planning programs is not as precise as that of short-term programs. Many organizations have not effectively developed how to assess the effectiveness of their training programs. Often organizations end up assessing the overall productivity level of the entire department or organization.

Long-Term Human Resources Planning

Any planning designed for the future beyond three years is considered long-term. An example of long-term planning is succession planning. The need for long-term human resources planning is instigated by the rapidly changing and highly competitive, worldwide marketplace and the understanding by organizations that the workforce cannot be altered at will in a short time. Long-term human resources planning requires the integration of the skills and knowledge of the human resources planners and all other executives responsible for strategic planning.

Forecasting Long-Term Demand and Supply. What types of managers are needed to run the organizations into the first quarter of the twenty-first century and how an organization makes sure it has such managers constitute the major, long-term organizational concern. Jackson and Schuler (1990) indicate that the answer to such questions is *succession planning.* They went further to cite the assertion of McManis and Leibman (1988) that:

Exxon is so far ahead in the succession planning game that it has already hired its CEO [chief executive officer] for the year 2010. Although it is not public knowledge who that person is, he or she is already being challenged, assessed, and groomed for the top spot. (p. 24)

Succession planning and human resources development programs are a complex planning system designed to protect and promote the long-term health of the organization. The principal activities in succession planning and development include:

- identification of high-potential employees
- identification of needed competencies and skills
- provision of learning experiences to develop these skills and competencies where they do not exist (Deluca, 1988; Jackson and Schuler, 1990)
- provision of developmental experiences to a greater number of employees (Jackson and Schuler, 1990) through rotating employees through many principal jobs throughout their careers (McCall, 1988).

The survival of any organization in the future depends on its competitive strategy. According to Jackson and Schuler (1990), there are three types of competitive strategies, namely, "quality enhancement," "emphasis on innovation," and "cost reduction." Each of these strategies is achieved through the long-term demand-and-supply planning of an organization, thus implicating human resources planning and development as a major force in organizational reorientation and change. The innovation strategies help an organization to develop products and services that are different from those of other competitors The objective is to offer consumers new and different products constantly. Enhancement strategy, on the other hand, focuses on product service quality, while in cost reduction strategy the organization typically attempts to gain a competitive advantage by producing goods or providing services at the lowest cost.

The pursuit of these three strategies requires the adoption of different patterns of behavior by the employees. For organizations pursuing innovation, the pattern of behavior required includes "creativeness, cooperation, risk taking, flexibility, a long-term focus, and willingness to assume responsibility for outcomes" (Jackson and Schuler, 1990). When cost reduction is the focus, the behavior required is predictability and reduction of wasteful behavior.

Implementing Long-Term Objectives. This is accomplished through the use of tests, assessment centers, and performance evaluation. Organizations use psychological tests to integrate their business needs and long-term human resources planning. Psychological tests help human resources planners to evaluate existing talents and project organizational, long-term manpower needs and to develop a talent pool that includes the essential characteristics to meet the organization's future needs or to meet future competitive strategies that the organization is striving for. Tests are also used to help human resources managers identify high-potential employees early in their careers (Bentz, 1983).

A second program design for the implementation of long-term objectives of human resources planning and development is performance evaluation. Performance appraisals serve to continually revalidate and monitor initial judgments of future ability potentials and emotional stability.

Finally, assessment centers have been used by organizations (e.g., American Telephone and Telegraph [AT&T] as a method for selecting managers for promotions. Jackson and Schuler (1990) indicate that, in addition to using assessment centers to develop managers' ability to cope with ambiguity, AT&T tried to ensure that the organization as a whole was prepared for the future by developing two different types of leaders. One type is people with high levels of functional expertise, and the other has the broad expertise needed to be successful general managers.

Evaluation of Long-Term Human Resources Programs. Jackson and Schuler (1990) acknowledged that AT&T has generated some useful infromation about how ability and personality factors contribute to managerial effectiveness and how patterns of change over the life span and between generations affect managerial effectiveness. The authors also maintain that research on the evaluation of succession planning programs at AT&T succeeded in predicting individual outcomes such as career progress and satisfaction, thus making organizational outcomes proper methods of evaluating long-term human resources planning.

PERSONNEL RECRUITMENT AND CLASSIFICATION

The remaining section of this chapter considers some of the other functions of the human resources planning and development department in a well-integrated and developed organization. Personnel selection is the most traditional function performed by psychologists in industries and organizations. The modern era of personnel selection had its beginning in 1917 in the United States during World War I. Psychological tests were employed to select soldiers to win the war. Men were tested for the American army, job specifications were written, and job knowledge tests (trade tests) were invented. Officer rating forms were devised, and training and psychological counseling programs were mounted. All these marked the beginning of the large-scale use of psychological tests and other systematic methods to aid personnel selection, placement, and other personnel decisions in the world of work. This also pushed publication of tests into a big business in the developed economies of the world.

This is dissimilar to what obtains in African organizations, where indigenous tests for recruitment do not exist. The French colonial government and its psychologists saw the need for tests to improve selection and placement of African workers in colonial organizations. Some of the tests that they employed lacked qualities that would have made them useful in the selection of Africans for specific organizational work. In many African countries job specifications are not codified. Workers are simply told, following employment and placement, what they are supposed to do on the job.

In some medium-sized and small owner-manager companies, recruitment and placement are not based on aptitude, education, skill, or experience. Owners prefer to recruit close relatives. These organizations are usually run as a family business involving the head of family and his or her primary and sometimes extended family members. Whenever there is the need to recruit more workers, close relatives are preferred over outsiders, who may possess better knowledge and skill. Sometimes these relatives are recruited as apprentices. Under such unwritten contract, the relative-apprentices receive no salaries but live in the owner's house with the members of the household, and are provided with meals, medical care, and other necessities. When the apprentices qualify (i.e., have learned the business) the owner-manager provides them with money as capital to start their own business. As the owner-managers' business expands into other areas such as banking, estate management, transportation, printing, and electronic media, they begin to recruit more qualified and better educated managers and supervisors. Even at this stage supervisors and managers are selected either because they are relatives or because the individuals seem to the owner-managers to be the best workers (Onyemelukwe, 1966).

In large organizations there are distinct departments with defined functions such as marketing, production, sales, and accounts. If the organizations are government parastatals, departments, agencies, or public liability companies where government has shares, there is a high probability that politicians and military regimes exercise undue and unhealthy influence in matters of recruitment, appointment, promotion, and retirement of managers. In many African countries a radical political party, military regime, or military dictator comes into power and, under the pretense of reinventing government, retires most of the top managers in government departments, parastatals, agencies and public liability companies and then replaces them with the ruling party's own people. Most of these new appointees may not possess the professional skills necessary to head such organizations. Government's undue interference sometimes also leads to indiscriminate appointment and promotion procedures.

Personnel recruitment and placement are not accorded the seriousness that they deserve in African organizations. The careful and modern procedures for selection and placement that are used in industrialized countries are yet to be adopted by many organizations, including large, indigenous ones. Generally, if there are vacancies to be filled in an organization, the manager may invite relatives and friends to apply for the positions. The manager may also inform those who are already working for the organization about the vacancy. Those of them who have relatives and friends who are looking for job would recommend such individuals. Other methods of recruitment in African organizations can be designated external sources, such as advertisements through newspapers, the radio, professional magazines, handbills, and local television. Some of the multinational and international organizations extend their recruitment drives to the campuses of institutions of higher learning. Very few companies still conduct such outreach programs as visiting higher institutions to recruit graduating students, probably due to the high rate of unemployment in Africa at present. A few private employment agencies confine their search for applicants at the professional, managerial, and technical levels. They use the national newspapers to advertise job openings without indicating the organization that is looking for applicants. The technique of recruiting through private employment agencies is not well developed in Africa.

With the exception of international organizations, government departments and many indigenous organizations do not know how to recruit and place workers internally by using computerized data banks where information about the skills, knowledge, and abilities of each employee is stored. Indeed, such data bank information is beginning to be initiated in some of the organizations. Through procedure of using stored information on employees, when a vacancy, organizational growth, or the retirement of an employee occurs, and the organization needs to add an employee to a particular line, the computer can survey the entire workforce in a short time. Studies show that the best source from which an organization can obtain applicants is employee referrals. Job analysis is required in order to determine organizational demand and supply. Many organizations in Africa do not possess the personnel or the expertise to conduct proper job analysis to determine the human resources needs of their organizations. Many of these managers worked themselves up the organizational ladder as a function of the number of years that they have been in the organizations that they manage.

The Handbook of Industrial and Organizational Psychology (Dunnette, 1976; Dunnette and Hough, 1991) contains several chapters relevant to vocational diagnosis and personnel selection and classification. The reader is referred especially to the chapters by Guion (1976, 1991), for a general overview of personnel selection issues.

The caliber of people employed by an organization is a good prediction of organizational effectiveness, while the method of recruitment affects the efficiency of the organization's selection and placement programs in the number of qualified applicants who are motivated to apply for a particular position in the organization. If the organization selects its workers from a small number of applicants, the selection ratios will be high. The higher the selection ratios, the lower the utility of the selection instruments. When an organization has to make decisions about hiring two people out of three or four applicants sent down by friends, it becomes meaningless to employ tests to help make the selection decision.

The method of recruitment also influences the attitude, motivation, and level of commitment of employees. In Africa it begets the concept of "godfatherism," a feeling among some employees that "after all my brother or in-law who gave me this job is the managing director of this place, so you can't do anything to me." It usually signifies the beginning of insubordination and indiscipline of some employees. If employees are employed through the recommendations of cronies, godfathers, or brothers, on the basis of ethnicity, or religious affiliation, or because the manager is befriending the sister who happened to be the manager's secretary, such employees may never develop the appropriate motivation and attitudes for the performance of their responsibilities.

Finally, this method affects negatively the processes of interview, job preview, and compromise selection and placement system of any organization.

JOB ANALYSIS

The first thing to do when developing a selection or placement program is to conduct a job analysis. Each job for which applicants are considered should be analyzed in order to obtain a description of it and its specifications. Many African organizations do not have the advantage of a nationally codified job characteristics that will enable them to compile meaningful job descriptions. The type of information needed to carry out job analysis includes the answer to the questions, What type of job is it? Here the job-oriented activities, including descriptions of work in "job" terms such as carpentry, weaving, driving, packaging, or binding, are clearly stated. The second question to be answered is, What type(s) of behaviors is expected in the performance of the job? Here one expects to see a description of work-oriented work activities or the behavior in which the worker engages, such as decision making, performance of physical actions, or communicating. Others questions concern a detailed outline of whether the performance of the job requires the use of machines, tools, or work aids; what level of knowledge is covered by the job; what the working conditions are; and what the personnel requirements should be.

The form of job analysis can be descriptive, in which working conditions, social context, and personnel requirements are descriptively rendered, while quantitative analysis is rendered in "units" of job information expressed in numerical terms, such as ratings of job characteristics, time required to complete the job, or oxygen consumption on the job per unit of time. Concerning methods employed by the job analyst in collecting the information, he or she may observe a worker performing the job, interview a worker, personally perform the job, or compile the information through technical conferences of experts. The analyst may collect the necessary information through a structured questionnaire consisting of job activities and other aspects of jobs to be used in checking or rating each item as it applies to a job. Finally, the job analyst may obtain the information from work diaries that workers use in recording what they do during a workday or through other sources such as maintenance records and mechanical recordings, such as heart rate, films, and blueprints of equipment.

Position Analysis Questionnaire

The Position Analysis Questionnaire (PAQ) is another major technique for obtaining job analysis. The method is not yet popular among managers in organizations in Africa. McCormick, Jeannenet, and Mecham (1972) developed the technique. It uses a questionnaire approach to obtain the detailed characteristics of a given job position. The PAQ consists of 194 job elements within six divisions. These include:

- Information input (where and how does the employee get the information used in the job?), for example, use of written materials (35 job elements).
- Mental processes (what reasoning, decision making, planning, etc are involved in the job?), for example, coding/decoding (14 job elements).
- Work output (what physical activities does the worker perform, and what tools or devices does he or she use?), for example, use of keyboard devices (49 job elements).
- Relationships with other persons (what relationships with other people are required in the job?), for example, interviewing (36 job elements).
- Job context (in what physical and social contexts is the work performed?), for example, working in high temperatures (36 job elements).
- Other job characteristics, for example, irregular hour (24 job elements).

The basic assumption underlying PAQ is that jobs can be described objectively with a standard checklist, and the results can be used to deduce which personal attributes may be most important for doing the jobs. Such knowledge is of obvious use in developing "job-related" selection procedures Knowledge about jobs and deduced attributes can be useful on a much broader scale to help assure improved matches between jobs and people. This can be done by using checklist information to evaluate more objectively each person's previous job experiences and relevant, on-the-job activities and preference, and to design training and orientation programs that are more directly job-related.

With proper job analysis performed, the other aspects of selection and placement processes, such as personnel testing, biographical information or application blank, interview, and assessment center will neatly fall in place.

METHODS OF OBTAINING INFORMATION ABOUT JOB CANDIDATE

Following application, the organization must endeavor to obtain reliable and valid information to enable it make hiring decisions. Organizations use various methods to collect such information. These methods differ in terms of their popularity, validity, and utility. In this section the following methods are discussed: biographical data, letters of recommendation, interviewing, testing, and assessment centers. Of all these, the application form, letters of recommendation, and interviewing are the most common methods of gathering information about applicants in African organizations.

Biographical Information Blank

All organizations in Africa employ the application blank in obtaining initial information about an applicant. The motives for collecting the information may differ from one organization to another. The first step in the process of selection in any well-run organization is to ask the applicant to complete some kind of application form called an application blank. The form usually contains items requesting factual statements regarding the applicant's biography such as name, age, sex, education, previous employment, health, references, and such personal items as leisure activities. In Africa this form goes further to request information on job-irrelevant variables such as ethnicity and religious affiliation. In Nigeria the government application blank contains items such as ethnic group and state and local government of origin. For a government appointment, the job-irrelevant variables such as ethnic and religious affiliations and local government and state of origin may be the determining factors in whether the applicant gets the job or not.

The collection of biographical information for some companies and organizations in Africa is one of those formalities with no organizational objectives attached to it. Some use it to gain knowledge of applicants' ethnic and religious background to enable them to know whether the applicants are members of their religious and ethnic group. No laws protect African workers from discrimination on the basis of gender, ethnic group, and religious affiliation. Application blanks are haphazardly developed. They are not usually weighted or structured to predict success on the job. Some organizations design their own application blanks by gathering samples of forms from other organizations and then copying these forms. This results in biographical information items that have no significance and relevance to predicting the applicant's job behavior.

Contrary to how application blanks are utilized in African organizations, in the United States and other industrialized countries of the world biographical information of applicants is regarded as a picture of where the applicant "has been," that is, a record of a person's life path (Owens, 1976). Owens also argues that a person's past job experiences can aid greatly in predicting where the person is "likely to go" in the future. A person's biographical information blank should be regarded as providing the individual's life and work history.

When constructed well, a weighted biographical information blank is one of the most valuable selection and placement devices. Studies show that well-constructed application blanks can be used effectively to predict success in a variety of jobs. Ghiselli's (1976) review of validity studies indicated that biographical information was the most successful kind of predictor both for training and for job proficiency criteria. Several other studies (see Dunnette and Borman, 1979) confirm that the method can, indeed, yield high validities. Wexley and Yukl (1984) pointed out that biographical items found on typical application forms often yield higher validity than other predictors such as intelligence, aptitude, interests, and personality tests.

Biographical information forms do not usually receive the type of treatment that they deserve in many African organizations. Many organizations do not have weighted application forms. Biographical information blanks should consist mainly of those specific items that have been empirically found to be related to future success on the job in question, by examining statistically the relationship between each biographical information item and some subsequent measures of job success, for example, the number of jobs previously held and the rate of job performance or experience and effective decision making. An item is retained for use in the biographical information blank if and only if it correlates positively with future job success. Once the valid items are identified, each item is then weighted in proportion to the magnitude of this correlation.

When this is done, it becomes easy to reach selection and placement decisions based on the biographical information, which is scored by summing the weights of the applicant's responses to the items in the same way tests are scored. Second, since no two jobs are the same, it follows that separate scoring procedures must be constructed for each job within the organization. Finally, the biographical information should be cross-validated. This means that the validity of the blank must be examined on a sample of people separate from those originally used in developing the scoring procedure.

Letters of Recommendation

In Africa, many organizations including government ministries, departments, and their agencies, do not often require letters of recommendation from prospective job applicants. From the author's experience in Nigeria as the head of a major department for over twenty years in one of Africa's top universities, records show that less than 10 percent of the students who graduated at three different levels of bachelors' degree, master's, and doctorate requested letters of recommendation during the entire period. Those who requested recommendations were seeking admission for either postgraduate education in universities or a teaching job in an institution of higher learning. A few who sought employment in banks also requested letters of recommendation.

One explanation of this phenomenon is that success at job hunting in Africa is more a function of "who you know than what you know." In other words, one gets a job at an organization most often through contact, friends, and relatives who are already employees of the organization. Organizations, on their part, assume that since the applicants are brought by their employees, business friends, and politically powerful individuals, these applicants must be good for the organizations. This assumption may not always be correct.

Universities, banks, international and multinational organizations usually request letters of recommendation. A few of them require the reference to write a letter of recommendation; others send a short form containing some questionnaire items to the reference to complete. Neither the form that the organizations send to the reference nor the letter gives the reference opportunity to critically assess the applicants. The items of the form that the reference completes for the organizations may not be related to specific job behavior in organizations. Letters of recommendation in Africa are assumed to be positive. References often forget that they are called upon to vouch for applicant's character and ability. In doing so, they put their professional dignity on line. They are thus expected to balance their assessment of the applicant by pointing out the applicant's strengths and weaknesses. An organization or manager who delegates the applicant to collect the recommendation letter from the reference does not expect to get an objective evaluation from the reference.

There are no laws in any African countries that make it mandatory for organizations to reveal the contents of an applicant's letters of recommendation to the applicant, as is the case in the United States. In spite of this, letters of recommendation in the United States are more evaluative and more predictive of job performance and aid decision making better in employee selection than letters of recommendation in African organizations.

Selection Interviews

The selection interview is the most commonly used method of recruiting and placing applicants in jobs in African organizations. No major organizations in Africa hire workers without some type of interviewing. It is expected that this trend will continue in future organizations in Africa.

An interviewing situation can be likened to a dyadic interaction or communication with a purpose. It is also important to exclude interviewers from participating in the making of selection decisions. The role of the interviewer is to collect information about a job applicant. Such information should be added to other types of information, such as biographical information, letters of recommendation, test scores, and performance at an assessment center, in order to make the final decision about an applicant or a job candidate. But in most African organizations where the interview is the only means of making hiring decisions the interviewers, not management, often make these decisions for organizations.

Cultural Problems with Interviews in African Organizations. Interviewers in African organizations must be aware of the specific errors that emanate from cultural response set among African workers. Interviews take place in a face-to-face communication situation. Interviewers who are usually older than the interviewee. Many cultural problems arise at this stage. Interviewers are trained to look out for the level of the interviewee's eye contact as a sign of assessing his or her honesty. Many African societies socialize youths not to look their elders in the face. In such societies youths listen to the elders or take instruction from them with their heads tilted down. Eye contact with an elder when taking instruction is regarded as a sign of disobedience or insubordination.

Another cultural response set among Africans is the influence of African hospitality and tendency toward courtesy. This predisposes African youths to not disagree with the views of their seniors even when they know that such views are incorrect. Related to this tendency is the general respect for the elderly in the African culture. In some cultures the young are socialized to be ingratiating. Such applicants will be prone to intentional distortion of relevant behaviors in order to win immediate approval from interviewers who come from cultures where such behaviors are valued in the young ones.

Other general interviewing problems are peculiar to African organizations. Interviewer and interviewee bring to the interviewing situation differing backgrounds and characteristics such as differences in gender, age, social status, and ethnic origin. These backgrounds and characteristics provide cues to the interviewer and interviewee about one another, thus affecting the result of the job interview. Characteristics and backgrounds are the sources of many attitudes, perceptions, expectations, stereotypes, and motives. Other general problems emanate from psychological and behavioral factors. These factors play an important role in determining patterns of interviewee response in an interview situation. They determine interviewee level of sensitivity to the interviewers' attitudes, to interviewers' style of asking questions, and to tone and nonverbal communication.

In order to minimize the effects of cultural response set and other general problems associated with interviewing in African organizations, interviewers must be knowledgeable of the cultural response set of interviewees in a dyadic interview interaction situation. The composition of the membership of the interviewing panel is very important. Interviewing panels must be representative with respect to gender, ethnicity, religious affiliation, geographical representation, and language. Such panels increase interviewees' trust and improve their communication.

Most interviews conducted in African organizations are badly done because it is believed that anybody can conduct interviews. For many people interviewing is just asking the applicant any questions. As a consequence most interviews are conducted in an unstructured manner; that is, interviews are usually conducted in an unplanned, casual, and loosely organized conversational manner between the interviewer and the interviewee. The interview questions are not usually structured. Rather, questions vary from one interviewer to another. The evaluation of the interviewee's responses also varies from interviewer to interviewer and from applicant to applicant. Organizations do not concern themselves with the predictive validity of interview processes. In the rating system used, one interviewer's ratings can determine the outcome of the process. Most personnel administrations are not aware that, when interviewing experienced applicants, they should use structured, patterned interview question that should be more technical in nature than when interviewing less experienced applicants.

Bingham (1949) maintains that a good interviewing session includes the interviewer's providing the interviewee with a frank job preview; that is, the interviewer provides the applicant with correct information about the job by answering questions about the business, the job, and working conditions. The interviewer must have attempted to convince the person interviewed that the organization is a good organization to work for by showing the opportunities that exist for the person to grow and advance if the applicant decides to join the company. The interviewer must be skillful in selling the organization to the interviewee. This is the public relations function of the interview process. The interviewer must have succeeded in steering the interviewee toward the job to which he or she is best suited in the organization. The interviewer through inter-personal skills should leave the interviewee with the feeling that a personal friendship has been established.

The Validity of Selection Interviews. This can be improved by structuring the interviews. Before conducting an interview, decide its purpose, that is, goals to be achieved. Interviewers should know the requirements of the job to be filled; they should recognize the public relations implications of the interview. They should allow the applicant time to talk and be aware of the need to avoid bias in interviewing persons of different gender, ethnic group, and beliefs.

No interviewer can remain oblivious to the gender, ethnic, and religious differences of the interviewees. These factors have been shown to affect interview results. Interviewers are prone to form sex-role, ethnic, and religious affiliation stereotypes (Seibel, 1967; Sanda, 1976; Ugwuegbu, 1994; Ugwuegbu and Obi, 1994). Negative and positive information affect interviewers' decisions (Constantin, 1976). Studies suggest that negative information is more salient than positive information; that is, the interviewer's decision is much more influenced by negative information about the interviewee than by positive information. The type of information available to the interviewer shows that when much information is available about the job, interviewers rely primarily on relevant factors in making selection decisions; when they have little information about the job, they rely more on factors less relevant to the job. The temporal placement of negative and positive information shows that when negative information about the interviewee surfaces early in the interview, it has more impact on interview decisions than when it surfaces later (latency and recency effects).

An effect of attitude similarity exists when applicants with attitudes similar to those of the interviewer receive more favorable ratings than applicants with attitudes different from those of the interviewer. More talkative candidates are rated more favorably. Interviewers are vulnerable to a "halo effect," that is, the tendency to allow one's overall impression of an applicant to generalize across trait ratings in either a positive, negative, or neutral direction. Attractive applicants are typically preferred, regardless of sex. Handicapped and older applicants tend to receive lower ratings. Training also improves interviewees self-presentation in employment interviews. Interviewer training always improves the reliability of the interview process and minimizes rating errors.

Personnel Testing

Personnel testing is not yet very popular in contemporary African organizations. Some multinational and banking organizations employ personnel tests and testing. In some instances the testing is limited to verbal and quantitative tests of abilities. The problem with the use of Western-designed tests for an African population is that such tests lack validity and reliability because they are not designed, standardized, and normalized for the African population. Tests are not generally culture-free. Aptitude tests do not predict managerial ability; where they are used at all, their use should be confined to initial screening of applicants.

Types of Tests

Most existing psychological tests for personnel selection were not standardized for the African population. In order to employ them for personnel purposes in Africa, the tests first have to be revalidated. The *Mental Measurements Yearbook* (Buros, 1978, 1998) contains thousands of published psychological tests for use in Western cultures. These tests cover the measurement of human behavior such as intelligence, interest, and psychomotor, mechanical aptitude, and clerical aptitude. Projective technique and tests measure personality characteristics. Psychologists who are members of the American Psychological Association can purchase the tests for use. Organizations that have a professional psychologist on their staff can also do so. Tests are so guided to ensure that scores in psychological tests are properly interpreted. Second, the ethical principles of psychologists are specifically directed toward the proper use and administration of psychological tests and the protection of the rights of clients or those to whom the tests are administered.

There are certain characteristics that all well-constructed tests must have in common, including standardization, norms, reliability, and validity. Every consumer of tests should consider these qualities when selecting a test for use. They constitute the ideals that every published test should strive to meet. These characteristics indicate the adequacy and suitability of a test that an organization intends to use.

Standardization. This refers to the demand that a test meets the characteristics of a good test. It also refers to the consistency or uniformity of procedures for administering and scoring a test. Since test scores obtained by job applicants are to be compared, test conditions must be identical for all those to be tested. Otherwise, any change in the testing procedures may disadvantage certain applicants. In order to maintain consistency in the administration of a test, the test developer must specify in the test manual the exact procedures to be followed when the test is being administered, such as time limits, oral instructions, ways of handling specific questions from those being tested, test materials needed, physical testing conditions such as seating facilities, and illumination, and scoring procedures. Organizations are supposed to follow the standardization procedures outlined in the manual very rigidly if the test is not to be compromised.

Norms. These indicate the relative standing of a job applicant among his or her comparison group, usually called the norm group. If you were told that a job applicant scored 60 percent on a mechanical reasoning test, this score would convey little information about the applicant's relative standing on mechanical reasoning ability. In order to give meaning to the score, 60 percent it must be compared with the scores obtained by a sample of similar individuals. This process is accomplished by means of test norms. Precisely, norms are a distribution of test scores obtained from a large sample of persons representative of the population of applicants being considered for the job. The distribution of scores of such a reference group serves as a yardstick against which a job applicant's score can be measured. The questions to be answered about the applicant's test score are, Does it coincide with the average score of the norm group, or is the applicant considerably above or below average? An applicant whose score comes within the 90th percentile has a score exceeding the scores obtained by 90 percent of those in the norm group.

Human resources planners and personnel managers involved in testing should make sure that they have the published characteristics of any test that they wish to use: validity, reliability, norms, and standardization. Norms presented in test manuals should state clearly the populations, that is, the groups with which users of the test will ordinarily compare the person tested. Unfortunately, many of the "tests" marketed by test developers in the African subregion may be worth less than the paper on which they are printed if the norms of such tests are not clearly stated. Most of these tests have no manuals, and the norms, validity, reliability, and other test characteristics are not demonstrated. Such tests are useless and should never be used in making any organizational decisions.

Reliability. This is one of the most important characteristics of any test. Reliability is the consistency with which the test measures a given behavior. It is the reproducibility or stability of a test over time. When making personnel decisions, a personnel manager must be fairly certain that when applicant Paul obtains a higher score on a selection test than applicant Peter, the difference between these two individuals would be the same if the test were given to them again at some other time. If test scores lack stability, the value of the test for selecting the better applicant is reduced.

No test is completely (i.e., 100 percent) reliable, no matter how ideal the testing conditions. This is because all tests are affected, to some extent, by uncontrollable, random changes that may affect the examinee, such as fatigue, emotional strain, and the testing conditions, such as unexpected noises, sudden changes in the weather, and changes in the examination environment, such as a sudden failure of electricity supply during the examination or shortage of water in the toilet nearby. It is very important that before a test is used for selection purposes, its reliability be shown to be adequate.

Reliability of a test can be determined in three ways. One is the *test-retest method,* which involves administering the same test on two different occasions to the same groups or sample and then correlating the scores on the first occasion with the scores on the second occasion. The closer the correlation coefficient is to 1.00, the more consistent are the test items. It is important for test manuals to report the time interval between administrations of the first test and the second test. This is because reliability coefficients tend to decrease the longer the interval between two test administrations. Anastasi (1982) maintains that the test-retest method is not appropriate with many psychological tests due to memory and practice effects. But the test-retest method is appropriate for tests requiring perceptual speed and for motor tests.

The second way of determining reliability is *equivalent form,* which requires that two equivalent forms of the same test be prepared and used rather than administering the test twice. Since the equivalent forms are administered once, it reduces the problem of memory and learning or practice that characterizes the test-retest method. The disadvantage of the equivalent form includes the problem of designing two forms that are similar in all respects except for their specific items. Second, it is more expensive to develop equivalent forms than to use other methods.

The third approach, which is concerned with the internal consistency of the test rather than with its temporal consistency, is the *split-halves method.* In order to find the split-half reliability, one should administer the test once, then divide the test by assigning the even-numbered items to one-half of the test and odd-numbered items to the other half, score the halves separately for each of the examinees, correlate the scores by the examinees on each half, then correlate both halves. Accentuate the correlation by means of the Spearman-Brown formula (see Anastasi, 1982). The split-halves reliability method is quite popular because it requires that the test be administered only once. Regardless of the method employed for the calculation of reliability of a test, the reliability estimates or correlation coefficient should fall in the range of r = .80 to r =.90 to be considered satisfactory for selection purposes.

Validity. This is the degree to which a test measures what it claims to measure. Each test is meant to measure a particular set of psychological domain, characteristics, or trait, or their behavioral components. Validity answers the question, How far does the test actually measure the specific domain? The specific methods employed for determining a test's validity are many. But criterion-related validity and content validity are the two main types of validity relevant to personnel selection and placement.

Criterion-related validity is determined by correlating the scores obtained by the individuals on the selection test with some available criterion of their job performance. For example, sales aptitude scores might be correlated with actual sales figures available for the period of a year or two. There are two kinds of criterion-related validity: predictive validity and concurrent validity. Wexley and Yukl (1984) maintain that of the two, predictive validity is the more convincing validity for selection purposes, since it comes closer to assessing the actual power of the selection test for predicting later job performance. To assess predictive validity, a test is administered to job applicants at the time of hiring and their scores are correlated with criterion measures (actual job performance) obtained at a later time (at the end of one year or so).

On the other hand, *concurrent validity* is determined by administering the test to employees presently on the job and correlating their scores with currently available measures of their job proficiency. Finally, *content validity* is usually employed for validating an achievement (or trade) test. It involves a systematic review of the test content by experts to determine whether it adequately measures the skills, knowledge, and abilities required by the job of interest. Each expert involved in the evaluation is given a set of test questions and asked to independently judge whether the skill, knowledge, or ability measured by each item is (1) essential, (2) useful but not essential, or (3) unnecessary to perform on the job (Cascio, 1982; Lawshe, 1975; and Wexley and Yukl, 1984).

Assessment Centers
Executive versatility involves adapting and performing effectively across a wide range of new situations and changing contexts (Sloan, 1994). It requires many different types of competencies and therefore must be appraised through multiple and integrated methods of assessment.

One of these assessment procedures is the assessment center method, which combines assessment techniques (such as tests, structured interviews, and simulations) and exposes participants to a variety of new, but realistic and job-relevant, situations. The technique is an ideal tool for assessing executive competencies as well as overall managerial versatility in handling a wide range of strategic organizational and interpersonal situations. Howard (1992, 1993), following a review of the status of the assessment center method, recommended its broader use as an excellent executive assessment tool.

The assessment center has been defined as a standardized, off-the-job procedure used for the identification of managerial potential for purposes of selection, placement, promotion, and/or development (Finkle, 1976; Moses and Byham, 1977; Wexley and Yukl, 1984). The procedure employs multiple methods of assessment, including observation of behavior in simulated situations. The development of assessment centers in the United States is ascribed to the efforts of psychologist Henry Murray and his associates at Harvard University. The procedure was set up for the Office of Strategic Services (OSS) to aid in choosing intelligence agents. The OSS center added interactive exercises and individual behavioral simulations to the method used by Murray at Harvard, making the technique a full-fledged assessment center in the contemporary meaning of the term.

The assessment center approach to selection has gained much popularity in recent years in the technologically advanced countries. There are presently no assessment centers in any African country. Some multinational companies in Africa, including banks, insurance companies, oil companies, and some manufacturing and distributive organizations, send their managers to their metropolitan centers in Europe and America to participate in assessment center evaluation when such officers are being considered for promotion to a more senior position. It is hoped that these organizations are aware of the negative experimenter effects of having Western psychologists to conduct assessment center exercises for these Africans.

Several studies have demonstrated the effectiveness of assessment centers in the United States. Fitzgerald (1980) in surveying large public jurisdictions (state and local governments) found that about 44 percent were using assessment centers in selecting persons for widely divergent departments, such as fire, police, and sanitation engineering. The American federal government is a heavy consumer of assessment centers. In addition to using this technique for evaluating managers, assessment programs have been developed to estimate the potential for success in sales (Bray and Campbell, 1968); police work at four levels (Dunnette and Motowidlo, 1975); the pharmacy profession; and stockbroker jobs (Hellerrik, Hunt, and Silzer, 1976). Thus, the assessment center method is sufficiently flexible to evaluate the potential for many occupations.

Objectives of Assessment Centers. These according to McCormick and Ilgen (1980), are the evaluation of individuals for future development and growth. The candidates for assessment centers are individual employees in organizations who are in supervisory and management positions or who are candidates for such positions. In some instances, too, assessment centers are organized for the selection of applicants for employment or for new employees, in the case of the latter, to provide an assessment of their future assignments or development and for the former, to assess their potential for employment.

The activities and exercises employed in assessment centers include such things as management games, group discussions, tests, interviews, self-ratings, and problem-solving exercises. The final assessment by the staff is based on "data" resulting from these activities and observations of the participants by the staff.

Techniques of Assessment. In the centers these include *An In-basket Test,* which is a technique used for management training as well as for selection purposes. The name comes from the fact that the test consists of an assortment of items such as might be found in a manager's in-basket. Such a basket might contain letters, reports, memos, notes, requests, and directives. Each candidate taking such a selection or training test is confronted with these and must "do" something with each of the items or note down what action he or she would take about them if in a manager's job. For example, the candidate may be asked to "answer" a letter and in some instances may be asked to give reasons for the "action." There is a standard procedure, which includes taking into consideration the content of the behavior, the type of behavior, and rating on overall performance.

A *leaderless group discussion* is another method that is often used in assessment centers. This method is a conference of several people in which no formal leader has been assigned. The discussion is often of a competitive nature in which each participant takes a position and tries to win its adoption by the group. For example, each participant is assigned the role of a general manager (human resources, sales, manufacturing, etc.) of a company. The company is said to be considering purchasing three new sites. The six general managers are meeting to decide which of the sites should be selected. The conflict for each manager is to win selection of the site that he or she favors versus the selection of the best possible site for the company. Sometimes the leaderless group discussion is of a cooperative nature in which each participant is assigned a role and told to help the group make an important decision (e.g., whether or not to acquire another company).

Dyadic situations are also employed, in which, for example, the candidate is interviewed in a face-to-face situation about the action taken in clearing the in-basket or is asked to play the role of a manager interviewing a capable, but troublesome, employee, a standardized role played by a member of staff. Others are *individual exercises*, which are usually included to test written communication skills or a speaking exercise as an example of oral communication skills. The biographical inventory blank, which the candidate has filled out earlier, forms the basis of conducting a *life history interview* with the candidate. Such an interview covers the candidate's personal history, work history, and history of goals and values. Peer ratings, sociometric ratings, and self-ratings are often collected. Projective tests such as the Thematic

Apperception Test (TAT) and Sentence Completion Tests are used to reveal the quality and strength of the candidate's motivations for a career in management In some centers psychometric tests, measuring mental ability, interests, values, and personality, are also administered. Typically, test scores are not used in making recommendations or decisions about candidates.

Assessment components of some centers may take four days. During the simulation   participants (maximum of 12) assume the role of the general manager of a division in a large organization and work independently and in groups on both division and specific, company-wide issues. Specifically trained organizational psychologists serve as assessors and role players in one-on-one meetings.

The dimensions assessed in assessment centers are those believed to reflect characteristics important in a managerial career, such as general mental ability, and those that might be affected by managerial experience, such as organizational value orientation. A dimension that is expected to be both important in careers and affected by them is primacy of work; how important satisfaction from work is compared to satisfaction from other areas of life.

The validity of the assessment center has been demonstrated by several studies. For example, Ritchie (1994) confirmed the predictive validity of the assessment center ratings of senior management potential. Among all the participants in the study sample, those who received ratings of excellent potential were more likely to advance to senior management positions than those seen as having less potential. Ritchie's finding is consistent with findings from other studies of the validity of the assessment center programs targeted at middle-level and lower-level management potential (Bray and Grant, 1966; Kraut and Scott, 1972; Moses, 1972).

In spite of the predictive validity of assessment centers, some observers still have some criticism about the procedure. Such criticism maintains that much of the practice of professional assessment relies primarily on tests and interviews and does not add the powerful tool of simulation, through which an individual's ability to apply aptitudes in action and handle new challenges can be directly assessed.

PLACEMENT

Placement is choosing from a number of possible jobs the one best suited to a given job candidate. In such an instance, the individual is already employed, and the placement decision is made to assign the employee to the job for which he or she is considered best qualified.

Decisions about placing a specific individual employee in a specific job or position in the organization or training that person for a specific job are important aspects of the function of human resources planning. The function is that of "matching" an individual to a job after weighing the actual or potential skill qualifications of the employee and the requirements of the job. Such decisions are usually based on data or on judgments of the candidate's qualifications as related to the requirements of the job to be performed. Classification, on the other hand, refers to a process of assigning pools of individuals to pools of jobs on the basis of a match between each individual and each job.

Job Requirement and Employee Specification

The objective of personnel selection should be to identify those who are most likely to succeed in performing the job in question. That implies that the individuals have the prerequisite skills, knowledge, and motivation to successfully accomplish the tasks of the job. This assumes knowledge of the job characteristics and the characteristics of a successful candidate through job specifications and personnel specifications.

McCormick and Ilgen (1980) distinguished two different classes of traits associated with success in a given occupation or job, namely intrinsic characteristics or traits and those associated with the environment of work. Intrinsic characteristics are peculiar to the successful performance of each job (e.g., visual acuity and finger dexterity). In addition to the intrinsic requirements, such jobs require aptitude and sensory and physical abilities of candidates who would be successful in the performance of the jobs. The intrinsic requirements vary from job to job.

Environmental characteristics include the type of workers available for work at a given time. Types of workers in a given environment vary from time to time. This variability requires that personnel specifications be modified in accordance with changes in the population or pool of available workers. Some of the personnel specifications are work experience, education and training, biographical data (such as those given on application forms), and physical data (such as height, weight, and general health).

Following job specifications and personnel specifications, the personnel manager can employ *regression equation* and/or *profile analysis* in making placement decisions. Regression analysis is used to predict an applicant's success in each of the job openings available. The personnel decision would then be to place individuals on that job for which each has the highest predictor criterion score. A profile analysis, on the other hand, is used to place an applicant on a job for which the applicant's profile matches the profile of the currently successful workers on the job.

SUMMARY

In many large organizations in Africa the general managers, in addition to their specific management responsibilities, usually perform the functions of human resources planners, because the functions and need for human resources planning and development sector are not adequately understood. Instead, many organizations have as one of the top managers a human relations officer whose job description is confined to the management of the relationships among the labor union, the employers' association, and the government. Human resources planning and development encompass personnel management and human relations functions and include the short-, medium-, and long-term forecasting, planning, provision, and management of personnel, compensation, staff development and training, and, above all, the development of improved work methods.

African governments are committed to the development of human resources. They do this through the formal and informal education systems, vocational and technical skills institutes, training in agricultural skills, management development institutions, and private organizations. In spite of all the efforts of these agencies, Africa is still in short supply of managerial, professional, and technical manpower needed for the management of its industries and agricultural organizations. One problem has been that governments' human resources planning through schools and other agencies is not closely tied to industrial planning and development.

While organizations in the developed countries have a three-stage human resources planning and development, African organizations can engage only in the short-term planning because of the dearth of relevant information for planning, lack of expertise, and the level of instability and unpredictability in the environment. Sometimes the medium and the long-term human resources planning of the multinational and expatriate organizations is drawn in Europe or North America without any input from the African line managers. Such grafted human resources planning does not meet the realities of the African management environment.

Overstaffing, which is common in African organizations, is a result of faulty job analysis. A major function of job analysis is to enable the manager to know how many job openings are to be filled and at what levels and the skill requirements of those openings. Following job analysis, other aspects of selection and placement processes, such as information gathered through application blanks, letters of recommendation, selection interviews, personnel testing, and assessment center outcomes, would be properly used to aid selection and placement decisions. African organizations need improved and well designed application blanks and knowledge of how to utilize the information in the application blanks, letters of recommendation, and interview processes to help select good job candidates. Studies have shown that when constructed well, a weighted biographical information blank is one of the most valuable selection and placement devices that can be successfully used to predict effective performance on a variety of jobs.

Another aspect of the selection process that is not properly utilized in frican organizations is the selection interview. This partly emanates from the erroneous belief that anybody can conduct a job interview. Other peculiar major problems with selection interviews are cultural response set, influence of behavioral tendencies such as African hospitality and courtesy, and characteristics of the interviewee and the interviewer. These tend to affect interpersonal interactions in interview sessions and to bias the outcomes. Managers should not only know the objective of a given interview but communicate the purpose to every interviewer in addition to structuring the interview. Tests are useful if the manager knows how to go about selecting the most relevant and valid tests for use. Many organizations in Africa presently employ aptitude tests, but none has cared about the criterion-related or the ccncurrent validity of these tests.

8

Evaluation of Employee Performance

Organizations are concerned with performance at the individual, group or departmental, and entire organizational levels. The assumption underlying such concern is that job performance can be measured in concrete terms. Two problems, however, confront efforts to measure job performance. One is that people do not know what constitutes good work behavior. For most aspects of work, people do not know how to distinguish good workers from those who are not so good. This is because people do not agree on the appropriate criteria for specifying good performance.

The second problem is that sometimes experts know what to measure but do not know how to measure it adequately. Jobs vary considerably. Howell and Dipboye (1982) point out that some jobs, such as routine production jobs, permit a relatively good measurement of output. For example, it is easy to count the number of matchboxes packed by a laborer in an hour or a day, while other jobs, such as higher-level managerial jobs, have no clearly defined link with production. The only way commonly used to measure performance is to rely on the subjective judgment of managers or the board of directors' opinions.

The objective of this chapter is to assess the stage of development of employee appraisal in African organizations. The areas to be covered include performance evaluation, the need to appraise employees, how to select and develop performance appraisal, and common errors to avoid in the use of subjective performance appraisal in African organizations.

PERFORMANCE EVALUATION IN AFRICAN ORGANIZATIONS
Performance evaluation is a systematic attempt to gauge how well an employee is doing a job. In most small and medium-sized organizations in Africa and most government jobs employees do not have a thorough knowledge of what they are expected to do or what their job position entails. Equity theory

is concerned with the balance between what a worker puts in and what is received relative to what a comparison-other gets. In an equitable incentive system, a person is paid relative to the worth of the job and relative to the contributions to that job through the employee's performance. In many African countries these relationships are neither clearly specified, nor are the employees and employers conscious of them. For the most part, nobody can justify why an employee is paid what he or she receives. For example, at a point in Nigeria, before the recent salary increases for government workers and university staff, a driver at the Nigerian National Petroleum Corporation earned more pay than a university professor or a high court judge. Incentive systems in most African countries are ill defined, irrational, and downright inequitable, thus creating opportunities for labor conflict, dissatisfaction, and corruption.

Very few organizations pay performance appraisal the attention that it deserves. In some companies or organizations, the performance appraisal is carried out annually for the junior and intermediate workers in an environment where there are no precise job descriptions or job specifications. There is also no standardized system that can compare with the *Dictionary of Occupational Titles* (DOT) (U.S. Training and Employment Services [USTES], 1972).

Appraisal instruments are not commonly available. Those that exist have questionable validity or reliability and may be impractical to use. Formal performance appraisal is designed to achieve the following ends:

- to provide systematic judgments to support reasons for salary increases, promotions, transfers, and sometimes demotions or terminations
- to inform subordinates how well they are doing on the job and to suggest needed changes in the employees' behavior, attitudes, skills, or job knowledge
- to serve as a vehicle for letting the employees know "where they stand" with the managers
- to serve as a basis for the coaching and counseling of the individual employee by the manager

Performance appraisal is inevitable if African organizations are to achieve their goal of having a competitive edge, if incentive systems are to develop and work well, if the performance-reward contingency is to be properly developed and implemented, and if training programs are to be properly targeted at the individuals and groups of employees that need them. Employee evaluation would be meaningless without some explicit specification of what workers are expected to do on their jobs. The employee as well as the appraising person must agree on what the job entails. In other words, there must be a frame of reference before a worker's performance can be satisfactorily measured. This is essential for a fair and accurate appraisal system.

A vivid example of the appraising situation in Africa is the numerous common school examinations that students go through every year. Take the Senior Secondary School Certificate Examination, which is conducted by the West African Examinations Council (WAEC). The syllabus contains an explicit specification of what the students are supposed to master given a specific time period. The teachers, students, and the appraising body, WAEC, are agreed on this. WAEC is guided by the syllabus when setting the students' final examination papers. WAEC's evaluation of each student's performance is valid if, and only if, the questions of each examination paper are based entirely on the syllabus. As the senior secondary school syllabus is to WAEC examinations, so is job description to performance evaluation. There must be a job description before one can have a valid performance evaluation.

Similarly, government trade centers have standards by which they measure whether an individual has completed the training successfully or not. An individual's success is measured by looking at details spelled out in the center's syllabus and then asking whether the individual has acquired the expected skills and the requisite behaviors that go with those skills. In developed countries the details of the job that an individual is expected to perform in a given job position and the expected behaviors are codified and made available to the employee. Such compiled duty information is called job description.

JOB DESCRIPTION

This is defined as a written statement describing the duties and responsibilities of a job. A job description specifies what a job incumbent does and how, why, and under what circumstances it is done. The type of qualifications and skills needed by the employee to carry out these duties is called job specifications or job requirements.

In addition to performance appraisal, an accurate description of job characteristics in organizations has other functions. Job description is the basis of the incentive system in organizations. It is very useful for the development of effective selection, placement, training, and compensation programs. It serves as the basis for the evaluation of selection, placement, and training programs and for the determination of recruitment and planning for new employees. Efficient job description is, to some degree, the principal determinant of all personnel functions in an organization

Howell and Dipboye (1982) insist that a worker's compensation should reflect not only how much the job that the employee is performing is worth but also how much the worker is worth in the job. Pay systems based on this age-old philosophy are known as *incentive systems.* We are also reminded that performance is not the only possible basis for pay, nor is pay the only reward for performance, according to Howell and Dipboye (1982). Nevertheless, the logic of incentive compensation is widely accepted everywhere, including in African organizations. This illustrates the importance of accurate performance evaluation; without it, incentive systems make no sense. Accurate performance evaluation makes incentive systems work through making employees understand the performance-reward contingency. Where this does not exist, as in many African countries, workers may not perceive the relation between reward and performance.

This observation is instructive to Oloko (1977), who asserted that since Nigerian workers do not increase their productivity in response to government salary awards, "they do not perceive the relationship between reward and performance." What the proponent forgot is that such national salary awards to workers are not made contingent upon supported good performance. Salary awards come as a function of labor union agitation and pressure. They are not a result of an employee's job efforts. They are usually awarded to all workers, those who have worked hard and those who have not worked hard. They do not discriminate between levels of efforts of workers and therefore cannot teach employees the value of good work performance.

Approaches to Job Description

If it is important to describe precisely what is expected of employees in various work roles, how does one accomplish this description? Job analysis is one way of achieving that objective (see Chapter 7). The second is through the use of standard classification systems by which one matches the to-be-described jobs to the standard definitions—where such definitions exist.

In most African countries there are no standard definitions that are generally accepted. Most international and big, indigenous organizations in Africa depend on definitions and titles borrowed from European countries and the United States. The most widely used standard system is furnished by USTES. This agency of the American government surveys, analyzes, and classifies America's population of jobs on a periodic basis. The results of such efforts appear in the DOT, which lists brief definitions of several thousands of current job titles. Howell and Dipboye (1982) maintain that the ultimate ideal of what USTES is doing is to produce "an integrated set of analytic procedures, descriptive terms, rules for combining those terms into task statements, and scheme for classifying jobs that would apply to any job whatsoever and would leave almost nothing to the interpretation of the analyst." (p. 180) Such a system makes it possible to achieve the same precise meaning of any job, no matter who described it. In addition to aiding the job analyst and facilitating the personnel functions, a standard set of descriptions and the availability of description rules give people a common language with which to communicate about work and work characteristics. Finally, it shows the employee and the organization how jobs are related to each other.

The digital divide between the United States and African countries will increase the problem of utilizing the DOT as a guide to job description in Africa. Soon most of the job titles that exist in DOT will not have corresponding job titles in African organizations. Another problem with any standardized system is that it does not usually capture all the aspects of any specific job. It often leaves out the details of the environment in which jobs are performed. Consider, for example, the duties of a secretary in one organization, which may be different from those in other organizations, or the duties of a secretary in an African organization and an American organization. In most African organizations the position of secretary is made up of five levels: in descending order of rank, personal secretary, secretary I, II, and III and typist. In African organizations these five levels of employees share the functions of secretary. They may also have the help of a full-time messenger whose duties include handling mail and files and running errands, while in most organizations in the United States the functions of secretary (administrative assistant) may be performed by one individual. It becomes important, therefore, for an organization to conduct it own job analysis to get appropriate descriptions of its jobs. Once what people do is known, the next step is to tag a monetary value on it. This whole process, according to Howell and Dipboye (1982), is known as *job evaluation.*

There are several ways of assessing what a given job is worth. Bass and Barrett (1972) listed four methods of establishing the value of each job in an organization: *ranking, classification, factor comparison,* and the *points system.* Job evaluation usually arouses labor objections since it is not based on seniority. Attempts to determine the value of each job touches on several interest groups, such as organized labor, individual employees, management personnel, and the various divisions or departments. In order to minimize objections, these groups should be involved in a committee or team, which would be charged with this responsibility of determining the value attached to jobs in the organization. Such a committee or team should establish the standards or criteria to be used to measure the jobs.

Ranking requires that the committee or team in charge of this function rank and list all the jobs from the most to the least valuable. In ranking, each job is considered as a unit. Classification is similar to ranking with the exception that it requires the initial specification of a set of ordered value categories into which jobs are then sorted. Once the jobs are ordered or classified, a pay scale is applied to each rank.

Factor comparison and the points systems are similar to each other and differ from the other methods in that both involve evaluating jobs in terms of underlying factors or common dimensions rather than as complete entities. Howell and Dipboye (1982) maintain that in order to carry out an evaluation, the manager should first determine the common factors that underlie the set of jobs to be evaluated, how much of each factor is present in each job, and how much each level of each factor is worth.

How the manager determines how much each level of each factor is worth indicates whether one is dealing with factor comparison or the points method, according to Howell and Dipboye (1982). For the factor comparison approach, a small, representative sample of key jobs is selected, and to each is assigned what is agreed upon as an equitable salary range. Salary levels are then set for the other jobs by comparison of their factor composition with that of the key jobs. An example makes this clearer. Suppose driving is a key job in a long-distance trailer company, and it pays ₦30.00 (Nigerian naira) per hour. Of this, 50 percent (or ₦15.00) is for a stress demands factor, 30 percent (or ₦9.00) is for a working condition factor, and 20 percent (or ₦6.00) is for a skill factor. Having established these standards, they are applied across the board. That is, all jobs having comparable physical demands in that company would be awarded ₦15.00 for this factor, all with comparable working conditions would earn ₦9.00 for this factor, and those with comparable skills would earn ₦6.00 for this factor. The total salary for a given job would be the total of all its factor values.

If the points method is used, each possible level of each factor is first evaluated in terms of points. Stress demands, for example, might be judged to exist at four levels (depending on whether the driving is done during the day or night), worth 40, 30, 20, and 10 points, respectively, while the skills factor exists at five levels worth 50, 40, 30, 20, and 10 points, respectively. Each job is evaluated on the basis of the points that it accrues for its particular level of each factor. The truck driver might get 40 points for physical demands, 30 points for working conditions, and 30 points for skills. After the total point value has been established for all the jobs the points are converted to monetary value. If each point were set to equal 30 kobo (100 Nigerian kobo in one naira) per hour, for example, the truck driver would earn ₦30 per hour (100 points multiply by 30 Nigerian kobo). The points system, according to Howell and Dipboye (1982), sets up an internally consistent evaluation structure within which jobs are located before any consideration is given to their monetary value. The whole structure is thereafter converted to money. New jobs need only to be fitted into the structure, and their pay rates are determined automatically. Any future change in the point conversion would affect all jobs proportionately. The factor-based methods have advantages over the others in that they tend to produce more objective, consistent, and complete estimates of a job's worth. Their disadvantage is that the procedures are more complex and time-consuming.

REASONS FOR APPRAISING EMPLOYEE PERFORMANCE

How to determine workers' benefits, wages, and promotion constitutes a central problem for managers of African organizations. This problem has led, in each of the African countries, the government's being the major determinant of workers' benefits, wages, and salaries. The unfortunate thing about government-determined wages is that it is devoid of market forces. Workers are not distinguished within their ranks. For example, all professors irrespective of their areas of specialization or the status of their university, are paid at the same salary rate. All personal or confidential secretaries irrespective of their proficiency, receive the same scale of pay. Again, workers, whether they work in the cities or rural areas, are paid at the same rate. Individual performance and contributions are not taken into consideration when workers are rewarded. The nonspecificity of government-determined wages and benefits is the chief cause of controversies, labor conflicts, worker dissatisfaction, low morale, and low motivation, which manifest themselves in Africa's low productivity and low economic capacity. In Europe and the United States workers are appraised for several reasons.

Reward

This is the workers' return for their contributions such as the nature of the work they do and their level of education, skill, expertise, and experience. Other factors that influence reward or the worth of the job are working conditions, degree of responsibility, and physical demands. But the difference between two workers within the same job is a function of both tenure and job performance.

The principle that workers should be rewarded on the basis of these attributes as well as their productivity is the rule of thumb in the developed countries of the world but not in any system where government controls workers' wages. One important reason for evaluating employee performance is to provide a fair basis for determining an employee's reward, compensation, or salary. Rewards that are not based on performance violate the principle of contingency. Other reward systems that violate this principle are those based on seniority, mass awards, automatic annual increases, and awards based on political manipulation of workers.

Promotion
This is another important reason that organizations appraise their employees. Workers are appraised to determine who should be promoted and who should not. Some organizations with strong unions promote on a seniority basis. In the civil service and the parastatals, employees are considered for promotion after a minimum number of years. The number of years that workers are supposed to stay on a given job before being considered for promotion is specified. Workers' motivation thus becomes the completion of the minimum number of years of service rather than effective performance. Many workers take this as a right and usually demand to be recommended for promotion by their head of department or supervisor in spite of their record of poor performance.

It is not always true that the best performers are promoted as against poor performers. Promoting the best or most senior employee often results in the so-called *Peter Principle*—the promotion of employees until they reach their highest level of incompetence. Aamodt (1996) has warned that if performance evaluations are to be used to promote employees, care should be taken to ensure that the employee is well evaluated, using on-the-job dimensions that are similar to the higher position's dimensions.

Sometimes some governments in African countries freeze employment of new applicants and promotion of employees as a means of holding inflation down or reducing government costs. When such is the case, evaluation processes in organizations play no relevant roles in management for the employees.

Performance Deficiencies
Workers' deficiencies are revealed through appraising employee performance. Regular performance evaluations have the added advantage of revealing performance deficiencies to be corrected in the workforce of an organization as well as appropriate competencies to be strengthened and rewarded. Organizations that do not conduct regular evaluations of their workforce have no knowledge of employees' competence and cannot provide them with appropriate feedback about their performance.

Aamodt (1996) maintains that improving employee performance is, by far, the most important use of performance evaluation. This is achieved by providing workers with feedback about what they are doing right or wrong. Performance evaluation also helps the organization to develop training programs for building appropriate skills for use in the near future. It provides excellent opportunities to meet with employees to discuss their strengths and weaknesses and how the strengths can be enhanced and weaknesses eliminated or minimized. It also helps the organization to assess the effectiveness of training programs by comparing employees' performance before and after participating in a training program.

Personnel Research

Another reason for appraising employees is for purposes of organizational research. Employee evaluation provides the data for some aspect of the human resources department functions. Furthermore, initial judgments of the potential of employees must be continually revalidated, as must the employment tests, which should be continuously monitored. One way of doing this is by correlating test scores with some measure of job performance. This requires that an accurate and reliable measure of job performance or the initial judgments about employee performance be available.

PROCESS OF PERFORMANCE APPRAISAL

The major problem that confronts a manager when considering the process of appraisal includes who should be used in evaluating the employees. Where does the manager obtain reliable performance appraisal instruments since they are not readily accessible in the African environment? This section discusses how managers go about obtaining good assessment of their employees' performance. The role of managers or supervisors, peers, subordinates, and customers in performance appraisal is discussed. The problem of determining an individual worker's good or poor performance remains the main problem of performance appraisal and reemphasizes the central importance of frame of reference in the evaluation process.

Authorities

Managers, heads of department, and supervisors, are the authorities most frequently used by organizations in Africa to obtain indices of employee performance. These evaluations are obtained in the form of questionnaire ratings. In African organizations such evaluations are not obtained regularly as is the case in industrialized countries. In many of these organizations employee evaluations are not conducted; in others they are carried out only once a year, often only for nonmanagement personnel.

The manager or the head of department conducts almost all performance appraisals in African organizations. This is due to the belief that managers or heads of department are best able to evaluate the extent to which employees perform their respective responsibilities and contribute to the overall success of the organization. It is believed that the manager or head of department interacts with each employee and, through such interaction, is better able to judge the effectiveness of each employee. Often managers may not see every aspect of an employee's behavior; they do, however, see the end result of his or her performance efforts. For example, a manager may not see the actual behavior of a telephone operator but receives reports of attitude and performance from other employees and customers. By reviewing a teller's daily records of transactions, a bank supervisor gets to know the level of the teller's performance. Managers, heads of departments, and supervisors receive official and unofficial reports of the employees under them. They can thus be reliable judges of workers under them because they see more than the *results* of employees' work efforts. In very large organizations with a large number of employees, the head of department or the manager sometimes may delegate the responsibility of evaluating the employees to the section head.

Peers
Those people who work with each other often see the actual work behavior of each other. Peer ratings are usually ratings of work behavior and performance by employees who work directly with another employee. For example, a secretary may be rated by other secretaries in the same department or section, while bank tellers in the same bank or branch of a bank would rate other bank tellers. Other employees, too, especially those who come into constant contact with the employee in the organization, can provide useful ratings. This procedure is not often followed in African organizations. For one thing, employees see themselves as exploited by the organization and management. They are unified in this perception and support union activities against management. Asking them to evaluate each other may produce resistance to management and the organization, resulting in more biased positive ratings for each other.

Research results from advanced economies show that peer ratings are fairly reliable only when the peers who make the ratings are similar to, and well acquainted with, the one being rated (Aamodt, 1996; Landy and Guion, 1970; Mumford, 1983). Peer ratings have also been found to be highly predictive of the future success of promoted employees, and they tend to correlate highly with supervisor ratings (Cederbloom, 1989). Most African organizations are probably unaware that peer ratings are a useful tool of employee appraisal. Fahr, Cannella, and Bedeian (1991) found that peer ratings are lenient when used for evaluation purposes but not when they are used to provide feedback to employees (Aamodt, 1996).

There are also suggestions from research that some employees are more lenient in their peer ratings than others. For example, Saavedra and Kwun (1993) showed that high performers evaluate their peers more strictly than do low performers. Aamodt (1996) suggests that this is probably due to the fact that employees compare others to themselves, resulting in high-performing peers not being impressed by "less productive" peers. Another explanation could be that subjects used in the studies are not members of a cohesive group or members of a union.

Subordinates
These are sometimes used to rate their supervisor or head of department. Subordinates' ratings are unheard of in African organizations. Even in the developed economies of Europe and North America, subordinates' ratings can be difficult to obtain because employees fear reprisals and a backlash if they rate

their supervisor unfavorably. Cultural deference for elders and people in authority position and management distance between the supervisor and the subordinates make the introduction and use of subordinates' ratings in African organizations improbable at the present time.

Subordinates' feedback can be encouraged in African organizations provided supervisors and department heads appear tolerant to employees' comments and opinions (Baumgartner, 1994). Other research works (Furnham and Stringfield, 1994; Riggio and Cole, 1992) show that subordinates' ratings correlate highly with upper-management ratings of supervisors' performances. Upward feedback, or feedback from subordinates to their supervisors, has been found to improve the performance of poorly performing managers (Atwater, Roush, and Fischthal, 1995; Smither, London, Vasilopoulos, Reilly, Millsap, and Salvemini, 1995).

Customers

Sometimes are used to appraise the organizations that they patronize. "If you like our service, tell your friends. If you do not, tell us." This is a notice commonly displayed in some shops in Nigeria. This shows that some organizations realize the importance of feedback from customers. It is unlikely that organizations would ask their customers to fill out performance appraisal questionnaires on an employee. In some organizations in Africa it is mandatory to mount suggestion boxes in their general offices where customers can drop any complaints. Feedback may be obtained when customers compliment a manager about one of the employees. Formerly, customers could provide feedback by completing evaluation cards after they had been served in a restaurant, for example, as displayed in Figure 8.1. Here customers are handed a card containing four or more short questions about the food that they were served, the manner of service, and their intention to return to the restaurant in the future.

Figure 8.1
Chicken Grotto Fast Foods : Customer Evaluation Card

Dear Customer
We value your patronage and we endeavor to make each of your visits a dining pleasure. To help us reach our goal of serving you better, we would appreciate your completing this card and placing it in our suggestion box on your way out.

1.	Was your food cooked properly?	Y	N
2.	Was your server friendly?	Y	N
3.	Was your server efficient?	Y	N
4.	Do you plan to return?	Y	N
5.	Who was your server? _____		
	Comment:_____		

Source: Adapted from Aamodt (1996, p. 262).

The customers complete the card and drop it as they leave the restaurant. In the United States organizations seek feedback through what they call *secret shoppers*. These are current customers of a company who have been secretly enlisted to periodically evaluate the service that they receive from the organization. In return for their ratings, secret shoppers receive favors from the organizations ranging from free meals to monetary rewards.

Self-Appraisal

In this method the employees are asked to rate themselves or their performance. Asking employees to evaluate their own work behavior and performance is also not very common in African organizations. Do employees actually know their own behavior and performance level? Even if they know, are they likely to be sincere in rating themselves? Research in self-appraisals in the United States shows that self-appraisal tends to suffer from a leniency effect (Holzbach, 1978; Meyer, 1980). Self-ratings also correlate moderately with actual performance (Mabe and West, 1982) and poorly with subordinate ratings (London and Wohlers, 1991). Whether these findings in North America will hold true in the African subregion is yet to be demonstrated. The prediction, however, is that African employees will tend to rate themselves as average performers. Their ratings will tend to suffer from a central tendency effect, which is a function of the African culture.

To maximize the benefits of these performance appraisal approaches and minimize their individual disadvantages, an organization is advised to combine the approaches. For example, supervisors' ratings can be combined with self-appraisal and peer ratings. Second, before introducing performance appraisal in any African organization, the raters must be trained so as to minimize leniency and central tendency effects and other biases that may affect the validity and reliability of the ratings.

Human Errors in the Use of Subjective Methods

Subjective measures are, by their nature, subject to distortions arising from individual differences in perception, attitudes, and beliefs. Often the individuals who hold such perceptions and attitudes are not aware of their consequences. Others who are aware but persist in their attitudes and perceptions are motivated by factors that are not consistent with the objectives of performance appraisal procedures. Human error is one of the variables that bias subjective performance appraisal procedures. The primary consequence of such errors is that crucial organizational decisions about promotion, remuneration, transfer, or termination are made based on invalid and unreliable data. An organization protects itself from such errors through constructing better performance appraisal instruments, providing special training and awareness for the raters, and motivating raters to appraise more accurately. There are several common human errors often discussed by authors.

Leniency, Strictness, and the Central Tendency. These are some of the errors that characterize subjective assessment of workers' performance.

Anybody who is familiar with the behavior of raters in the field will have noticed that when some people are asked to evaluate others, they are reluctant to give extremely high or low ratings. This is true in the African cultural environment, where it is regarded as inappropriate to be judgmental and where it is preferable to agree with a consensual position than exercise individual views. Some workers tend to concentrate their ratings toward the upper end, while others tend to concentrate theirs toward the lower end of the scale.

Central tendency errors occur when raters continuously concentrate their rating scores at the center or at the average point on a rating scale, in spite of actual large differences in proficiency among those being rated. Leniency errors occur when raters concentrate their ratings toward the upper end, while the strictness errors occur when raters bias their ratings by piling their scores at the lower end of the scale. The problem that these errors create for an appraisal program is that they give an apparent impression that there are no significant differences in proficiency between those being rated when, indeed, actual differences exist. It messes up an appraisal program by creating difficulty in cross-departmental or organizational comparisons.

Characteristics of Rater. These can influence the accuracy of ratings. For example, research has shown that supervisors who are effective in their own jobs are more capable of differentiating between good and poor employees and are less likely to commit leniency errors (Kirchner and Reisberg, 1962). Other traits that affect supervisors' ratings include ethnicity, religiosity, and being authoritarian or production-oriented. Landy and Farr (1980) have shown that production-oriented supervisors tend to be less lenient than those who are employee-oriented when rating subordinates. Korman (1971) demonstrated that better raters have a higher level of intelligence and better analytical thinking ability than poor raters.

Halo Effect. This is the tendency to rate an employee high on many factors because the rater assumes that employees who have one positive characteristic must have others or the tendency to rate an employee low on many factors because the rater assumes that employees who one negative characteristic must have others of that type. For example, a supervisor whose cultural values encourage compliance and conformity may tend to rate conforming subordinates high on characteristics other than compliant behavior. The high value that the supervisor places on compliance and conformity should not influence the rating of the subordinates on other more relevant and important characteristics such as self-reliance, learning ability, emotional stability, and team spirit. The problem is, How does an organization prevent such a supervisor from being influenced by these cultural orientations? Wexley and Yukl (1984) suggest that supervisors can reduce errors from the halo effect by rating all subordinates on the first dimension, then rating all subordinates on the second dimension, and so on until the subordinates are rated on all the dimensions. Making the rating scale benchmarks more behavioral and expressing the factors to be rated in precise terms so that the raters are quite clear about each characteristic that they are rating also help to reduce halo errors. This suggestion may not eliminate completely the effect of culturally embedded behavioral orientation and expectations that influence halo effects.

Rater's Organizational Position. This has been associated with the level of accuracy of the ratings. The more organizational distance between the rater and the worker being rated, the less accurate and relevant the ratings (Wexley and Yukl, 1984). In other words, supervisors who are near the employees, can observe their work behavior, and can see the finished product give a more accurate rating of the subordinates, while those who are two or three organizational levels from the subordinates and have no opportunity to observe the subordinates' work behavior or finished products have inadequate information for rating the subordinates' performance. They would, of course, call for the employees' files, but in African organizations, with the exception of management queries, other performance records and ratings of employee performance are not often kept. Appraisals should be conducted by supervisors who have had the opportunity to observe employees' job behavior.

Personal Bias. This emanates from some social psychological factors and aspects of biographical background of the raters and ratees, such as physical attractiveness, ethnic and religious affiliation, seniority in the organization, level of education, age, social standing in the society, perceived job experience, and personality. These can cause distortions in managers' or supervisors' ratings of their subordinates. A large number of studies show that physically attractive people are evaluated more positively than are unattractive people (Berscheid and Walster, 1978). Other studies also show that similar individuals receive more positive ratings than dissimilar people (Byrne and Wong, 1962; Hendrick and Hawkins, 1969; Ugwuegbu, 1976).

Sex-role stereotypes may also operate to distort performance ratings. For example, in a well-designed study to investigate sex-role bias in personnel decisions involving selection in Nigerian industrial organizations, Ugwuegbu and Obi (1994) requested actively employed personnel managers to read manipulated background information of applicants, either male or female, following which the personnel managers were requested to rate the applicants on the following job-related dimensions: qualifications, probability of being considered for the position, expected level of performance, and probability of success on the job if eventually hired. The results indicated that a male applicant is significantly rated higher on access, judged as better in performance, rated better on background, and expected to be more successful if eventually hired than a female applicant.

Ugwuegbu (2000, 1994, 1986) demonstrated in several studies that ethnicity increases the social distance of interacting individuals. Managers with greater social distances from their workers tend to evaluate employees who are from different ethnic groups more negatively than employees from the same ethnic group.

Proximity Errors. These occur when a rating on one dimension generalizes to the dimension that immediately follows it by influencing the rating that the latter receives on the rating scale. The difference between proximity errors and the halo effect is in the cause of the error and the number of dimensions that are affected (Aamodt, 1996). With the halo effect, all dimensions are affected, while with the proximity errors, only the dimensions physically located next to a given dimension on the rating scale are affected (Aamodt, 1996). This is a function of the physical proximity of the dimension rather than an overall impression of the rater.

Contrast Errors. These emanate when the performance rating that one employee receives is influenced by the performance rating of a previously evaluated person or by the stand of the employee on previous ratings. When a frame of reference is not provided in a rating task, raters usually create their own individual frames. For managers either the best or poorest performance rated is used as a frame of reference. The ratings of an employee should be based on some objective criteria rather than contrasted with the performance ratings of the best or worst employee.

Contrast errors can also occur between separate performance evaluations of the same employee, that is, when raters allow the ratings received on one performance appraisal to affect the ratings made on an appraisal six or twelve months later. The employees' files are available to the managers when they are rating their employees. A copy of the employees' previous ratings is usually filed in the employees' files; also contained there are copies of other negative work behaviors such as queries, conflicts, and records of tardiness and absenteeism. Managers may rely on copies of these previous records to guide their evaluations; if they do, the ratings may suffer contrast errors. Smither, Reilly, and Buda (1988) call this type of rating error *assimilation.* Rating of the employees requires information of the employees' standing on performance as of the present and not as a function of previous performance.

Recency Effect Errors. These are due to human cognition. In some organizations in the United States and Europe performance appraisal is typically conducted quarterly or biannually. Most African organizations that conduct appraisals do so annually. The evaluation is designed to cover all of the behaviors that have taken place during the period. Research shows that raters tend to recall more accurately recent behaviors than behaviors that occurred previously. They thus tend to weight recent behaviors more in their performance evaluation than previous behaviors that occurred earlier before the evaluation period. If a worker performed well in the earlier months of the evaluation period but "trailed off towards the end," such an employee "would be penalized while employees who save their best work until just before the evaluation" are rewarded (Aamodt, 1996, p. 285). Keeping accurate daily records of employees' positive and negative job performance behaviors minimizes recency effect errors.

Psychological State. This affects the way raters evaluate people. Emotional factors such as stress, depression, anxiety, and even ill health and feelings of insecurity affect raters' judgment. Srinivas and Motowidlo (1987) found that raters who were placed in a stressful situation produced ratings with more errors than raters who were not under stress. This finding is important because managers and supervisors, especially in African organizations, do not take performance evaluation as an important aspect of their function. Studies show that raters who like the employees whom they are rating are more lenient (Adams and Delucca, 1987) and less accurate in rating them than raters who neither like nor dislike the employees whom they are rating (Cardy and Dobbins, 1986).

Minimizing Rating Error

One major way to promote the use of subjective ratings of African workers and at the same time minimize the number of rating errors in performance evaluation is to *train* the people who will be making the performance evaluations in the organization, whether managers, supervisors, heads of departments, peers, or the workers themselves. Several research results have demonstrated that training managers and supervisors to become aware of the various rating errors that tend to bias performance appraisal and how to avoid them often increases appraisal accuracy (Smither, Barry, and Reilly, 1989), reduces leniency and halo errors (Bernardin and Buckley, 1981; Fay and Latham, 1982), increases the validity of tests with which the ratings are compared (Pursell, Dossett, and Latham, 1980), and increases employee satisfaction with the ratings (Ivancevich, 1982). These results occur if the training techniques employed are discussion, practice in rating, and feedback about rating accuracy rather than the lecture method (Smith, 1986).

The training format also influences the effectiveness of rater training. Research by Athey and McIntyre (1987) and Sulsky and Day (1992) shows that raters who receive frame-of-reference training make fewer rating errors and recall more training information than do untrained raters or raters who were given information only about job-related behaviors.

Frame-of-Reference Training. This is a training technique that provides raters with job-related information, practice in rating, and examples of ratings made by experts as well as the rationale behind those expert ratings (Aamodt, 1996; Hauenstein and Foti, 1989; McIntyre, Smith, and Hassett, 1984).

In all, the enthusiasm, support, and understanding of the supervisors or managers and all others who are involved in rating others are essential for a performance evaluation program to be successful in an organization. Since people support what they have helped to create, it would be necessary to include the managers, supervisors, and labor unions in the actual development of any comprehensive performance appraisal program. This motivates supervisors and other raters to participate with a high sense of commitment in any company appraisal programs.

Performance Appraisal Instruments. Finally, performance appraisal instruments must be properly constructed. The instruments must be valid, reliable, and practical. Wexley and Yukl (1984) insist that proficiency measures should be acceptable to management and the employee being evaluated. In a unionized organization, it is important that the consent and support of the union should be obtained. This is because unions traditionally favor seniority in the determination of promotions and wages rather than formal evaluation programs. Whichever appraisal instruments are used by an organization in Africa they must be readily accessible and easily administered and measure accurately employee performance.

PERFORMANCE MEASUREMENT METHODS

Psychologists have developed several instruments for evaluating work performance. Each technique, however, has its advantages and disadvantages. The human resources manager should choose the method(s) most appropriate for the organization's needs, as a function of what the organization wants to achieve with the performance appraisal instrument. This is because instruments used for performance evaluation to implement remuneration should be different from instruments used for the selection of employees for training. Most performance appraisal techniques fall into one of two broad psychological classifications, *objective* and *subjective* measures. Objectivity refers to the extent to which a measure is independent of human judgment. The measurement of an event is objective if it remains the same regardless of who made the observation. objectivity, on the other hand, refers to observations where there is a likelihood of disagreement. Different observers of the same event would be likely to give differing reports.

When objectivity and subjectivity are applied to performance appraisal techniques, they refer to the level of latitude in interpretation permitted by the specific instrument (questionnaire, checklist) used to make the measurement (Howell and Dipboye, 1982). Some methods do not allow any latitude. For example, the total of how many boxes of Kampala soap a worker packs in an hour remains constant irrespective of who counts it. Others allow a lot of latitude (and are therefore subjective), for example, making a judgment on how well an employee gets along with coworkers. While the former is a matter of fact, the latter is usually "pure judgment" (Howell and Dipboye, 1982). There is a very thin line between objectivity and subjectivity. Counts and ratings can be more or less subjective. If a supervisor is asked to estimate the number of boxes of Kampala soap that an employee packs in an hour or to rate a worker's ability to get along with colleagues by considering how frequently he or she disagrees with them, one can see that it is not the measurement techniques used or the kind of criteria that determines the objectivity of performance appraisal measures. Rather the specific device and criterion define objectivity. When one thus classifies graphic-rating procedures as subjective, their subjectivity depends on how the scales are worded.

Objective Measures

Aamodt (1996) refers to objective measures as result-focused systems because they assess what employees accomplish as a result of what they do. They employ "hard" criteria, such as quantity of work, quality of work, attendance, and safety, as a means of evaluating employees' performance.

Quantity of Work. This is obtained by counting or naming the number of relevant job behaviors that the employee has completed or that have taken place. For example, one can evaluate a salesperson's performance by counting the number of units that he or she sold, an assembly-line worker's performance in an automobile company by the number of car doors that he or she installed, or a police officer's performance by the number of arrests that were made. The number of students who passed the Cambridge Secondary School Certificate in Division One measures the status of some secondary schools in some African countries.

Any salesperson knows that quantity measures are often misleading, although they appear to be objective measures of performance, because many factors, some of them outside the salesperson's control determine the quantity of work. The number of air conditioners that are sold may be more a function of geographical location than of any other factor. Finally, quantity of work output is not a practical measure for the work of many employees, such as doctors, lecturers, computer programmers, governors, and higher levels of managers, who deal with more decision making-related functions.

Quality of Work. This measures how good the finished product is as compared to the standard. Quality is measured in terms of errors, which are defined as deviations from a standard. For example, the number of typographical errors per page would measure a secretary's quality of performance. In order to measure quality, there is always a standard against which the output is measured. If a standard-quality meat pie for a fast-food restaurant includes two ounces of minced meat, any production that exceeds or is less than that amount is an error, since an error is any deviation from a standard. The quality-control section of organizations is in the best position to compile quality work statistics. To take quality of work assessment to the level of the individual worker, there must be a system of associating each unit of production with specific teams or employees.

Attendance. This is a common method for objectively measuring one aspect of an employee's performance. Aamodt (1996) separated attendance into three distinct criteria: absenteeism, tardiness, and tenure. Both absenting oneself from regular attendance at work and tardiness have important implications for the performance appraisal process, according to Aamodt (1996). The weight that each has in the overall evaluation of the employee depends on the nature of the job.

Safety. This is another method employed in the evaluation of how successful an employee has been on a given job. Employees who know the safety rules and follow them and who have no occupational accidents do not cost the organization as much money and time as those who break rules and equipment and hurt themselves. Those who are accident-prone cost the organization more, and this ought to be taken into consideration when making employment decisions on promotion and remuneration or bonuses. For example, in some organizations in some countries, such as Nigeria, vehicle drivers usually receive bonuses if they do not register any accidents in a year.

SUBJECTIVE MEASUREMENT METHODS
In the United States the human resources manager has a large number of subjective methods from which to select for evaluating the job performance of employees in the organization. Some of these measurement techniques can easily be utilized by African organizations with little or no adaptation. Among these techniques are rating scales, behavior description, comparative judgment procedures, and the critical incident method.

Rating Scales
These include the graphic rating scales, behaviorally anchored rating scales (BARS), and behavioral observation scales (BOS).

Graphic Rating Scales. These are the most common and the simplest scales for rating work behavior. An example of a graphic rating scale is shown in Figure 8.2.

Figure 8.2
Example of Graphic Rating Scale

Motivation	Low	1	2	3	4	5	High
Initiative	Poor	1	2	3	4	5	Excellent
Cooperation	Poor	1	2	3	4	5	Excellent
Dependability	Poor	1	2	3	4	5	Excellent

Graphic rating scales are fairly simple and usually have five to seven points accompanied by adjectives or evaluative concepts such as good-bad and excellent-poor that anchor the ends of the scale. They are easy to construct. When not properly constructed they, are highly susceptible to human errors such as halo and leniency effects. Instructions require the rater to circle the appropriate number of each item.

Behaviorally Anchored Rating Scales (BARS). These were developed by Smith and Kendall (1963). BARS were intended to reduce the rating problems associated with the graphic rating scales. An example of BARS is illustrated in Figure 8.3. As this figure shows, BARS use critical incidents to formally provide meaning to the numbers on a rating scale. The construction of BARS is time-consuming, but managers can seek help from professional psychologists for construction and interpretation of BARS.

Figure 8.3
Example of Behaviorally Anchored Rating Scale (BARS)

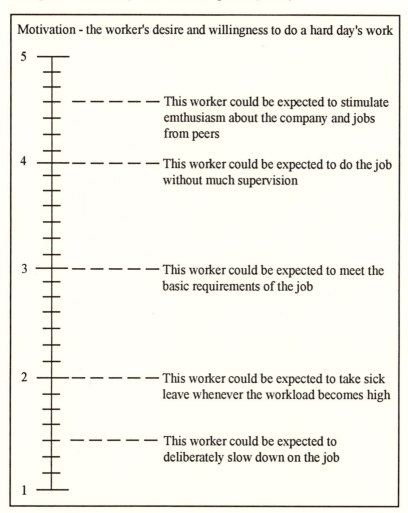

Motivation - the worker's desire and willingness to do a hard day's work

5

— — — — — This worker could be expected to stimulate emthusiasm about the company and jobs from peers

4 — — — — — This worker could be expected to do the job without much supervision

3 — — — — — This worker could be expected to meet the basic requirements of the job

2 — — — — — This worker could be expected to take sick leave whenever the workload becomes high

— — — — — This worker could be expected to deliberately slow down on the job

1

Source: Wexley and Yukl (1984, p. 348).

In order to use BARS when actually rating performance, the manager or supervisor compares the incidents previously recorded for each employee to the incidents on each scale. This can be done in two ways. In the most accurate and the most time-consuming method, the rater compares each of the recorded incidents to the anchors and records the value of the incident on the scale that most closely resembles the recorded incident. This is done for each recorded incident. The value for each incident is summed and divided by the total number of incidents recorded for that dimension; this yields an average incident value. This average incident value is the employee's rating for that particular job dimension.

The second method, which is probably easier and less accurate, involves reading all the recorded incidents to obtain a general impression of each employee. The general impression is then compared to the incidents that anchor each scale point. The scale point next to the incident that most closely resembles the general impression gained from the incidents becomes an employee's score for that dimension. A third way that people use BARS is to use the incidents contained in BARS to arrive at a rating of the employee without recording actual incidents. Aamodt (1996) says that this procedure is not recommended. Instead, BARS are used only to provide meaning to the five scale points.

Behavioral Observation Scales (BOS). These were originally developed by Latham and Wexley (1977). They are a more sophisticated method for measuring the frequency of desirable work behaviors (see Fig. 8.4). BOS have no psychometric advantages over BARS (Aamodt, 1996; Bernardin and Kane, 1980). Their physical advantages are that they are simpler to construct and easier to use. They are used to provide high levels of feedback and are better than simple rating scales at motivating employees to change their behavior (Tziner, Kopelman, and Livnech, 1993).

Figure 8.4
Example of Behavioral Observation Scale (BOS)

1 = Employee engaged in behavior less than 65% of the time
2 = Employee engaged in behavior 65 – 72% of the time
3 = Employee engaged in behavior 73 – 84% of the time
4 = Employee engaged in behavior 85 – 94% of the time
5 = Employee engaged in behavior 95 – 100% of the time

Job knowledge (for example, behavior expected of a bank worker)
   1.____is aware of the current interest rate?
   2.____offers suggestions to customers about how they can make the most
          interest?
   3.____ knows various ways to reduce taxes on interests for customers?
Employee relations

   1. ____offers to help other employees when own workload is down?
   2.____ praises other employees when they do well?

Source: Wexley and Yukl (1984, p. 344-345).

The development of BOS is relatively straightforward. The first steps are similar to those of BARS. Critical incidents and behaviors are obtained from employees, then the incidents are placed into categories, and each incident is rated as to the level of job performance that it represents. In the example, the behaviors are listed, and supervisors read each behavior on the list and use the following scale to find the frequency for an employee performing that specific behavior. After each employee has been rated on each behavior, the scores from each item in each dimension are summed to obtain the dimension score. BOS have been criticized for actually measuring *recalled* behaviors rather than measuring the actual *observation* of behaviors (Aamodt, 1996; Murphy, Martin, and Garcia, 1982).

Behavior Description

This technique consists of forced choice-rating scale, weighted checklist, and mixed standard scale.

Forced-Choice Rating Scales. These are sometimes called forced-choice checklists. They are a very unpopular, statistically sophisticated performance appraisal technique. The scales are developed to reduce leniency problems in BARS. Forced-choice rating scales use critical incidents and relevant job behaviors, as do BARS, but, unlike BARS, the scale points are hidden.

In using the forced-choice rating scale to evaluate employee performance, the supervisor selects the behavior in each item that appears most typical of that performed by a given employee. The supervisor's choices are then scored by a member of the personnel department to yield the employee's rating on each dimension. The scores on each dimension can be summed to form an overall rating.

Forced-choice rating scales are not commonly used, even in industrialized countries, because they are very complicated to develop and take considerable time. Their advantages are that they eliminate common rating errors such as leniency and halo effects and yield more accurate performance evaluations.

On the other hand, their disadvantages are that they are subject to faking. Second, because the key for forced-choice rating scales is kept secret, supervisors have no control over the appraisal process, thus reducing the level of cooperation and participation of the supervisors. Finally, the secrecy makes feedback impossible, although this is usually expected to be an important part of employee evaluation. As a result of these disadvantages, Aamodt (1996) suggests that forced-choice rating scales be employed only when the major goal of the performance appraisal system is accurate employee evaluation for the purposes of promotion and salary increase.

Weighted Checklists. These and the forced-choice techniques are the most highly structured of all subjective evaluation techniques. Like the forced-choice rating scale, the weighted checklists are aimed at reducing rater biases by requesting the rater to focus on very specific attributes or items of behavior.

The development of weighted checklists requires three steps. First, a large number of statements describing work behavior are collected. Some of these behaviors are effective behaviors, and some are ineffective. The best source of such statements is written or oral statements from managers and supervisors.

Second, the statements are given to about 10 to 15 independent judges, who place the statements in a scale as to the degree of proficiency that an employee so described would possess. The judges sort the statements into degrees of desirability ranging from piles 7, representing desirable, through 9, to 11 being undesirable. Only the statements that have a low level of variability, that is, a high level of consistency in the judges' scaling, would be employed in the final checklist. A statement scaled by 10 different judges as 5, 6, 6, 6, 5, 5, 5, 5, 5, and 5 would be judged to have low variability or high consistency among the judges. Such a statement would be included in the final checklist. If the 10 judges failed to agree among themselves by giving such judgments as 2, 7, 11, 5, 4, 6, 7, 9, 1 and 8, such a statement would be excluded.

The final step is to determine the scale value or weight of each statement by averaging the judges' individual estimates. The weight or scale value of the statement characterized by low variability and high consistency among the judges, in this instance, is 5.3.

Figure 8.5 is an example of some items taken from a weighted checklist used to measure the human relations competence of line supervisors by their

Figure 8.5
Example of a Weighted Checklist

Instructions:
The following form is designed to evaluate the human relations competence of (name _____). Included in the checklist are examples of behavior you may have observed on the part of this supervisor in the past. Would you please read each statement and carefully consider whether or not you have observed the behavior described .Then do one of the following:
a. If you can recall having observed the described behavior, please place a check mark (x) in the space at the left of the statement.
b. If the behavior described has not been observed, or if you do not immediately recall having observed the behavior, leave the space blank.
1. _____When making a job assignment, discusses significant detail of the job with subordinates.
2. _____Unable to settle personal differences between subordinates
3. _____Solicited subordinates' opinions and ideas and tried them, whenever possible.
4. _____Delegated responsibility for an important job, but refused to let subordinate perform it without interfering.
5. _____Went out of the way to give credit to subordinates and compliment them for a job well done.
6. _____Failed to keep promises to subordinates
7. _____Failed to apologize to subordinates when wrong.

Source: Wexley and Yukl (1984, p. 353).

managers as presented by Wexley and Yukl (1984). Managers who use the checklist simply place a check mark next to any behavior that they have seen the subordinates exhibit in the past. The raters do not see the weights. The final score of a person being rated on the checklist is obtained by averaging the weights of all the items marked by the managers. The weighted checklist is an excellent technique for the development of subordinates who benefit from feedback based on actual observation of their behavior. Among its disadvantages are its complexity and the time required to construct it.

Mixed Standard Scales (MSS). These were originally developed by Blanz and Ghiselli (1972). In order to develop mixed standard scales employees are asked to rate job behaviors and critical incidents on the extent to which they represent various levels of job performance. For each job dimension, a behavior or incident is chosen that represents excellent performance (E), average performance (A), and poor performance (P). These behaviors are then shuffled, and the end result may look like Figure 8.6.

Figure 8.6
Example of Mixed Standard Scale

<u>Direction</u>. Place a "+" after the statement if the typical behavior of the teller is usually better than that represented in the statement, a "0" if the typical behavior of the teller is about the same as that represented in the statement, and a "–" if the typical behavior of the teller is worse than that presented in the statement.

		Rating
1.	Teller constantly argues with other employees (P)	_____
2.	Teller smiles at customers (A)	_____
3.	Teller asks customers how their families are doing (E)	_____
4.	Teller helps other employees where possible (A)	_____
5.	Teller asks customers what they want (P)	_____
6.	Teller is always friendly to and talks with other employees (E)	_____

Note: Items 1, 4, and 6 are from the Employees Relations Dimension
Items 2, 3, and 5 are from the Customer Relations Dimension

Source: Adapted from Aamodt (1996, p. 267).

In order to appraise a subordinate with the mixed standard scale, a manager reads each behavior and places a plus (+) next to it when a particular subordinate's behavior is usually better than the behavior listed, a zero (0) if the employee's behavior is about the same as the behavior listed, or a minus signs (–) if the subordinate's behavior is usually worse than the behavior listed.

To arrive at a score for each scale, the manager uses a chart such as the one in Table 8.1. An overall score can be obtained by summing the scores from each of the scales. The advantage of mixed standard scales is that they are less complicated than forced-choice and weighted checklists. Their disadvantage is that they are subject to "logical rating errors." Logical errors arise from the

tendency of managers to rate a subordinate's performance "as better than the
tendency of managers to rate a subordinate's performance "as better than the
example of excellent performance or worse than the example of poor
performance" (Aamodt, 1996).

Table 8.1
Example of Original Scoring System for Mixed Standard Scale

	Statement Type		
Good	Average	Poor	Dimension Score
+	+	+	7
0	+	+	6
–	+	+	5
–	0	+	4
–	–	+	3
–	–	0	2
–	–	–	1

Source: Adapted from Blanz and Ghiselli (1972), as cited by Aamodt (1996, p. 268).

Such errors are very common with mixed standard scales. Logical rating errors
are minimized by using the revised scoring method as developed by Saal (1979)
(see Table 8.2). Aamodt (1996) insists that, in spite of the solution provided by
the revised scoring method, the existence of logical errors still casts some doubt
on the accuracy of mixed standard scales as a performance appraisal instrument.

Table 8.2
Example of Revised Scoring System for Mixed Standard Scale

Good	Average	Poor	Dimension Score
+	+	+	7
0	+	+	6
+	+	0	6
+	0	+	6
+	+	–	5
+	0	0	5
+	–	+	5
0	+	0	5
0	0	+	5
–	+	+	5
–	0	+	4
+	0	–	4
+	–	0	4
0	+	–	4
0	0	0	4

Table 8.2 (Continued).

Good	Average	Poor	Dimension Score
0	–	+	4
–	+	0	4
–	–	+	3
+	–	–	3
0	0	–	3
0	–	0	3
–	+	–	3
–	–	+	3
–	0	0	3
–	–	0	2
0	–	–	2
–	0	–	2
–	–	–	1

Source: Adapted from Saal (1979), as cited by Aamodt (1996, p. 268).

Comparative Judgment Procedures

This class of employee evaluation procedures includes ranking, paired comparisons, and forced-distribution.

Ranking. This requires that the evaluator rank all subordinates from the best to worst performer. This may be done separately for different traits. The ranks are then averaged across each dimension to yield an overall rank for each evaluated subordinate, as in Table 8.3.

Table 8.3
Example of Ranking Method of Evaluating Performance

		Dimension		
Employee	Knowledge	Dependability	Quality	Total
Chima	1	1	1	1.00
Kojo	2	3	2	2.33
Ojo	3	2	3	2.67
Ben	4	5	4	4.33
Musa	5	4	5	4.67

Ranking methods are easy to use when there are only a few employees to rank. They are difficult, however, when there are larger numbers of subordinates to evaluate. Ranking the top few and bottom few employees is relatively easy, but deciding which 2 of 60 subordinates should be placed at the fortieth and forty-first ranks is more difficult.

Paired Comparisons. Paired comparisons were introduced to make the process of ranking larger numbers of employees easier. The paired comparison method involves comparing each possible pair of employees and choosing which one of each pair is the better employee. An example is shown in Figure 8.7.

The problem with the paired comparison method is that with large number of employees, the time necessary to make all of the comparisons becomes prohibitive. For example, comparing 12 employees would require 66 comparisons. Although this number is not too cumbersome, one can imagine evaluating 150 employees. That would amount to a total of 11,175 comparisons. With five performance dimensions, the manager would be required to make 55,875 separate comparisons. No supervisor would appreciate such a task even with the aid of a computer, not to mention African organizations, where the aid of a computer may not even exist. The time and energy expenditure required for large comparisons may not justify the benefits of the outcome.

Figure 8.7
Example of Paired Comparison Method

Employees: Ben, Chima, Kojo, Musa, and Ojo

Paired comparisons: Select the better employee in each pair.

Chima*	Kojo
Chima*	Ojo
Chima*	Ben
Chima*	Musa
Kojo*	Ojo
Kojo*	Musa
Ojo	Ben*
Ojo*	Musa
Ben*	Musa

Scoring

Employee	Number of times selected.
Chima	4
Kojo	3
Ojo	1
Ben	2
Musa	0

Note: * Selected employee.

Forced Distribution Procedure. This can be likened to grading by normal curves where a predetermined percentage of employees are placed into five categories such as very poor, poor, average, good, and excellent. That is, the evaluator must assume that employee performance is normally distributed, with the top 10 percent judged excellent and the bottom 10 percent very poor, irrespective of the absolute level of group performance, 40 percent judged average, and the next 20 percent above and below the average judged good and poor, respectively.

Aamodt (1996) indicates that the greatest problem with all the employee comparison methods is that they do not provide information on how well an employee is actually doing. Take for example, a plant where every employee had been selected very carefully and where all continued to perform very well. Someone has to be at the bottom. Similarly, in a class of gifted students where, in a mathematics test, the scores ranged from 98 percent to 100 percent, 98 percent is the bottom score. The scorer is by no means doing poorly. All the students are doing well, contrary to the information that the comparison method provides.

Critical Incident Technique

Previously, the critical incident method was considered a technique for employee performance evaluation. Recent approaches consider it an aid to more accurate performance appraisal of employees (Aamodt, 1996). Critical incidents are written in a log consisting of formal accounts of excellent and poor employee performance that the supervisor has observed and recorded. Such documentation helps the managers to recall behavior when they are evaluating subordinates' performance. Without documentation, Aamodt (1996) maintains that research has shown that supervisors and managers tend to recall certain types of behavior more than others. The behaviors that managers tend to recall are first impressions and recent behaviors that are consistent with managers' opinion of workers under them.

Studies in psychology have demonstrated that people tend to remember *first impressions* of other people more than they remember later behaviors. This phenomenon is called primacy effect. Consequently, managers tend to recall behaviors that are consistent with the first impression of an employee, even though those first behaviors may not be representative of the employee's typical performance. Managers and supervisors also tend to recall the most recent behaviors that occurred during evaluation periods. Unusual or extreme behaviors or what Jones and Davis (1965) call "uncommon behaviors" are remembered more than common behaviors. A police officer who turns in a large sum of money that he picked up at the scene of an accident is evaluated inappropriately as higher on honesty than ordinarily he would have been evaluated. Also, a good officer who makes an unfortunate mistake is likely to receive an inappropriately low evaluation. Once managers form a good opinion about some employees and their behaviors, they will tend to look for those behaviors that conform to the original opinion.

Further functions of documentation and accurate recordings in the files of employees in an organization are that they increase the accuracy of performance appraisal as well as help to protect the organization against legal action by an employee who was terminated or denied promotion or a raise.

In order to use critical incidents to document performance rather than entries in the employees' files, as is the case in many African organizations, managers maintain a log of all the critical behaviors that they observe the employees performing in a specially prepared critical incident record. Those behaviors are then used during the performance appraisal review process to assign a rating for each employee. A more formal method for using critical incidents in evaluating performance was developed by Flanagan and Burns (1955) for use by the American General Motors Company. They called it *employee performance record.* It consists of a two-color forms. Half the sheet is used to record examples of good behaviors, the other half, to record examples of poor behaviors exhibited by each employee. On each side, there are columns for each of the relevant performance dimensions such as level of knowledge, employee relations with others (management, personnel, and customers), and level of accuracy of work or efficiency. These dimensions are crossed by type of performance (either poor or excellent) exhibited by the employee. Managers have separate records for each employee and at the end of the day can record the observed behaviors.

The employee performance record has the advantage of allowing managers to record only job-relevant behaviors. At the end of the performance appraisal period, which should be every 6 months, the manager has a record of job-relevant behaviors recorded in an organized manner. It also informs the manager of the consistency of the employee's good or poor performance.

COMMUNICATING APPRAISAL RESULTS TO EMPLOYEES

The most important use of performance appraisal data is to provide feedback to employees and to assess their strengths and weaknesses so as to determine further training to help remedy deficiencies and enhance their areas of strength. Employee feedback and assessment of training needs should be an on-going process in every organization. Aamodt (1996) maintains that the semiannual evaluation is the best time to formally discuss employee performance. Another benefit of the "formal review interview" with the manager is to protect the organization legally in case of a lawsuit.

In organizations with a routine employee performance appraisal system, the manager holds a formal review interview with every employee semiannually to discuss the scores received during the recent evaluation appraisal exercise. The manager also uses the interview as an occasion to "tell and sell" (Aamodt, 1996); that is, the manager tells the employees one by one everything that they have done poorly and then sells to them the techniques of how they can improve.

Making adequate preparation and scheduling sufficient time for them can make performance appraisal interviews more effective by giving the exercise the importance that it deserves. The performance appraisal interview should never be held in a hurry. The ratings by the manager should have been made available to the employee to study in preparation for the performance appraisal interview. Prior to the interview, enough time should be budgeted by the manager and the employee for this exercise. The manager should have time to prepare. The employee must be informed when the performance appraisal interview will take place and must be given at least one hour in which to prepare. The manager should budget sufficient time for each employee for preparation and actual interview.

New employees go through their performance appraisal interview after their first 6 months on the job and after that as often as deemed necessary. The performance appraisal interview should be scheduled to take place in a neutral location that ensures privacy, and is away from the manager's intimidating office, and allows the manager and the employee to be in a face-to-face situation without a desk between them. The manager should prepare for the interview by reviewing the ratings given to the employees one by one and the reasons that the employees received those ratings. The managers also review the employees' self-ratings and their reason for scoring themselves the way they did. When the manager and the employee meet at the interview session, the manager should begin the discussion by informing the employee of the purpose and objective of the organization's appraisal programs. The manager should explain how the performance appraisal was conducted, why the instruments that were used were preferred over other instruments, and why the supervisor or peers or customers were used in the rating.

The initial discussion should be handled in a friendly manner to reduce employee anxiety and stress and to lower employee defenses. Step 2, according to Aamodt (1996), should permit the employee to discuss the self-ratings and the justifications for such ratings. The employee is then given an opportunity to discuss the ratings that the worker received and to indicate agreement or disagreement with the ratings on each item. If the employee does not agree with any of the ratings, these form areas for further discussions and persuasion. If the employee agrees with the ratings by the manager, the employee is asked to endorse the evaluation to indicate agreement with the result of the performance evaluation. The manager should be a good listener. Following the employees' assessment of their performance, the manager informs the employee of positive work behaviors first. The manager later discusses the negative aspects of the employee's work performance. Positive work behaviors are discussed first to maintain the employee's self-esteem. Any differences in the manager's and employee's scores should be discussed until both of them are satisfied or understand the difference.

The third step is to discuss why the employee did not receive perfect evaluation ratings. This may be due to the fact that the employee lacks some knowledge as to how to perform the job properly, may have been assigned too many duties, or may have a low level of motivation. Performance appraisal feedback, according to Aamodt (1996), should be "candid, specific, and behavioral rather than personal."

The next step, once the difficulties and problems have been identified, is to reach decisions on how the manager should help the employee to find solutions to the problems. What should the employee do? What role should the organization play? The manager as part of the performance appraisal should document answers to these questions. Factors that can affect the employee's performance can be classified into person-specific factors, such as ability and motivation, and company-specific factors, such as leadership, company policy, training, coworkers, physical environment, and economic matters. The manager in the evaluation must be aware of these factors. Finally, the manager and the employee should mutually set goals for future performance and work behaviors. They also should establish an understanding of how these goals can be attained.

SUMMARY

The objective of this chapter was to X-ray the importance of periodic employee evaluation to African organizations. For performance evaluation in organizations to be meaningful, employees must have a good knowledge of the details of the work they are to perform as well as the appropriate behavior that is expected on their jobs. The codification of details of a job for which an employee is responsible is called job description. Many small and medium-sized organizations in Africa, including government departments and parastatals, do not have detailed job descriptions for their employees. In these organizations workers' benefits, wages, and promotions are not closely tied to the details of the work that employees do.

Most international and large, indigenous organizations in Africa borrow job description concepts from Europe and North America, in spite of the fact that the numerous job titles available in the developed countries do not exist in Africa. Trade unions in Africa have a negative attitude toward job description and employee job performance evaluation. They associate performance evaluation with wage considerations, promotions, and termination of employees. The reasons that organizations appraise their workers go beyond those three reasons. Performance evaluation helps organizations to reveal areas of performance deficiencies. Consequently, it enables organizations to design training development programs that will correct deficiencies, aid personnel research, and determine the types of skills required.

In African organizations the manager is assigned the responsibility of evaluating the employees, unlike in Europe or North America, where organizations can use peers, subordinates, customers, and the employees themselves to complete appraisal forms. While every worker is subject to being appraised in the industrialized world, in most African organizations such evaluation forms, in most cases, only exist for junior and intermediate staff. Another difference between organizations in the developed countries and those in Africa is that many small and medium-sized owner-manager African organizations have no program of employee evaluation, and some of the larger indigenous organizations conduct evaluations for their junior and intermediate employees annually, while in organizations in Europe and the United States most employees are evaluated at least twice a year. One of the reasons for these differences is that African organizations do not realize the importance of employee appraisal in the effective management of organizations. Second, African organizations do not have much access to employee appraisal instruments. A vital use of regular performance evaluation of employees in organizations is to provide data for the purpose of informing the employees of their performance strengths and weaknesses and to determine training programs to enhance employee performance strengths and remedy their weaknesses. In order to accomplish these goals through employee appraisals, African organizations must learn the processes of performance appraisal, employ valid and reliable techniques, minimize human errors in handling subjective procedures in appraisal, and learn to keep performance records so as to produce dependable evaluations from which the organization can benefit.

9

Principles and Methods of Effective Management Training and Development

Colonial administrators in most French-speaking African countries placed emphasis on the selection and placement of African supervisors and foremen and women. Given the very low proportion of Africans literate and willing to work in industrial and organizational settings, the emphasis was, indeed, misplaced. What was needed at that stage were training and development. Africa also inherited the colonial belief that management can best be learned through long, on-the-job experience. The consequence of that attitude is that even today many managers in African organizations rose to their present positions through the ranks. Such managers require constant management training and development.

Managerial training refers to a specific program of instruction designed to equip managers, supervisors, and foremen and women with knowledge, skills, attitudes, values, rules, and concepts to enable them to perform their present management functions effectively. Training is sometimes distinguished from development. Development is a preparation for growth for a person to assume higher responsibilities in the future. At times, too, development may be applied to all such programs meant to improve the performance of the organization (organizational development, OD) or the performance of managers, supervisors, foremen and women or other employees in the present as well as in the future. One may assume in this context that training and development practically mean the same thing. This is because the methods of training and development overlap to a great extent, and their essence is to produce learning experience for the employees involved.

The term *method* refers to the techniques and media of communicating the learning experience to the learners, while *principles* are rules or statements to guide future action. The purpose of this chapter is to outline the necessary procedure for determining organizational training needs, methods, and principles of managerial training and development, as well as the necessity to evaluate managerial training results in African industrial organizations.

TRAINING AND DEVELOPMENT IN AFRICAN ORGANIZATIONS

The shortage of professionals and people with the required technical and management skills to manage African organizations made manpower development a priority for many African governments. The response to this shortage was that African governments and other agencies increased opportunities for management training and development of workers. Governments in each African country, employers' associations, public enterprises, the civil service, management development institutes, and agricultural and technical skills institutes are all involved in personnel training and development efforts in Africa.

Recently, universities have established faculties of business management. These faculties offer full-time degree courses in business management, some up to the doctoral level. There are also diploma and certificate courses in management and industrial labor relations in some universities, colleges, and polytechnics. At the University of Ibadan, Nigeria, the Department of Psychology took a bold step in establishing a novel management course called Managerial Psychology. The program is a professional master's degree targeted at managers in different organizations. In spite of all these efforts, African countries still lack skilled maintenance personnel, skills in development innovation, and an appropriate attitude to increase workers' commitment to reducing constant breakdown in organizational and infrastructural facilities and equipment and to lowering high operation cost.

In addition to these institutionalized training and development, managerial training and development programs are implemented in most private and public organizations in Africa. The need for organizations to improve their performance has led to the mushrooming of many managerial and development training programs. Thousands of private consulting agencies offer training programs at exorbitant cost to different organizations. There are also overseas training programs to which government and multinational companies send managers for training. The objective of most managerial training and development programs is to teach or improve various managerial skills that will lead to improved on-the-job performance (Burke and Day, 1986; Goldstein, 1980; Wexley and Latham, 1981). A great deal of managerial training focuses on teaching managers how to lead (people skills) improving job performance in the areas of general human relations, self-awareness, problem solving and decision making, motivation, values reorientation, creativity, time management, and general management. Many African organizations, unfortunately, do not know how effective these training programs are for which they pay so much. This lack of knowledge concerning the results of managerial training is primarily due to the lack of evaluative research on these programs. Often most organizations do not even know which of the available managerial programs will be beneficial to their organization as a whole or to individual managers or supervisors.

African organizations, like others elsewhere, normally train their managers and other employees as a result of increased responsibility. This may be caused by reengineering, turnaround, downsizing, the introduction of new technology, or a new management system. A second reason that may necessitate training is promotion, the hiring of new executives, or upgrading of existing managers' skills, knowledge, attitude, and job behavior. Finally, no manager or employee has all the technical and interpersonal skill, and knowledge necessary to function in today's organization. Therefore, training becomes a part of effective organizational management and development. Modern organizations realize that training relates to the overall critical success factor. This chapter considers steps necessary for effective training and learning in organizations and emphasizes the need for trainers to insist on transfer of skills acquired in training and development to job performance in organizations.

NEEDS ASSESSMENT

Organizations as living organisms are made up of subsystems, which, in turn, are made up of identifiable tasks performed by workers. Efficient management requires that managers understand the organization and what it will take in terms of resources to run it effectively. In order to plan effective training and development programs, managers ought to carry out an assessment of needs for the organization, including analysis of the organization, tasks, workers available, and the type of skills that they possess for carrying out all the organizational functions. There are several public and private training and development institutions in Africa, yet a close examination shows that most African organizations do not benefit from or utilize, the services provided by these training institutions. Those that do often do not determine for what type of training and development they send their employees to the institutions. The attitude of employees toward participation in training programs is that it is generally regarded as paid free time away from work when the employee is entitled to free accommodations in a nice hotel and good meals at the expense of the organization and some extra money. They do not have organizational reasons to understand why one manager is sent to a particular training and a second to another. The choice of training is often not determined by the needs of the organization but determined by other considerations. Managers who are in good favor with the chief executive rarely attend locally mounted training programs no matter how good and relevant those programs are. They usually go overseas to Europe and North America for their training and development. Attending training overseas is often more financially rewarding for managers. A company-sponsored, two-to-three-week training in Europe or North America earns an employee extra income to purchase and ship home a used Mercedes-Benz. In the civil service there is usually a heated competition to be selected to attend training and development overseas, even to countries such as India.

Top management personnel are reluctant to attend locally mounted training and development programs. Often the organizations send intermediate and lower-ranking officers to programs meant for managers. These officers may not benefit from the training and development program. On their return to the organizations, they usually write a report, which they submit to their immediate supervisor. The supervisor, in turn, may submit the report to the sectional manager, who asks the secretary to file the report without the organization's bothering to learn whether the training program that the employee received could benefit the organization in any way. Most organizations in Africa do not give their employees opportunity to put into practice the skills and knowledge gained at training and development programs.

The first step in developing a managerial training system is to conduct *needs* analysis. Needs analysis is the process of determining the short-term, inter-mediate, and long-term training needs of an organization. Three types of needs analysis are typically conducted; organizational, task, and person analysis (Aamodt, 1996; Sleezer, 1993).

Organizational Analysis

This involves the determination of organizational factors that either facilitate or inhibit the effectiveness of managers' training. Numerous small and medium-sized owner-manager organizations in Africa do not participate in any type of training and development programs for their employees. Indeed, most indigenous organizations still do not know that there is any need for training in their organizations. Most do not have training units in their organizations. In large organizations trainers have to battle with the attitudes of personnel managers whose responsibility is to authorize training for the workers in their organizations. Often one finds that these personnel managers are committed to a particular training organization that gets all their training programs. If other agencies have a good program that will benefit the manager's organization, the personnel manager will not patronize it.

Another problem is that organizations may realize the importance of management training but may not have the necessary budget to properly fund its programs. Others may not rank training in its appropriate position in their prioritization of activities. Training of managers in an organization will be effective if the organization creates a conducive environment for training, if it has developed a good training program, and if the goals of the training program will aid the achievement of the overall organizational goal.

The second function of organizational analysis is to help determine the organizational objectives and how far the organization is achieving each objective. Is the organization failing to perform in some areas, or does it have managers with the appropriate human skills, knowledge, and attitudes and managerial leadership style to motivate their subordinates to perform? Is the organization effective in its team-building efforts, and are the existing teams being effectively utilized? Finally, organizational analysis reveals immediate, intermediate, and long-term organizational problems so that training programs will be designed to avoid such problems before they actually arise.

Task Analysis

Some authors regard this as operational analysis (Howell and Dipboye, 1982). It involves employing the job analysis and employee evaluation methods to obtain information about the job itself and the overall performance of the employees in an organization who are responsible for each of the tasks (Sims, Veres, and Heninger, 1989). Task analysis is important because if an organization is to benefit from training programs, such programs must be aimed at areas where the employees evidence weakness.

Training needs that emanate from task analysis should be stated in the form of concrete and achievable objectives (Aamodt, 1996; Mager, 1984). These objectives should include the specific ways that trainees are expected to work differently after attending a training and development program. The conditions under which the trainees are supposed to perform the learned behaviors must be specified. The level of the trainees' performance and how the training is expected to generalize to actual job performance in the organization should be stated.

Person Analysis

This deals with the question of which managers and employees need training and in which areas. Being sent to a training program by an organization is not a form of paid holiday, for the employee, nor is it a reward for employees who are loyal to the manager or a bribe to buy the loyalty of critical employees. The author is familiar with how a given manager of an organization in Nigeria once tried to buy critical labor leaders in his organization with offers of training overseas. One overseas organization awarded five three-month training programs in Ireland. The manager's organization was having problems with the labor union at the time. The five officers who benefited from the training program were all executive members of the very labor union that was in conflict with management.

Person analysis is important because further training is not required for every employee and every job task. The objective of person analysis is to use the evaluation results of one or more employees to make decisions about which individual manager needs further training. Some of the performance evaluation methods employed in person analysis are performance appraisal scores, surveys, interviews, and skill and knowledge tests.

Performance Appraisal Scores. These are the easiest method of person analysis. The method uses employee evaluation scores (see Chapter 8). Generally, high scores by employees in a particular task dimension are a clear indication that there is no need for training. Low scores or ratings on a dimension by most employees are an indication of training needs. Table 9.1 demonstrates the use of performance evaluation in determining the training needs for managers. As the table indicates, the managers, as a whole, need little training in problem solving or decision making but need further training in self-awareness and leadership. Even though most managers can handle problems in their respective departments, Layi needs further training in this area; both Chima and Usman probably can skip the training in leadership.

Table 9.1

Example of How Performance Evaluation Scores Can Be Used for Needs Analysis

Performance Dimension			Managers			
	Chima	Chidi	Ojo	Layi	Usman	Average
Self Awareness	2	1	2	5	1	2.2
Problem solving	5	5	5	1	4	4.0
Decision making	5	5	5	5	5	5.0
Motivation	2	2	2	2	2	2.0
Leadership	5	3	1	2	5	3.2
Average	3.8	3.2	3.8	3.0	3.4	

The use of performance evaluation scores to determine training needs appears very easy and feasible, but there are three problems that a user must guard against. As discussed in Chapter 8, several types of rating errors can reduce the accuracy of performance appraisal scores. The most relevant here are leniency and strictness errors, which can make the performance evaluation scores very high or very low. If the scores are consistently high due to leniency errors, an organization might incorrectly conclude that its managers are all proficient in a particular task area and therefore need no training. Likewise, consistently low scores due to strictness errors might lead to a wrong conclusion that the managers are poor in a particular dimension and thus need training when, in fact, the actual cause of the low scores is rater error (Aamodt, 1996).

The second problem arises from the use of an average score to determine whether or not a group of managers needs training. Normally, not all the managers in an organization will score consistently high on a given task dimension. Some will score high in performance evaluation, while others will score low. In such a situation, it would be incorrect to conclude that the managers do not need training. The correct interpretation should be that training would be conducted for those managers whose scores were low for that task dimension. Finally, some authors have raised questions about whether the present performance evaluation system can, indeed, provide the type of information that is required to conduct effective training needs analysis (Aamodt, 1996; Herbert and Doverspike, 1990). They suggest that performance appraisal systems must be specific to be useful.

Survey. These are a very common approach to determining training needs. A well-designed and-administered survey that asks employees what knowledge and skills they believe should be included in the future training of managers has been found useful in determining training needs. The advantages of such surveys are that they tend to eliminate the problems of performance evaluation errors. Managers often are in the best position to know their own strengths and weaknesses. If one wishes to know the manager's strengths and weaknesses, one should ask the managers themselves. Surveys can be used even in the absence of an organizational performance evaluation system or adequate job descriptions.

Surveys to determine training needs can be carried out in different ways The most common method involves the use of a questionnaire that requires managers to list the areas in which they would like further or future training. A second method was suggested by Graham and Mihal (1986). The method requires the provision of a list of job-related tasks and knowledge, and the managers are asked to rate their need for training on each task and knowledge. The results of these ratings are made available to the chief executive or his or her representative, who validates and cross-checks the results with the critical incident records of each manager. This is done to determine the correspondence between the chief executive's and managers' perception and to help prioritize training needs.

Interviews. These are methods of determining training needs for managers. The technique requires that some managers be randomly selected and interviewed about their opinions and views on training needs. Aamodt (1996) maintains that interviews are not used as extensively as surveys but that interviews have the advantage of yielding in-depth answers to questions and greater awareness about training needs. A second advantage is that interviews reveal managers' attitudes and feelings more clearly than the survey approach. Steadham (1980) points out that a problem of the interview method is that data generated through it are usually difficult to quantify and analyze.

Skill and Knowledge Tests. These are used to diagnose the training needs for managers. These include tests of knowledge of company laws, labor laws, lending policy, and government trade regulations and skills test such as for human and leadership skills. If managers score poorly on these tests, training across the organization is indicated. If only a few managers score poorly, such low-scoring managers are singled out for individual training. The advantages of using these types of tests for the determination of training need is that measures of knowledge of labor laws, company laws, and government trade policies and regulations vary according to countries and are available in each African country. Questions of reliability and validity do not arise for such tests.

Critical Incidents. These are completed each day for each employee (see Chapter 8) and provide a good method for determining training needs. Critical incidents are demarcated into good and poor performance. Task dimensions with many poor performance entries are considered to be areas in which many managers are performing poorly and therefore should be areas where training is needed.

PRINCIPLES OF LEARNING AND TRAINING

It is important to consider a few principles of learning and training that those who train managers ought to consider in designing and implementing training programs in African organizations.

Principles of Learning

For training to be effective, there must be effective learning. Psychologists define learning as a relatively permanent change in behavior, that results from practice or experience. Some authors have attempted to distinguish between learning and performance. As we have defined *learning*, its products are carried with the individual on a fairly permanent basis and are available as a basis for action as the occasion demands. *Performance,* on the other hand, refers to the translation of learning into behavior. The level of performance depends on relatively short-term factors such as motivation, the availability of appropriate environmental circumstances, and fatigue. This is important when evaluating a training program. Hull (1943) maintained that learning sets an upper limit to performance. Depending on temporary conditions, therefore, performance may provide a relatively accurate or inaccurate index of learning.

No other human behavior has been researched by psychologists as much as learning. In the process, elaborate models, paradigms, and theories have been evolved about learning and the transfer and retention of learned behavior. In spite of all the elaborate and elegant knowledge in the area of learning, very little of it has been applied to actual organizational training. Some of the promising learning principles that can effectively influence managerial training include effects of reward or reinforcement, knowledge of results, goal setting, imitation, practice, and the nature of the task to be learned.

Reinforcement (Reward) and Instrumental Conditioning. The basic principles of learning are concerned with the process by which new behaviors are "stamped in" and old behaviors are strengthened. The most important principles of learning articulated by most theories and models of learning revolve around the concept of reinforcement or reward. In organizations, rewards for employees include wages, promotion, and recognition. The basic paradigm through which reinforcement is demonstrated is called *instrumental conditioning.*

Instrumental conditioning is a process whereby an organism learns to respond in a given manner so as to achieve certain consequences. The manner of responding is instrumental in the attainment of reward or positive reinforcement or the avoidance of punishment or negative reinforcement. Organisms, including human beings, have the tendency to repeat responses that are followed by positive reinforcement (reward) and to avoid behaviors that attract negative reinforcement or punishment. In training, therefore, when we have discovered what kinds of things are positively and negatively valued by the individual, we have at our disposal a very powerful means of programming that person's learning behavior.

Things that have the power to influence behavior in this way are called reinforcers (or rewards). The process whereby these reinforcers are presumed to operate is called reinforcement. Some potential reinforcers that are operational in work situations include pay, positive social interaction, achievement, the feeling of being appreciated, and promotion. If workers value good salaries, they work in desired ways to obtain them. Such inducements can serve to bring about the learning of the desired behavior. For example, incentive systems can be used to promote learning as well as to influence performance level through the manipulation of employees' motivation.

In order to achieve conditioning, different ways of arranging reinforcement are desired. At the beginning of conditioning attempts, every acceptable response is reinforced. When the response is well mastered, its occurrence can be maintained at a high level by an occasional reinforcement. When every acceptable response is followed by reinforcement, we call the scheduling *continuous reinforcement;* otherwise, we call the reinforcement schedule *partial reinforcement.* A number of different partial reinforcement schedules have been identified. Each of these schedules produces patterns of response of its own.

For example, in laboratory studies, the results of which may not transfer to organizational setting, experimenters can maximize the effects of reinforcement or reward through fixed ratio and fixed interval schedules. In a fixed ratio schedule the learner is reinforced every second, third, fourth, or nth response. A fixed ratio schedule induces the learner to respond at a very high, steady rate. In a fixed interval schedule, on the other hand, the reinforcement is given on a time basis, that is, only the first response after each n-minute interval. The response behavior instigated by a fixed interval schedule is that the response rate will be high just before the reinforcement and very low right after it. According to Howell and Dipboye (1982), partial reinforcement schedules such as fixed ratio and fixed interval tend to "control performance to a greater extent than learning."

Second, partial reinforcement-conditioned responses are more likely to be permanent than those under continuous reinforcement. In other words, behaviors learned under continuous reinforcement are less resistant to extinction than those learned under partial reinforcement. As training progresses, therefore, it is necessary to vary the number of reinforcements once the response or behavior has been acquired or mastered.

Feedback or Knowledge of Result (KR). This is a very important principle of learning. Our consideration of performance evaluation indicated that the important value of KR is to provide the employees with knowledge of their performance on the job. Information regarding a person's performance is very important for learning (Howell and Dipboye, 1982). Such information can influence learning in two ways, through reinforcement of past behavior and through serving as a guide for future behavior. The individual is reinforced by the knowledge that positive past behavior was noticed and appreciated and is motivated to engage in similar behaviors in the future in order to earn further reinforcement or reward. Reinforcement principles are useful for maintaining learned behavior as well as for controlling future behavior (Howell and Dipboye, 1982). If "well done" (said to a subordinate by a superior officer following good performance) is an effective reinforcing agent for the performance of a high-quality piece of work, the managing director or any other superior officer can maintain quality performance among subordinates by a judicious administration of "well done," which has acquired the value of a reinforcer. The managing director's subordinates will now work harder to earn the recognition. But to maintain the high value placed on this commendation, the managing director must make sure that no subordinate receives the commendation frequently (partial reinforcement), that exceptional performers receive it occasionally (variable interval schedule), and that only those who demonstrate a work performance that is above standard receive the commendation (contingent reward).

Another contribution that feedback or knowledge of result makes to learning is that it informs the learners of the correctness or incorrectness of their responses. In order to learn to respond correctly, the learner must have some way of knowing what is within the acceptable limits and what is not.

Research evidence demonstrates that providing feedback to trainees regarding correct and incorrect responses enhances learning (Howell and Dipboye, 1982). Komaki, Heinzmann, and Lawson (1980) found that training employees in safe work practices was not sufficient for them to maintain safe behavior; the training must be followed with on-the-job feedback from supervisors. In other words, both training and feedback were necessary for employees to learn to maintain high levels of safe behaviors.

Goal Setting. Research results tend to link goal setting and feedback. The conclusion from several research findings is that feedback is more effective when it is combined with goal setting than when feedback is provided alone without goal setting. Goal setting has important implications for learning. Locke (1968), for decades, pointed out that an employee's behavior is regulated by the individual's goals and intentions. Other research findings also show that setting specific goals, such as giving a certain level of performance, has a greater effect on performance than a generalized goal (e.g., try your best). Still others show that more difficult goals result in a higher performance than easy and unchallenging goals, provided the set goals are not beyond the ability of the employee and are acceptable to the employee. Feedback and goal setting are learning principles that every trainer needs to take into consideration in programming effective training and development.

Shaping, Guiding, and Imitation. These are techniques of training. A response must first occur before it is reinforced. For example, a baby must verbalize before the mother responds with reinforcement. Many responses do not occur in their desired form spontaneously enough to be reinforced, so it requires several devices to initiate the desired response. These devices include imitation or modeling, shaping, and guiding.

In *imitation* or *modeling,* the learner is shown the proper response and then taught to replicate the response, for example, when someone is teaching a person to dance. The trainer demonstrates the steps and allows the trainee to imitate the steps. The trainee can also be *guided* to make the correct response. This is the method used when teaching a child to ride a tricycle or a beginner to change gears when learning to drive a car.

A third procedure is shaping. In *shaping,* every successive approximation to the desired response is reinforced, for example, when a friend is being taught to play golf. The successive approximations to a successful hitting of the ball include the stance, proper handling of the golf club, tilting of hip, swinging, and, finally, hitting the ball. Each of these successive approximations is reinforced when it is mastered until the trainee progresses to the final stage, which is mastering what is considered a correct golf swing. At each stage, positive reinforcement would be administered only for a performance that meets or exceeds the set criterion. Through shaping, the trainee's pattern of response would be brought to meet the desired form. Howell and Dipboye (1982) indicate that this principle is very important for training. The problem with the application of shaping in many training situations is that it requires a very keen distinction between rewarded and nonrewarded responses. Many trainers may not distinguish the difference. Second, the reinforcement of a remote approximation may, indeed, slow down learning. Because of these disadvantages, trainers who wish to use this method should receive special training to prepare them in the art of shaping as well as have good knowledge about the job for which they wish to shape the trainees' behavior.

Learning Materials and Conditions of Practice. Effective human learning is a function of the material to be learned and the manner in which this material is arranged. Research findings have consistently shown that meaningful material is easier to learn than meaningless material such as nonsense syllables. It is necessary, therefore, to organize the material to be learned in such a way that it makes sense to the learner; that is, the learning is faster and more effective if the learner can impose meaning and organization on the task to be learned.

The method of presentation of the material to be learned can be whole or partial. If the material is simple and highly integrated, the whole presentation method should be adopted. If the material is complex, the part method should be recommended, in which subsets are presented and learned, and, finally, the parts are integrated into a whole. In other words, the trainer works from subsets to a whole if the task is complex.

Massed and Distributed Practice. This concerns whether learning is massed or distributed. For example, when studying for an examination, if the material to be learned is distributed over time, such as several days or weeks, we have distributed learning. This strategy makes the learning easier, less stressful, and easier to recall. In massed learning, on the other hand, sometimes called cramming, we learn a lot of material in a short time, such as in a seminar or workshop where trainers try to make trainees cram in a day or two a lot of materials one would take two weeks to learn. Another example is reading a whole textbook during one night for an examination the next day when we should have been reading it gradually over a semester.

Distributed practice seems to be superior for lengthy or difficult material, while massed practice is adequate for short, very simple material. Material learned in training should be presented in small, easily remembered chunks. If too much material is presented at one lecture (massed), trainees will not be able to follow, concentrate on, or remember all that is being taught. This calls for the trainer to be aware of the intellectual and skills background and previous knowledge of the trainees or the audience.

Transfer of Training. This is the influence of prior learning or experience in one task on the performance or learning of another. It refers to the utilization of habits, skills, associations, or knowledge acquired under one set of training situations in a new, later situation, such as on the job. The appropriate evaluation of any training program is the extent to which what is learned in the training situation transfers to the actual job. Unless the trainee performs better on the job, is more motivated or more satisfied, manages the subordinates better, or in some way is a better employee than before the training, a training program may not be considered a success.

Depending on the characteristics of the original training or learning and transfer tasks, the effects that carry over will vary. They can vary both in amount and in kind, that is, how much the training influences job behavior and whether the change is positive (facilitative), negative (inhibitive), or negligible. Performance following training can be better than, worse than, or show no difference from, what it would have been without training.

According to psychological theories, the principal determinant of transfer of training is the similarity between the training and transfer situations. The more similar the "response elements," the more likely that what is learned will positively influence performance. According to Bourne (1966), one factor that determines the degree of positive transfer of training is *overlearning* of individual problems. Overlearning is practicing a task even after it has been successfully learned. Driskell, Wills, and Cooper (1992) indicate that overlearning significantly increases the retention of training material. Another factor is discovery of a *general rule* for solution of problems. According to Bourne (1966), the generation of a sufficient number of problems gives rise to the generation of a rule for successful learning. A rule combines given attributes in some way so as to prescribe a meaningful, specific grouping of objects. Attributes, on the other hand, are the particular, usually "point-at-able qualities" of things that are "labelable" by words.

For skills, knowledge, and response behavior learned in training to transfer to behavior on the job, employees must have the opportunity to apply what they learned (Ford, Quinones, Sego, and Sorra, 1992). Employees are more likely to be given opportunities to perform what they have learned if their supervisor perceives them as competent and if the organizational climate is supportive (Baldwin and Ford, 1988, Ford, Quinones, Sego, and Sorra, 1992). Aamodt (1996) further indicates that some employers neither are supportive nor provide opportunities for their employees to apply what they have learned. This is more pronounced if the training is in the form of employees going to school to obtain degrees (Posner, Hall, and Munson, 1991). In African organizations lack of opportunity for employees to put into practice what they learned from training and development programs is accounted for by the generally negative attitude of the managers and their unawareness of the contributions that training could make in their organizations.

Principles of Training

Gagne (1962) criticized the principles of learning and training in psychology and showed how unrelated they were to actual training such as training in military tasks. He advocated different learning and training principles that would embrace task analysis, intratask transfer, component task achievement, and sequencing, which Gagne claimed were important variables that influence learning and transfer of training. Howell and Dipboye (1982) maintain that the importance of Gagne's principles is that every task involves a set of distinct component activities and that the proper sequencing of those activities facilitates the learning of those tasks. The most efficient sequence, according to Howell and Dipboye (1982), involves intratask transfer (the positive effect of learning one component maximizes the learning of the next).

Principles of Training for African Managers. This training should be result-oriented and cover training and development for managers who rose from the ranks, who form the majority of African managers, and those who are managers by virtue of their professional education. The design of a training program for these managers should be preceded by diagnosis of the organizational needs and managerial talents of these trainees, as well as analysis of the task to be learned. There must be a concrete identification of what is to be learned and how it is to be learned. The trainer must also break down the task into behavioral components and classify them. A thorough diagnosis of the goals, objectives, and cultures of the organizations from which the managers come is needed, and decisions must be made about the most efficient sequence for learning the components in order to facilitate the transfer of learning. Training for African managers must emphasize the transfer to work situation of behaviors learned in training and development and other seminars and workshops.

The trainer should enlist the views of trainees about areas where training may be needed, and their views should be validated with those of their organizations. This is achieved through surveys and interviews of the managers and their superiors. Diagnosis is needed of the typical, day-to-day problems that arise out of the managers' performance of their duties. Some of these should form the practical problem-solving aspect of the training. The objective that the trainer defines for a given training program must be explicit. The content of the training program should be relevant to the needs of the managers and should be guided by the goals and objectives of their organizations as well as the needs of their subordinates. The content should emphasize the skills and knowledge involved in the process of "managing" a resource mix of money, materials (including "raw material," equipment, machine technology), and people Trainers should not be slaves to one method. There is no one best general training method. But depending on the objective that a given training program wishes to achieve, there is a best method for it. Methods should be varied, emphasizing those that have been empirically tested and experimenting with innovations. Group interaction management should be included as one of the techniques of training. A training program must always be followed up and evaluated. As already emphasized, the essence of training is in its learning experience and the transfer of such learning behaviorally to the job. Follow up and evaluation ensure the organization whether or not the training is producing the changes in behavior that are expected.

METHODS OF TRAINING AND DEVELOPMENT

Organizations offer their employees different types of training. They also employ different methods to communicate the training experience. This section discusses different methods used by African organizations to train their employees and considers techniques of training under the broad categories of on-the-job and off-the-job methods of training. While on-the-job methods consist in learning by doing at or near the actual job site under the watchful eyes of an experienced worker, off-the-job methods are carried out at a remote site designed exclusively for training. Private and public consultancy companies, institutes, universities, and polytechnics usually conduct off-the-job training programs for African organizations.

On-the-Job Methods

The three most popular on-the-job training methods employed in many African organizations are apprentice training, coaching, and job rotation.

Apprenticeship Training. This method is very commonly used in African organizations. It is typically the most common training method adopted by small and medium-sized owner-manager enterprises, such as trading firms, farming, and craft and building trades. Training in retail business, carpentry, plumbing, and commercial driving also adopts the apprenticeship method. Apprenticeship training is often informally organized, and there are no government regulations for apprenticeship in many African countries.

In countries where apprenticeship training is professionally organized, the trainee is involved in formal classroom work for a given period in a year and then in practical work with an expert in the field for several years. At the end of a successful apprenticeship, the trainee becomes eligible to join a trade union. Apprenticeship provides the trainee with opportunity to learn a valuable trade, while the expert (master) or the organization gets cheap labor. In the developing African countries with a large population of unskilled illiterates, the apprenticeship training method provides young men and women with the opportunity for skills acquisition.

Job Rotation. This is an excellent method of on-the-job training; an employee performs several different jobs within an organization or across an organization's branches. The method is very popular for training managers or young graduates who are being prepared for future managerial responsibilities, because it allows a trainee-manager to experience and understand most or all of the jobs that the subordinates will perform in the organization (Aamodt, 1996). The principle underlying job rotation is the belief that managers perform better if they understand clearly how each worker does his or her job.

As example of job rotation, Jiji, a recent graduate, is employed by the Nigerian Breweries. Jiji majored in finance and was recruited as one of the organization's young managers. For the first year Jiji worked in four different branches of the organization, in Lagos, Aba, Kaduna, and Ibadan. In each branch, Jiji was placed in a management department different from the one in which she had worked in previous company branches. Different superiors with differing levels of expertise supervised her. These supervisors were required to write a report of the employee's performance during the period when she worked in their respective departments. What Jiji went through is job rotation. Job rotation is also employed for the training of nonmanagerial employees. Many multinational organizations employ job rotation as a training method by having an employee spend a few months in different departments performing different functions such as sales, underwriting, cash control, personnel, and marketing. Sometimes some aspects of such rotation training are extended to branches of the organizations in Europe or North America.

Through job rotation, employees increase their awareness, knowledge, and skills. It also creates for the organization the opportunity to easily replace an absent worker. Job rotation improves job satisfaction by reducing the fatigue and boredom that result from repetitive tasks (Aamodt, 1996; Wilbur, 1993). It also exposes managers to more management skills by having them work in different organizational departments or units. Some organizations have tried to enhance the advantages of job rotation by assigning the same trainer to supervise the trainee throughout the trainee's period of job rotation (Nadler, 1993) instead of placing the trainee under different trainers.

Coaching. This is another method of training new employees. The method requires a new employee to be assigned to an experienced employee who is required to teach the new employee how the job is performed. Coaching has the advantage of allowing the trainee to learn from the expert. Comer (1989) reported that coaching is more effective than mere orientation in training new employees.

The problem with coaching is that often good workers do not make good trainers and good trainers, may not be good workers (Rae, 1994). The trainer may also end up serving as a model for the new employee, thus communicating to the trainee the trainer's positive and negative attitudes and work behavior. Second, taking on a trainee tends to slow down the expert's work productivity.

Aamodt (1996) indicates that many organizations now adopt a new system called *pass-through program* in which experienced workers are temporarily assigned to the training department, where they are taught training techniques. At the end of their training they are given responsibilities in the training department for some months before they resume work in their respective departments (Geber, 1987).

The overall advantages of on-the-job methods of training are, first, that the training situation is the same as the job situation in which the trainee will be working. As such, the issue of transfer of training will not constitute any problems. Second, the trainee contributes to productivity while in training, thus partially offsetting the cost of training. Howell and Dipboye (1982) criticized on-the-job training schemes on the basis of their implementation, which they claim is poorly organized. According to these authors, on-the-job methods ignore "all the systematic planning and evaluating," which are important aspects of effective training.

Off-the-Job Techniques
Unlike on-the-job methods, which focus on the trainee's practicing the whole job, off-the-job techniques focus on specific aspects of the job or specific skills. Off-the-job methods provide information to the trainee, who is expected to learn from such verbal and visual information, while with on-the-job training, the trainee is expected to learn from experience (Howell and Dipboye, 1982). There are several off-the-job methods. Those mostly used in African organizations are seminar, lecture method, the case method, role-playing, and simulation. Programmed and individual methods, T-groups, and behavioral modeling are not very much in use in organizations in Africa.

Seminars or Lecture Method. These seminar methods are the most common in-company and out-company training techniques employed by many African organizational training experts. In some organizations it forms over 95 percent of all the methods of training. This is very understandable for companies in African countries, given the low level of technological development. The lecture method allows a member of the training staff or an outside consultant to impart training by giving a particular amount and type of information to a few employees or a large number at the same time. The seminar can involve a large number of people, and the trainer could be required to speak to hundreds of employees at once. These trainees may come from one company or from different organizations. At the other extreme, a consultant may lecture to a small number of employees to help them improve skills such as interpersonal communication, conflict management, or handling problems of discipline among subordinates.

The specific approach adopted depends on the type of information that employees need to acquire. Thousands of consultants in Africa, for example, offer hundreds of thousands of seminars every year in addition to in-company seminars and workshops organized by different companies annually. The problem with many such seminars is that the trainers do not often conduct needs analysis to determine whether such seminars are indeed needed. Second, the absence of relevant seminar materials for African organizations means that the main method used in such seminars is pure lecture technique. The few visual materials available for seminars in Africa, such as videos, films, and other visual aids, were not originally prepared for use in the African environment.

Seminar has been criticized as providing one-way communication without any provision for feedback from the trainees. But anyone familiar with seminars knows that many activities take place in a seminar, including lectures, the use of learning aids such as slides and videotapes, discussion sessions, and question-and-answer periods. The choice of activities to complement the lecture depends on the skill, ability, and sophistication of the lecturer as well as the task or skill to be imparted. If the skill is complex, such as operating a new and unfamiliar machine or how to deal with insubordination among subordinates, a lecture alone is not enough. An effective seminar should also include some type of practical aspect, illustrations, or role-playing.

There has been much criticism of the lecture method, but it must be remembered that, in spite of its negative aspects, the lecture method has survived over the centuries. It is economical, as important training information can be imparted to thousands in a short time. Second, research has shown that the lecture is still an effective training method (Goldstein, 1993; Miner, 1963).

The Case Study Method. This is sometimes referred to as the best training technique for training managers and other executives in problem solving and decision making (Aamodt, 1996; Niemyer, 1995; Newstrom, 1980). With the case study method, a trainer assigns a real or hypothetical case that might be encountered on the job to each member of a small group. The trainees are assigned the task of studying the cases and identifying the kinds of problems, their parameters, and some of the alternative solutions based on the information provided by the trainer. After the individuals have prepared their analyses, they are allowed to present their solutions. Following each presentation, the trainer leads a group discussion. The group evaluates the alternative solutions, their advantages and disadvantages, and then arrives at what the group thinks is the best solution to the problem. Meanwhile, the group learns that there are alternative approaches to resolving a given problem, as well as the existence of a generally systematic approach in problem solving and decision making.

Inguagiato (1993) insists that for a case study to be successful, the problems presented for solution should be taken from actual problems within the organization or at least taken from actual situations or from the participants' own experience. Aamodt (1996) indicates that the use of cases from the participants' experience or organizations is more effective for the typical case study. This is because the solutions reached by the group could be used to solve a real problem. White, Dittrich, and Lang (1980) had a group of nursing supervisors describe problems that they had confronted frequently in the course of their work. In a workshop environment the nursing supervisors were asked to generate solutions to the three most common problems. The supervisors then attempted to implement the solutions, and, in a follow-up session, they discussed their attempts at implementation. Based on the self-reports of the trainees, the conclusion was that this application of the case study method was successful in solving some real-world organizational problems.

The disadvantage of the case study method, as for all the methods that involve group discussion, is that all the trainees do not actively participate in the discussions. A few talkative ones usually dominate the group discussions and prevent other trainees from benefiting as much as they could from the case analysis. Trainers should be aware of this and should maintain equitable participation among all the trainees. A second problem is that there is often no opportunity for providing participants with detailed feedback on their individual analysis or contribution. The general conclusion regarding the case study method is that it is a useful training technique, but reaping its benefits depends heavily on the skill of the trainer. Case studies are realistic and interesting and should be made difficult enough to be challenging to the trainees.

Role Playing. This involves directing the trainees to act out some roles, such as taking the part of a manager in a performance appraisal interview with an insubordinate junior staff member. The trainees are told to imagine themselves in a situation created for them by the trainer and to try to empathize with the feelings, emotions, and attitudes of the people whose role the trainees are playing. Once the acting starts, interactions among the trainees are usually spontaneous. The participants discuss critically the playing of the problem at the end of each acting episode. Sometimes role-playing is videotaped for self-criticism by the group. Several authors have indicated that the role-playing method is one of the best for learning interpersonal skills (Aamodt, 1996; Carrol, Paine, and Ivancevich, 1972; Newstrom, 1980).

Wexley and Yukl (1984) presented two variations of role-playing methods: role reversal and multiple role-playing. Role reversal requires trainees who have differences of opinions or perspectives to act each other's role, for example, managers and labor union leaders, supervisors and their subordinates, or even two managers with overlapping responsibilities such as supply and finance managers. Reversed roles give the participants insight into what is involved in each other's expected roles, thus providing them with the opportunity to solve problems from viewpoints other than their own. The expectation is that the reversal of roles will reduce differences by making each manager aware of the other's needs and attitudes. Several attitude-change studies show that when people are forced to verbalize opinions opposite to those they already have and to defend these contrary views before others, the experience modifies their own personal attitudes in the direction of the role being played (Janis and King, 1954; Janis and Mann, 1965; Ugwuegbu, 1982). This finding holds true regardless of how much the trainee is satisfied with his or her role performance (King and Janis, 1956; Wexley and Yukl, 1984).

In multiple role-playing, about 20 to 30 trainees are subdivided into groups of five to six persons each. A trainee is requested to introduce a problem, and each of the subgroups is asked to role-play the problem. Following the subgroup's role-playing, the entire group of the trainees is reassembled to share and compare their experiences (Maier and Zerfoss, 1952; Wexley and Yukl, 1984).

Role-playing allows employees to practice what is being taught, but it is not for everyone. Many trainees find it difficult to participate enthusiastically in acting. The technique has been shown to be effective in studying small group leadership skills (Maier, 1953; Maier and Hoffman, 1960; Maier and Maier, 1957), in increasing sensitivity to subordinates (Bolda and Lawshe, 1962), in improving interviewing skills (Van Schaack, 1957), and in modifying attitudes (Culbertson, 1957; Ugwuegbu, 1982).

Compared with other executive training methods, role-playing is time-consuming. Another problem is that some trainees find it difficult to participate in role-playing, while others may go too far and overreact. It is also often difficult in role-playing to provide immediate feedback on correct behavior, while incorrect behavior may be reinforced by other participants. Similarly, with the T-group, few evaluative research works have assessed the effectiveness of role-playing in bringing about attitude change or improvement in trainee performance. Kidron's (1977) study suggests that the primary effect of role-playing as a method of managerial training is that it produces changes in trainee attitudes, but the results are usually short-lived; that is, such changes suffer "sleeper effect" or decrease as a result of time lag.

Simulation. In the United States and other technologically advanced countries, researchers in psychology and management often employ management simulation in their study of some aspects of an organization, just as soldiers simulate war conditions in war games. Simulation methods are adopted in teaching would-be pilots to fly airplanes or drivers to drive cars. In a simulation, a model of the real-world situation or a replica of the operational task is employed for the purpose of instruction or training. Simulation has the advantage of ensuring a high level of positive transfer. Second, it allows the trainee to work under "actual working conditions" without the probability of accident, either to the operational equipment or the trainee. Third, training on simulators does not tie up operational equipment.

Simulation exercises vary. Some are complex and expensive, while others are simple and inexpensive. Any learning situation can be simulated, from a manager's office, to the cockpit of an airplane, to the driver's seat in a car, to a restaurant counter. Examples of management simulations include training in oral communication, planning, and decision making (Aamodt, 1996; Keel, Cochran, Arnett, and Arnold, 1989). Others are business games, which have become a popular method for training executives in decision making and conflict resolution.

The level of resemblance between the simulator and the actual job situation has become an area of concern. Does the simulator exactly replicate actual physical and psychological job conditions? Howell and Dipboye (1982) designate this the *fidelity* question. A simulator is characterized by high *physical fidelity* if it bears a high level of physical resemblance to the operational situation. If the resemblance is low, it bears low physical fidelity. If the behavioral requirements of the model are similar to those required by the operational situation, the model is said to possess high *psychological fidelity* (Goldstein, 1974). Howell and Dipboye (1982) suggest that the only real proof of psychological fidelity is the level of transfer to the operational task of what is learned with the simulator. Aamodt (1996) admits that most simulators may not have high physical and psychological fidelity but that employing them in training managers is better than using only the lecture or actual practice methods.

Programmed Automated and Individualized Methods. These are a variety of programmed learning. One celebrated disadvantage of the lecture method is that it fails to take into consideration the individual differences among the learners. All the learners in a class are taught at the same pace. When there is a significant difference among the learners, those who are brighter and more experienced may tend to be bored if a lecture moves too slowly. Those who are slower and less experienced or less familiar with the equipment being employed for the learning, such as a computer, may feel frustrated and express more anxiety if the pace of the lecture moves too fast. Programmed instruction is a major device that has been introduced to allow employees to learn the material at their own pace. The techniques of programmed automated and individualized methods "are centered around the application of reinforcement principles" (Howell and Dipboye, 1982).

According to Aamodt (1996), programmed instruction can be delivered in several ways. With the oldest method, each trainee is provided with a step-by-step booklet that provides the material to be learned as well as a series of tests that measure the trainee's mastery of the material. If the trainees do not pass the test at the end of each unit, they must go back and reread the material and retake the test until they pass. The method affords trainees the chance to proceed at their own rate, and the tests ensure that the trainees understand the material before proceeding further.

The second method is rooted in immediate feedback to the trainee. Like the first technique, it also employs booklets, with tests that are printed in "a special latent ink" (Aamodt, 1996). The trainee reads and answers questions based on the reading and then uses "a felt-tipped, latent-image developer pen to uncover the correct answer." Each test item has four multiple-choice answers, of which only one is correct. The trainee is allowed to continue making choices until the hidden feedback is discovered about the correctness of the chosen answer.

The correct choice allows the felt-tipped, latent-image developer pen to go through the answer board indicating correct answers, thus providing immediate feedback about the correctness or otherwise of each chosen answer. In addition to the immediate feedback, the trainer has a written record of the answers given and the way the trainee went about the answers, for example, the number of attempts made by the trainee before the correct answer to each question was found. This lets the trainer know how thoroughly the trainee mastered the material.

The third method of programmed instruction uses computers. This method is commonly called computer-assisted instruction (CAI). It employs the same learning principles as programmed instruction but differs from it in the way the material to be learned and subsequent tests are delivered. With CAI, employees or trainees study at a computer terminal at their own pace. At the end of the study material, the computer poses a number of questions to the trainee. If the trainee does not answer enough questions correctly and so fails to satisfy the computer, the computer informs the trainee about the area in which help is needed and returns the trainee to the appropriate material.

King (1986) maintains that programmed instruction is effective because it employs some of those principles that help to make learning effective. For example, learning is self-paced; that is, all trainees proceed at their own individual pace. Slow learners and fast learners are happy to proceed at their own rates. Learners are also involved in active participation in the learning process. This differs from learning in a lecture method, where the learner may not be involved in any activities.

Finally, information in programmed instruction is presented in *small units.* This method of presenting material to be learned is more effective because studies on memory indicate that material presented in small units is easier to learn than large amounts of material.

Interactive video is a recent development added to programmed instruction. Interactive video allows the trainee to view a videotaped situation on a television screen. At the end of the display, the trainee makes a choice of response to the situation, and the computer selects a video that shows what would happen based on the trainee's response (Aamodt, 1996; Packer, 1988). Interactive video is not yet commonly employed for managerial training and development in African organizations probably because it is expensive and less adaptable than other types of programmed instruction.

Aamodt (1996) classifies programmed instruction as a very successful training method. Research results maintain that it achieves higher levels of faster learning than other methods (Nash, Muczyk, and Vettori, 1971) and facilitates improved performance at relatively low cost. A general criticism of all programmed instruction when compared to the lecture method comes from Howell and Dipboye (1982). They maintain that the emphasized advantages of programmed methods, such as individualization, participation, and planning, are all advantages normally associated with learning and not training per se.

T-group or Sensitivity Training. This was popularized in the mid-1960s as a method of training executives. It is an outcome of humanistic theories of management. It assumes that successful management is a function of the level of the manager's skill in interpersonal relations. The approach assumes that managers need to be trained in the following areas:

- how to listen to subordinates
- how their behavior affects their subordinates and how their subordinates' behavior affects them
- how to develop a real understanding of their personal relationship with those who work with them.

The T-group is a direct result of these new demands on the executive. The technique is known by varied names: T-group, D-group, h-group, and laboratory training. It developed enthusiastic followers and attracted controversy. The techniques employed by the T-group are similar to group therapy and encounter group approaches. Usually a small group of trainees meet regularly about once a week. The group is usually unstructured, like the leaderless discussion group, and the trainer or therapist is nondirective. The subject of discussion is each individual participant and what is going on in the group. As the participants confront each other, emotions rise, and resistance increases. How each member handles the intense emotion that is aroused forms a further aspect of the group discussion; that is, the social interactions that occur during the session itself form the core of group exploration. Events such as comments, arguments, outbursts, opinions, and denials from participants are analyzed with the aim of understanding the social process involved.

Howell and Dipboye (1982) indicate that the basic premise underlying T-group processes is that it allows people to gain insight about themselves and their behavior. Self-understanding is assumed to produce changes in attitude, behavior, and perception. Increased insight is assumed to result in increased sensitivity to the needs of subordinates and improved skill in their management.

As already indicated, the communications that go on in T-groups are often emotionally charged, but the group setting provides the participants with a psychologically safe atmosphere within which they may feel free to handle such emotional areas. The major controversies surrounding the T-group as an executive training method concern issues of ethics and the effectiveness of the technique. Critics question the right of the organization to compel employees to undergo sensitivity training that may end up changing the way they see the world through a change of attitude. If they possess the right, the criticism continues, do the results usually obtained make it worthwhile when one considers the level of psychological stress that the participants go through during the training sessions? On the level of the effectiveness of T-groups, the evidence in support of overwhelmingly positive outcomes remains discouraging. Campbell and Dunnette (1968) report that only a few of the evaluative studies on the T-group have been accepted on scientific grounds.

Behavioral Modeling. This is one of the most successful managerial training methods. Behavioral modeling differs from role-playing in that trainees play ideal behavior, not the behavior they might normally perform. Behavioral modeling is said to be loosely based on Bandura's (1971) social learning or vicarious learning theory. The theory proposes that individuals do not have to experience directly the consequences of their behavior in order to learn but can do so through observation of another person's enactment of same behavior. Social learning theory effects have been overwhelmingly supported by several well-designed experimental and clinical psychological studies (Bandura, 1977; Wexley and Yukl, 1984). Studies have found that social learning theory is effective in changing employee behavior in work organizations (Burnaska, 1976; Moses and Ritchie, 1976; Smith, 1976). Goldstein and Sorcher (1974) were the first to demonstrate the relevance of social learning theory to industrial training. They applied the theory of vicarious learning to the training of managers in human relations skills. The step-by-step procedure employed by these authors still provides the steps employed today. Those steps include, first, verbal presentation of the specific behaviors or skills that the trainees are expected to acquire. This is followed by presentation of film models displaying these behaviors. The trainees then role-play these behaviors displayed in the film. Correct enactments of behaviors that are correctly role-played are reinforced (Mann and Decker, 1984). Finally, each of the trainees plans how to ensure the transfer of the skills back to the job situation.

The training session schedule lasts for about nine weeks, during which period the trainees meet for about two hours per week. Each training session follows the same format as just outlined. Goldstein and Sorcher (1974) indicated that behavioral modeling has been shown to be successful in improving supervisory skills in:

- orienting new employees
- teaching job duties to employees
- motivating poor job performers
- correcting inadequate work quantity and quality
- conducting performance reviews
- handling racial and ethnic discrimination complaints

Although the behavioral modeling method has been shown to be a very effective managerial training technique, some research workers continue to question the design of such work (McGhee and Tullar, 1978). Latham and Saari (1979) employed a much-controlled study that again lent substantial support for the behavioral modeling method as an effective training technique. The general observation at present is that when proper procedures for employing behavioral modeling in managerial training are followed, employee performance is significantly improved (Meyer and Raich, 1983; Sorcher and Spence, 1982).

THE MOST EFFECTIVE METHOD

As we come to the end of our discussion of management training techniques, the question that rocks the reader's mind is, Which method is the best? As indicated earlier, the trainer should not be a slave to any given training method. All of them can be effective provided they are employed in the right situations. The method or technique to be selected for training and development must be guided by the needs of the organization, the characteristics of the managers to be trained, the nature of the goal to be attained, the objectives of the instruction, the nature of the curriculum, and organizational environmental constraints. Newstrom (1980) maintained that each training objective has a different "best" method. That best method is selected following a careful analysis of needs. Howell and Dipboye (1982) insist that the method chosen should consider the goals of the course, the abstractness of the material to be learned, and the motivation and level of skills of the managers to be trained. Among the second class of things to be considered are the resources available to the trainees for purposes of the training, such as time and opportunity for practicing what will be learned on the job situation. The trainers should be conscious of their skills and values and be knowledgeable of the personality and profiles of the trainees. Finally, no one single training method is sufficient. Trainers should assess the training environment and adopt a combination of techniques to achieve their organizational goal of effective training.

EVALUATION OF TRAINING

Literature on managerial training development in Africa can best be described as nonexistent. Unfortunately, the numerous management and development training programs that go on in any African organization are still based neither on management nor on psychological theories. Many of these private and corporate training and development programs are of low utility and anecdotal in presentation. African organizations are very fond of adopting new training methods even when they do not understand such methods. Others expend a lot of money on imported training development videos and films without giving thought to the relevance of such visual aids to the African background and the characteristics of the employees. African trainers must learn to pay attention to relevant theories and research in the area of managerial training and development if organizational training in Africa is to achieve the purpose that is intended.

An unpublished survey of the rate at which managers are trained in organizations in Nigeria showed that 93.5 percent of those surveyed claimed that they knew that the evaluation of training programs was very important but that they did not usually conduct evaluations (Ugwuegbu, 1995b). If organizations are willing to pay so much for training development, they should make sure that what they are getting is worth more than the paper on which the training procedures are written.

Criteria for Training Evaluation

Howell and Dipboye (1982) outlined four criteria suggested by Kirkpatrick (1977) by which training programs should be evaluated: trainee reactions, level of actual learning, behavior of trainees, and results.

Trainee Reactions to a Training Program. The trainers at the end of a program take a survey of how well the trainees liked a particular training program. The problem with this type of on-the-spot evaluation is that it suffers from bias. The trainees tend to engage in effort justification. For example, they tend to conclude that the course cannot be anything other than a good course since the company has spent so much money on it and since they have been involved in it for so long. Furthermore, it is a privilege to be selected for a training course. "In order to impress those who sent me and justify their decision a good reaction must be what is desirable." This attitude results in what the author calls a "They can have a good evaluation syndrome."

Learning. Here the evaluation is aimed at measuring the principles, facts, and techniques of doing thing, or solving problems that were imparted, learned, understood, and absorbed by the trainees. A further evaluation of learning would overlap with monitoring behavior on the job.

Behavior. This requires that the behaviors of participants be monitored for positive changes. In other words, the training program should result in observable trainee behavior that transfer positively to the actual job situation.

Results. These are ascertained by measuring the extent to which the training program results in long-term improvements in actual job performance as evidenced by a reduction in costs, turnover, absenteeism, and grievances or by an improvement in the quantity and quality of performance and the overall satisfaction of employees. For the evaluator to measure these criteria successfully, a baseline should be established before the start of training. Such a baseline will guides the evaluator to know when a training program has an effect as expected.

During training, the training development program should be monitored at frequent intervals to ensure that everything is progressing as planned and that all the participants are participating actively. This can be accomplished through feedback from films and videotapes, which can be assessed on the spot. Other techniques for such feedback are tests and interviews with trainees. The analysis of filmed or videotaped records allows trainers to isolate sources of wasted time, confusion, and other areas of ineffectiveness in the training program.

Research Design for Training Evaluation

It is likely that many training development managers in African organizations and other organizational consultants do not engage in the evaluation of training development because they do not know how to do it. There are many experimental ways of evaluating the effectiveness of training development programs. One may employ the *pretest-posttest* method. This technique requires the evaluator to obtain measurements of job behavior or knowledge twice, once before the training is given (pretest) and later, after training has been given (posttest). Any changes in performance observed following posttest are attributed to the effect of training.

Critics of this approach maintain that it is simple, but the findings are difficult to interpret for several obvious reasons. One reason is that the technique does not provide any control group against whose behavior the experimental group's behavior would be compared in order to rule out the Hawthorne effect, or extraneous variables that have the potential to cause the observed effect. In order to overcome these extraneous variables, a control group becomes necessary.

A second approach is the *pretest-posttest experimental group* with control group design. For purposes of clarity, the experimental group consists of subjects who are tested (pretest) first, then given training, and then tested again (posttest), while the control group consists of employees who are tested (pretest) and tested again (posttest) without receiving any training. The control group usually receives all the experimental treatments given to the experimental group such as pretest and posttest, with only one exception: they receive no training, while the experimental group receives training.

The advantage of this evaluative design is that it allows the evaluator to assess the effect of training while ruling out the influence of extraneous factors. It is also a far better design than the first design. The problem with this design is that taking a test twice may end up sensitizing the trainees, causing them to perform better when they take the test the second time. If this happens, it would incorrectly be attributed to the effect of training.

A more advanced method of assessing training outcome is Solomon's *four groups design* (see Table 9.2). This was introduced by Campbell and Stanley (1963) to solve the problems inherent in other designs. It can be adopted in evaluating training development programs. Ugwuegbu (1982) employed this technique in his study of self-persuasion and attitude change.

Table 9.2
Example of Solomon's Four Groups Design

Groups	Pretest	Training	Posttest
1	No	Yes	Yes
2	Yes	Yes	Yes
3	Yes	No	Yes
4	No	No	Yes

The design employs four distinct groups of subjects. Group 1 undergoes no pretesting, undergoes training and takes a posttest; group 2 is subjected to a pretest and also undergoes training and a posttest; group 3 takes a pretest, undergoes no training, and takes a posttest, while group 4 does not undergo a pretest or training but receives posttest. The total configuration of Solomon's four groups design would look as in Table 9.2.

The advantage of the Solomon's four groups design is that it allows the evaluator to control for both extraneous effects as well as pretest effects. Its disadvantage is that it is too difficult for most people, who may not have the statistical rigor. It is also often not practical in some moderately sized organizations to line up enough subjects to participate in this design.

SUMMARY

There are two types of managers in African organizations: those who rose from the ranks as a function of their long experience in the organizations and who form over 70 percent of all managers in African organizations and those who reached that level as a function of their professional education. Irrespective of their background and experience, no manager or employee has all the technical and interpersonal skills and knowledge necessary to operate effectively in today's organizations. This makes it necessary for organizations in Africa to put emphasis on managerial training and development.

Numerous government agencies engage in managerial training and development, including the civil service, institutes, universities, colleges and polytechnics, and private consulting organizations. In spite of all these, African countries still suffer from a shortage of skilled and competent maintenance personnel for their infrastructure and industrial equipment, skills in development innovation, and appropriate attitude and commitment to reducing constant breakdown and lowering high operational costs.

Many organizations in Africa do not utilize the training and development services that are offered them. Those organizations that do often fail to conduct needs analysis. Needs analysis is the process of identifying the short-term, intermediate, and long-term training needs of an organization. Needs analysis covers organizational, task, and person analyses. Such analyses help organizations identify what types of training and development programs are required for their employees, the type and nature of organizational tasks that are to be performed, and which managers need to be sent to a particular training and development program.

Lack of needs analysis in African organizations is responsible for the erratic nature of their training programs and has led employees and management alike to develop the wrong notions about the purpose of organizational training. Such notions include regarding periods for participation in off-the-job training programs as paid holidays for the employee. This attitude results in the lack of management demand for accountability from their employees following sponsorship in training and development programs. Thus, the organizations usually do not demand to know what impact training programs have made on their employees, nor do they create opportunity for the employees to put into practice the skills and knowledge gained from such programs.

The principles for training African managers should be guided by results. This is achieved if the design of a training program is preceded by diagnosis of the needs of the organization, managerial talents of the trainees, and analysis of the task to be learned. The training objective and the material to be learned should be identified, and the sequencing of the material or tasks to be learned should ensure transfer to actual work situations.

Methods of training and development in Africa include on-the-job and off-the-job methods. The on-the-job methods mostly used in Africa are apprenticeship training, job rotation, and coaching, while off-the-job techniques are seminars, lectures, case study, role-playing, and simulation. Programmed automated and individualized methods, T-groups and behavioral modeling are not used as often as the rest of on-the-job techniques.

As for the irking question of which training and development methods African trainers should use, a contingency view is advocated. The method or methods a trainer should employ in order to maximize the benefits of training and development programs should be guided by the needs of the organization, characteristics of the participating managers, the nature of the organizational goal to be attained, the objective of the training, and organizational environmental constraints. Trainers should bear in mind that there is no one best method but that there is a "best" method to achieve a particular objective.

African organizations should also learn to lay emphasis on evaluation of training and development programs. Evaluation of training programs helps consuming organizations to determine which programs are valuable and which are not. Such evaluations are accomplished through experimental procedures.

References

Aamodt, M.G. (1996). *Applied industrial organizational psychology.* 2nd ed. New York: Brooks-Cole.

Abdi, Y. (1975). The problems and prospects of psychology in Africa. *International Journal of Psychology,* 10, 227–235.

Abelson, R.P. (1976). Script processing in attitude formation and decision making. In J.S. Carroll and J.W. Payne (Eds.), *Cognition and social behavior.* Hillsdale, N J: L. Erlbaum Associates.

Achebe, C. (1958). *Things fall apart.* London: Heinemann.

Ackelsberg, R.; and Yukl, G.A. (1979). Negotiated transfer pricing and conflict resolution in organizations. *Decision Sciences,* 10, 387–398.

Adams, J.S. (1965). Inequity in social exchange. In L. Berkowitz (Ed.), *Advances in experimental social psychology.* New York: Academic Press, vol. 2, 267–299.

Adams, J.S. (1963). Toward an understanding of inequity. *Journal of Abnormal and Social Psychology,* 67, 422–436.

Adams, J. S.; and Freedman, S. (1976). Equity theory revisited; comments and annotated bibliography. In L. Berkowitz and E. Walster (Eds.), *Advances in experimental social psychology.* New York: Academic Press, vol. 9, 43–90.

Adams, L. (1965). *Managerial psychology.* Boston: The Christopher Publishing House.

Adams, L.; and Delucca, J. (1987). Effect of confidentiality and likability in performance evaluations. *Proceedings of the 8th Annual Graduate Conference on Industrial/Organizational Psychology and Organizational Behavior,* 183–184.

Adewumi, F. (Ed.) (1997). *Trade unionism in Nigeria: Challenges for the 21st Century.* Lagos: Friedrich Ebert Stiftung.

Akinola, O.A. (1986). The effect of feedback and goal setting on the productivity of bank cashiers. Unpublished M.Sc. thesis, Department of Psychology, University of Ibadan, Nigeria.

Alderson, W. (1957). *Marketing behavior and executive action.* Homewood, IL: Richard D. Irwin.

Anastasi, A. (1982). *Psychological testing.* New York: Macmillan.

Anderson, N.H. (1974a). Algebraic models in perception. In E.C. Carterette and M.P. Friedman (Eds.), *Handbook of perception.* New York: Academic Press, 215–298.

Anderson, N.H. (1974b). Information integration theory. A brief survey. In D.H. Krantz, R.C. Atkinson, R.D. Luce, and P. Supps (Eds.), *Measurement, psychophysics and neural information processing.* San Francisco: Freeman, 236–305.

Argyle, M. (1990). *The social psychology of work.* 2nd ed. London: Penguin Books.

Argyris, C. (1957). *Personality and organization.* New York: Harper and Row.

Argyris, C. (1960). *Understanding organizational behavior.* Homewood, IL: Dorsey Press.

Armer, J.M. (1974). *African social psychology: A review and annotated bibliography.* New York: African Press.

Athey, T.R.; and McIntyre, R.M. (1987). Effect of rater training on rater accuracy: Levels of processing theory and social facilitation perspectives. *Journal of Applied Psychology, 72,* 567–572.

Atwater, L.; Roush, P.; and Fischthal, A. (1995). The influence of upward feedback on self-and follower ratings of leadership. *Personnel Psychology, 48,* 35–60.

Baker, C. (1980). The Vroom-Yetton model of leadership—model, theory or technique? *Omega, 8,* 9-10.

Bakke, E.W. (1953). *The fusion process.* New Haven, CT: Labor and Management Center, Yale University.

Baldwin, T.T.; and Ford, J.K. (1988). Transfer of training. A review and directions for future research. *Personnel Psychology, 41,* 63–105.

Balogun, S.K.; and Daodu, I. (1994). Sex and time pressure effects on bargaining outcomes in open markets. *African Journal for the Psychological Study of Social Issues,* 1 (2), 185-194.

Bandura, A. (1977). *Social learning theory.* Englewood Cliffs, NJ: Prentice-Hall.

Bandura, A. (Ed.) (1971). *Psychological modeling: Conflicting theories.* Chicago: Aldine.

Barnard, C.I. (1938). *The functions of executives.* Cambridge: Harvard University Press.

Bass, B.M. (1983). *Organizational decision making.* Homewood, IL: Richard D. Irwin.

Bass, B.M. (1985). *Leadership and performance and beyond expectations.* New York: Free Press.

Bass, B.M. (1990). *Bass and Stogdill's handbook of leadership.* 3rd ed. New York: Free Press.

Bass. B.M.; and Barrett, G.V. (1972). *Man, work, and organizations.* Boston: Allyn and Bacon.

Batstone, E. (1979). The organization of conflict. In G.M. Stephenson and C.J. Brotherton (Eds.), *Industrial Relations: A social psychological approach.* Chichester: Wiley and Sons, 55-74.

Baumgartner, J. (1994). Give it to me straight. *Training and Development Journal, 48,* 49–51.

Bazerman, M.H. (1983). Negotiator judgment. *American Behavioral Scientist, 27,* 211–228.

Bazerman, M.H.; Magliozzi, T.; and Neale, M.A. (1985). Integrative bargaining in a competitive market. *Organizational Behavior and Human Decision Processes, 35,* 294–313.

Bechet, T.P.; and Maki, W.R. (1987). Modeling and forecasting: Focusing on people as a strategic resource. *Human Resource Planning,* 10, 209–219.

Bennis, W.G.; and Nanus, B. (1985). *Leaders: The strategy for taking charge.* New York: Harper and Row.

Bentz, V.J. (1983, August). Executive selection at Sears. Update paper presented at the fourth Annual Conference on Frontiers of Industrial Psychology, Virginia Polytechnic Institute, Blacksburg.

Bentz, V.J. (1985, August). A view from the top: A third-year perspective of research devoted to discovery, description and prediction of executive behavior. Paper presented at the 93rd Annual Convention of the American Psychological Association, Los Angeles.

Bentz, V.J. (1987, August). Contextual richness as a criterion consideration in personality research with executives. Paper presented at the 95th Annual Convention of the American Psychological Association, New York.

Bentz, V.J. (1990). Contextual issues in predicting high-level leadership performance. In K.E. Clark and M.B. Clark (Eds.), *Measures of leadership*. West Orange, NJ: Leadership Library of America, 131–143.

Berg, E.J. (1963). The role of trade unions in African economic development. Cambridge: Harvard University Press.

Berlew, D.; and Hall, D. (1966). The socialization of managers: The effects of expectations on performance. *Administrative Science Quarterly*, 1, 202–223.

Bernardin, H.J.; and Buckley, M.R. (1981). Strategies in rater training. *Academy Management Review*, 6, 205–242.

Bernardin, H.J.; and Kane, J.S. (1980). A second look at behavioral observation scales. *Personnel Psychology*, 33, 809–814.

Berscheid, E.; and Walster, E.H. (1978). *Interpersonal attraction*. 2nd ed. Reading, MA.: Addison-Wesley.

Bingham, W.V. (1949). Today and yesterday. *Personnel Psychology*, 2, 267-275.

Blake, R.R.; and Mouton, J.S. (1964). *The managerial grid*. Houston: Gulf.

Blanz, F.; and Ghiselli, E.E. (1972). The mixed-standard scale. A new rating system. *Personnel Psychology*, 25, 185–200.

Bolda, R.A.; and Lawshe, C.H. (1962). Evaluation of role-playing. *Personnel Administration*, 25, 40–42.

Bourne, L.E., Jr. (1966). *Human conceptual behavior*. Boston: Allyn and Bacon.

Bray, D.W. (1982). The assessment center and study of lives. *American Psychologist*, 37, 180–189.

Bray, D.W.; and Campbell, R.J. (1968). Selection of salesmen by means of an assessment center. *Journal of Applied Psychology*, 52, 36–41.

Bray, D.W.; Campbell, R.J.; and Grant, D.L. (1974). *Formative years in business: A long-term AT&T study of managerial lives*. New York: Wiley–Interscience.

Bray, D.W.; and Grant, D.L. (1966). The assessment center in the measurement of potential for business management. *Psychological Monographs*, 1–27.

Bray, D.W.; and Howard, A. (1983). The AT&T longitudinal studies of managers. In K.W. Schaie (Ed.), *Longitudinal studies of adult psychological development*. New York: Guilford Press, 112–146.

Brett, J.M. (1986). Commentary on procedural justice papers. In R. Lewicki, M. Bazerman, and B. Sheppard (Eds.), *Research on negotiations in organizations*. Greenwich, CT: JAI. Press, vol. 1, 81–90.

Brett, J.M.; and Goldberg, S.B. (1983). Grievance mediation in the coal industry: A field experiment. *Industrial and Labor Relations Review*, 37, 49–69.

Brett, J.M.; Goldberg, S.B.; and Ury, W.L. (1990). Designing systems for resolving disputes in organizations. *American Psychologist*, 45, 162–170.

Burack, E.H. (1988). A strategic planning and operational agenda for human resources. *Human Resource Planning*, 11, 63-68.

Burk, R.J. (1970). Methods of resolving superior-subordinate conflict: The constructive use of subordinate differences and disagreements. *Organizational Behavior and Human Performance*, 5, 393–411.

Burke, M.J.; and Day, R.R. (1986). A cumulative study of the effectiveness of managerial training. *Journal of Applied Psychology*, 71, 232–245.

Burnaska, R.F. (1976). The effects of behavior modeling training upon managers' behaviors and employees' perceptions. *Personnel Psychology*, 29, 329–335.

Burns, J.M. (1978). *Leadership*. New York: Harper and Row.

Buros, O.K. (Ed.), (1978). *The mental measurements yearbook*. Lincoln: University of Nebraska.

Buros, O.K. (Ed.),   (1998). *The measurements yearbook*, Lincoln: University of Nebraska.

Byrne, D., and Wong, T.J. (1962). Racial prejudice, interpersonal attraction and assumed dissimilarity of attitude. *Journal of Abnormal and Social Psychology*, 65, 245–253.

Calder, B.J. (1977). An attribution theory of leadership. In B.M. Staw and G.R. Salancik (Eds.), *New directions in organizational behavior*. Chicago: St. Clair Press, 179–204.

Campbell, D.P. (1991). *Manual for the Campbell Leadership Index*. Minneapolis: National Computer System.

Campbell, D.T.; and Stanley, J.C. (1963). *Experimental and quasi-experimental designs in research*. Chicago: Rand-McNally.

Campbell, J.P.; and Dunnette, M.D. (1968). Effectiveness of T-group experiences in managerial training and development. *Psychological Bulletin*, 70, 73–104.

Cardy, R.L.; and Dobbins, G.H. (1986). Affect and appraisal accuracy. Liking as an integral dimension in evaluating performance. *Journal of Applied Psychology*, 71, 672–678.

Carrol, S.J.; Paine, F.T.; and Ivancevich, J.J. (1972). The relative effectiveness of training methods: Expert opinion and research. *Personnel Psychology*, 25, 495–510.

Cascio, W.F. (1982). *Applied psychology in personnel management*. Reston, VA: Reston.

Cederbloom, D. (1989). Peer and supervisor evaluations: An underused promotion method used for law enforcement. *Proceedings of 13th Annual Meeting of International Personnel Management Association-Assessment Council*.

Cell, J.W. (1970). *British Colonial Administration in the Mid-Nineteenth Century: The Policy -Making Process*. New York: Yale University Press.

Chidester, T.R.; Helmreich, R.L.; Gregorich, S.E.; and Geis, C.E. (1991). Pilot personality and crew coordination. *International Journal of Aviation Psychology*, 1, 25–44.

Cohn, B. (1988, August). A glimpse of the "flex" future. *Newsweek*, 38–39.

Comer, D.R. (1989). Peers as providers. *Personnel Administrator*, 34, 84–86.

Constantin, S.W. (1976). An investigation of information favorability in the employment interview. *Journal of Applied Psychology*, 61, 743–749.

Culbertson, F. (1957). Modification of an emotionally held attitude through role-playing. *Journal of Abnormal and Social Psychology*, 54, 230–233.

Cummings, L. L.; and Harnett, D.L. (1969). Bargaining behavior in a symmetric bargaining triad. *The Review of Economic Studies*, 36, 485–501.

Curphy, G.J. (1991). An empirical investigation of Bass (1985) theory of transformational and transactional leadership. Diss. University of Minnesota, Minneapolis.

Curphy, G.J. (1993). An empirical investigation of the effects of transformational and transactional leadership on organizational climate, attrition and performance. In

K.E. Clark, M.B. Clark, and D.P. Campbell (Eds.), *Impact of leadership*. Greenboro NC, Center for Creative Leadership, 177–188.

Dale, E. (1969). *Management: Theory and practice*. 2nd ed. New York: McGraw–Hill.

Dawson, J.L.M. (1967). Traditional versus Western attitudes in West Africa: The construction, validation and application of a measuring device. *British Journal of Social and Clinical Psychology*, 6, 81–96.

Dearborn, D.C.; and Simon, H.A. (1958). Selective perception: A note on the departmental identification of executives. *Sociometry*, 140–144.

Deluca, J.R. (1988). Strategic career management in non-growing volatile business environments. *Human Resource Planning*, 11, 49–62.

Deutsch, M. (1973). *The resolution of conflict: Constructive and destructive processes*. New Haven, CT: Yale University Press.

Deutsch, M. (1980). Fifty years of conflict. In L. Festinger (Ed.), *Retrospections of social psychology*. New York: Oxford University Press, 46-77.

DeVries, D.L. (1992). Executive selection: Advances but no progress. *Issues and Observations*, 12, 1–5.

Doob, L.W. (1960). *Becoming more civilized*. New Haven, CT: Yale University Press.

Driskell, J.E.; Wills, R.P.; and Cooper, C. (1992). Effect of overlearning on retention. *Journal of Applied Psychology*, 77, 615–623.

Drucker, P. (1964). *Managing for results*. New York: Harper and Row.

Dumaine, B. (1989, July 3). What the leaders of tomorrow see. *Fortune*, 48–62.

Dunnette, M. D. (Ed.), (1976). *Handbook of industrial and organizational psychology* Chicago: Rand-McNally.

Dunnette, M.D.; and Borman, W.C. (1979). Personnel selection and classification systems. *Annual Review of Psychology*, 30, 477–525.

Dunnette, M.D.; and Hough, L.M. (Eds.), (1991). *Handbook of industrial and organizational psychology*. Palo Alto, CA: Consulting Psychology Press.

Dunnette, M.D.; and Motowidlo, S.J. (1975). *Development of personnel selection and career assessment system for police officers for patrol, investigative, supervisory, and command positions*. Minneapolis: Personnel Decisions.

Ejiofor, P. (1981). *Management in Nigeria*. Onitsha: African Press.

Emerson, R.M. (1962). Power dependency relations. *American Sociological Review*, 27, 31–41.

Etuk, E. (1983). Factors that motivate executive officers in the public service section: The case of Cross River State. Paper presented at the First National Workshop on Organization Behavior and Management, University of Ibadan.

Evans, M.G. (1970). The effects of supervisory behavior on the path-goal relationships. *Organizational Behavior and Human Performance*, 5, 277–298.

Eysenck, H.J. (1963). The measurement of motivation. *Scientific American*, 208(5), 130–140.

Eze, N. (1995). *Human resources management in Africa: problems and solution*. Lagos: Zomex Press.

Fahr, J.; Cannella, A.A.; and Bedeian, A.G. (1991). Peer ratings: The impact of purpose on rating quality and user acceptance. *Group and Organization Studies*, 16, 367–386.

Farmer, R.N.; and Richman, S.M. (1965). *Comparative management and economic progress*. Homewood, IL: Richard D. Irwin.

Fay, C.H.; and Latham, G.P. (1982). Effects of training and rating scales on rating errors. *Personnel Psychology*, 35, 105–116.

Fayol, H. (1949). *General and industrial management*. Translated by Constance Storrs. London: Sir Isaac Pitman and Sons.

Feder, D.B. ; and Ferris, G.R. (1981). Integrating O.B. mod with cognitive approaches to motivation. *Academy of Management Review,* 6, 115–125.

Federal Republic of Nigeria (1988). *Implementation guidelines on the civil service reforms.* Lagos: Federal Government Printer.

Fiedler, F.E. (1967). *A theory of leadership effectiveness.* New York: McGraw-Hill.

Fiedler, F.E. (1977). A rejoinder to Schriescheim and Kerr's premature obituary of the contingency model. In J.G. Hunt and L.L. Larson (Eds.), *Leadership, the Cutting Edge.* Carbondale: Southern Illinois University Press, 45–51.

Finkle, R. B. (1976). Managerial assessment centers. In M.D. Dunnette (Ed.), *Handbook of industrial and managerial psychology.* Chicago: Rand-McNally, 861- 888.

Fisher, R.; and Ury, W. (1981). *Getting to yes: Negotiating agreements without giving in.* Boston: Houghton Mifflin.

Fitzgerald, L.F. (1980). *The incidence and utilization of assessment centers in state and local governments.* Washington, DC: International Personnel Management Association.

Flanagan, J.C.; and Burns, R.K. (1955). The employee performance record: A new appraisal and development tool. *Harvard Business Review,* 33, 95–102.

Flander, A. (1965). Industrial relations: What is wrong with the system? London: Faber and Faber.

Ford, J.K.; Quinones, M.A.; Sego, D.J.; and Sorra, J.S. (1992). Factors affecting the opportunity to perform trained tasks on the job. *Personnel Psychology,* 45, 511–527.

Forrester, J.W. (1961). *Industrial dynamics.* Cambridge: M.I.T. Press, 93.

French, J.R.P., Jr.; and Raven, B. (1959). The bases of social power. In D. Cartwright (Ed.), *Studies in social power.* Ann Arbor, MI: Institute of Social Research. 150–167.

Furnham, A.; and Stringfield, P. (1994). Congruence of self and subordinate ratings of managerial practices as a correlate of superior evaluation. *Journal of Occupational and Organizational Psychology,* 67, 57–67.

Gagne, R.M. (1962). Military training and principles of learning. *American Psychologist,* 17, 83–91.

Galton, F. (1869). *Hereditary genius: An inquiry into its laws and consequences.* London: Macmillan; Paperback edition, New York: Meridian Books, 1962.

Geber, B. (1987). Who should do the sales training? *Training,* 24, 69–76.

Ghiselli, E.E. (1976). The validity of aptitude tests in personnel selection. *Personnel Psychology,* 26, 461–477.

Goldberg, L.R. (1993). The structure of phenotypic personality traits. *American Psychologist,* 48, 26–34.

Goldberg, S. B.; Green, E.D.; and Sanders, F.E.A. (1985). *Dispute resolution.* Boston: Little, Brown.

Goldstein, A.P.; and Sorcher, M. (1974). *Changing supervisor behavior.* New York: Pergamon Press.

Goldstein, I.L. (1974). *Program development and evaluation.* Monterey, CA.: Brooks-Cole.

Goldstein, I.L. (1980). Training in work organizations. *Annual Review of Psychology,* 31, 229–272.

Goldstein, I.L. (1993). Training in organizations. 3rd ed. Pacific Grove, CA: Brooks-Cole.

Graham, J.K.; and Mihal, W.L. (1986). Can your management development needs surveys be trusted? *Training and Development Journal,* 40, 38–42.

Guion, R.M. (1976). Recruiting, selection, and job replacement. In M.D. Dunnette (Ed.), *Handbook of industrial and organizational psycholog.,* Chicago: Rand-McNally, 777–828.

Guion, R.M. (1991). Personnel assessment, selection, and placement. In M.D. Dunnette and L.M. Hough (Eds.), *Handbook of industrial and organizational psychology*, Palo Alto, CA.: Consulting Psychology Press, 32–397.

Hackman, J.R.; and Oldham, G.R. (1975). The development of the Job Diagnostic Survey. *Journal of Applied Psychology,* 60, 159–170.

Hackman, J.R.; and Oldham, G.R. (1980). *Work redesign.* Reading, MA: Addison-Wesley.

Haire, M. (Ed.), (1959). *Modern organizational theory: A symposium of the Foundation for Research on Human Behavior.* New York: John Wiley and Sons.

Hammond, K.R.; and Summers, D.A. (1972). Cognitive control. *Psychological Review,* 79, 58–67.

Hamner, W.C.; and Carter, P.L. (1975). A comparison of alternative production management co-efficient decision rules. *Science, 6,* 324–336.

Harbinson, F. H. (1959). Egypt. In W. Galenson (Ed.), *Economic Development.* London: John Wiley, 146-185.

Harnett, D.L.; Cummings, L.L.; and Hughes, C.D. (1968). The influence of risk taking propensity on bargaining behavior. *Behavioral Science,*13, 91–101.

Harris, G.; and Hogan, J. (1992). Perceptions and personality correlates of managerial effectiveness. Paper presented at the 13th Annual Psychology in the Department of Defense Symposium, Colorado Springs.

Hauenstein, N.M.A.; and Foti, R.J. (1989). From laboratory to practice: Neglected issue of implementing frame-of-reference rater training. *Personnel Psychology,* 42, 359–378.

Hazucha, J.F. (1991). Success, jeopardy, and performance: Contrasting managerial outcomes and their predictors. Diss., University of Minnesota, Minneapolis.

Hellerrik, L.W.; Hunt, A.; and Silzer, R.F. (1976). *An assessment center for selecting account executives.* Minneapolis: Personnel Decisions.

Hendrick, C.; and Hawkins, G. (1969). Race and belief similarity as determinants of attraction. *Perceptual and Motor Skills,* 29, 710.

Herbert, G.P.; and Doverspike, D. (1990). Performance appraisal in the training needs analysis process: A review and critique. *Public Personnel Management,,*19, 253–270.

Herzberg, F. (1966). *Work and the nature of man.* Cleveland, OH: World.

Herzberg, F.; Mausner, B.; and Snyderman, B.B. (1959). *The motivation to work.* New York: Wiley and Sons.

Hogan, R. (1994). Trouble at the top: Causes and consequences of managerial incompetence. *Consulting Psychology Journal,* 46, 9–15.

Hogan, R.; Curphy, G.J.; and Hogan, J. (1994). What we know about leadership effectiveness and personality. *American Psychologist,* 49, 493–503.

Hogan, R.; Hogan, J.; and Roberts, B.W. (1996). Personality measurement and employment decisions. *American Psychologist,* 51, 469–477.

Hogan, R.; Raskin, R.; and Fazzini, D. (1990). The dark side of charisma. In K.E. Clark and M.B. Clark (Eds.), *Measures of leadership.* West Orange, NJ: Leadership Library of America, 343–354.

Hollander, E.P. (1964). *Leaders, groups, and influence.* New York: Oxford University Press.

Hollander, E.P. (1978). *Leadership dynamics: A practical guide to effective relationships.* New York: Free Press.

Hollander, E.P.; and Julian, J.W. (1969). Contemporary trends in the analysis of leadership processes. *Psychological Bulletin,* 71, 387–397.

Hollander, E.P.; and Offermann, L.R. (1990). Power and leadership in organizations: Relationship in transition. *American Psychologist,* 45, 179–189.

Holmes, J.G.; Throop, W.F.; and Strickland, L.H. (1971). The effects of prenegotiation expectations on the distributive bargaining process. *Journal of Experimental Social Psychology,* 7, 582–599.

Holzbach, R.L. (1978). Rater bias in performance ratings: Supervisor, self and peer ratings. *Journal of Applied Psychology,* 63, 579–588.

Homans, G.C. (1961). *Social behavior: Its elementary forms.* New York: Harcourt Brace Jovanovich.

Homans, G. C. (1974). *Social behavior: Its elementary forms.* Rev. ed. New York: Harcourt Brace Jovanovich.

House, R.J. (1971). A path-goal theory of leader effectiveness. *Administrative Science Quarterly,* 16, 231–338.

House, R.J. (1977). A 1976 theory of charismatic leadership. In J.G. Hunt and L.L. Larson (Eds.), *Leadership: The cutting edge.* Carbondale: Southern Illinois University Press, 189–207.

House, R.J.; and Mitchell, T.R. (1974). Path-goal theory of leadership. *Journal of Contemporary Business,* 3, 81–87.

House, R.J.; Spangler, W.D.; and Woycke, J. (1991). Personality and charisma in the U.S. presidency. A psychological theory of leadership effectiveness. *Administrative Science Quarterly,* 36, 364–396.

Howard, A. (1992). Selecting executives for the 21st Century. Can assessment centers meet the challenge? Presentation at the Executive Selection Conference, Center for Creative Leadership. Greensboro, NC.

Howard, A. (1993). Will assessment centers be obsolete in the 21st century? Replies to the critics. Paper presented at the 21st International Congress on Assessment Center Method, Atlanta, GA.

Howard, A.; and Bray, D.W. (1988). *Managerial lives in transition.* New York: Guilford Press.

Howard, A.; and Bray, D.W. (1990). Predictions of managerial success over long periods of time: Lessons for the Management Progress Study. In K.E. Clark and M.B. Clark (Eds.), *Measures of leadership.* West Orange, NJ: Leadership Library of America, 113–130.

Howell, W.C.; and Dipboye, R.L. (1982). *Essentials of industrial and organizational psychology.* Homewood, IL: Dorsey Press.

Howells, J.M. (1972). Causes and frequency of strikes in New Zealand. *Industrial and Labor Relations Review,* 25, 524–532.

Hull, C.L. (1943). *Principles of behavior.* New York: Appleton-Century-Crofts.

Ijewere, G.O. (1958). Rail and road in post-world war Nigerian economy. Ph.D. thesis, Oxford University.

Inguagiato, R.J. (1993). Case studies: Let's get real. *Training and Development,* 47, 20–24.

Ivancevich, J.M. (1982). Subordinates' reactions to performance appraisal interviews: A test of feedback and goal-setting techniques. *Journal of Applied Psychology,* 67, 581–587.

Jackson, S.E.; and Schuler, R..S. (1990). Human resource planning; challenges for industrial organizational psychologists. *American Psychologist,* 45, 223–239.

Jacoby, J. (1975). Perspectives on a consumer information processing research program. *Communication Research,* 2, 203–215.

Jacoby, J. (1976). Consumer psychology: An octennium. *Annual Review of Psychology,* 27, 331–358.

Janis, I.L. (1972). *Victims of groupthink.* Boston: Houghton-Mifflin.

Janis, I.L.; and King, B.T. (1954). The influence of role-playing on opinion change. *Journal of Abnormal and Social Psychology,* 49, 211–218.

Janis, I.; and Mann, L. (1965). Effectiveness of emotional role-playing in modifying smoking habits and attitudes. *Journal of Experimental Research in Personality,* 1, 84–90.

Janis, I.L.; and Mann, L. (1977). *Decision making: A psychological analysis of conflict, choice, and commitment.* New York: Free Press.

Jones, E.E.; and Davis, K.E. (1965). From acts to dispositions: The attribution process in person perception. In L. Berkowitz (Ed.), *Advances in experimental social psychology,* New York: Academic Press, vol. 2, 219-266.

Kaplan, R.E.; Drath, W.H.; and Kofodimos, J.R. (1991). *Beyond ambition: How driven managers can lead better and live better.* San Francisco: Jossey-Bass.

Karambayy, R.; and Brett, J. M. (1989). Managers handling disputes. Third-party roles and perceptions of fairness. *Academy of Management Journal,* 32, 687–704.

Katz, D.; and Kahn, R.L. (1966). *The social psychology of organizations.* New York: John Wiley and Sons.

Katz, R.L. (1974, September/October). Skills of an effective administrator. *Harvard Business Review,* 90–102.

Katzell, R.A.; and Thompson, D.E. (1986). Empirical research on a comprehensive theory of work motivation. Paper presented at the 21st International Congress of Applied Psychology, Jerusalem, Israel.

Katzell, R.A.; and Thompson, D.E. (1990). Work motivation: Theory and practice. *American Psychologist,* 45, 144–153.

Keel, S.B.; Cochran, D.S.; Arnett, K.; and Arnold, D.R. (1989). AC's are not just for the big guys. *Personnel Administrator,* 34, 98–101.

Kelley, H.H. (1966). A classroom study of dilemmas in interpersonal negotiations. In K. Archibald (Ed.), *Strategic interaction and conflict.* Berkeley: Institute of International Studies, University of California.

Kidron, A.G. (1977). The effectiveness of experimental methods in training and education: The case of role-playing. *Academy of Management Review,* 2, 490–495.

Kilby, P. (1960). Some determinants of individual productivity in Nigeria. *Proceedings of the Nigerian Institute of Social and Economic Research,* 171-180.

King, B.T.; and Janis, I.L. (1956). Comparison of the effectiveness of improvised role-playing in producing opinion changes. *Journal of Human Relations,* 9, 177–187.

King, J. (1986). Computer-based instruction. In L. Donaldson and E.E. Scannell (Eds.), *Human resource development: The new trainer's guide.* Reading, MA: Addison-Wesley, 79–85.

Kipnis, D. (1976). *The powerholders.* Chicago: University of Chicago Press.

Kirchner, W.; and Reisberg, D.J. (1962). Differences between better and less effective supervisors in appraisal of subordinates. *Personnel Psychology,* 15, 295–302.

Kirkpatrick, D.L. (1977). Evaluating training programs: Evidence versus proof. *Training and Development Journal,* 31, 9–12.

Kolb, D.A.; and Boyatzis, R. (1970). On the dynamics of helping relationship. *Journal of Applied Behavioral Science,* 6(3), 267-289.

Kolb, D.A.; Rubin, I.M.; and McIntyre, J.M. (1971). *Organizational psychology: An experimental approach.* Englewood Cliffs, NJ: Prentice-Hall.

Komaki, J.; Heinzmann, A.T.; and Lawson, L. (1980). Effects of training and feedback: Component analysis of a behavioral safety program. *Journal of Applied Psychology,* 65, 261–270.

Koontz, H.; and O'Donnell, C. (1968). *Principles of management: An analysis of managerial functions.* 4th ed. New York: McGraw–Hill.

Korman, A.K. (1971). *Industrial and organizational psychology.* Englewood Cliffs, NJ: Prentice-Hall.

Kraut, A.L.; and Scott, G.J. (1972). Validity of an operational assessment program. *Journal of Appied Psychology,* 56, 124–129.

Lambo, T.A. (1978). Psychotherapy in Africa. *Nature,* 3, 32–39.

Landy, F.J.; and Farr, J.L. (1980). Performance rating. *Psychological Bulletin,* 87, 72–107.

Landy, F.J.; and Guion, R.M. (1970). Development of scales for the measurement of work motivation. *Organizational Behavior and Human Performance,* 5, 93–103.

Latham, G.D.; and Saari, L.M. (1979). Application of social-learning theory to training supervisors through behavioral modeling. *Journal of Applied Psychology,* 64, 239–246.

Latham, G.P.; and Wexley, K.N. (1977). Behavioral observation scale for performance appraisal purposes. *Personnel Psychology,* 30, 225–268.

Lawler, E.E. (1987). Pay for performance: A motivational analysis. In H. Nalbantian (Ed.), *Incentive, cooperation, risk sharing.* Totowa, NJ: Rowman and Littlefield, 69–86.

Lawshe, C.H. (1975). A quantitative approach to content validity. *Personnel Psychology,* 28, 563–575.

Lax, D.A.; and Sebenius, J.K. (1986). *The manager as negotiator.* New York: Free Press.

Leavitt, H.J.; and Bahrami, H. (1988). *Managerial psychology: Managing behavior in organization.* 5th ed. Chicago: University of Chicago Press.

LeVine, R.A. (1966). *Dreams and deeds: Achievement motivation in Nigeria.* Chicago: University of Chicago Press.

Liddell, W.W.; and Slocum, J.W. (1976). The effects of individual role compatibility upon group performance: An extension of Schutz's FIRO theory. *Academy of Management Journal,* 19, 413–426.

Likert, R. (1959). A motivational approach to modified theory of organization and management. In M. Haire (Ed.), *Modern organizational theory: A symposium of the foundation for research on human behavior.* New York: John Wiley and Sons, 193.

Likert, R. (1961). *New patterns of management.* New York: McGraw-Hill.

Likert, R. (1967). *The human organization.* New York: McGraw-Hill.

Lind, E.A.; and Tyler, T.R. (1988). *The social psychology of procedural justice.* New York: Plenum Press.

Lloyd, I.S. (1949, December). The environment of business decisions: Some reflections on the history of Rolls Royce. *The South African Journal of Economics,* 457–479.

Locke, E.A. (1968). Towards a theory of task motivation and incentives. *Organizational Behavior and Human Performance,* 3, 157–189.

Locke, E.A. (1991). *The essence of leadership.* New York: Lexington Books.

Locke, E.A.; Cartledge, N.; and Koepl, J. (1968). Motivational effects of knowledge of results. A goal setting phenomenon. *Psychological Bulletin,* 70, 474–485.

Locke, E.A.; Feren, D.B.; McCaleb, V.M.; Shaw, K.N.; and Denny, A.T. (1980). The relative effectiveness of four methods of motivating employee performance. In K.D. Duncan, M.M. Gruneberg, and D. Wallis (Eds.), *Changes in working life.* New York: Wiley and Sons, 363–388.

Locke, E.A.; Latham, G.P.; and Erez, M. (1988). The determinants of goal commitment. *Academy of Management Review,* 13, 23–39.

Locke, E.A.; Shaw, K.N.; Saari, L.M.; and Latham, G.P. (1981). Goal setting and task performance 1969–1980. *Psychological Bulletin,* 90, 125–152.

Lombardo, M.M.; Ruderman, M.N.; and McCauley, C.D. (1988). Explanations of success and derailment in upper-level management positions. *Journal of Business and Psychology,* 2, 199–216.

London, M.; and Wohlers, A.J. (1991). Agreement between subordinate and self-ratings in upward feedback. *Personnel Psychology,* 44, 375–390.

Mabe, P.A.; and West, S.G. (1982). Validity of self-evaluation of ability. A review and meta-analysis. *Journal of Applied Psychology,* 67, 280–296.

Maccoby, M. (1976). *The gamesman, the new corporate leaders.* New York: Simon and Schuster.

Maccoby, M. (1981). *The leader.* New York: Simon and Schuster.

MacCrimmon, K.R.; and Taylor, D.N. (1976). Decision and problem solving. In M.D. Dunnette (Ed.), *Handbook of industrial and organizational psychology.* Chicago: Rand-McNally, 1393–1454.

MacKinnon, D.W. (1944). The structure of personality. In J. McVicker Hunt (Ed.), *Personality and the behavior disorders.* New York: Ronald Press, vol. 1, 1- 48.

Maehr, M. (1974). Culture and achievement motivation. *American Psychologist, 29,* 887–896.

Maehr, M.L.; and Sjogren, D. (1971). Atkinson's theory of achievement motivation. First step toward a theory of academic motivation? *Review of Educational Research, 41,* 143–161.

Magenau, J. M.; and Pruitt, D.G. (1979). The social psychology of bargaining: A theoretical synthesis. In G.M. Stephenson and C.J. Brotherton (Eds.), *Industrial relations: A social psychological approach.* Chichester: John Wiley and Sons, 181– 210.

Mager, R.F. (1984). *Preparing institutional objectives.* Belmont, CA: Pitman Learning.

Maier, N.R.F. (1953). An experimental test of the effect of training on discussion leadership. *Human Relations,* 6, 161–173.

Maier, N.R.F.; and Hoffman, L.R. (1960). Using trained developmental discussion leaders to improve further the quality of group decisions. *Journal of Applied Psychology,* 44, 247–251.

Maier, N.R.F.; and Maier, R.A. (1957). An experimental test of the effects of developmental versus free discussions on the quality of group decisions. *Journal of Applied Psychology,* 41, 320–323.

Maier, N.R.F.; and Zerfoss, L.R. (1952). MRP: A technique for training large groups of supervisors and its potential use in social research. *Human Relations,* 5, 177–187.

Mann, R.B.; and Decker, P.J. (1984). The effect of key behavior distinctiveness on generation and recall in behavior modeling training. *Academy of Management Journal,* 27, 900–910.

Maslow, A.H. (1954). *Motivation and personality.* New York: Harper and Row.

Mayo, E. (1933). *The human problems of industrial civilization,.* New York: Macmillan.

Mayo, E. (1960). *The human problems of industrial civilization, 2nd ed.* New York: Viking Press.

McCall, M.W., Jr (1988). Developing executives through work experiences. *Human Resource Planning,* 11, 1–11.

McCall, M.W., Jr.; and Lombardo, M.M. (1983). *Off the track: Why and how successful executives get derailed* (Tech. Rep. No. 21). Greensboro, NC: Center for Creative Leadership.

McClelland, D.C. (1961). *The achieving society.* Princeton, NJ: D. Van Nostrand.

McClelland, D.C. (1965a). Achievement motivation can be developed. *Harvard Business Review,* 43, 6–24.

McClelland, D.C. (1965b). N'achievement and Entrepreneurship: A longitudinal study. *Journal of Personality and Social Psychology,* 1, 389–392.

McClelland, D.C. (1965c). Towards a theory of motive acquisition. *American Psychologist,* 20, 321–333.

McClelland, D.C. (1971a). *Assessing human motivation.* New York: General Press.

McClelland, D.C. (1971b). *Motivational trends in society.* New York: General Press.

McClelland, D.C. (1975). *Power: The inner experience.* New York: Irvington.

McClelland, D.C.; and Boyatzis, R.E. (1982). Leadership motive pattern and long-term success in management. *Journal of Applied Psychology,* 67, 737–743.

McClelland, D.C.; and Burnham, D.H. (1976, March/April). Power is the great motivator. *Harvard Business Review,* 100–110.

McClelland, D.C.; and Winter, D.G. (1969). *Motivating economic achievement.* New York: Free Press.

McCormick, E.J.; and Ilgen, D.R. (1980). *Industrial psychology.* London: George Allen and Unwin.

McCormick, E.J.; Jeanneret, D.R.; and Mecham, R.C. (1972). A study of job characteristics and job dimensions as based on the Position Analysis Questionnaire (PAQ). *Journal of Applied Psychology,* 56, 347–368.

McEwen, C.A.; and Maiman, R.J. (1981). Small claims mediation in Maine: An empirical assessment. *Maine Law Review,* 37, 237–268.

McFarland, D.E. (1974). *Management: Principles and practices.* 4th ed. New York: Macmillan.

McGhee, W.; and Tullar, W.L.A. (1978). A note on evaluating behavior modification and behavior modeling as industrial training techniques. *Personnel Psychology,* 31, 477–484.

McGregor, D. (1960). *The human side of enterprise.* New York: McGraw-Hill.

McIntyre, R.; Smith D.; and Hassett, C. (1984). Accuracy of performance ratings as affected by rater training and perceived purpose of training. *Journal of Applied Psychology,* 69, 147–156.

McManis, G. L.; and Leibman, M. S. (1988, April). Succession planners. *Personnel Administrator,* 33, 24–30.

Meyer, H.H. (1980). Self-appraisal of job performance. *Personnel Psychology,* 33, 291–296.

Meyer, H.H.; and Raich, M.S. (1983). An objective evaluation of a behavior modeling training program. *Personnel Psychology,* 36, 755–761.

Miller, G.E. (1980). A method for forecasting human resource needs against internal and external labor markets. *Human Resource Planning,* 3, 189–200.

Mills, D.Q. (1985, July-August). Planning with people in mind. *Harvard Business Review,* 97–105.

Miner, J.B. (1963). Evidence regarding the value of a management course based on behavioral science subject matter. *The Journal of Business of the University of Chicago,* 36, 325–335.

Moses, J.L. (1972). Assessment center performance and management progress. *Studies in Personnel Psychology,* 4, 7–12.

Moses, J.L.; and Byham, W.C. (Eds.), (1977). *Applying the assessment center method.* New York: Pergamon Press.

Moses, J.L., and Ritchie, R.J. (1976). Supervisory relationships training: A behavioral evaluation of behavior-modeling program. *Personnel Psychology,* 29, 337–343.

Moskowitz, H. (1974). Regression models of behavior for managerial decision making. *OMEGA, International Journal of Management Science,* 2, 677–690.

Mumford, M.D. (1983). Social comparison theory and the evaluation of peer evaluations: A review and some applied implications. *Personnel Psychology,* 36, 867–881.

Murphy, K.R.; and Cleveland, J.N. (1991). *Performance appraisal.* Boston: Allyn and Bacon.

Murphy, K.R.; Martin, C.; and Garcia, M. (1982). Do behavioral observation scales measure observation? *Journal of Applied Psychology,* 67, 562–567.

Murray, H.A. (1938). *Exploration in personality.* New York: Oxford University Press.

Nadler, P. (1993). How to start job-rotation training on the right track. *American Banker,* 158 (12), 7.

Nash, A.N.; Muczyk, J.P.; and Vettori, F.L. (1971). The relative practical effectiveness of programmed instruction. *Personnel Psychology,* 24, 397–418.

Neale, M.A.; Northcraft, G.B.; and Earley P.C. (1988). Joint effects of goal setting and expertise on negotiator behavior. *Unpublished working manuscript.* Northwestern University, Evanston, IL.

Neff, W.S. (1985). *Work and human behavior.* 3rd ed. New York: Aldine.

Newstrom, J.W. (1980). Evaluating the effectiveness of training methods. *Personnel Administrator,* 25, 55–60.

Niemyer, E.S. (1995). The case for case studies. *Training and Development,* 49, 50–52.

Noujaim, K. (1968). Some motivational determinants of effort allocation and performance. Unpublished Ph.D. thesis. Sloan School of Management, Massachusetts Institute of Technology.

Nwachukwu, C.C. (1994). Effective leadership and productivity, evidence from a national survey of industrial organizations. *African Journal for the Psychological Study of Social Issues,* 1, 38–46.

Obi-Keguna, H.U. (1994). A survey of job satisfaction in two Nigerian establishments. *African Journal for the Psychological Study of Social Issues,* 1, 67–76.

O'Connell, J.O. (1962). Some social and political reflections on the plan. Cited in C.C.Onyemelukwe (1966), *Problems of industrial planning and management in Nigeria.* London: Longmans, 24.

Odejide, A.O. (1979). Traditional healers and mental illness in the city of Ibadan. *African Journal of Psychiatry,* 3, 99–106.

Odiorne, G.S. (1981, July). Developing a human resource strategy. *Personnel Journal,* 534–536

Odumosu, O. (1994). Influence of sanctions on employee performance. *African Journal for the Psychological Study of Social Issues,* 2, 129–155.

Oloko, O. (1977). Incentive and reward for efforts. *Management in Nigeria,* 13, 13–25.

Olson, P. (1986, July). Entrepreneurs: Opportunistic decision makers. *Journal of Small Business Management,* , 29–37.

Onah, J.O. (1984). Management education and training in Nigeria. In V.A. Aniagoh, and P.N.O. Ejiofor (Eds.), *The Nigerian manager: Challenges and opportunities.* Ikeja, Lagos, Nigeria: Longman.

Onyemelukwe, C.C. (1966). *Problems of industrial planning and management in Nigeria.* London: Longman Group.

Onyemelukwe, C.C. (1973). *Man and management in contemporary Africa.* London: Longman Group.

Onyemelukwe, C.C. (1983). Challenges of management in an African context. Paper presented at the First National Workshop on Organization Behavior and Management, University of Ibadan, Ibadan.

Osborn, A.F. (1957). *Applied imagination.* New York: Charles Scribner and Sons.

Osuji, L.O. (1984). Problems of effective utilization of trained manpower in Nigeria. In V.A. Aniagoh and P.N.O. Ejiofor (Eds.), *The Nigerian manager:. Challenges and opportunities.* Ikeja, Lagos, Nigeria: Longman Nigeria.

Otobo, D. (1995). *The trades union movement in Nigeria.* Lagos: Malthouse Press.

Ouchi, W.G. (1981). *Theory Z: How American business can meet the Japanese challenge.* Reading, MA: Addison–Wesley.

Owens, W.A. (1976). Background data. In M. D. Dunnette (Ed.), *Handbook of industrial and organizational psychology.* Chicago: Rand-McNally, Ch. 14, 609 - 644.

Oyemakinde, J.O. (1970). A history of indigenous labour on Nigerian railway 1895–1945. Unpublished Ph.D. thesis, University of Ibadan, Ibadan.

Packer, A. (1988). America's new learning technology. *Personnel Administrator, 33,* 62–132.

Peterson, D.B. (1993). Measuring change: A psychometric approach to evaluating individual training outcomes. In V. Arnold (Ed.), *Innovations in training evaluation: New measures, new designs.* Symposium conducted at the Eighth Annual Conference of the Society for Industrial and Organizational Psychology, San Francisco.

Peterson, D.B.; and Hicks, M.D. (1993). How to get people to change. Workshop presented at the Eighth Annual Conference of the Society for Industrial and Organizational Psychology, San Francisco.

Planning with People (1984, May 3). *Bulletin to Management,* 2–7.

Plunkett, W.R. (1992). *Supervision.* 6th ed. Boston: Alleyn and Bacon.

Plunkett, W.R.; and Attner, R.F. (1994). *Introduction to management.* 5th ed. Belmont, CA: Wadsworth.

Popoola, D. (1983). Fundamentals of personnel training and development in Nigeria. Paper presented at National Workshop on Organizational Behavior and Management, University of Ibadan, Ibadan.

Posner, B.Z.; Hall J.L.; and Munson, J.M. (1991). A first look at the benefits of educational benefits programs. *Applied H.R.M. Research, 2,* 128–152.

Pruitt, D.G. (1972). Methods for resolving differences of interest. A theoretical analysis. *Journal of Social Issues, 28,* 133–154.

Pruitt, D.G. (1981). *Negotiation behavior.* New York: Academic Press.

Pruitt, D.G.; and Carnevale, P.J.D. (1982). The development of integrative agreements. In V.J. Derlega and J. Grezlak (Eds.), *Cooperation and helping behaviour.* New York: Academic Pres, 151–181.

Pruitt, D.G.; and Drews, J.L. (1969). The effect of time pressure, time elapsed, and the opponent's concession rate on behavior in negotiation. *Journal of Experimental Social Psychology, 5,* 43–60.

Pursell, E.D.; Dossett, D.L.; and Latham, G.P. (1980). Obtaining valid predictors by minimizing rating errors in the criterion. *Personnel Psychology, 33,* 91–96.

Rae, L. (1994). Choose your method. *Training and Development, 48,* 19–25.

Raiffa, H. (1982). *The art and science of negotiation.* Cambridge: Harvard University Press.

Rice, R.W.; and Kastenbaum, D.R. (1983). The contingency model of leadership: Some current issues. *Basic and Applied Social Psychology, 4,* 373–392.

Riggio, R.E.; and Cole, E.J. (1992). Agreement between subordinate and superior ratings of supervisory performance and effects on self and subordinate satisfaction. *Journal of Occupational Psychology, 65,* 137–158.

Ritchie, R. (1994). Using the assessment center method to predict senior management potential. *Consulting Psychology Journal, 46,* 16–23.

Roberts, L. (1990). Human resource in Africa. In L. Nadler and Z. Nadler (Eds.), *The handbook of human resource development,*. 2nd ed. New York: John Wiley and Sons, 25.1–25.25.

Robins, S.P. (1974). *Managing organizational conflict. A non-traditional approach.* Englewood Cliffs; NJ: Prentice-Hall.

Roethlisberger, F.J.; and Dickson, W.J. (1939). *Management and the worker.* Cambridge: Harvard University Press.

Rush, M.C.; Thomas, J.C.; and Lord R.G. (1977). Implicit leadership theory: A potential threat to the internal validity of leader behavior questionnaires. *Organizational Behavior and Human Performance,* 20, 93–110.

Russo, J.E.; and Rosen, L.D. (1975). An eye fixation analysis of multi-alternative choice. *Management and Cognition,* 3, 267–276.

Saal, F.E. (1979). Mixed-standard rating scale: Consistent system for numerically coding inconsistent response combinations. *Journal of Applied Psychology,* 64, 422–428.

Saavedra, R., and Kwun, S.K. (1993). Peer evaluation in self-managing work groups. *Journal of Applied Psychology,* 78, 450–462.

Sanda, A.O. (1976). The ethnic factor in urban social relations. In A.O. Sanda, (Ed.), *Ethnic relations in Nigeria. Ibadan:.* University of Ibadan, Department of Sociology. 189.

Sanusi, H.U. (1992). Public policy coordination as capacity building. In H.O. Sanusi (Ed.), *Public policy coordination in Nigeria.* Kuru: National Institute for Policy and Strategic Studies, 128–137.

Schein, E.H. (1970). *Organizational psychology.* Englewood Cliffs, NJ: Prentice-Hall.

Schelling, T. C. (1960). *The strategy of conflict.* Cambridge: Cambridge, M.A.: Harvard University Press.

Schopler, J. (1965). Social power. In L. Berkowitz (Ed.), *Advances in experimental social psychology.* New York: Academic Press, vol. 2, 177 -218 .

Schriesheim, C.A.; and Kerr, S. (1977). RIP, LPC: A response to Fiedler. In J.G. Hunt and L.L. Larson (Eds.), *Leadership: The cutting edge.* Carbondale: Southern Illinois University Press 51–56.

Seibel, H.D. (1967). Some aspects of inter-ethnic relations in Nigeria. *Nigerian Journal of Economic and Social Studies,* 9, 217–228.

Senghor, L. (1960). Cited in David Lamb (1985). *The Africans.* London: Methuen Paperback.

Shanteau, J. (1975). An information-integration analysis of risky decision making. In M.F. Kaplan and S. Schwartz (Eds.) *Human judgement and decision processes.* New York: Academic Press, 109-137.

Sherkovin, Yu. A. (1985). *Social psychology and propaganda.* Moscow: Progress.

Shutz, W.C. (1955). What makes groups productive? *Human Relations,* 8, 429-465.

Simon, H.A. (1957). *Administrative behavior: A study of decision-making processes in administrative organization.* 2nd ed. New York: The Macmillan.

Simon, H.A. (1977). *The new science of management decision.* Englewood Cliffs, NJ.: Prentice-Hall.

Sims, R.R.; Veres, J.G.; and Heninger, S.M. (1989). Training for competence. *Public Personnel Management,* 18, 101–107.

Sirippi, S.B. (1979). Decision-making: An organizational behavior. *The Journal of Management Studies,* 11, 36–46.

Sleezer, C.M. (1993). Tried and true performance analysis. *Training and Development,* 47, 52–54.

Sloan, E.B. (1994). Assessing and developing versality: Executive survival skill for the brave new world. *Consulting Psychology Journal, 46,* 24–31.

Slovic, P.; Fischhoff, B.; and Lichtenstein, S. (1977). Behavioral decision theory. *Annual Review of Psychology,* 28, 1–39.

Small Business Reports (1988, July). Group decision-making: Approaches to problem solving, 30–33.

Smith, D.E. (1986). Training programs for performance appraisal: A review. *Academy of Management Review,* 11, 22–40.

Smith, M.B. (1968). International conference on social psychological research in developing countries. *Journal of Personality and Social Psychology,* 8, 95–98.

Smith, P.C.; and Kendall, L.M. (1963). Retranslating expectations: An approach to the construction of unambiguous anchors for rating scales. *Journal of Applied Psychology,* 47, 149–155.

Smith, P.E. (1976). Management modeling training to improve morale and customer satisfaction. *Personnel Psychology,* 29, 351–359.

Smither, J.W.; Barry, S.R.; and Reilly, R.R. (1989). An investigation of the validity of expert true score estimates in appraisal research. *Journal of Applied Psychology,* 74, 143–151.

Smither, J.W.; London, M.; Vasilopoulos, N.L.; Reilly, R.R.; Millsap, R.E.; and Salvemini, N. (1995). An examination of an upward feedback program over time. *Personnel Psychology,* 48, 1–34.

Smither, J.W.; Reilly, R.R.; and Buda, R. (1988). Effect of prior performance information on ratings of recent performance: Contrast versus assimilation revisited. *Journal of Applied Psychology,* 73, 487–496.

Sorcher, M.; and Spence, R. (1982). The interface project: Behavior modeling as social technology in South Africa. *Personnel Psychology,* 35, 557–581.

Soyibo, A. (1996). *The power of ideas and the ideas of power.* Ibadan: University of Ibadan Press.

Srinivas, S.; and Motowidlo, S.J. (1987). Effects of rater's stress on the dispersion and favorability of performance ratings. *Journal of Applied Psychology,* 72, 247–251.

Stagner, R. (1956). *Psychology of industrial conflict.* New York: Wiley and Sons.

Stagner, R.; and Rosen, H. (1965). *Psychology of union-management relations.* Belmont, CA: Wadsworth.

Steadham, S.V. (1980). Learning to select a needs assessment strategy. *Training and Development Journal,* 30, 56–61.

Stogdill, R.M. (1974). *Handbook of leadership.* New York: Free Press.

Stone, E.F. (1986). Job scope-job satisfaction and job scope-job performance relationships. In E.A. Locke (Ed.), *Generalizing from laboratory to field settings.* Lexington, MA: Lexington Books, 189–206.

Stoner, J.A.F. (1961). A comparison of individual and group decisions involving risk. Unpublished Master's thesis, Massachusetts Institute of Technology, School of Industrial Management.

Sulsky, L.M.; and Day, D.V. (1992). Frame of reference training and cognitive categorization: An empirical investigation of rater memory issues. *Journal of Applied Psychology,* 77, 501–511.

Survey Research Center, University of Michigan (1971). *Survey of working conditions.* Washington, DC: U.S. Government Printing Office.

Svenson, O. (1974). A note on thinking aloud. Protocols obtained during the choice of a home. *Psychological Laboratory Reports, No.421.* University of Stockholm, Sweden.

Sweetland, J. (1978). Work in America institute. Studies in productivity: Highlights of the literature *Managerial Productivity.* Scarsdale, NY: Work in America Institute.

Tamuno, T.N. (1964, December). Genesis of the Nigerian railway-1, *Nigeria Magazine*, no. 83.

Taylor, F.W. (1911). *Scientific management*. New York: Harper and Row.

Thomas, K. (1976). Conflict and conflict management. In M.D. Dunnette (Ed.), *Handbook of industrial and organizational psychology*. Chicago: Rand-McNally, 889 - 935.

Thompson, L. (1988). Social perception in negotiation. Unpublished Ph.D. thesis, Northwestern University, Evanston, IL.

Tichy, N.M.; and Devanna, M.A. (1986). *The transformational leader*. New York: Wiley and Sons.

Toffler, A. (1990). *Power shift*. New York: Bantam Books.

Tubbs, M.E. (1986). Goal-setting: A meta-analytic examination of the empirical evidence. *Journal of Applied Psychology, 71*, 474–483.

Tversky, A. (1972a). Choice by elimination. *Journal of Mathematical Psychology, 9*, 341–361.

Tversky, A. (1972b). Elimination by aspects: A theory of choice. *Psychological Review, 79*, 281–299.

Tziner, A.; Kopelman, R.E.; and Livnech, N. (1993). Effects of performance appraisal format on perceived goal characteristics, appraisal process satisfaction, and changes in rated job performance: A field experiment. *The Journal of Psychology, 127*, 281–292.

Ubeku, A.K. (1983). *Industrial relations in developing countries: the case of Nigeria*. London: Macmillan.

Ubeku, A.K. (1994). The statutory machinery for the resolution of industrial disputes in Nigeria. *African Journal for the Psychological Study of Social Issues, 1*, 14–28.

Ugwuegbu, D.C.E. (1976). Black jurors' personality trait attribution to a rape case defendant. *Social Behavior and Personality, 4*, 193–201.

Ugwuegbu, D.C.E. (1977). The stop sign is for the other guy: A naturalistic observation of driving behavior of Nigerians. *Journal of Applied Psychology, 62*, 574–577.

Ugwuegbu, D.C.E. (1982). Effectiveness of self-persuasion in producing healthy attitudes towards polygyny. In I. Gorss, J. Downing, and A. d'Heurle (Eds.), *Sex role attitudes and cultural change*. Dordrecht, Holland: D. Reidel, 151-155

Ugwuegbu, D.C.E. (1983a). The impact of cultural predisposition on employee work satisfaction. Paper presented at the First National Workshop on Organization Behavior and Management, University of Ibadan, Ibadan.

Ugwuegbu, D.C.E (1983b). Psychology and management. Keynote address delivered at the National Workshop on Organization Behavior and Management, University of Ibadan, Ibadan.

Ugwuegbu, D.C.E. (1987). Introduction to social research and information gathering. In D.C.E. Ugwuegbu and S.O.Onwumere (Eds.), *Social research and information gathering*. Lagos: Federal Government Press, 1 -6.

Ugwuegbu, D.C.E. (1989a). Effective leadership in the civil service. Paper presented at the Workshop for Honorable Ministers, Directors General, and Heads of Extra-Ministerial Departments, and Principal Officers in the Federal Civil Service, ASCON, Lagos.

Ugwuegbu, D.C.E. (1989b). Implications of motivation theories in Nigerian organizations. Paper presented at the National Workshop on Bank Management Appreciation, Department of Psychology, University of Ibadan, Ibadan.

Ugwuegbu, D.C.E. (1990a). Are our gains and pains in our stars? Psychology and national development: The case of Nigeria. Paper presented at Nigeria in a Changing

Continent, a postgraduate seminar for CSC 2, Command and Staff College, Jaji, Kaduna, Nigeria.

Ugwuegbu, D.C.E. (1990b). Motivation: Techniques for fostering motivated work behavior in organizational staff. Paper presented at the Management Appreciation Course organized by the Nigerian Tobacco Company, Ibadan.

Ugwuegbu, D.C.E. (1991). Psychology and bank management. A keynote address at Bank Management Seminar, Department of Psychology, University of Ibadan.

Ugwuegbu, D.C.E. (1994). The beautiful ones are yet to be born: Inter-ethic acceptance among Nigerian school children. *African Journal for the Psychological Study of Social Issues,* 1, 1–13.

Ugwuegbu, D.C.E. (1995a). Discipline in National Development. Paper prepared for the National Orientation Agency for a Workshop on Work Ethic and Queue Culture, Federal Capital Territory, Abuja.

Ugwuegbu, D.C.E. (1995b). Training and training evaluation in Nigerian industrial organizations. Working paper, Ibadan.

Ugwuegbu, D.C.E. (1999). Contact, ethnic attitudes and attraction. Seminar paper presented to the Workgroup on International Racism, Institute of Social Research, University of Michigan, Ann Arbor.

Ugwuegbu, D.C.E. (2000). The unfinished business of the contact hypothesis. Paper presented to the Social Division of the Department of Psychology, University of Michigan, Ann Arbor.

Ugwuegbu, D.C.E.; and Obi, N.A. (1994). Gender bias in selection of applicants for managerial and non-managerial jobs. *African Journal for the Psychological Study of Social Issues,* 1 (2), 156–170.

Ugwuegbu, D.C.E.; and Onwumere, S.O. (Eds.), (1987). *Social research and information gathering.* Lagos: Federal Government Press.

U.S. Training and Employment Services (1972). *Dictionary of Occupational Titles.* 4th ed. Washington, D.C.: U.S. Government Printing Office.

Uvieghara, E.E. (1987). *Nigerian labor laws: The past, present, and future.,* Lagos: University of Lagos Press.

Van Schaack, H, Jr. (1957). Naturalistic role-playing: A method of interview training for student personnel administrators. *Dissertation Abstracts,* 17, 801.

Vetter, E.W. (1967). *Manpower planning for higher talent personnel.* University of Michigan, Graduate School of Business, Bureau of Industrial Relations, Ann Arbor.

Vroom, V.H. (1973, Spring). A new look at managerial decision-making. *Organizational Dynamics,* 67.

Vroom, V.H.; and Yetton, P.W. (1973). *Leadership and decision making.* Pittsburgh, University of Pittsburgh Press.

Wainer, H.A.; and Rubin, I.M. (1969). Motivation of research and development entrepreneurs: Determinants of company success. *Journal of Applied Psychology,* 53, 178–184.

Walker, J.W. (1988). Managing human resources in flat, lean and flexible organizations: Trends for the 1990s. *Human Resource Planning,* 11,125–132.

Walker, J.W.; and Armes, R. (1979). Implementing management succession planning in diversified companies. *Human Resource Planning,* 2, 123–133.

Walster, E.; Walster, G.W.; and Berscheid, E. (1978). *Equity theory and research.* Boston: Alleyn and Bacon.

Walton, R.E.; and Dutton, J.M. (1969). The management of interdepartmental conflict. A model and review. *Administrative Science Quarterly,* 14, 73–84.

Walton, R.E.; and Mckersie, R.B. (1965). *A behavioral theory of labor negotiation.* New York: McGraw-Hill.

Wells, F.A.; and Warmington, W.A. (1962). *Studies in industrialization: Nigeria and the Cameroons,* London: Oxford University Press.

Wexley, K.N.; and Latham, G.P. (1981). *Developing and training human resources in organizations.* Glenview, IL.: Scott, Foresman.

Wexley, K.N.; and Yukl, G.A. (1984). *Organizational behavior and personnel psychology.* Homewood IL: Richard D. Irwin.

White, S.E.; Dittrich, J.E.; and Lang, J.R. (1980). The effects of group decision-making processes and problem situation complexity on implementation attempts. *Administrative Science Quarterly,*25, 428–440.

Wickert, F.R. (1967). *Readings in African psychology: From French Language sources.* Lansing: African Studies Center, Michigan State University.

Wilbur, L.P. (1993). The value of on-the-job rotation. *Supervisory Management,* 38 (11), 6.

Wober, M. (1975). *Psychology in Africa* London: International African Institute.

Wrightsman, L.S. (1972). *Social psychology in the seventies.* Monterey, CA: Brooks-Cole.

Yukl, G.A. (1974a). Effects of opponent's initial offer, concession magnitude, and concession frequency on bargaining behavior. *Journal of Personality and Social Psychology,* 30, 332–335.

Yukl, G.A. (1974b). The effects of situational variables and opponent concessions on a bargainer's perception, aspirations and concessions. *Journal of Personality and Social Psychology,* 29, 227–236.

Yukl, G.A. (1989). *Leadership in organizations.* 2nd ed. Englewood Cliffs, NJ: Prentice-Hall.

Yukl, G.A.; Wall, S.; and Lepsinger, R. (1990). Preliminary report on the validation of the management practices survey. In K.E. Clark and M.B. Clark. (Eds.), *Measures of leadership.* West Orange, NJ: Leadership Library of America, 223–238.

Yusufu, T.M. (1962). *Introduction to industrial relations in Nigeria.* London: Oxford University Press.

Zaleznik, A.; and Kets de Vries, M.F.R. (1975). *Power and the corporate mind.* Boston: Houghton Mifflin.

Zwicky, F. (1969). *Discovery, invention, research through the morphological approach.* New York: Macmillan.

Author Index

Subject Index

About the Author

DENIS CHIMA E. UGWUEGBU is Professor of Social and Organizational Psychology and Chair of the Department of Psychology, which he founded, at the University of Ibadan, Nigeria. Currently a visiting professor at the University of Michigan and the Center for Afro American Studies, both in Ann Arbor, he is an internationally recognized psychologist with more than 100 highly regarded publications in books and journals, both in the United States and Nigeria. Dr. Ugwuegbu is a recipient of several prestigious awards and fellowships and serves as a consultant to various organizations and government ministries abroad.

DATE DUE